DEVELOPMENTAL READING, K-8
Teaching from a Psycholinguistic Perspective

Second Edition

Daniel R. Hittleman
Queens College, City University of New York

in collaboration with

Carol G. Hittleman
Huntington Public School District, New York

HOUGHTON MIFFLIN COMPANY   BOSTON
Dallas   Geneva, Illinois   Hopewell, New Jersey
Palo Alto   London

Acknowledgement is made to the following authors and publishers to reprint selections from copyrighted material.

Barbara S. Wood, *Children and Communication: Verbal and Nonverbal Language Development,* 2d ed., ©1981, p. 230. Reprinted by permission of Prentice-Hall, Inc., Englewood Cliffs, NJ.

Degrees of Reading Power Test Booklet, copyright ©1980 by College Entrance Examination Board, New York. Reprinted by permission.

Roach Van Allen and Claryce Allen, *Teacher's Resource Book, Language Experiences in Reading.* Copyright 1970, 1966 by Encyclopedia Britannica Press.

O. L. Davis et al., *Exploring the Social Sciences: Asking About the U.S.A. and Its Neighbors;* and *Exploring the Social Sciences: Investigating Communities and Cultures.* Copyright 1971. American Book Company.

Kenneth S. Goodman et al., *Choosing Materials to Teach Reading.* Copyright 1966 by Wayne State University Press.

Marguerite Henry, *Misty Chincoteague.* Copyright 1947 by Rand McNally & Company.

Thomas F. Monteleone, "The Thing from Ennis Roack," in *More Science Fiction Tales,* edited by Roger Elwood. Copyright 1974 by Rand McNally & Company.

Ross Hutchins, *Tonka, the Cave Boy.* Copyright 1973 by Rand McNally & Company.

Anne Emery, *A Spy in Old West Point.* Copyright 1965 by Rand McNally & Company.

Anne Alexander, *Noise in the Night.* Copyright 1960 by Rand McNally & Company.

Children's Literature in the Elementary School, 2d ed. by Charlotte S. Huck and Doris Young Kuhn. Copyright ©1961, 1968, by Holt, Rinehart and Winston. Adapted by permission of Holt, Rinehart and Winston, CBS College Publishing.

Photo Credits

Russell Abraham, page 1 / Elizabeth Crews, pages 7, 86, 99, 159, 240, 255, 340 / Elizabeth Crews, Jeroboam, Inc., page 60 / Joe DiDio, National Education Association, page 283 / Michael Goss, page 64 / B. Griffith, page 106 / Elizabeth Hamlin, Stock, Boston, pages 183, 219 / Meri Moutchens-Kitchens, page 353 / Anna Kaufman Moon, Stock, Boston, pages 176 / Jean-Claude Lejeune, Stock, Boston, pages 128, 138, 196, 272, 324 / Julie O'Neil, Stock, Boston, page 170 / Frank Siteman, Stock, Boston, page 314 / Michael D. Sullivan, page 45.

Production by Phil Carver & Friends, Inc.

Copyright © 1983, 1978 by Houghton Mifflin Company. All rights reserved. No part of this work may be reproduced or transmitted in any form or by any means, electronic or mechanical, including photocopying and recording, or by any information storage or retrieval system, except as may be expressly permitted by the 1976 Copyright Act or in writing by the publisher. Requests for permission should be addressed in writing to Houghton Mifflin Company, One Beacon Street, Boston, Massachusetts 02108.

Printed in the U.S.A.

Library of Congress Catalog Card Number: 82-83378

ISBN: 0-395-327709

Contents

PREFACE	ix
CHAPTER 1 READING PROGRAMS IN TODAY'S SOCIETY	1
Focus Questions	1
Reading and Writing in a Changing World	2
Relevant Reading Programs	3
Reading Defined	4
Assumptions About Reading Programs	4
Organizing for Reading Instruction	5
The Informed Teacher	11
Discussion Questions and Activities	12
Further Readings	13
CHAPTER 2 HUMAN COMMUNICATION AND THE DEVELOPMENT OF THINKING AND LANGUAGE	16
Focus Questions	17
Human Communication	17
Barriers to Communication	19
Signaling Meaning	21
The Structure of All Languages	23
The Structure of English	28
Human Thinking	39
Schema Theory	40
Human Cognition	42
Developmental Stages of Human Thinking	43
The Structure of Human Intellect	46
The Structure of Human Memory	49
Conclusion	53
The Development of Language in Children	54
Implications for Education	59
Discussion Questions and Activities	61
Further Readings	62
CHAPTER 3 THE READING PROCESS	64
Focus Questions	65
Significance of a Psycholinguistic Model of Reading	66

Psycholinguistic Models of Reading	67
The Goodman Model of the Reading Process	68
The Interactive Model of Reading	72
A Model of Text Comprehension	75
The Reading Act: A Continuum of Moments	78
The Reader	80
The Text	80
The Environment	81
The Process of Reading	82
The Interaction	82
The Relationship of Writing to Reading	82
Implications	83
Discussion Questions and Activities	84
Further Readings	85

CHAPTER 4 PRINCIPLES OF ANALYTICAL TEACHING THROUGH STANDARDIZED TESTS — 86

Focus Questions	87
Analytical Teaching	87
Objectives of Assessment	88
Standardized Tests	89
Characteristics of Standardized Tests	90
Standardized Reading Tests	94
Limitations of Standardized Tests	96
Effective Use of Standardized Reading Test Results	102
Obtaining Information About Academic Potential	102
Discussion Questions and Activities	104
Further Readings	105

CHAPTER 5 STRATEGIES FOR ANALYTICAL TEACHING THROUGH INFORMAL TESTS — 106

Focus Questions	107
Useful Background Information	108
Information About Academic Potential	109
Obtaining Information About Reading Performance	109
Assessing Oral Reading Performance	110
Assessing Silent Reading Performance	127
Obtaining Information About Writing Performance	132
Discussion Questions and Activities	135
Further Readings	136

CHAPTER 6 STRATEGIES FOR DEVELOPING READINESS FOR READING INSTRUCTION 138

Focus Questions	139
Readiness for all Reading	140
Parents and Reading	141
Development of Reading Readiness	141
Readiness for Formal Reading Instruction	143
The Place of Writing in Beginning Reading	144
Strategies for Developing Readiness to Use Print	145
Activities for Developing Readiness	146
Determining Readiness to Read	159
Developing Readiness for Participating in Group Activities	162
Group Functions	163
Forming Groups in a Classroom	164
Resources for the Teacher	165
Discussion Questions and Activities	167
Further Readings	168

CHAPTER 7 STRATEGIES FOR GUIDED READING DEVELOPMENT 170

Focus Questions	171
The Language Experience Approach	172
Implementing the Language Experience Approach	173
Implementing a Thematic Unit	180
Resources for the Teacher	181
Strategies for Guiding Student's Learning	183
Strategies for Questioning	187
Writing as a Strategy for Comprehension	193
Discussion Questions and Activities	194
Further Readings	195

CHAPTER 8 STRATEGIES FOR RECONSTRUCTING AND CONSTRUCTING MEANING 196

Focus Questions	197
The Reader Reconstructs the Author's Message	199
Writing as a Strategy for Reconstructing Meaning	199
Prediction Strategies	200
Strategies for Understanding Textual Material	206
Developing Strategy Learning Lessons	219
Implementing Reading Strategies	224

Activities for Reconstructing Meaning	231
Resources for the Teacher	235
Discussion Questions and Activities	238
Further Readings	239

CHAPTER 9 STRATEGIES FOR VOCABULARY DEVELOPMENT AND WORD RECOGNITION — 240

Focus Questions	241
Strategies for Developing and Extending Word Knowledge	242
Increasing General Vocabularies	243
Developing General Vocabularies	244
Activities for Developing General Vocabularies	245
Using Context to Determine Unknown Words	248
Contextual Signals to Word Meanings	248
Using Context Signals	250
Activities for Using Context Signals	251
Strategies for Using Graphophonological Information	253
Clarification of Misunderstandings About Graphophonological Information	253
Effective Instruction in Graphophonological Information	256
Immediate Word Recognition	256
Mediated Word Recognition	257
Spelling	259
Dictionary Usage Strategies	261
Activities for Developing Dictionary Strategies	266
Resources for the Teacher	267
Discussion Questions and Activities	269
Further Readings	270

CHAPTER 10 DEVELOPING STRATEGIES FOR CONTENT AREA READING — 272

Focus Questions	273
The Structure of Content Area Materials	274
Writing Patterns in Content Area Texts	274
Vocabulary	275
Paragraph Structures	277
Graphics	280
Guiding Reading in the Content Areas	283
Strategies for Independent Reading in the Content Areas	286
Activities for Content Area Reading	290
Strategies for Locating Information and Using Reference Materials	294
Locating Information in Books	294
Locating Information in Libraries	295

Strategies for Using the Encyclopedia	296
Strategies for Locating Information on Maps	297
Strategies for Reading the Newspaper	298
Activities for Developing Newspaper Reading Strategies	299
Functional Literacy	301
Strategies for Organizing Information	304
Strategies for Using Outlines	305
Developing Outlining Strategies	307
Writing as a Strategy for Content Area Understanding	309
Resources for the Teacher	310
Discussion Questions and Activities	312
Further Readings	313

CHAPTER 11 DEVELOPING STRATEGIES FOR LITERATURE READING — 314

Focus Questions	315
Strategies for Developing a Literature Program	316
Recognizing the Categories for Literature	318
Recognizing Literary Forms	318
Recognizing Elements of Style	320
Uses of Literature	323
Strategies for Bringing Children and Literature Together	324
Using Library Resources	325
Selecting Children's Literature	325
Literature and the Media	328
Writing and Literature	329
Resources for the Teacher	330
Activities for Developing Literary Appreciation	333
Strategies for Using Bibliotherapy	335
Discussion Questions and Activities	336
Further Readings	337

CHAPTER 12 STRATEGIES FOR STUDENTS WITH SPECIAL NEEDS — 340

Focus Questions	341
The Needs of Divergent Dialect Speakers	341
Black American Dialects	342
Barriers to Comprehension	344
Developing Comprehension Across Dialects	345
The Needs of Speakers of English as a Second Language	347
Strategies for Teaching	349
The Needs of Students Who Have Difficulty Learning to Read	352

Identification of the Reading Disabled	355
A Developmental Concept of Disability	357
Assessment of Disability and Instruction	358
The Needs of the Gifted and Talented	360
Discussion Questions and Activities	362
Further Readings	363
REFERENCES	366
INDEX	379

Preface

PURPOSE

Developmental Reading, K-8: Teaching from a Psycholinguistic Perspective provides teachers-in-training, preservice and inservice, with a theoretical framework about the reading process and with procedures for creating instructional strategies consistent with that perspective. The text is intended for use in an introductory course in the methodology of reading instruction for the elementary and intermediate grades.

Our position is that reading is a process. We explain that process by relying on insights provided by our experiences and those of scholars, investigators, and other practitioners in the field of psycholinguistics. We present a single interpretation of the reading process because we believe it provides a consistent, logical, and natural picture of the nature of reading and how students learn to read.

THE SECOND EDITION

In this second edition, the learning and teaching of reading and writing (composing) are integrated. Based upon the current thinking of researchers and scholars in the field and upon our experiences in aiding students to become literate, we show how reading comprehension is enhanced through the composing process. We view reading and writing as part of a total written communications approach to functioning in today's world.

ORGANIZATION AND COVERAGE

The chapters in the text provide a broad overview of the nature and extent of a reading program in kindergarten through eighth grade. In Chapter 1, we review the general needs for and functions of reading and writing in society. In Chapter 2, we provide the background for understanding the psycholinguistic perspective of the reading process through an examination of how spoken and written language convey meaning, how language and thinking develop, and what the natures of schemas and human memory seem to be. In Chapter 3, we provide information about the significance of psycholinguistic models of reading and discuss three representative models of the reading process, a model of the reading act, and the relationship between writing and reading. In Chapters 4 and 5, we examine what it means to engage in analytical teaching. In Chapter 6, we show how the readiness to read can be developed for any type of materials at any stage of development. In Chapters 7 and 8, we develop strategies for leading students to understand how sentence patterns and structure words within sentences can be used to determine authors' meanings in sentences, paragraphs, and extended discourse. We distinguish between teacher-led reading procedures and student-self-guided reading procedures. In Chapter 9, we discuss strategies for extending vocabulary and recognizing words in context. In Chapter 10, we provide strategies for understanding content area texts. In Chapter 11, we present literary techniques used by authors and offer suggestions for developing literature appreciation and reading strategies. In Chapter 12, we identify the special needs of some students and provide suggestions for accommodating the previous chapters' strategies and understandings to those needs.

ACKNOWLEDGMENTS

This edition is more than a collaboration between husband and wife. It is a collaboration with the ideas and insights of our colleagues, students, and friends. We find it extremely difficult sometimes to distinguish original ideas from those of others with whom we share a framework and who exchange their ideas freely through personal communications and professional writings. Throughout the text, we try to acknowledge the sources of ideas; however, the expression and interpretation of those ideas' final forms remain our responsibility. We must single out H. Alan Robinson, teacher, colleague, and, most importantly, friend, for his immeasurable ongoing contribution to our professional growth.

For their reviews and insightful comments on the preliminary revision plan and on the revised manuscript, we wish to acknowledge the efforts of Richard L. Allington, Patricia L. Anders, David Bloome, and Diane DeFord. Their contributions through formal reviews and to us personally were extremely helpful. We wish also to acknowledge Kenneth S. Goodman, Walter J. Moore, P. David Pearson, and Esther Schatz, who provided reviews and comments during the preparation of the first edition.

The first edition was a family affair in an emotional sense. The collaboration on this edition resulted from our recognition of the influence each professionally has had on the other. We dedicate this book with love and affection to our daughters, Margo and Jill.

Daniel R. Hittleman
Queens College,
City University of New York
Carol G. Hittleman
Huntington Public School District,
New York

Chapter 1

READING PROGRAMS IN TODAY'S SOCIETY

Focus Questions

1. How does reading fit into a world in which ideas are to a greater extent than ever being transmitted through multimedia devices?

2. What kind of school instructional program is appropriate to the teaching and learning of reading and writing in today's society?

3. What does a teacher need to know in order to implement an effective literacy program in today's society?

4. How can the classroom teacher maintain a current knowledge of reading theory and practice?

During the late 1960s and early 1970s, the teaching of reading came under severe attack. Reading was characterized as "irrelevant" and even "antisocial." It was contended that print was no longer the dominant medium of communication in our culture, even though the schools acted as if it were (Postman, 1973). This polemic was reminiscent of McLuhan's argument (1964) that our information about the world now comes more through multimedia devices than through print alone. (But note the following line from an advertisement: "Marshall McLuhan says the printed word is 'obsolete' and to prove it, he wrote fifteen books.")

During the late 1970s and early 1980s, reading again came under attack, but from a different perspective. This new attack from the "back to basics" movement in American education emphasizes strict standards, the extensive use of phonics in reading instruction, and the teaching of reading at a very early age (Heckinger, 1980; Maeroff, 1981). It is the belief of back-to-basics advocates that adherence to these principles will overcome the problems they see in teaching reading.

Obviously, there are many people who do not think that reading will become an "art form" limited to an elitist group. And there are those who feel that the back-to-basics movement merely disguises the indecision and confusion in American educational philosophy and society's expectations of the public schools (Johnson, 1979). There can be no denying that "reading instruction" has become and will remain a volatile political issue. However, one of the reasons for this explosive polemic is the misconception about the nature of reading as well as confusion over the differences between "reading" and "the instruction of reading."

In this chapter we will examine (1) some of the functions of the print medium in our society today and in the future, (2) how a reading instructional program might be formulated to meet the demands of society, (3) the components of that instructional program, and (4) how teachers can maintain a current knowledge of reading theory and practice in relation to the changing demands of society.

The remaining chapters will attempt to explain the reading process, distinguish the "process" from instruction developing that process, and provide models and suggestions for implementing an instructional program consistent with human growth and the development and the character of our society.

READING AND WRITING IN A CHANGING WORLD

Where do reading and writing fit in a changing world? There is, of course, McLuhan's point of view: technological changes have made the printed word obsolete—therefore eliminating the need for reading—and instruction in the schools should focus on developing "literacy" in the other modes of communication.

Yet, reading and writing are acts of communication, and as such, they share many characteristics with other modes of communication. Now and in the future, we will have various alternatives for gaining information and communicating with other people. The educational process should provide for the development of enlightened selection of the means of communication.

Reading is vital to our complex society to develop understanding citizens. It is important for improving our understanding of government, expanding our understanding of contemporary conditions in conflict with the rights and responsibilities of a free people, and accepting our obligation to participate in social and political discussions.

Reading, moreover, is the one means of communication in which the receiver of the message is in almost full control of the communicative situation. The author's intended sequence can be followed or not. Communication can begin and terminate at the reader's will. The reader can find other sources to verify meanings or find sources with differing ideas. The rate at which the ideas will be processed and how many of the ideas will be processed can be adjusted. No other medium allows us this much flexibility. Even the use of pictures does not give the viewer total control, for pictures have one basic shortcoming in relation to printed ideas—"you cannot make a picture of the concept of a statement" and all "statements cannot be transcribed into images" (Gombrich, 1974).

There surely are limitations in using the printed word to convey ideas, and surely many ideas can be conveyed in ways other than through print. But that is not the question. That alternative modes of communicating exist does not decrease the need for reading in our society: just observe the growing interest in and use of word processors in businesses and homes.

We cannot stop or retard the explosion of knowledge, nor can we usurp the freedom of the press or the freedom of authors to write and publish. The responsibility lies in teaching students to discriminate between what is worthy and what is not. We must be concerned with educating students to become efficient and discriminating processors of all language. It is not *whether* we should be taught to read but *what* we are taught about communicating. Are we taught to question and analyze the information we receive regardless of its source? Are we literate with language in whatever form?

These questions have particular importance in light of the study by the National Assessment of Educational Progress of the reading ability of nine-, thirteen-, and seventeen-year-olds for the 1979–1980 academic year. The conclusion of the report was that although American school children are learning to read a wide range of materials, the majority do not develop adequate thinking skills or the ability to interpret what they read beyond a superficial level (Fiske, 1981).

As teachers, then, our concern is not to be caught up in the polemic of whether reading is outmoded, irrelevant, or politically stultifying. Our concern is with developing citizens who can select the most advantageous means for learning at a particular time, at a particular place, and for a particular subject. Our values and knowledge of the world will be in constant flux. No one can ever be sure what the world over the "edge of history" will be like (Thompson, 1972). But students will be shortchanged if educational practices are not adjusted so that they can "learn what to want" and can explore the "range and quality of experiences" available to them (Bell, 1974). If students are not given the opportunity to learn to read, they will be forever limited in their range of choices and in the satisfaction they will be able to obtain from life.

RELEVANT READING PROGRAMS

In this book we will offer some ideas about a school reading program for grades N–8. These ideas should be relevant to the world in which today's students must function and at the same time prepare them for a world that may be quite different by the time they are adults. As such, the "program is part of the message": not that *what* is done, the substance of the program is unimportant but that *how* the program is implemented has a great impact on pupil learning. The acquisition of the reading process is an interaction among the learner, the teacher, the instructional material, and the environment in which the learning occurs. "The ways in which the child is taught to read have direct bearings on both his productivity as a reader and his aspirations about being a reader" (Jacobs, 1971).

At this point, it seems fitting to make a general statement about the reading process and how the *process of reading* differs from the *teaching/learning situation* in which the process develops.

Reading Defined

Reading is a verbal process interrelated with thinking and all the other communication abilities—listening, speaking, and writing. Specifically, reading is the process of reconstucting from printed patterns the ideas and information intended by the author. It is somewhat like the process of listening to someone talk and then reconstructing his or her ideas from sound patterns. Learning to read develops from learning to use and understand oral and written language. The ability to use language in its printed form has to be preceded by the ability to communicate in language in its oral form. Learning to read adequately requires applying existing thinking strategies to written ideas; therefore, the cultivation of the cognitive learning processes is integral to any program to develop the reading process.

"Reading," Gephart (1970) says, "is a term used to refer to an interaction by which meaning encoded in visual stimuli by an author becomes meaning in the mind of the reader." That interaction involves a number of factors, some of which are not inherently part of the text being read or are not within the reader. The factors in the reading interaction include (1) the purposes for which we read; (2) the types and formats of the materials being read; (3) the situations and contexts in which the reading occurs; (4) the means by which understanding is determined or measured; and (5) the reader's skills, abilities, and experiences. In chapters 2 and 3 we will discuss the theories behind this definition of the reading process. One should not assume that the meaning intended by the author automatically becomes the meaning assumed by the reader. The five factors of reading interaction prevent such a one-for-one correspondence.

What constitutes the process of reading will affect the instructional program. However, the teaching of reading and reading itself must be kept conceptually apart. The environment of the classroom, the methodology of the teacher, the materials used, the strategies presented, and the amount and effectiveness of practice all interact to aid or inhibit the development of the reading process by children. Teachers should ask not "How can I teach reading?" but "How can I best promote the learning of reading?" The major portion of this text is devoted to providing some answers to that question.

Assumptions About Reading Programs

A few basic assumptions about reading programs underlie our recommended strategies for the efficient and productive development of the reading process in children. These assumptions are

1. All language activities have communication as their prime purpose. Reading is learned only through the attempt to "communicate" with and through written language.
2. Knowing how to read and write will help people cope with the demands of society.
3. Instruction in composing messages accompanies instruction in reading messages. By creating their own texts students gain insights into how to reconstruct the intended meaning of others.
4. Instruction directed toward developing the reading process is planned and purposeful, involves children in direct experiences in using reading and writing strategies in meaningful situations, and allows children to assume some of the responsibilities for their learning.

ORGANIZING FOR READING INSTRUCTION

Reading curriculums should be based on the premise that reading is "using language" and that the function of language is the communication of thoughts: "reading is not reading without some level of comprehension, and reading materials, however simple, must have something to say; there must be some thought to be comprehended" (Goodman, 1969).

An instructional program in reading should have educationally sound general curricular principles. The program should have a theoretical foundation and relate the means of instruction to what has been confirmed about human potential and human development. Bruner (1966) described some general characteristics of instruction, which are summarized in the following paragraph.

Learning and problem solving should depend on the exploration of alternatives, and instruction should aid and guide these explorations. The teacher should activate the exploration of alternatives, maintain the learner's interest and constantly direct the learner's search for solutions to problems. Any idea, problem, or fact can be presented to students in a form simple enough so that any of them can understand it. The efficacy with which the information is understood and recognized will depend on the interaction of certain variables. Instructional techniques should be selected with consideration for (1) the learners' age, (2) the learners' style of learning, (3) the subject matter, (4) the mode of presentation, (5) the concepts to be learned, and (6) the learners' conceptual capacity. The learners should be led through sequences of statements and restatements that increase their ability to grasp, transform, and transfer what is learned. Essential to learning is a knowledge of results at a time when the knowledge can be used for corrections. Learners should be aided in developing self-sufficiency in problem solving. This should be accomplished by always translating the information to be learned into the learners' way of solving problems.

The organized procedures for teaching reading strategies should provide for multiple and varied learning situations. There should be specific guidance in the development of the students' thinking strategies. The instructional activities should include teaching and learning that allows the teacher and students to mutually assess the students' needs. Instructional activities and experiences should be created to allow the development of those strategies relevant to the students' learning needs and capabilities.

The structure of a reading program is commonly thought of as the school or classroom organizational pattern. Many beginning teachers have wondered whether to "group" or "individualize" their teaching of reading.

The type of organizational pattern used in a whole school or in a single classroom should be selected because it "fits" the learning environment. A school or class organizational pattern should be selected after considering various factors: (1) the concepts about learning and reading held by the school administration and the classroom teacher, (2) the recognized role(s) of the teacher, (3) the facilities available for instruction and the daily classroom interpersonal interactions desired, (4) the perceived needs of the learners, and (5) the subject matter and the format in which the subject matter is presented.

Philosophical Assumptions Different philosophical assumptions about learning underlie three current learning theories: Behavior-Control Model, Rational Model, and Discovery-Learning Model (Nuthall & Snook, 1973). With the Behavior-Control Model, teaching is considered a method of controlling both the students and the conditions of learning. In the Rational Model, the aim of teaching is the transmission of knowledge. The Discovery-Learning Model has various descriptions consolidated in teaching models based on information processing. These models call for (1) the active participation of the student in the learning process; (2) the creation of attractive alternatives; (3) the encouragement and development of divergent, convergent, and creative thinking; (4) the rearrangement and transformation of evidence; and (5) the learning of the process of "discovery" through various kinds of learning. The psychological theory supporting the information-processing models is not as precise as that supporting the Behavior-Control Model. The Discovery-Learning Model, however, is very strongly supported by the research of cognitive psychology, child development, and the study of creativity (this will be brought out in Chapters 2 and 3).

A reading program consistent with the ideas in this book would be developed along the guidelines of the information-processing, or Discovery-Learning, teaching models. In such models, the instructional program aims at (1) establishing learning environments in which the students accept some responsibility for educational decisions, rather than merely following directives; (2) tying learning not only to performing some task but also to making decisions about what is appropriate at any given time; and (3) encouraging the generation of many answers rather than simply accepting a "right" answer.

Teacher Roles The roles that teachers can play in an instructional setting depend on their perceptions of the expectations of others in the immediate social and educational system, the teachers' self-concepts, and their value systems

(Morine & Morine, 1973). Among the roles teachers could decide to play are reporter, model, problem-poser, counselor, diagnostician, systems manager, police officer, experimenter, and consumer.

An instructional program should always be flexible enough to accomodate and develop the special talents of all concerned— teachers and learners—in a manner that will be self-rewarding, educationally sound, and socially effective. The question is not "Which role should I perform?" but rather "Which role is appropriate for a particular instructional purpose, with a particular child or group of children, and with a particular subject matter?"

Facilities The physical environment most assuredly places some limitations on the type of instructional organization. Quite often, however, the size and arrangement of rooms and the age and construction of the school building are used as excuses for adhering to one particular organizational pattern. The facilities of a school should not hinder the creative teacher who wishes to use a particular organizational structure or a variety of organizational structures. The decision of what pattern or pattens to use should be only indirectly influenced by the school's physical conditions.

The Learner's Needs Havighurst (1964) found evidence that children have a "drive" to learn. It is not fully known whether this drive is innate or acquired. Some evidence also points to the possibility that there may be crucial periods in

which certain learning is easier. The crucial period for learning language and communicative tasks seems to be the first twelve years of life. What is most evident, though, is that children need a cirriculum that

1. Provides experiences in exploring and explaining the unfamiliar in both the social and physical worlds;
2. Offers experiences in a variety of sensory modalities and experiences while talking about these sensory impressions;
3. Develops experiences with increasingly complex social relationships;
4. Gives practice in the fundamentals of reading that are tied to relevant discussion and explantions of these fundamentals; and
5. Allows for experiences in expanding control of language and meanings as expressed in speech.

Learning does not seem to occur rapidly—at least not that needed for long-term decision making. Facts are learned rather quickly, but the processes of thought and communication are acquired slowly and in a cumulative fashion. These processes require practice and are undertaken with some sort of anticipation of reward. Factors that influence the extent to which learning is acquired are such things as intelligence, the mode or modes of learning, motivation, and the expectations developed through family relationships (Havighurst, 1964). (See Chapters 2, 3, and 4.)

The school organizational pattern should reflect a responsiveness to the children's various needs in any learning situation. The teacher should not follow one specific organizational pattern if it does not meet the needs and purposes of all the learners.

Subject Matter Every subject area has some unique features of organization. Some subjects are more efficiently presented in certain formats and require certain strategies for their effective processing by the reader. Subsequent chapters will deal in greater detail with strategies for reading specific subject areas.

Organizational Patterns The modern concept of school organization is to offer "flexibility" (Congreve & Rinehart, 1972), that is, to provide options and alternative patterns for learning and teaching opportunities that would not otherwise be available. The following is a discussion of a number of schoolwide and intraclass organizational patterns for reading instruction commonly used in elementary schools.

Schoolwide plans:
1. *Grade level classes.*
2. *Nongraded units:* random groups or multiage groups.
3. *Cross-class or cross-grade groupings:* children from different classrooms regrouped for instruction in particular content area, usually composed of children at same grade level.

4. *Team teaching:* an instructional program planned by two or more teachers, each responsible for teaching a particular subject area or a particular group of children.
5. *Learning laboratory:* sometimes called a reading laboratory, skills center, or learning center.
6. *Differentiated staffing:* team teaching based on skill differentiation.
7. *Scheduling or departmentalization:* class periods as in junior or senior high school.

Intraclass plans:
1. *Homogeneous grouping:* based on some characteristic—reading or intelligence achievement test score—that reduces range of achievement in the group.
2. *Heterogeneous (or random) Grouping.*
3. *Individualized reading:* students selecting their own reading material and reading at will; plus (a) students teacher conferences, (b) comprehensive exams, (c) temporary groups for specific skills instruction, and (d) sharing of children's reading experiences.
4. *Needs grouping* or *activities grouping:* shared instructional need or group project.
5. *Independent* or *contract learning:* specific assignments based on student-teacher contracts.
6. *Student groups:* peer tutoring or pair/group project.
7. *Diagnostic/prescriptive instruction:* individual assignments based on diagnosed needs and follow-up diagnosis to determine progress.
8. *Open classroom.*

The above patterns of schoolwide or intraclass organization should not be considered mutually exclusive; many, in fact, rely on other plans for their implementation. Returning to the question of whether to group or individualize the teaching of reading, we can now see that no simple answer can be given. Research into the effective use of classroom organization for meeting students' individual differences seems to substantiate the belief that all of the above forms of organization have at least some potential. A comparison of research between intraclass and interclass organization, heterogeneous and homogeneous groupings, and divided-day and whole-day instruction (Oliver, 1970) reveals implications for teaching. The research seems to indicate that the best organizational plan for reading instruction is the one that permits the most appropriate teaching for the teacher, the students, and the reading lesson. Also, homogeneous groups of children selected according to only one criterion will be composed of children with different instructional needs. And teachers tend *not* to move students from group to group to the extent that individual differences would suggest is necessary.

This research did not make it possible to state conclusively that the advantages of the ungraded school outweigh the disadvantages. It seems that the claims of the proponents are excessive and that many advantages claimed for those who favor the ungraded structure can be achieved by excellent teachers working in a "traditional" school organization. The literature shows that there are many different types of ungraded organizations in schools and that it is hard to determine whether a cause-and-effect relationship exists between many of the advantages and disadvantages of these patterns (Kingston, 1969). The research on the open classroom has shown that there has not been sufficient consistency to warrant an unqualified endorsement of it as a superior means of organizing classrooms (Horowitz, 1979). In general, the term open classroom is used ambiguously, and so it has become difficult to determine the actual degree to which teachers have implemented "openness" (Marshall, 1981). The main advantage of ungraded and open structures seems to be that they reveal the inflexibility and impracticality of the self-contained classroom as a form of organization.

A summary of the issues and principal findings of research on homogeneous and heterogeneous ability grouping (Esposito, 1973) shows, in part, that

1. There is consistent positive value for students in general, for a particular group of students to achieve more academically, or for more efficient learning conditions in a homogeneous ability grouping.
2. There is evidence of an unfavorable effect on the affective development of students because of homogeneous ability grouping.
3. No improvement of achievement under either homogeneous or heterogeneous grouping patterns seems to be a factor unique to the organization and could be considered a factor separate from curriculum modifications.
4. Teaching methods, materials, and other variables, rather than the type of grouping pattern, have a cause-and-effect relationship with achievement.

Research on the sociological conditions for effective student/teacher interactions and the effect of classroom environmental variables on learning seems to verify the conclusions found in the above research. The physical characteristics of a conventional classroom seem to have little impact on the students' achievement, though the classroom environment may affect their nonachievement behaviors and attitudes (Weinstein, 1979). Student growth and learning seem to be directly related to the kind of classroom teaching. Certain personal characteristics of a teacher may be as important in determining success in teaching as any particular knowledge or set of skills is. Effective teaching seems to occur when there is some kind of explicit rationale for the relationship between what the teacher does and what the students do. Good teachers ask "Do instructional activities take place as planned, and are they producing the outcomes intended?" Also, the relationship between the teacher's activities and the students' learning depends on the social system in the classroom. In school, the teacher has the right and the obligation to control and evaluate the students. Learning appears to depend on how this authority is used (Cohen, 1972).

Another conclusion about learning in the classroom is that it depends on a number of interacting variables. In any determination of the success of a learning situation, we therefore should consider the developmental history of each member of the group, including background conditions, personality variables, cognitive variables, socioeconomic status, and sex. These variables, in fact, seem to interact with the behavior of the participants in a certain environment (Randhawa & Fu, 1973).

From the above research, the inference can be drawn that there is no one organizational pattern that is ideal for all instructional situations. The question ceases to be one of selecting an "open" or "individualized" approach in contrast to a "self-contained" or "grouped" approach, but rather how best to integrate the various kinds of instructional organization patterns and procedures into an efficient and effective learning climate. As such, organizational patterns will be viewed primarily as an administrative device that never eliminates individual differences. "Openness" and "individualization" seem to be as much attitudes as they are organizational procedures. Since there can never be a true homogeneous or heterogeneous group, organizing the classroom should not become an end in itself but must always be a means for realizing the goals and objectives of a relevant reading program. The ways in which the various organizational patterns are important to learning and teaching reading and writing will be explored throughout this text.

The degree to which children undertake directed and independent study will vary in different circumstances. In individualized instruction, each child does not need to work independently (which can sometimes be a very lonely undertaking), nor does each child need to do something completely different from what all the others do, nor do all children need to work simultaneously. Individualized instruction means providing for the growing needs of every student by giving each the type of organizational structure that student needs to learn.

THE INFORMED TEACHER

In order to develop lifelong learners among their students, teachers themselves must be lifelong learners. A continuously growing body of knowledge exists in almost every subject area. Teachers should, of course, be knowledgeable about the world in which they live. They should also be familiar with the field of education. The purpose of this book is not to inform teachers about their world. This they must do on their own. Suffice it to say, that teachers should not only live their lives "as a teacher"; to be complete human beings they must also have interests that go beyond their vocational training. As Thompson stated, if an individual "could not survive the subtraction of his job from his identity, then there wasn't really much to him in the first place" (1972).

Yet educators need to keep abreast of current research, publications, theoretical positions, and instructional practices. Since reading and writing are communicaton, they are concerns of many people and not just educators. Many allied fields of study have both their own specialized knowledge of and their own techniques for approaching the study of reading and writing. From sociology, mass media and social class structure, social psychology, child development, cognitive and language development, linguistics, psycholinguistics, educational psychology, the media of instruction and behavior analysis, ophthalmology, and perception will continue to come contributions to our knowledge of the reading process. The classroom teacher must decide which information is valid for the guiding of learning in a relevant reading and writing program. Just as children should cultivate the art of critical and questioning acceptance of written communication, so must the classroom teacher. We must be wise consumers in the scholastic market.

As a teacher concerned with providing an educational program to foster the growth and development of the reading and writing processes you must be a reader and writer yourself. To develop readers who are independent and self-reliant, who are comfortable and proficient in handling reading matter from many sources and disciplines, who search for alternatives to problems without dogmatically accepting the "printed word" just because it is printed, and who realize that education does not occur only in the classroom, to develop readers who can do all these things you must be able to do them yourself. To develop the complete human potential of their students, schools must be staffed with teachers who recognize their own qualities and who continually search to fulfill their potential as informed teachers and citizens of our society. As Jacobs asserted, "The essence of being human is to be in charge of one's life—to assume responsibility for oneself, to be willing to renew and remake oneself on the basis of evidence that renewal and remaking are essential to one's well-being as an individual" (1971).

Discussion Questions and Activities

1. How would you explain to a group of parents why their children should learn to read? What characteristics of the school population would you have to consider when formulating your answers? After deciding how you would explain this issue, how would you present it?
2. Explain how proponents of two different school or classroom organizational patterns might react to the following statement by William Armentrout (1970).

    School has the obligation to provide flexibility and diversity for the vast differences and rates of growth children come to school with.

3. Explain what the following statement by John Goodlad (1969) means to you:

   Take the educational environment beyond school and classroom and learning can be humanized.

4. What is your reaction to the following statement by H. Alan Robinson (1969)?

   The saddest scene is to observe those teachers who work in the midst of a changed environment but don't recognize it—who go on trying to do what they have learned and, in the face of failure, blame their failure on the learners.

5. What has appeared in the professional literature about classroom organizational procedures—grouping, individualizing instruction, "open" classroom—in the last year?

For students who are currently teaching:

6. Keep a record for one week of the different grouping procedures you followed in your classroom. What kind of activities did you use in each grouping? Would any particular instructional lesson have been more effective if done with a different grouping procedure? What kind of activities and groupings seemed to go together best?
7. Keep a record for one week of the different roles you used as a classroom teacher. Did you use the same type of role in all instructional situations? Did you use a different role for teaching arithmetic or social studies? Did you ever start out to function in one role and find that you had to change roles? If so, what made you change?

Further Readings

The name may have changed from "Right to Read" to "Basic Skills," but the political and legal issues surrounding the teaching of reading continue. The first entry is an answer to those who call for simplistic basics as the cure-all for children with problems in learning to read. The second is a collection of articles by educators and lawyers on the complex relationship between reading and the law.

Gutknecht, Bruce, and Donna Keenan, "Basic Skills: Not Which, but Why and Enlightened How," *The Reading Teacher* 31 (1978): 668-674.

Harper, Robert J., II, and Gary Kilarr, eds., *Reading and the Law* (Newark, DE: International Reading Association and the Clearinghouse on Reading and Communication, 1978).

To help teachers understand how information-processing models can be implemented in classrooms, the following book shows six ways to enhance learning in any classroom:

Eggen, Paul D., Donald P. Kauchak, and Robert J. Harder, *Strategies for Teachers: Information Processing Models in the Classroom* (Englewood Cliffs, NJ: Prentice-Hall, 1979).

For resources related to the study and teaching of reading, the following guide should be helpful:

Davis, Bonnie M., *A Guide to Information Sources for Reading* (Newark, DE: International Reading Association and ERIC/CRIER, 1972).

There are professional organizations that publish journals, books, and other materials that teachers will find informative and useful. The journals contain articles, comments from readers, news of recent materials or instructional and professional literature, summaries of research, advertisements of educational products, and information about the organization.

The Reading Teacher, The Journal of Reading. The International Reading Association (IRA), 800 Barksdale Road, P.O. Box 8139, Newark, DE 19711

Language Arts. The National Council of Teachers of English (NCTE), 11 Kenyon Road, Urbana, IL 61801

Reading World. The College Reading Association (CRA), c/o Ellen Fuchs, Oxford University Press, 200 Madison Avenue, New York, NY 10016

Other magazines pertaining to reading and language arts are

Reading Newsreport. Multi Media Education, Inc., 11 West 42nd Street, New York 10036

Instructor. The Instructor Publications, Inc., P.O. Box 6099, Duluth, MN 55806

Teacher. CGM Professional Magazines, Inc., 22 West Putnam Avenue, Greenwich, CT 06830

The Elementary School Journal. The Elementary School Journal, 5835 Kimbark Avenue, Chicago, IL 60637

Two references for general and research articles on reading and its related topics are the *Education Index* and the *Current Index to Journals in Education.* These are monthly publications with semiannual and annual cumulations, indexes to periodicals, book reviews, government documents, conference proceedings, and yearbooks. *The Education Index,* which has subheadings arranged by author and subject, and the *Current Index to Journals in Education,* which has only subject subheadings, have some duplication of articles, but not enough to warrant the use of one index over the other.

As an aid to educators in locating and using information about the American educational system, a national network of information clearinghouses was established and is supported by the Department of Education, National Institute of Education (NIE). The purpose of the Educational Resources Information Center (ERIC) is to provide ready access to current research results and related information to the people who need it—teachers, administrators, researchers, educational policy makers, and interested members of the general public. The ERIC Clearinghouse on Reading and Communication Skills (ERIC/RCS) is one center in the nationwide network whose task is to organize, analyze, and make available documents and products to people interested in the field of reading. There has been a wide variety of resources produced, including the *Guides to Information Sources in Reading,* state-of-the-art monographs (produced in conjunction with the International Reading Association and/or the National Council of Teachers of English), interpretive monographs directed to special audiences, special bibliographies and reviews, broad subject bibliographies, basic references on reading, and bibliographies related to special ERIC collections. Many of the above documents are reproduced in hard copy, and all of them are available in microfiche. The ERIC materials are found in the educational/periodicals section of most college and university libraries and in the periodicals section of many public libraries. All resources of the ERIC system are catalogued in the monthly journal *Resources in Education* (RIE).

Teachers interested in children's literature and its related aspects will want the materials and newsletters of the Children's Book Council, 67 Irving Place, New York, NY 10003. Their materials, some of which have a nominal fee, report on new publications, events for stimulating the use of books in the schools and libraries information about authors and illustrators, free or inexpensive materials provided by commercial publishers, and suggestions for fostering the "reading habit." Send them a large, stamped, self-addressed envelope to obtain more information.

Teachers wishing to be placed on mailing lists so that they can receive catalogs and brochures can contact the publishers of instructional materials advertised in the professional journals. Quite often, publishers are willing to send teachers examination copies of instructional materials appropriate to their teaching situations. Names and addresses of the major educational publishing houses are easily obtained from the advertisements in any of the journals and magazines mentioned previously.

Of course, the teacher, wanting to know how the educational scene is viewed by the general public, should be aware of the many reports, articles, and critiques published in the mass media. Newspapers and popular magazines often carry articles pertaining to the teaching and/or learning of the reading process.

Chapter 2

HUMAN COMMUNICATION AND THE DEVELOPMENT OF THINKING AND LANGUAGE

Focus Questions

1. What do verbal and nonverbal communication systems have in common? How do they differ?
2. What can cause a breakdown in the communication process?
3. What are the basic structures of human language?
4. How is meaning signaled in present-day American English?
5. What are the developmental stages of growth in Human thinking?
6. What are the traits of human intelligence?
7. What is the difference between the way long-term memory and short-term memory retain information?
8. What are the developmental stages of language acquisition?

In the broadest sense, communication is all the procedures by which one mind may affect another. Human communication is the process by which people relate to one another. Language is the vehicle of verbal communication, an arbitrarily agreed-upon pattern consisting primarily of vocal sounds that retain their significance in different situation. This chapter and the next discuss the structures and patterns of language and how they represent meaning. An understanding of the nature of verbal communication and the thinking, reading, and writing processes is necessary for the effective instruction of reading and writing. The ideas presented are used to create the instructional strategies presented throughout the remainder of the text.

In this chapter we first define human communication and some factors that may cause its breakdown. Then the discussion demonstrates how English is structured and how children acquire and develop the ability to think and to use spoken language.

HUMAN COMMUNICATION

Communication is the process by which information is transmitted from one person to another or from one group to another. It generally has three stages: transmission, perception, and evaluation (see Figure 2–1).

A message may be transmitted by actions that are either verbal (in spoken or written language) or nonverbal (in previously agreed-upon or accepted patterns of meaningful signals or body movements). Another person perceives the message and may retain it for future reference. Or after evaluating it, the receiver may find it necessary to respond. In that case, the receiver may become a transmitter, and the process of communication continues.

Human communication must be examined within the context in which it is used, that is, the cultural situation. "Every cultural pattern and every single act of social behavior involve communication in either an explicit or an implicit sense" (Sapir, 1967). Competence in using cultural patterns or codes is reflected in a person's ability to participate in social activities. This means that no manner of communication, either verbal or nonverbal, is learned outside a social setting. Human communication is learned only in contact with and in relation to other humans. How well we learn to communicate with others determines how well we will function within that social setting. Therefore, it may not be possible to take

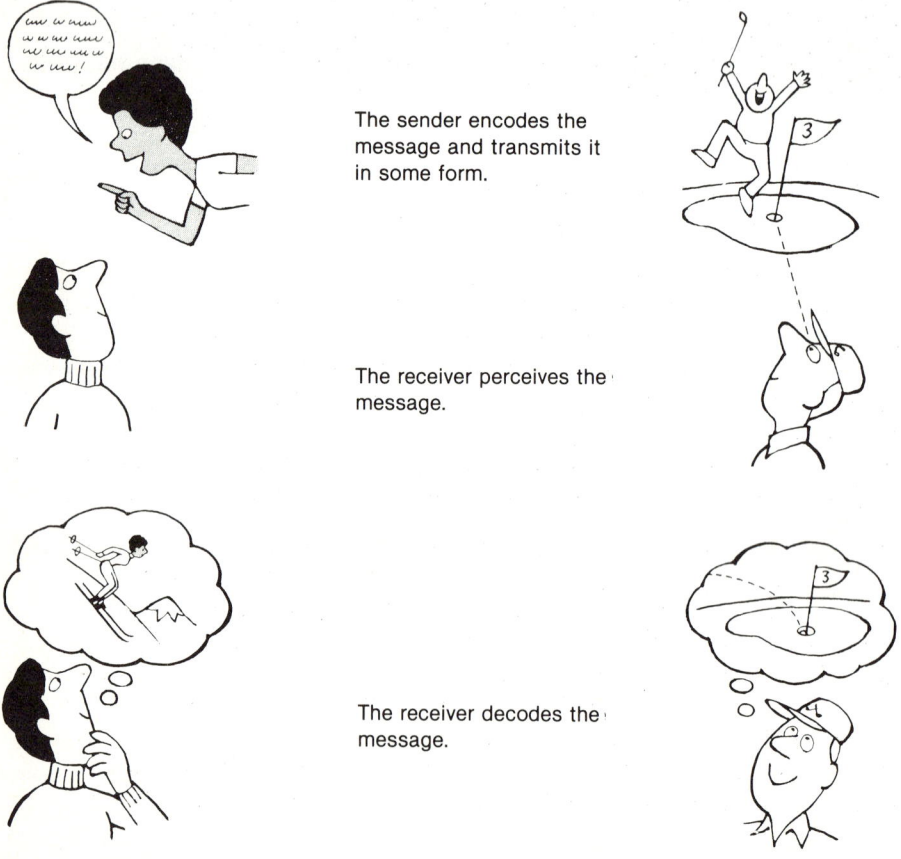

Figure 2-1 The Communication Process

on the cultural practices of another group except through participation in that other group (Byers & Byers, 1972).

Nonverbal communication is sometimes referred to as *paralinguistic communication*. It is the way individuals convey information, feelings, and attitudes without words. These are referred to as languages because, like verbal communication, they are patterns of cues and signals meaningful to the members of a cultural group or social organization. They are usually learned intuitively by the group's members. The paralinguistic system comprises sign languages, body movements and gestures, pantomime and dance, and the intentional display of material things (kinds of dress, car, and house, for example, communicate feelings, beliefs, and attitudes).

There is a strong relationship between the verbal and nonverbal communication systems of a culture. So much so that many verbal messages are conveyed on two levels: (1) the statement itself, and (2) the factors pertaining to its interpretation. The receiver of a message unconsciously uses the nonverbal signals accompanying the message. The transmitter of the message may, either unconsciously or consciously, use paralinguistic signals. These signals may be used to help the receiver understand the message or to obscure the true meaning of the message. The role of gesture in daily communications is so important that "one may intuitively interpret the relatively unconscious symbolisms of gesture as psychologically more significant in a given context than the words actually used" (Sapir, 1967). This may create misunderstandings, as discussed in the next section.

Other nonverbal communication signal systems to which all people respond are the intonational patterns of speech and the use of space. The volume of a verbal message often conveys meanings that reinforce or contradict the message delivered verbally. In addition, the pitch of one's voice indicates attitudes and feelings. Often there is a response to the openness of a speaker's voice, that is, the hollow or resounding effect of the voice, rather than to the message itself. Listeners are often affected by the softness or sharpness of speech (drawls or tight-lipped staccato speech). The tempo of speech also influences the way a message is received.

In summary, human communication is an arbitrary, systematic set of symbols associated with ideas, feelings, and attitudes. The verbal signals—signs, actions, gestures, vocal features—transmit meaning usually on an unconscious level. The verbal and nonverbal signaling systems are learned intuitively in a cultural setting in interaction with other people.

BARRIERS TO COMMUNICATION

Some breakdown in the communication process may occur if an individual is unaware of the features of a communication code. The most immediately apparent and striking situation is when two individuals speak different languages. However, there are more subtle barriers to effective communication. These, because they are not consciously realized, can be confusing to the sender and the receiver of the message. The subtler aspects of communication are very important. In fact, one who is not familiar with the subtleties is likely to be baffled by the significance of certain kinds of behavior, even though there is thorough awareness of the general external forms and the verbal symbols that accompany them (Sapir, 1967).

Although all communication depends on some accord between the sender and the recipient of the message, it is impossible to know ahead of time the degree of agreement. Only after the message has been sent and attempts have been made to receive and evaluate it do breakdowns become evident.

Failures in communication may occur when

1. The receiver has a limited capacity—that is, any physical or cognitive inability to receive and evaluate a message effectively.
2. Unwanted emotional noise is interjected. Emotional noise may take the form of unstated assumptions by the receiver about the intended message. These prior expectations are the connotations given to certain words. When the receiver's connotations differ from those of the speaker, the intended communication is not conveyed.
3. The message is transmitted in a confounding manner. The speaker might make ambiguous statements or deliver the message with nonverbal signals that contradict the verbal ones.

Effective communication results from active participation in the life activities of a social group. We are deemed competent in a group if we can use the group's communication system. Skill in using verbal language is usually judged by looking at the message itself to see if it matches what was expected. When there is a high degree of correlation, the person is considered competent in using language skills. An individual's nonverbal communication competence is judged by examining what is occurring among communicators. When there seems to be reciprocal understanding among the communicators, efficient communication has occurred.

These insights have consequences for the classroom. "When we teach children how to participate in communication with others, we are teaching them how to learn" (Byers & Byers, 1972). Quite often, an individual's failure to learn is due to the presence of a barrier to effective communication. Simple translation of a verbal message will not overcome the lack of communication between a teacher who speaks English and a child for whom English is a second language. Also, dialogues between speakers of different dialects are not always successful because of felt, but not consciously realized, linguistic or emotional static. More about this will be discussed in Chapter 12.

Figure 2-2
Source: From *Amelia Bedelia* by Peggy Parish, illustrated by Fritz Siebel. Text copyright 1963 by Margaret Parish. Pictures copyright 1963 by Fritz Siebel. Reprinted by permission of Harper & Row.

Effective classroom communication between the teacher and the students, and among the students as well, is the result of a classroom environment in which all share knowledge. Teachers are responsible for detecting differing social or cultural viewpoints that might impede communication. Once these have been identified, a common system of communication can be developed. The result might well be the reduction of classroom misunderstandings and conflicts.

SIGNALING MEANING

The following generalizations about language are accepted by linguists:

1. Language, any language, is a system of arbitrary vocal symbols used for human communication. The key to understanding languages in general is that they are systematic. The structure of any language can be described and predicted.

2. All languages allow their speakers to deal with the world. In fact, no known natural language is any more advanced than any other is. Each language can express any experience understood by its users.
3. Vocal symbols are associated by convention, with objects, ideas and actions. The users of a language agree (usually implicitly) to a relationship between the sounds uttered and the concepts to which the sounds refer. The relation of word to meaning, in short, is arbitrary.
4. Every language is unique and can be described only in terms of its own structure. It might be possible to compare languages, but only their similarities and differences can be noted. The structure of another language or the rules of how one language signals meaning cannot be used to explain these procedures in another language. For example, a knowledge of the rules of how Latin conveys meaning will not necessarily help in understanding the way in which English conveys meaning.
5. All languages presently used by some group or society are constantly changing. Examples of changes in present-day American English are most evident in the new words entering the language and the new meanings being assigned to already existing words. More subtle changes are evident, for example, in the dropping of the adverbial *ly* in a statement such as "Go slow!" Other changes include the use of alternative pronunciations of words (*add VER tiz ment* and *add ver TIZE ment*), variant spellings of the same word (programmed and programed), and the different ways for constructing what become accepted, grammatical statments ("I think I should go" and "I think that I should go").
6. The details of a language system must be learned in a social setting.
7. A spoken language generally varies from place to place, with social or occupational status, and in differing social situations.
8. Every language has built into its structure a factor of redundancy, that is, a feature in which meaning is signaled in more than one way. For example, in English, in the sentence "The boys are here," the information regarding plurality is signaled not only by the *s* but also by the form of the verb *to be* (Wardhaugh, 1977; Marquardt, 1965).

A distinction is usually made between the *structure* of language and the *function* of language. Structure refers to the form of the language. Function refers to the purpose of language, and pragmatics is the study of that use. Aside from its role as a means of expressing and recording thoughts, language functions as the medium in which we think. In a subtle way, it may help shape our thought processes.

The meaning of the term *psycholinguistics* may now become clearer. Psycholinguistics is the science that investigates the mental processes that underlie language use. Psycholinguists distinguish between language as a communication system and cognition as the thought processes of the language user. Because of the increasing evidence that thought and language are mutually inclusive, some researchers have concluded that "thinking is always thinking in some language"

(Schaff, 1973). Language is conceived as a template or screen through which the world is codified. The language of a society or group provides the categories into which the events of the world are placed. These are the "schemas" about which we shall say more in a later section. When a language does not have a specific category for an event, a distinction, or some aspect of reality, then one of two things seems to happen: (1) the event or distinction is totally ignored, or (2) it is placed into another category, and the two events, although observed by members of another group as different, are conceived to be the same thing. This is another way of saying that unless two people share similar social and linguistic contexts, then communication is impossible. For example, American English divides the color spectrum into six main categories (red, orange, yellow, green, blue, purple) and then subdivides these categories into tints, shades, and hues—gradations of the colors. The result is that we "see" a vast array of colors on a paint-shop color chart. However, some native American languages categorize the color spectrum into four units and thus do not have as many color gradations as American English does.

The Structure of All Languages

In the 1940s, psycholinguistics originated when researchers combined the knowledge and insights from both behaviorist psychology (followers of Skinner and others) and descriptive linguistics (followers of those who examined and described the structure of language). In the 1950s, another version of psycholinguistics emerged. In this version, cognitive psychologists joined transformational linguists in studying the mind through studying language. This later version of psycholinguistics emphasized the powerful regularities of the underlying language system rather than the way sentences sound or look when we hear, speak, read, and write them (Malmstrom, 1977).

Many of the psycholinguistic insights discussed here start with the theory of language developed by Noam Chomsky and called *generative* or *transformational grammar*. His theory is called generative because it tries to explain how speakers are able to produce, or generate, all of the sentences of their language. A generative grammar of a language is a "system of rules that can ... generate an indefinitely large number of structures" (Chomsky, 1965). Figure 2-3 represents the components of a natural language grammar.

Chomsky's theory postulates that languages have three components: (1) The *syntactic component* explains the formation of sentences, and the study of syntax examines how sentences are formed in a language. (2) The *semantic component* assigns meanings to strings of words, and semantics investigates how meaning is assigned and interpreted. (3) The *phonological component* determines how strings of words are put into sounds and transmitted. Because we are concerned with written language, we can, without damage to Chomsky's model, call this component graphophonological and specify that it also determines how words are written.

```
                    ┌─ Base
                    │    ↓
SYNTACTIC           │  Deep Structures ─────────▶ SEMANTIC COMPONENT
COMPONENT           │                              (yields semantic
(generates          ┤     transformations          interpretations)
grammatical         │
structures)         │    ↓
                    └─ Surface Structures ───────▶ PHONOLOGICAL COMPONENT
                                                   (yields phonetic
                                                   interpretations)
```

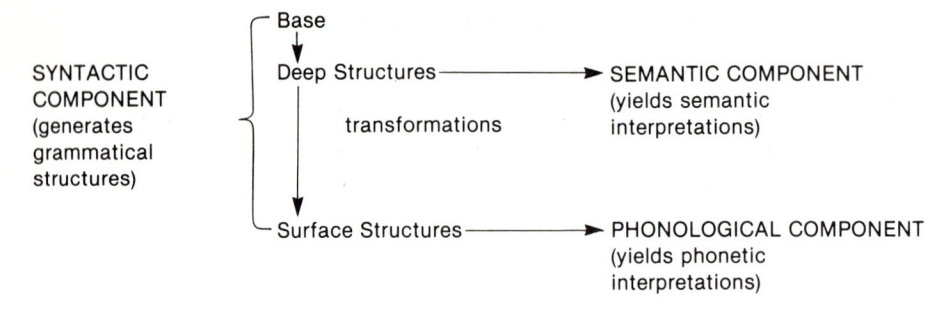

Figure 2-3 Chomsky's Transformational Theory of Grammar (1965)
Note: Chomsky has recently modified his theory so that the Semantic Component interprets Surface Structures rather than Deep Structures. For our purposes, it will be worthwhile to ignore this refinement.

Chomsky's theory states that every sentence has a *deep structure* that determines the semantic interpretation of that sentence. This deep structure specifies the basic syntactic relations among the elements of the sentence and is close to the basic underlying meaning of the sentence. The *surface structure* is the form of the sentence that is either spoken or written, the only form of a language that we can observe and describe. The surface structure arises from the deep structure through certain formal operations called grammatical transformations.

The syntactic component contains two subcomponents, the base and the transformation rules. The base is the collection of rules that define and determine the ordering of the sentence's parts. It also contains a dictionary of terms (a denotative lexicon). The relationship of symbols to referents in this dictionary is fairly consistent, and there are no emotional or attitudinal overtones. The transformation subcomponent determines which of a number of alternative rules will be used to arrive at the surface structure. Here is an example of two sentences that have the same deep structure (meaning) but that have undergone different transformations and thus are represented by two different surface structures:

The hungry cat ate the bird.

The bird was eaten by the cat that was hungry.

The rules governing sentence production and transformations in all languages determine such things as word order, inflectional endings, and structure words.

1. Languages differ in the order of the subject and its modifiers and in the ways they may reorder words to change simple statements into questions.
2. Inflectional endings are used to indicate tense, parts of speech, plurals, mood, the status of the speaker or hearer, agreement among different parts of speech, and voice.

3. Structure words do not usually have any direct meaning in the themselves but indicate relationships among other words. They also assist other words in expressing meanings.

Languages may employ rules in one or more of these categories. The rules may parallel or be completely different from those of another language.

The semantic component pairs the sentence's deep structure with its meaning. The semantic component interprets terms, "colors" the multiple meanings of words, deals with certain aspects of specialized vocabulary, places limitations on the common speech that may be used in various situations, and changes meanings within the context of a social situation.

The graphophonological component determines what sounds or graphic representations the message will have. This component also selects such things as intonational patterns, stress, accent, and pitch, and the junctures, or pauses, used by speakers.

It should not be inferred that any part of this process actually goes on inside the speaker's head. The base, transformations, deep structures, and surface structures are convenient linguistic notions that help explain numerous phenomena. These notions may have biological correlates of some sort, though none have yet been identified.

Although Chomsky's work was an important breakthrough for understanding how languages are structured, psycholinguists began to realize that his theory provides insights only about the construction of sentences, not longer discourse, and that it emphasized grammar and not meaning. In the 1970s, psycholinguistics became more interdisciplinary as anthropologists, sociologists, and neuropsychologists joined cognitive psychologists, linguists, and educators in studying language and language development in children. What emerged from this study was an area that has become known as *generative semantics.* Researchers in this field are concerned with how language systems grow from meaning. Their work shows that a study of the grammar of language does not indicate meaning; rather, it is meaning that determines the form that sentences will take (Smith, 1978). The result has been a movement from studying specific, isolated samples of language, usually single sentences, to studying language in longer spoken or written passages and in relation to the purpose(s) for which they are intended and used.

Much of the work in generative semantics has been summarized by Graesser (1981), who identified six knowledge domains of natural language: (1) linguistic; (2) rhetorical; (3) causal conceptualization; (4) intentional conceptualization; (5) spatial; and (6) roles, personalities, and objects (see Figure 2-4).

The linguistic domain contains rules that govern the utilization and sequence of sounds (phonemics), the assignment of dictionary meanings (lexicon), the grouping and ordering of words in sentences (syntax), the construction of meanings in sentences (semantics), and the use of language in dialogue and social situations (pragmatics). The linguistic domain thus contains many of the insights of trans-

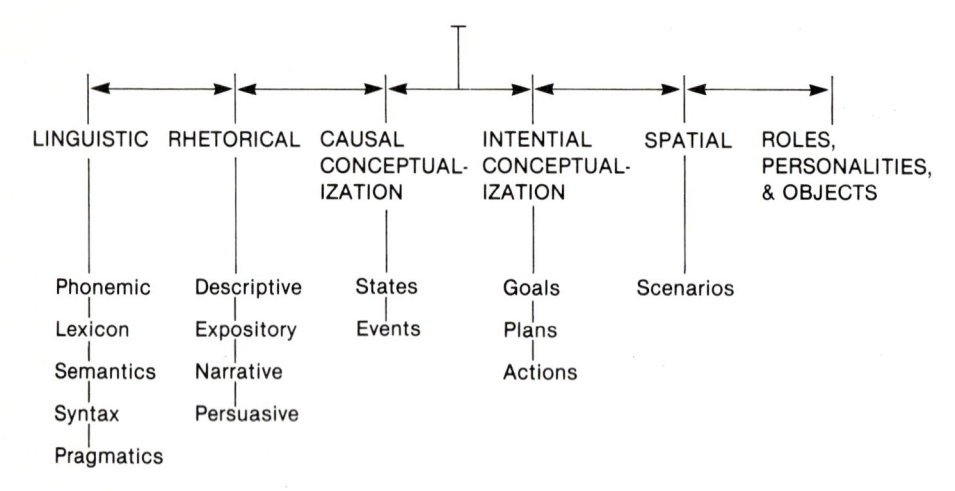

```
                    |
    |←——→|←——→|←——→ ⊥ ←——→|←——→|←——→|
    |     |     |         |     |     |
LINGUISTIC RHETORICAL CAUSAL  INTENTIAL SPATIAL ROLES,
                   CONCEPTUAL- CONCEPTUAL-        PERSONALITIES,
                   IZATION    IZATION             & OBJECTS

 Phonemic   Descriptive  States    Goals    Scenarios
    |          |           |         |
 Lexicon    Expository  Events    Plans
    |          |                    |
 Semantics  Narrative           Actions
    |          |
 Syntax     Persuasive
    |
 Pragmatics
```

Figure 2-4 Generative Semantics Knowledge Domains
Each domain contains information about the world and the way a language organizes and expresses that information. The domains are not discrete but interactive.

formational grammar theory. The least understood domain is pragmatics, the rules that govern the interactions of speaker and listener, author and reader.

Some researchers of pragmatics have constructed a theory of shared, or common, knowledge. Their work shows that when the sender and receiver of messages share background knowledge or when the communication occurs in a specific social context, the form of the message becomes more limited and more abstract than when the communicators have less in common. For example, a master craftsperson is more likely to comment to an apprentice "It won't fit unless it's rotated half a notch" than to say "The cam, in order to be aligned with the indicator, needs to be placed in a position so that it is first turned to the left the distance of half of the space of one notch."

From the study of the linguistic domain, a new view of the link between syntax and semantics has developed. Called case grammar (Fillmore, 1968), this is much more than the transformational grammar proposed by Chomsky. In case grammar, the verb is considered the key element of a sentence, and sentences are examined for their underlying syntactic-semantic relationship(s). Therefore, verbs are studied and analyzed according to the function of the nouns in relation to the verbs. There are six relationships between nouns and verbs:

1. Agent: person or thing doing the action denoted by the verb
2. Object: receiver of the action
3. Instrument: object used in performing the action on the object
4. Manner: modification or explanation of the action
5. Time
6. Location

These "cases" can be thought of as explaining the who, what or whom, with what, how, when, and where in sentences and groups of sentences.

The rhetorical domain contains rules regarding how statements should be introduced, ordered, and interrelated in different kinds of language, novels, speeches, newspaper articles, and so on so that the message has the best chance of making an impact on the listener or reader. Rhetoric is usually "descriptive," "expository," "narrative," or "persuasive."

The causal conceptualizations domain contains rules for how events and states are sequenced and influenced in a nonintentional manner. States are the more-or-less stable characteristics of the communicators' physical environment and social conditions. Events are changes within these environments and conditions. Languages have various links to the way two or more events are related in a causal way, to the way a state is the causation of an event, and to when an event results in a state. These links can be explicit or implicit in the language. For example, the knowledge that a person consistently reacts in the same way to specific actions or statements may influence the way you will make a request or offer a suggestion. Knowing this, a speaker might say "I have found that planting tomatoes at least one week after Mother's Day results in less loss to frost" in place of "Your plants died of last night's frost. You always should wait until later in May to plant tomatoes in this region."

The intentional conceptualizations domain contains the rules for organizing language depending upon the user's goals, plans, and actions. What the initiator of a message expects to achieve—a behavior, another statement, an act—and whether this goal is oriented toward the future or the past will influence how something is said or written.

The spatial domain contains the knowledge and rules of the "scenarios" that provide the context for the communicator's actions, events, and states. In other words, the specific place and situation in which the communication occurs affects the structure of the message.

The roles, personalities, and objects domain contains the rules governing the form of the language used when referring to messages concerning social roles and personality traits, characteristics, and aspects. These rules also govern language form in regard to stereotypes, impressions attributed to people, and to the physical properties of inanimate objects or the personification of such properties. These rules usually call for the use of nouns and adjectives which, in conjunction with rules from the intentional conceptualizations and rhetorical domains, might combine to have one say "John is a radical anarchist" when it is known that such labels will produce a specific action from others and that this is the speaker's intent.

These six knowledge domains are not discrete. They interact throughout the communication process. They form the basis for the message's surface structure as transmitted by the sender as well as the receiver's perception and evaluation of the message. Whether the message is received as intended or whether the communication is hindered by some barriers depends to a large extent on the shared knowledge of the rules by both parties in the communication act. Current psycholinguistic research shows that people usually focus on the meaning of a message, that is, they seem to remember the semantic and pragmatic aspects of the message rather than the exact words of its surface features. Therefore, any instruction in reading and writing must include attention to the total communication process and all features of the language rather than the surface features alone.

The Structure of English

The structure of modern American English might be better understood through examining its origin and its changes. The brief description of the history of the English language will be followed by a discussion of the phonological, semantic, and syntactic structures of present-day American English. We will then describe the features of written English and some of the differences between its written and spoken forms.

History of the English Language The known history of the English language began sometime during the sixth or seventh centuries when the Germanic Angle, Saxon, and Jute tribes invaded Celtic Britain. The Germanic languages belonged to the large family of Indo-European languages, from which almost all the languages of Europe and India are said to be descended. (At present, there is no known language ancestor for all of the known spoken languages.)

In the Middle Ages, texts written by English writers first appeared. The English of this period is called Old English or Anglo-Saxon. The English spoken from about 1100 to the Renaissance (about 1450 to 1550) is generally called Middle English. The language of Shakespeare, called Early Modern English, was spoken until about the beginning of the eighteenth century. The English spoken from that time to the present is called Modern English. These are general classifications and tend to distinguish social history rather than language characteristics. However, language historians use these distinctions to account for the gross differences in language between these periods.

In its early periods, the grammar and vocabulary of English was influenced greatly by other languages. Old English was influenced by the language of the invaders from Scandinavia and by the Norman invaders and conquerors. During the late Middle Ages, changes were caused by the strong influence of the French language. Early Modern English, that spoken during the age of world exploration, was affected by the contact of English with many different cultures. American English from the 1700s on developed separately from British English, through constant contact with Dutch, Spanish, French, the various Indian languages, German, the Scandinavian languages, Yiddish, and the speech of the Afro-American.

The sounds of English have undergone changes, too. Many of these changes are easier to follow for the Old English and Middle English periods because the spellings in these periods had a more direct relationship to the pronunciation of the words. After the Middle English period, spellings were more consistent. No longer were pronunciations always reflected in spellings. To identify the different present-day American regional pronunciations and to classify changes in these sounds, special records must be kept. As we shall see, consistent spelling patterns aid us today in written communications across regional speech patterns. On the other hand, they do not reveal the past and ongoing changes in pronunciations.

From this brief description of the development of present-day American English, certain conclusions can be drawn. Changes have occurred and continue to occur because of normal variation in society. As new ideas and technologies are produced, new language forms need to be invented to represent them. Also, as people move around the world, they create new language forms as they first become isolated and then interact with other languages and cultures. These language changes can occur in pronunciations, word forms, sentence structures, and vocabulary (Malmsrom, 1977).

Phonological Features The human voice can make hundreds of different sounds. However, each language uses no more than a few dozen. Even though there is considerable overlap among languages in the sounds used, no two languages share exactly the same sounds.

The particular sounds of a language are called *phonemes*. Individual phonemes do not carry any meaning; rather meaning is assigned only to sequences of phonemes. Within a speech community, there is an implicit agreement to group speech sounds into a few dozen classes. These are the particular sounds that constitute the phonemes of a language. When speakers of a language recognize two sounds as being significantly different, then two distinct phonemes exist. For example, the English sounds /t/[1] and /d/ are recognized as being distinct sounds.

All English speech sounds are made by the muscular movement of the speech organs as breath is expelled. Traditionally, phonemes are divided into two groups, consonants and vowels. A consonant is a speech sound in which the breath is stopped, hindered, or diverted while being emitted. A vowel is a speech sound in which the vocal tract is open and the tone is selectively changed as it passes through the resonating chambers of the throat and head. Differences in the vowel sounds depend on the postion of the tongue and changes in the shape of the mouth opening and cavity.

Some disagreement exists as to the exact number of phonemes in English. There is greater agreement on the number of consonant phonemes than there is on the number of vowel phonemes. Generally, it is felt that twenty-four consonant sounds are used. Depending on the source and method of categorizing, the

---

1. A letter in slash marks, such as /t/, represents the spoken sound usually associated with that letter or group of letters. When there is a possibility of confusion, examples will be used. An italicized letter or word represents the written form.

number may be higher or lower (Kean & Personke, 1976). Table 2-1 contains one listing of the phonemes of present-day American English.

The categories of consonants are (1) stops, (2) fricatives, (3) affricates, (4) nasals, (5) liquids, and (6) glides. The stops are produced by impeding the flow of breath by either the lips or some part of the tongue. The fricatives are produced by forcing air through an opening restricted by the lower lip or the tongue. Affricates are produced in a manner similar to the fricatives except that the tongue touches the roof of the mouth just behind the front upper teeth. The stops and the fricatives can be either voiced (that is, the vocal cords vibrate) or unvoiced. The only difference between /f/ and /v/, for example, is that the latter is voiced. The nasals, all of which are voiced sounds, are produced by emitting the sound through the nasal passage rather than through the mouth. The liquids are produced by emitting air over or around the tongue. Glides are like vowels in that the stream of air is relatively unimpeded in the oral cavity, but they nevertheless act like consonants in the flow of speech. In most cases, the consonants occur in contrasting pairs—one voiced and the other unvoiced.

There is, as mentioned, much less agreement among speech and language researchers on the exact number of vowel phonemes in present-day American English. Since the production of a vowel depends on the position of the tongue, a very large number of different sounds can be produced. All could conceivably be considered vowel sounds. It is only through ear training during the speech acquisition process that individuals learn to distinguish a few of these sounds as the usable vowels for any language. There is general agreement on the nine relative positions of the tongue during the production of English vowel sounds. In Table 2-1, "Front," "center," and "back" refer to the placement of the tongue in relation to the teeth (front) or the throat opening (back). The labels "high," "mid," and "low" refer to the height of the tongue in relation to the roof of the mouth. The low vowels are generally produced with a wider mouth opening than are the mid or high vowels.

Vowel combinations are called diphthongs. and are produced by combining vowels or a vowel and a semivowel (or glide). In this way, there are over thirty-five possible diphthongs; however, in actual practice, English uses fewer (Kean & Personke, 1976).

It is no wonder that reading teachers are confused about the teaching the "vowel sounds." All speakers of American English *know* the vowel sounds. Yet confusion arises when educators try to teach these sounds to students who already know them. When helping students associate the sounds of the language with the printed symbols representing these sounds, a great deal of frustration can be avoided if variant forms of the phonemes are recognized. No value judgment should be made regarding the various pronunciations themselves. Many of us probably do not pronounce the words *idea, father, dog,* and *merry* in the same way, and the main differences in the way they will be pronounced will be in the vowel sounds. We have learned to consider the variations in regional and

TABLE 2-1: The Phonemes of Present Day American English

Consonants

	Stops				Nasals		
*	/p/	pig, nipple, speak, rap			/n/	name, manner, fin
	/b/	big, tumble, stab			/m/	miss, hammer, ram
*	/t/	take, stop, little, fat			/ng/	ring
	/d/	dog, middle, mad				
*	/k/	Kite, skate, tickle, back		Liquids		
	/g/	got, bigger, rag			/l/	long, follow, fill
					/r/	rabbit, barrel, tear

	Fricatives				Glides		
*	/f/	fat, rifle, fluff			/w/	win, away
	/v/	vote, savor, save			/y/	yes
*	/th/	them, either, clothe		*	/h/	have
	/th/	think, ether, cloth				
*	/s/	sink, hassle, pass				
	/z/	zone, fuzz, quiz				
*	/sh/	shell, fashion, fish				
	/zh/	vision, mirage				

Affricates
* /ch/ chin, kitchen, such
  /dj/ fudge

* unvoiced

Vowels

		Front		Center		Back	
High	/ee/	feet				/oo/	pool
	/i/	it				/oo/	look
Mid	/ay/	table	/u/	up		/oh/	nose
	/e/	bed					
Low	/a/	act	/o/	ox		/aw/	saw
			/ah/	Amen			

Diphthongs
 /ie/ pie, final
 /ow/ cow, found
 /oy/ boy, soil
 /ai/ pail, stay, rake

individual speech patterns as normal and to treat variations in vowel sounds as usually not significant to meaning. These two ideas about teaching vowel sounds will be expanded later in Chapter 6 "Strategies for Developing Readiness to Read," and in Chapter 9, "Strategies for Using Graphophonological Information."

Other features of spoken English are the phonemic elements of *stress, pitch,* and *juncture.* These elements make up the intonational pattern of language. Stress refers to the relative loudness of a syllable or word, and there are usually four levels: primary, secondary, tertiary, and weak. They are signals to differences of meaning. For example, one way we know the difference between the noun *record* and the verb *record* is by the shift in stress. Also, /GROWING corn/ is not /growing CORN/.

Pitch is the relative level of a speaker's voice. English is considered to have four pitch levels. We can see by the example below that a change in pitch level can signal a change in meaning:

/we are all go^{ing} home/

/we are all going $^{home/}$

The first follows the normal intonational pattern for a declarative statement, and the second follows the normal intonational pattern for a question.

Juncture is a phonemic element closely related to pitch. Juncture refers to the pauses made between syllables, words, phrases, and sentences. Most of these pauses are so slight that they are almost imperceptible. Together with stress and pitch they combine to convey various meanings. The feature of juncture is what helps us, together with other syntactic and semantic features, to distinguish between *Seymour* and *see more, night rates* and *nitrates, scenic* and *see Nick,* and *syntax* and *sin tax.*

Syntactic Features The usual English sentence contains a subject and a predicate. In English, the order of words in a sentence is very important. In fact, the order of certain classes of words is often how meaning is signaled.

The main English word classes are nouns, verbs, adjectives, adverbs, and structure words. How a word should be classified is determined more by how it is used in the sentence than by dictionary designation. The first four classes of words are considered *content words.* These words have basic referents in the world and usually carry the content or subject of a message. The fifth class of words are considered *structure* or *function words.* They do not generally have any meaning in themselves but act as markers of the content words and establish relationships between the classes of words or between groups of these classes of words.

You will remember that the base of the syntactic component of a grammar generates deep structures. Transformations are then performed on the deep structure, and their final product is the surface structure. Linguists generally agree on the five common patterns of deep structure sentences. In the basic sentence patterns, the structure words are not considered to be important, since the meaning of the sentence is predominately carried by the word order of the four content word classes and by the relationship of the nouns and verbs in the sentence. To illustrate these classes we shall use sentences that have undergone a minimum of transformations and are thus very similar to their deep structures. We shall call such sentences "kernel sentences."

The deep structure sentence patterns are

1. *Noun-verb* or *subject-verb* structures.

   Birds fly.
   He works happily hour after hour.

2. *Noun-verb-noun* or *subject-verb-direct object* structures

   Freddy threw the stick.
   The gerbil ate the sunflower seed quickly.

3. *Noun-verb-noun-noun* or *subject-verb-indirect object-object* structures

   John gave Harry a watch.
   Father gave me a new bat.

The following patterns are often considered *noun-verb-noun-noun* patterns. Although our purpose is not to definitively describe sentence patterns but to explain the general patterns of classifying English sentences we have included these sentences to clarify these patterns.

   a. *Subject-verb-direct object-object of preposition* structures

      Billy took a letter to school.

   b. *Subject-verb-direct object-object complement* structures

      The class voted Jim door monitor.

4. *Noun-linking verb-noun* or *subject-linking verb-predicate noun* Linking verbs connect subject and complement so that the complement describes the subject.

   Walter is a monitor.

5. *Noun-linking verb-adjective* or *subject-linking verb-predicate adjective* structures

   Sheila is pretty.

Five common kinds of transformations that deep structure sentences can undergo are

1. Passive voice

    Kernel: John gave Harry a watch.
    Transform: A watch was given to Harry by John.

2. Questions

    Kernel: Freddy threw the stick.
    Transform: Did Freddy throw the stick?

3. Negative

    Kernel: Walter is a monitor.
    Transform: Walter is not a monitor.

4. Imperative

    Kernel: George gives Alice a new book.
    Transform: George, give Alice a new book!

5. Beginning with *it* and *there*

    Kernel: Answering a teacher is wise.
    Transform: It is wise to answer a teacher.
    Kernel: Birds are flying.
    Transform: There are birds flying.

Although not all English sentence patterns can be accounted for by the above categories, most of them can. From these basic patterns, an unlimited number of sentences can be formed. These new sentences are created through the application of rules governing the expansion and combination (also known as *embedding*) of whole sentences or parts of sentences.

Five common patterns of expansion and combination are

1. Compounding. Words, phrases and independent clauses are combined to form compound subjects, compound predicates, compound objects, and compound sentences.

    Kernel: Carol sat.
    Carol waited.
    Betty sat.
    Betty waited.
    Transform: Carol and Betty sat and waited.

2. Modification. Adjectives, adverbs, qualifiers, adjective and adverbial phrases, and adjective and adverbial clauses are added.

Kernel: The man gave away chickens.
Transform: The little man who wore a red hat gave away three chickens.

3. Apposition. Words, phrases, or clauses are used to restate a preceding noun.

Kernel: Gerald is secratary of the club. Gerald read the minutes of the previous meeting.
Transform: Gerald, secratary of the club, read the minutes of the previous meeting.

4. Subordination. Words, phrases, and clauses that are closely associated with and dependent on the main idea are added.

Kernel: John bought an ice cream cone.
John was not really hungry.
Transform: Although John was not really hungry, he bought an ice cream cone.

5. Parallel structure. A series of ideas in the form of equally important phrases or clauses is added.

Kernel: The children had to read a story.
The children had to draw a picture.
The children had to write three sentences.
Transform: The children had to read a story, draw a picture, and write three sentences.

Reading comprehension is the reconstruction of the meanings intended by authors. It occurs when readers understand how a text's particular syntactic surface features result from authors' decisions pertaining to the six knowledge domains of natural language. Since more than one syntactic form for a message is possible in English, authors choose forms to reflect their knowledge of the receiver(s) of the message, the intent of the message, and the situation in which the message is received. In later chapters we will explain the various strategies for guiding students to maturity in this reconstruction process.

Semantic Features Upon hearing the word semantics, one usually thinks first of word meanings. Semantics as a language study, however, is concerned with the ability of speakers to interpret sentences. Thus semantics is both the meanings or concepts attached to words, singly and in strings, and the relationship of meaning to syntactic and phonological structure.

In English, words have various functions as parts of a sentence. When words are discussed as parts of a sentence, they are called *parts of speech,* which signify the positions of certain words in sentences and the meaning that usage signals.

The first part of our discussion is not of semantics in its strict sense. Rather, it is a discussion of syntactic features that allow the reader to determine certain meaningful relationships between and among words and sentences. (It might be helpful at this point to refer back to the discussion of case grammar.) The syntactic roles and functions of words are important to understand because they signal the meaning of other words and phrases and sentences. (The reader's use of these signals for understanding an author's message is discussed in Chapter 8, and strategies for developing and expanding students' understanding of words are discussed in Chapter 9.)

The content words can often be recognized by certain structural features and by the changes that occur in these words according to the part of speech they take in a sentence. For example, the word *know* becomes *knowledge* or *knowledgeable* and the word *nation* becomes *national* or *nationalize* according to now they function as different parts of speech. In these cases, a signal to the meaning of the word can be found in the word itself.

The smallest sound unit, you will recall, is the phoneme. But a sound by itself usually does not convey any meaning. Only combinations of these sounds convey meaning. These combinations, *morphemes,* are minimal meaningful forms.

The English language has two forms of morphemes, free and bound. A free morpheme is a group of sounds that by themselves signal meaning. For example, *walk, tooth,* and *pretty* are free morphemes because they can be combined with other free morphemes to create sentences. A bound morpheme is a sound or group of sounds that signals meaning only when it is combined with other free or bound morphemes. For example, *s* is a bound morpheme that signals meaning when it is combined with *coat* to form *coats.*

Sometimes a morpheme can be both a free and a bound morpheme. For instance, *ball* and *meter* are considered free morphemes; yet they are bound morphemes in *football* and *thermometer.* The bound forms of the morphemes are spelled identically, but they do not always retain their original meanings or pronunciations.

Structure words are classified by the role they play in sentences. The various categories of structure words are

1. Noun markers. Words such as *a, an, the, their, this, my* and *some* signal the appearance of a noun or noun phrase.
2. Verb markers. Words such as (a) forms of *to be, to have,* and *to do* used as auxiliary verbs and (b) other auxiliaries such as *well, shall, ought, may,* and *can* signal an oncoming verb or verb phrase.
3. Qualifiers. Words such as *very, too,* and *much* signal the relative strength of an oncoming adjective or adverb.
4. Prepositions. Words such as *up, down, in, out, out of, above,* and *below* combine with noun forms to create phrases that modify other parts of speech.
5. Clause markers. Words such as (a) the relative pronouns *who, whom, which, what* and *that* and (b) the subordinating conjunctions *if, because, although, even, while,* and *until* all signal the onset of a dependent clause.
6. Question markers. Words such as *who, why, how, where, when what, did, are, is, have, do,* and *has* often begin sentences and signal question transformations.

7. Negatives. Words such as *no, not, never, nor* and *none*.

The semantic features of English also refer to (1) definitions of words—both denotative and conotative—(2) the concept of unity and coherence, and (3) the context of the communication situation. The latter point, the context of the communication situation, is discussed in the next section, "Pragmatics."

Dictionaries record the most common meanings of words, their denoted meaning(s); connotative meaning(s) are given to words because of how or when or by whom they are used. These meanings transcend a word's specific dictionary definition. For example, one meaning of *club* is an organization of individuals with a common goal, purpose, or interest. But to some people, a *club* implies an elitist group, snobbery, and exclusion. Word meanings, therefore, develop within the context of sentences and longer discourse and are related to specific communication situations.

In addition, certain features of English indicate the coherence of a message or prose passage (Schafer, 1981). When a message is coherent, it "holds together"; there are no abrupt jumps or missing links between ideas. The devices of cohesion are

1. Reference. The use of pronouns to refer to another word.
2. Substitution. The use of a synonym for the original word.
3. Ellipsis. The deletion of an intended term(s) from subsequent sentences, as in "I went to the movies last night and enjoyed the show. So did Mary." (So did Mary what? She went to the movies last night and enjoyed the show.)
4. Connection. The use of various terms (*therefore, although*) that connect or subordinate ideas.

Additional examples of these devices for cohesion can be found in Chapter 8, "Strategies for Reconstructing Meaning."

Pragmatics Closely related to the semantic features of language are the functions for which language is used. Pragmatics is the study of how and when language is used. The syntactic and phonological features are essential in signaling meaning; yet much of the meaning of a message results from the *manner* in which a speaker or writer uses language. This functional aspect of communication combines the other basic elements of communication—the content and the form of the message. The five dominant pragmatic functions of spoken English are

1. The controlling function. Statements to direct or affect the behavior of another person as well as responses to control. Examples are requests, suggestions, warnings, acknowledgments, refusals, and assents.
2. The sharing function. Statements and expressions of feelings to others.

Examples are praises, commiserations, ridiculings, approvals, apologies, and rejections.
3. The informing function. Statements occurring when we provide ideas and information to others. Examples are namings and giving examples, responses to information given by others, answers, questions, and denials.
4. The ritualizing function. Statements that help sustain social relationships with others. Examples are greetings, thank yous, introductions, and teasings.
5. The imagining function. Statements dealing creatively with reality through language. Examples are speculations, fantasizings, story tellings, and dramatizations. (Wood, 1981)

The social functions of a message can be obvious, as in "I want you to wear your mittens today," or it can be implicit, as in "It's rather cold today; I think you left your mittens on the floor of your closet," in which case, the pragmatic features of the message are not apparent unless one knows the complete communication situations, including the relationship between the speaker and receiver of the message. There is evidence that children learn first to attend to what is meant by a message and then learn to pay attention to what is said (Olson, 1981). This literal understanding of a message seems to be acquired as a result of learning to read and write.

In spoken language, the pragmatic features may be provided by nonverbal linguistic features such as sign language, symbols, and gestures. Also, as is most often the case, any communication involves the interplay of more than one function. For example, two functions come into play when someone controls a situation by using a ritualized means of introductions.

Graphic Features It is commonly heard that writing is talk written down. In a way it is. However, there are a number of stylistic features found in one form that are not found in the other. Written language is not merely speech in graphic form, just as reading, though similar to listening, is more than "listening with the eyes" (Olson, 1981). These differences include features of phonographemics, syntax, semantics, and pragmatics. The differences between the forms becomes most apparent when individuals attempt to transpose one form into the other (write down speech, read aloud expository prose).

Spoken prose and conversation differ in the use of tempo, juncture, and redundancy. Juncture in spoken prose is related to the written message and follows the pattern of punctuation. In conversation, juncture can be quite unpredictable. In spoken prose, tempo will be rather uneven. In conversation, there is much redundancy, not only for emphasis, but also for maintaining the continuity of one's ideas. Also, the pronunciation of words—especially articulation deviations—goes relatively unnoticed in conversation.

Written English at present is not directly phonetic. There is no longer a single, simple, one-letter-to-one-sound relationship. In some cases, one letter represents a sequence of sounds, as in /x/. In other cases, a sequence of letters represents a single sound, as in /th/. There has been a tendency to retain the same spelling a word had when it first entered the language or the spelling it had in the language from which it was borrowed. For example, the /sh/ pronounced in *ocean* reflects the spelling of its Greek origin; the same sound in *nation* reflects the spelling of its Latin origin.

There is difficulty, though, in drawing hard and fast conclusions about the differences between spoken and written English. First, there is a methodological problem in research. Researchers have used different types of oral language passages as a means for comparison, since it is impossible to obtain material on the same topic, intended for the same audience, and presented by the same communicator through both modes. Second, authors and speakers confront the problem of audience from different perspectives. The author must address unknown readers, in unknown contexts, and with unknown states of knowledge. Therefore, authors must use more explicit references and link propositions and ideas in a more logical manner than speakers do, who directly confront their audiences.

We must keep in mind that a writing system is one form the symbolization of a language, but it is not the language itself. Both spoken and written languages have many levels. They both have a standard and nonstandard form and a formal and an informal tone, and they both can be scholarly and "edited" or slangy and unrevised. We should not consider these variations as "corruptions of the language." Language changes continually, and should it cease to change, it no longer would be adequate for human communication: language change does not mean language decay.

In conclusion to this section on understanding verbal communication:

The effectiveness of a communication is not related to the use of an extensive vocabulary, careful articulation of speech sounds, or perfect grammatical phrasing. Instead, it is based on the appropriateness of what we say. The message must be appropriate to the person, the setting (time and place), the topic being discussed and the task at hand. The competent communicator carefully weighs the factors of the communication situation:

1. participants: the person(s) involved in communication
2. setting: the time and place of the communication event
3. topic: the subject matter of communication
4. task: the goal or purpose of communication (Wood, 1981)

HUMAN THINKING

Living entails thinking, and thinking entails resolving uncertainty (or at least the attempt). The term *problem solving* is applied to thinking that is aimed toward adjusting to a new situation or resolving some conflict. How people develop this problem-solving capacity, how it is related to the nature of language, and how it affects and is affected by the development of language are receiving increased attention by psycholinguistic researchers. Their findings regarding human thinking and language are rapidly changing our knowledge of thought and language. The following discussions represent a synthesis of current research on these topics. Although this information may be modified in the future, there is strong evidence that it will not change radically.

The basis for all current ideas about thinking is called *schema theory*. At one time the basis of thinking was believed to be the acquisition and use of concepts—categories of mental experiences learned by individuals during their lifetime. Although the idea of concepts is important to schema theory, the model of thinking involves much more than what is considered to be a concept.

Schema Theory

Schema theory is a theory about knowledge that postulates that a spoken or written text does not in itself carry meaning. In schema theory, we construct meaning by using our previously acquired knowledge (schemas). The theory specifies how our knowledge interacts with and shapes incoming information and how the knowledge we have must be organized to support this interaction (Graesser, 1981; Hacker, 1980; Rumelhart, 1981).

Features of Schemas Schemas are the building blocks of thinking. They are generic rather than specific knowledge structures. They are broad concepts that are stored in memory. Concepts, like schemas, are the categories we create for sorting out and responding to the world. The categories reflect our culture and serve to reduce environmental complexity, to identify objects around us, to reduce the necessity of constant learning, to provide direction for basic life activities, and to order and relate different kinds of events (Bruner et al., 1956). For a concept to be developed, we must have a series of earlier experiences that are similar in one or more respects. The common features of those experiences are generalized, and it is this general description of the similarity of the features that we consider a concept (Carroll, 1966). Schemas, though, are and do much more than concepts.

Schemas are structures for reproducing concepts that are stored in memory. They guide our interpretations, inferences, expectations, and attention. They are not merely memories of events but are an organized, structured set of summaries of the parts, attributes, and relationships that occur in specific "things" or "events" in our world. They are created after years of experiences (Graesser, 1981).

One main feature of schemas is the collection of variables forming their structures (Graesser, 1981; Hacker, 1980; Rumelhart, 1981). These variables can be categorized in the six knowledge domains of language discussed previously:

linguistic; rhetorical; causal conceptualizations; intentional conceptualizations; spatial; and roles, personalities, and objects (see Figure 2-4). The variables of schemas are like scripts or little plays stored in our memory. They allow us to know and understand such things as "going shopping" or "going to school." The scripts for such activities may include:

characters: customers, clerks, students, teachers, principals
objects: goods, counters, desks, pencils, paper
goals: the customer purchases goods and pays the bill; students learn; teachers teach
logical orders: obtain item from shelf, go to check it out, total bill, pay; arrive at school, morning routines, day divided into periods or subjects, related activities, lunch, recess, dismissal

A second feature of schemas is that they can be embedded, or nested, one within the other. Some schemas contain subschemas. For example, in the shopping schema, there is the subschema of "bill paying." In the school schema, each learning activity or subject area may have its own script or plot.

A third feature of schemas is that they can represent various levels of abstractness. Some schemas may be concrete, such as the schema for mixing colors from the three primary colors, and some can be very abstract, such as that for relating stylized map features to real geographic properties.

A fourth feature is that schemas represent broad aspects of knowledge rather than definitions (Graesser, 1981). With such a view of schemas, it is possible to understand that people may possess incomplete schemas for some aspects of the world. For example, to understand the schema of shopping, we need not only a definition of the term *shopping* but also an understanding of the general components of grocery stores or supermarkets, and general attributes of stores, the actions of shopping, and the relationships between shoppers and sellers. This understanding may not necessarily be a complete knowledge of all aspects of all stores and all shopping instances. What we develop is a universal or generic understanding so that we can shop in a large variety of food-selling establishments.

Finally, schemas are active processes. They are constantly examining incoming information in an effort to determine how it fits with existing schemas or whether it needs to be developed on its own as a new schema. This feature will become clearer as we study the processes of schemas.

Processes of Schemas   Schemas are used for identification and schema application. At first glance, this may seem circular, but it becomes more understandable when schemas are thought of as (1) templates in our memory against which incoming information is matched, (2) organizers in our memory that specify how all previously learned information (schemas and concepts) will interact with and shape the new information, and (3) processors that specify how the incoming information must be arranged to support the interaction. It is almost as if what we already know determines what and how we will understand and learn. Schema identification and schema application may work independently of each other or, as is more often the case, in an interactive, supportive manner.

Schema identification is a pattern recognition process. The schema is activated by information available to us and is then examined and evaluated for its appropriateness—to determine how it fits into the broader, generic categories. The incoming information may be a new experience with food shopping, perhaps in an exclusive gourmet shop. The new data are then placed in perspective to already existing schemas about food shopping (broad and subschemas) so that we then can decide on appropriate behavior(s) for the information.

Schema application seeks out information to satisfy and/or embellish already existing variables of schemas. It is also a process that provides knowledge and a context for interpreting incoming information, generating inferences, and guiding our attention to specific aspects or parts of the incoming information. Our schemas then determine whether or not the information contains aspects that are consistent with or deviant from existing schemas. Our schemas are corrected and adjusted according to the new input. For this reason, schemas can be considered knowledge specialists that govern what and how a message is received.

In summary, schemas are a generalized description both of the categories into which we place some of life's experiences and of the hierarchical arrangement into which we place others. They are our private theories about the nature of the world, its objects, and events. And they guide our predictions about how well the new information conforms to the old. They allow us to make predictions about unobserved or new events and guide us in acting in conventional and novel situations. In this way, *thinking* is the interaction between and among schemas, and *understanding* is realizing how any information conforms to or disagrees with what we already know.

Human Cognition

Presently, the most widely known name in research on the development of human thinking and cognition is Piaget. Piaget had been concerned with explaining the developmental process by which we learn to think and to use language. Although not as widely known, Vygotsky, a Russian psychologist, developed a theory of cognitive growth that parallels Piaget's. Vygotsky's stages of cognitive development have many of the same characteristics, but the onset and duration of each are different. Guilford, an American psychologist, is concerned with explaining how the mind is structured in order to identify the kinds of thinking that can occur. Many researchers are investigating the nature of human memory as a cognitive function. Many of them are using a computer analogy to assist them in their explanations. The following discussions of Piaget's developmental stages,

Guilford's structure-of-intellect model, and the research on the structure of human memory attempt to synthesize their ideas. These discussions provide the basis for understanding a psycholinguistic explanation of the reading process.

Developmental Stages of Human Thinking

According to Piaget, intelligence develops gradually over a long period. This growth shows itself in differences in the way an individual solves problems at different developmental stages (Furth, 1970, 1975). Acquiring knowledge is not just adding new information to old information. Acquiring knowledge is an active process of incorporating new information which Piaget, too, referred to as schemas. A thing in the world is not an object of knowledge until we relate it to something already learned. We then reorganize the new information into a new, larger meaning or understanding. However, the manner in which we relate new information to prior knowledge depends on our psychological frame of reference, or cognitive structure. Piaget's four developmental stages (see Table 2-2) are an attempt to explain how a child thinks while progressing through the stages of cognitive maturity.

Piaget considered humans to be primarily biological organisms. This means that we are responsive to our environment, and our reactions are not merely responses to outside stimulation They are attempts to incorporate the environmental information into our own intellect (schemas). We then make some changes in our cognitive structure to meet the newly incorporated information. These are what Piaget called *assimilation* and *accommodation*. As a biological organization, we have an innate tendency to preserve the status quo. But instead of our functioning state being a static one, it is a dynamic situation in

Table 2-2: Piaget's Stages of Intellectual Development

Approximate Age (years)	Characteristics
0-2	*Sensorimotor Development* Acquires skills and adaptations which are reflexive in nature. Coordinates and integrates information from senses; operates with a sense of object permanency; exhibits goal directed behavior.
2-7	*Preoperational Thought* Develops internal cognitive picture of external world. Begins language development; classifies on perceived attributes.
7-11	*Concrete Operations* Organizes through the logical structure of groups. Manipulates concrete ideas; develops concepts of reversibility and conservation.
11-15	*Formal Operations* Develops fundamentals of logical thought. Understands principles of causality and hypothesis testing.

which we try to maintain a balance between assimilation and accommodation. The process of maintaining this balance is, according to Piaget, *equilibration.* It results in developmentally successive changes that lead from the most elementary and basic knowledge (shown by adaptive reflex action) to abstract knowledge (shown by adult intelligent actions). The change represents a qualitatively different way of organizing and dealing with the world at each successive stage. These changes are cumulative, each building on the other, and they occur in four ways:

1. Addition. adding to an existing schema of new information
2. Substitution. replacing some or all of a schema with new information
3. Inclusion. adapting old information to a new schema
4. Mediation. using old information to bridge the gap to accommodate new information (Gray, 1978)

Intelligence, then, is considered the "regulating force" of a living organism that "tends towards a stable equilibration between the organism and environment" (Furth, 1969).

Piaget emphasized, somewhat, the effect of the environment. Although he stressed that children would progress naturally (mature) through the stages of development, he indicated other sources of change as well: biological, experiential, societal transmissions, and equilibration. Experience, he felt, could be passive—merely "experiencing" the physical world. Or it could be "logicomathematical," actions stimulating change. Societal transmission, according to Piaget, are learning and education (Gray, 1978). (For another Piagetian concept of learning with greater emphasis on environmental effects on the learner, see Chapter 12 in reference to Feuerstein's ideas about the assessment of retarded performers and his Instrumental Enrichment program.) Sketches of Paiget's four stages of development follow.

The *sensorimotor stage*, the first stage, occurs during the first two years of a child's life. During this time, the child develops the practical knowledge of the world that will structure all future knowledge of the world. The skills and adaptations developed during this stage are reflexive. The child organizes sensory information from the various sensory modalities and begins integrating this information in goal-directed, deliberate actions. Discoveries are still primarily through manipulation. The child begins to understand the permanency of space. However, there is not yet an internalized representation of the world. During this period, language beings.

The second stage, the *preoperational stage,* is filled with experiments with objects in play. The child begins to establish relationships between experiences and actions. The child imitates adults and begins to internalize observations of adult activities. The result is that these internalizations become the basis for imagery and language development. Although the child is developing consistent representational skills (schemas), these are not always acceptable representations to adults. At first, the child identifies words and symbols with an object and its characteristics. A cow is a cow because it has "cowness." By the end of the growth period the child begins to understand the arbitrariness of symbol-to-object associations. Different things and people may be called by different names. Thinking during this period is "transductive," which means that information can be related from particular to particular but not from particular to general. The child's activity is limited to concrete actions. Relationships are made because objects have some features in common. For instance, associations may be based on environmental conditions rather than on some inherent quality of the object. Things are grouped together because "Mommy uses them in the kitchen" rather than because they all are round or made of metal. Finally, the child cannot distinguish between the motives of the external world and those of the internal world. Egocentricity will not allow the child to take another's point of view. Thinking during the period is irreversible, as shown by the widely known experiments on conservation of mass.

The *concrete operations* stage, the third stage, occurs approximately during the ages of seven to eleven and covers the largest portion of the elementary school year. During this stage the child develops schemas of time, space, number, and logic. These control the child's understanding of events and objects, the logical structure of groups, and a sense of multiple classifications. The child realizes that objects have multiple characteristics and that the significance of each characteristic can change with a change of purpose. Objects can be grouped because they are red or round and then again because they are used for cooking or building. Although thought still remains tied to actual objects and events, the child has internalized the world. A need to manipulate objects physically no longer exists. By the end of this stage, the child can perform mental arrangements of objects.

The fourth stage, *formal operations* occurs during the eleventh to fifteenth years. The child develops in this period, an understanding of basic principles of causal thinking. The child can perform experiments, deduce implications, and grasp abstract, logical thought and hypothetical reasoning. The child, by the end of the period, can think through a full set of alternatives for a problem.

There is a very important distinction between the thinking of elementary school age children and that of adults. Quite often adults make assumptions about the way children think that are erroneous according to Piagetian principles (Elkind, 1974). One misconception is that children and adults are alike in the way they think and different in the way they feel about things. The opposite seems to be true. However, many adults treat children as if they do not have personal preferences or likes and dislikes and as if children's emotions are different from adults'. Another misunderstanding is that children learn by sitting and listening. From the description of Piaget's developmental stages, one should infer that children learn best by activity and movement. Children learn about the world through active minipulation of that world and by imitating the people they encounter in their lives. A third misunderstanding is that children learn best by learning rules. Again, the child learns by living and acting in the world, not by associating some abstract rule to a situation. A fourth misunderstanding concerns accelerating development. In general, the results of Piaget's work seem to indicate that children at each stage of development benefit more from enriching activities than from attempts to speed up their education.

The Structure of Human Intellect

Guilford's structure-of-intellect model is unlike Piaget's in that it is not hierarchical in nature (see Figure 2-5). Guilford cross-classifies the various intellectual abilities that adults seem to possess. His model classifies the intellectual abilities in three different ways so that the subunits, or categories, of each ability intersect with those of the other abilities. The three major classifications are mental operations, content, and product (Guilford, 1967; 1971).

Operations are the major kinds of intellectual activities, that is, the things we do in processing information. Five categories of operations are

1. *Cognition.* Awareness or recognition of information in its various forms.

2. *Memory.* Process of storing information, not to be confused with memory storage.
3. *Divergent production.* Generating logical conclusions from any given or known information with the emphasis on achieving variety, quantity, and relevance of outcomes.
4. *Convergent production.* Generating logical conclusions from any given or known information with the emphasis on achieving conventionally best outcomes.
5. *Evaluation.* Comparing information and making judgments about information.

Contents, Guilford's second classification, are the broad, substantive kinds of information as presented to or perceived by the individual. Four kinds of contents are

1. *Figural.* Information in concrete form, that is, the actual object or a realistic picture of the object involving perception by visual, auditory, or kinesthetic sensory modalities.
2. *Symbolic.* Information in the form of denotative signs having no basic significance themselves, such as letters, numerals, musical notes, codes, and words.
3. *Semantic.* Information in the form of conceptions or mental images.
4. *Behaviors.* Information, basically nonpictorial and nonverbal, that involves human interaction, that is, information representing attitudes, needs, desires, moods, and intentions.

INTERACTION AMONG

Kinds of Thinking (Operations)

Information

Forms of Presenting Information (Products)

Ways of Organizing Information (Contents)

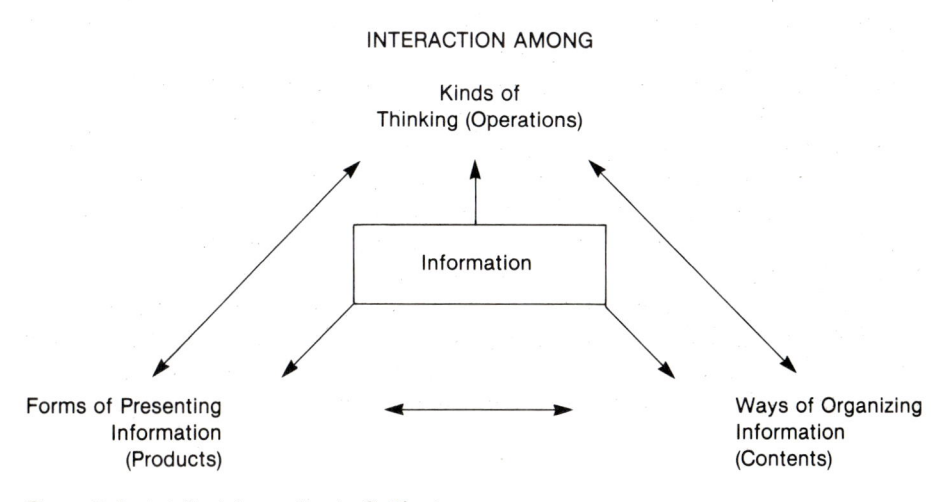

Figure 2-5 Intellect According to Guilford

Products, Guilford's third class, are the forms of information. Six categories of products are

1. *Units.* Sets of things, chunks of information, segregated wholes, or figures on grounds.
2. *Classes.* Sets of things having a common property or characteristic.
3. *Relations.* Connections based on a definable relationship among things or groups of information.
4. *Systems.* Organized or structured groups of items of information, that is, complex structures interrelated parts.
5. *Transformations.* Changes in information such as redefinitions, shifts, transitions, or modifications.
6. *Implications.* Circumstantial connections among different information—expectations, anticipations, or predictions to implications not usually verbalizable.

When the three classifications are combined in the cross-classification model, the result is a block of 120 cells. Each cell represents a combination of one kind of operation with one kind of content and one kind of product.

In his explanation of the model, Guilford (1967) advises us not to suppose that the 120 abilities represent all of the intellectual traits of human intelligence. There are reasons to suppose that the number might be much greater, since many of the cells seem to represent two or three kinds of related abilities. For example, figural memory of units seems to be of two kinds, auditory and visual. Cognition seems to consist of auditory abilities, visual abilities, and kinesthetic abilities. It thus appears that in the cognition and memory-operation categories, there may be some general differentiation of abilities along sense-modality lines.

The Guilford structure-of-intellect model parallels Piaget's classifications of developmental stages. Although Guilford does not attempt to explain the developmental nature of his structures, he does classify the kinds of thinking that can occur in adults. The basic implication is that there are different kinds of thinking for different situations. In the classroom, a child might be able to perform certain types of mental functions and yet not be able to perform others. For example, a child may understand individual things pictorially (represented by the intersection of the operation *cognition* with the product *units* and the content *figural*). But the child may not be able to remember symbolic relations (represented by the intersection of the operation *memory* with the product *relations* and the content *symbolic*).

Another classroom implication comes from the realization that the concept of product of information is represented in different ways in our language (Guilford, 1967). The information in the form of units and classes are things or groups of things to which we normally apply nouns. Relations, the connections or bridges between two or more bits of information, are commonly expressed by prepositions. Systems are generally verbally stated arithmetic problems, outlines, mathematical equations, or plans. Transformations are generally expressed through participles, that is, a verb in noun form such as *thinking, running,* or *reddening.* The ability to use these various parts of speech and to understand their use may depend on certain and separate mental abilities.

The Structure of Human Memory

A growing body of research indicates that human memory has the structure of a multiple storage system (Kumar, 1971; Lindsay & Norman, 1977; Andre, 1979). The components of the system are a sensory register, a short-term memory, and a long-term memory.

From the available evidence we have some

... reasonably good agreement that permanent storage of information takes place either through chemical or structural changes in the brain. There is little or no disagreement that the immediate, ongoing activities of thought, conscious processes, and the immediate memories—sensory information store and short term memory—are mediated through electrical activity. (Lindsay & Norman, 1977)

One possibility in regard to the location of the various functions in the brain is that memories do not seem to be stored in specific locations. Rather, they are found as patterns in different locations throughout the brain. Any specific memory, then, involves large sections of the brain. No one portion is absolutely necessary for memory processes; yet the more sections that function together, the clearer the recollection is (Lindsay & Norman, 1977).

The human brain is amazingly complex. The fact that its parts are interchangeable, or at least interdependent, has not allowed researchers to identify the specific sections functioning as memory system. If it should encounter injury in one section, the complexity of the brain allows it to have another of its sections perform certain life-sustaining activities. What have been localized are the specific regions where certain sensory stimuli enter the brain and the regions responsible for certain human activities. For example, motor areas, speech areas, and seeing areas have been identified. Still a mystery is precisely how information is transferred from one region to another and the exact process of solving problems and storing, retreiving, and analyzing information. Although the exact physical nature of the brain's activities is not yet known, enough evidence is available to sustain a theory of a multiple storage system model of memory (see Figure 2-6).

The sensory register is where all sensory images are deposited by the sensory modalities. The five senses are constantly at work, and all the incoming information from them, as well as information originating in the individual (like thoughts and attitudes) must be collected until it is determined what information is

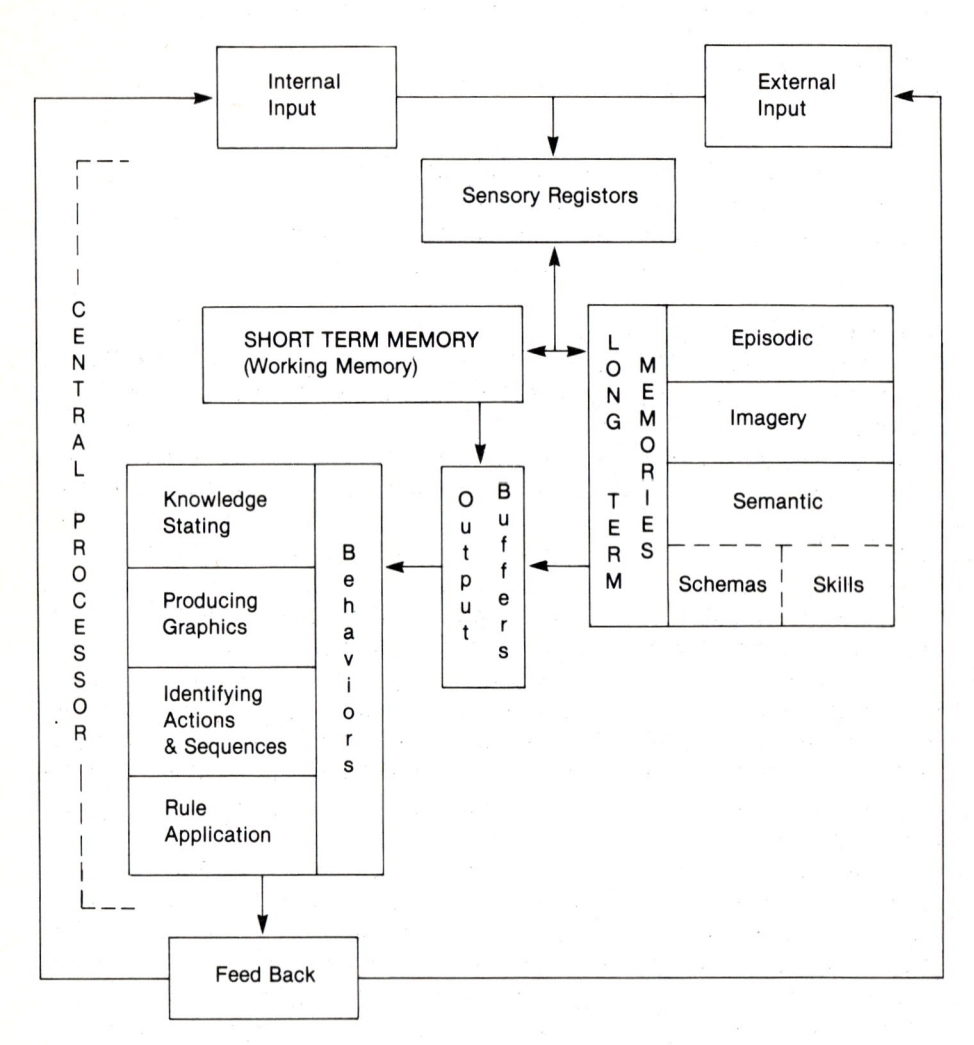

50 CHAPTER 2/HUMAN COMMUNICATION: THINKING AND LANGUAGE

Figure 2-6 An Information Processing Model of Memory
After Andre (1979) and Gagne and White (1978).

valuable and should be retained. That means that all information in one's fields of vision, hearing, touch, taste, and smell is stored. However, this information is stored only briefly and is subject to very rapid decay. Experiments show that the time limit for information stored in the sensory register must be measured in milliseconds. By half a second, a bit of registered information has disappeared. Information may also be forgotten or eliminated from the sensory register by the introduction of new information.

How is information, which will quickly disappear, transferred to the other memory storage systems? Transfer is perhaps best thought of as a "copying" of information. What information is copied on one system from another depends a great deal on the individual schemas. Each individual seems to employ procedures of selective attention. Information is selected from the sensory register according to the importance of the information to the individual. The information is then retained in the short-term memory storage. We all are aware of this phenomenon of "attenuating" as we direct our thinking to the heat in a room and do not listen to the lecturer, or as we are diverted by uncomfortable seats from the enjoyment of a theatrical performance.

The phenomenon of selective attention has both good and bad points. It is desirable because without it the collection of sensory inputs would be utterly chaotic. The world to us would be a jumble of sights, sounds, and smells. The procedure allows for the orderly selection of incoming sensory data based on what seems important at the moment. A negative feature is that more than one thing cannot be given attention in any one instant. Because of this we find it difficult to keep track of two conversations simultaneously or to read a book and follow the progress of a sporting event on television without rereading many pages and relying on instant replay for continuity of action.

The information in the sensory register seems to undergo some sort of change as it is copied for transfer into the short-term memory system. It seems the information is changed into a verbal code that retains the meaning of the information and not its original sensory image. An analogous situation exists with the computer. The symbolic language used for instructing the computer must be translated into machine language for the computer to function. The relationship between the symbolic language and the machine language is purely arbitrary; yet a computer must have the appropriate program before it can make the translation. In our brain, all information that is allowed to pass beyond the sensory register to the next storage system must be transformed into a basic meaning, regardless of its sensory source. In the hypothesized transformational grammar model, the information is transformed from its surface features to its deep structure features.

The short-term memory is a working memory. In it information is retained for a slightly longer period than is possible in the sensory register. Information is generally retained for as long as fifteen seconds before it decays. The information in the short-term memory is retined in what is called an auditory-linguistic-verbal store, since it is extremely difficult to separate these aspects of short-term memory. The capacity of short-term memory is much more limited than that of the sensory register; however, this information is much more select than the information in the sensory register. The short-term memory seems to be able to hold only about six units of information. The more meaningful the information is or the more closely related to one another the bits of information are, the more likely it is that it will be retained as a single unit of information. For example, the letters *x, y, l,* and *n* would probably be retained as four descrete units of information, whereas a rearrangement of those letters into a meaningful unit—*lynx*—would cause them to be retained as a single unit.

Information is eliminated from the short-term memory by either decay or replacement. Information is lost or forgotten after about six seconds or when new information enters the short-term memory to replace it. However, information may be retained for longer periods of time by a process of rehearsal. Rehearsal is a "silent, mental repetition of the material that is to be retained" and seems to serve two primary functions: (1) the indefinite retention in short-term memory of material and (2) the aid in the transfer of material to a more permanent storage in long-term memory (Lindsay & Norman, 1977).

The information that is transferred from short-term memory to long-term memory is, to a large extent unconsciously, under the control of the individual. The importance one places on information determines whether it is processed further (Kumar, 1971). An attentional aspect similar to that in the transfer of information from sensory register to short-term memory seems to be involved in the transfer of information from short-term memory to long-term memory. Information is transferred by the mental repetition of information (rehearsal) and by perceiving different aspects, attributes, or conceptual psychological dimensions of the information (Kumar, 1971). The encoding strategies are conscious efforts of the individual involving substitution (a replacement of the incoming information by another symbol), elaboration (the storage of additional information), and schema formation (the combining of information with past experience).

Long-term memory seems to consist of three subunits: episodic memory, imagery memory, and semantic memory (Andre, 1979; Gagne & White, 1978). Episodic memory consists of dated events and temporal-spatial relationships regarding those events retained in a sort of cognitive code (schemas). These memories are tied to places and time sequences. Episodic memory can be considered our diary of life's experiences.

Imagery memory contains representations both concrete and referential. These images are not stored in any verbal code; they are true images but can be activated by encoding, that is, by associations from other units of the long-term memory. For example, a mental picture can be created by hearing or seeing the words "Mount Rushmore."

The semantic memory contains all of a person's abstracted or generalized knowledge about concepts, principles, rules, and so forth. These abstractions are broader than episodes; they are the schemas that enable comprehension of incoming information. Semantic memory also contains a network of interrelated schemas—ideas and the connections between them. Semantic memory seems to have two subsections. One is the clusters of information and relationships mentioned above, and the other is a set of "action plans" or "routines;" These are concepts and rules that guide the application of rules. It is the "knowing how" portion of memory that complements the "knowing what" portion.

Long-term memory, the most important of the memory systems, is relatively permanent and resistant to forgetting. In comparison to the sensory register and the short-term memory, the capacity of long-term memory is almost limitless. Everything that is to be retained for more than a few minutes must be placed in long-term memory. Here are stored all one's knowledge of the world, language and cultural rules, and strategies for creating meaning out of the world. Piaget considered memory the active and selective restructuring of information and an entity that develops with age (Piaget & Inhelder, 1973).

Any discussion of long-term memory cannot be complete without considering *retrieval*. Assuming that information is adequately stored (that is, that appropriate schemas exist and that appropriate rules are applied to link new information to them), the recall of information depends on a number of factors. These include the means by which we search our memory, the means by which we initiate the recall process, and the length of time between input and recall (Berry, 1980; Gagne & White, 1978; Graesser, 1981).

Immediately after information is stored in long-term memory, our retrieval may be *reproductive*. We may be able to recall almost verbatim what the input contained. But over time our memory becomes *reconstructive*. Information consistent with our general schemas is preserved. What we remember is not so much the specific information that was received and stored but a generalization consistent with our schemas.

Retrieval may also be affected by our recall process. For example, returning to the analogy of the shopping schema and, in particular, the subschema of buying an object in a gourmet shop, information might be *conceptually initiated* by thoughts about a particular dinner party. Alternatively, retrieval might be *data initiated* by observing a particular food item and recalling the dish in which it is to be served.

Conclusion

The conclusions of Piaget, Guilford, and the cognitive psychologists studying the structure of human memory have many parallel features. They all conceive of thinking as a process in which the information an individual receives from the world is systematically organized. The manner in which the information is catalogued and the strategies of the process seem to depend on prior experiences and prior information. Piaget theorized that the growing child develops an internalized view of the world. This seems to be only another way of suggesting that the child has developed a strategy for encoding information into long-term memory. In addition, it seems that the structure of language is

... designed to complement the ability of the human to piece together the meaning of a communication from a few isolated fragments. ... The redundancy of the language ... allows us to attend selectively to bits and pieces of a communication, to anticipate what will come next, and to look selectively for the key words and phrases that convey the basic meaning of the message. (Lindsay & Norman, 1977).

Memory appears to develop as a problem-solving process in which information is routinely analyzed to determine its consistency with past experience. The way in which the problem is solved seems to be the result of

1. The kind and form of information.
2. The manner in which the information is presented.
3. The muturity of the individual.
4. The plans for solving problems devised by the individual.

All of these are acquired as part of our aculturation and are what we call "learning" and "knowledge."

THE DEVELOPMENT OF LANGUAGE IN CHILDREN

In this section, we will discuss the development of verbal (syntactic and semantic) structures in the language of children. Phonological development—that is, the development of the ability to produce the sounds of language—though interesting, has no direct bearing on the examination of our larger topic. We are concerned here with the development of the thinking process in children as reflected in their development of language. Little will be said now about the development of vocabulary because much evidence indicates that vocabulary development reflects the social situations in which the young child grows. Much more will be said about this last point in later chapters.

That language is learned as a process of communication is the most important result of the study of how speech develops in children. Young children seem to possess an innate ability to reduce and restructure adult language in a highly systematic way so as to fit their intellects. As the child matures, there is a progressive differentiation in word usage and the use of syntactic structures (Brown & Bellugi, 1966). The child's language is not, however, a miniature copy of adult speech—until the child is almost mature, patterns are used that do not normally appear in adult speech. These patterns are remarkably similar from language to language (Slobin, 1979). Further, it is clear that language cannot develop primarily from the memorization of words and lists of sentences. The known limitations of the memory of children of this age preclude memorization as the mechanism of language acquisition. Also, all speakers of a language are able to produce sentences that they have never heard previously.

Behavioral philosophy presents another view of how language is learned. However, psycholinguistic research demonstrates that the behaviorist view cannot adequately account for language acquisition (Lindfors, 1980). Specifically, the behaviorist approach to language acquisition cannot explain the uniformity with which language is learned by all humans, regardless of their ethnic, cultural, or geographic backgrounds. It cannot account for why or how children infer the deep structure from an exposure to only surface features, since reinforcement principles are not applied to these deep structure elements. And it cannot explain the relatively short period of time and the early onset of the acquisition of so much of a complex system of linguistic rules and applications.

Generally, children begin to speak around the age of one and a half years, a period that coincides with the Piagetian "preoperational thought" stage. In fact, language development occurs in most normal children during this period. It should be kept in mind that the preoperational thought stage is characterized by the internalization of the external world and that items and events are classified on attributes that the child can actually perceive.

The following explanation of the development of language in children, a synthesis of the ideas and contributions of researchers and scholars in the field (Anastasiow, 1979; Halliday, 1975; Lindfors, 1980; Wienmann & Backlund, 1980; Wood, 1981), begins with an explanation of the development of the verbal features of language—syntax and semantics—and then examines the development of nonverbal features. These three aspects are presented in an arbitrary order; yet they are concomitant, codeveloping aspects of language (see Table 2-3).

Table 2-3. Language Development

Syntactic Phase	Semantic Phase	Nonverbal Phase
Birth	*Approximately 9-16 months*	*Birth*
Imitation of intonation	Sounds and Meaning	Paralinguistics
Single word sentences	*Approximately 16-24 months*	
Two & three word sentences	Grammar and Dialogue	
Hierarchical constructions	*Approximately 24 months and on*	
Regularizations	Development of "scripts"	
Language transformations		
Approximately 10 years & on		*Approximately school age*
Continued learning		Continued learning

Syntax In acquiring the ability to order words into sentences, the initial phase of speech acquisition begins when the baby imitates adult intonational patterns. This is then followed by a period in which single words appear. These words, although they have no direct tie to words found in a standard dictionary, are word approximations and relate symbols to objects. At this time children show that they understand words spoken to them. In addition, they use various intonational patterns, and it may be possible to distinguish the consistent use of declarative, emphatic, and question intonations in their utterances.

The next stage of language development occurs when children can combine two words to make a sentenace. At first a child constructs a few of these sentences. Then, in a brief period of time, there is an effusion of them. These two-word sentences are not random combinations of words but consist of two classes of words: pivot words and open class words. The pivot words are high frequency words the child uses. Usually the number in this category is small and stable. They are words such as *on, more, big,* and *allgone*, and generally represent a quality or a process of something. The open class consists of a large and growing number of words representing attempts to name and classify the objects and events encountered by the child. The pivot words may occupy the first or the second position in the sentence. They are easily recognized as those words with which many of the open words in the child's vocabulary can be joined. Examples of two-word sentences with the pivot word at the beginning are "Allgone milk," "See Daddy," "Big dog." Two-word sentences with the pivot word at the end are "Baby down," "Shoe on," "Mommy off."

The pivot constructions serve various functions in a child's speech. However, they soon begin to show a subject-predicate construction, modification of quantity and quality, and negation.

Some two-word sentences seem to consist of only open class words, but careful examination shows they demonstrate the child's beginning awareness of the deep structure and surface structure features of language. For example, the utterance, "Mommy bottle," might mean any one of the following: "Mommy has the bottle," "Mommy, give me the bottle," or "Mommy, that is the bottle."

One determines the underlying meaning of the statement through the context of the situation. In the example, evidence for a specific interpretation exists, if on hearing "Yes, I have the bottle," the child cries. Observations of young children indicate that at different times the same statement, "Mommy bottle," will produce different responses by the child's mother and quite different subsequent behaviors by the child. The child, though demonstrating at least some understanding of adult syntactic and semantic structures, may not yet possess the capacity to produce more than two-word sentences.

After the child has begin to use two-word, pivot-open sentences, a stage of hierarchical constructions begins. The child takes the basic pivot-open sentences and begins to expand them by adding other syntactic features. The construction "More cooky" might be expanded to "Want more cooky" and then to "Want more cooky now." In each case of expansion, the child is not just stringing words together but is creating a hierarchical pattern according to the grammatical structure of the language.

The child then enters a period of regularization. This period is also marked by deviations from adult speech, and constructions are created that are not usually found in the adult speech the child hears. For example, *came* becomes *comed*, and *feet* becomes *foots*. Most often the high frequency irregular forms are learned correctly first, and then they are overregularized as the child becomes aware of generalizations inherent in the language. The child continuously attempts to create order out of the language the child hears.

The final stage is using language transformations. This is a highly complex phase of language acquisition, and investigation is only starting to reveal how children create transformations of basic sentences. Two early transformations made by young children are questions and negatives. When a child begins to construct questions, the tendency is to invoke the "question marker" rule but not the "subject-verb reversal" rule. For instance, a child who is asked to create a question about what Mommy has in her hand will ask, "What Mommy have in hand?" It seems that children of this stage have a limited performance capacity that blocks the application of both transformations together.

By the time children are four years old, they have mastered basic grammatical structures. During the fifth and sixth years, children begin to control the inconsistencies of language, and by the end of the seventh year—roughly corresponding to the end of first grade—children have developed a grammar that is almost equivalent to that of adults, although by age ten some children are still struggling with complex structures. Lacking are the extensive vocabulary and the ability to manipulate the many grammatical transformations of adult speech.

Semantics Along with learning the rules of word order, children acquire the ability to "mean." As explained previously, children acquire the semantic features of language when they begin using their language for communication purposes. There are three phases of semantic development. The first occurs approximately between the ages of nine and sixteen months. The child, in interactions with adults and older children, makes sounds, the beginnings of words (although not necessarily using the initial phonemes of the words), full words, and groups of words. These efforts are related to the general language functions of

regulating behavior	"Bring book"
obtaining objects	"Want cookie"
instructing others for activities	"Play game"
questioning or curiosity resolution	"What this"
personal statements	"Sleepy"
imaginative statements	"Choo-choo"

These statements are presented one at a time and may not be understood by everyone. They develop from interactions between the child and others in general family activities, games, and excursions into the world. These functions are not lost but are retained and expanded in later phases of semantic development.

The second phase occurs between the ages of approximately sixteen and twenty-four months. It is sometimes referred to as the stage of "grammar and dialogue." In it, the child can deal with two or more meanings simultaneously and uses ever-increasing forms of syntax through extended conversations with others. In addition to the functions acquired in the first phase, the child adds three more:

learning and exchanging information	"I saw Grandma"
	"That man hit the boy"
fulfilling practical or personal needs	"I can't tie this"
	"Lift me up"
extending imaginative function, including pretense	"I see the bus coming" (when there is no bus)

In this second phase the child combines functions to produce more complex meanings and expands syntax to signify meanings that are now comprhensible to almost all hearers. The child now uses language to obtain actions from others and to receive direct verbal responses to his or her statements. The child is both observer and participant in the communication process, using language in specific contexts with specific intentions.

The third phase begins at approximately twenty-four months and continues throughout life. The child begins to be able to distinguish between old and new information. This includes learning to use language for additional learning and learning to use language to act. During this phase the child develops the various "scripts" for behaving and speaking appropriately in different situations. As noted, the schemas underlying these scripts and the scripts themselves are developed as part of the total communication process, through communication with others in cultural and social settings.

Nonverbal Features Equally as important is the development of language's paralinguistic features. Wood (1981) and Lindfors (1980) have done much research on these paralinguistic features, and we summarize their findings here. Voice manipulation, intonational features, body use, space use all are learned along with the spoken language. The development of voice manipulations (pitch, pauses, loudness, tempo, and juncture) are known to begin with the earliest production of language. They have not been set down into precise phases of development, however, nor have the nonverbal features of body language; yet it is known that children by the age of two have acquired the body moves of gender. It is apparent that children learn early in life to communicate with their facial expressions. The use of space in the oral language system has been studied extensively, and children seem to understand and use spacing behavior in a zone fashion. They seem to understand personal space early and move from intimate and personal space to social space. By the time they enter elementary school, they have established the patterns of sex and ethnic background.

The importance of the nonverbal communication systems lies in children's ability to support or contradict a spoken message if conflicting messages are transmitted through the two systems. Children usually acquire these nonverbal features in conjunction with the verbal; the two develop simultaneously, not in isolation. So children usually acquire the appropriate nonverbal "support system" as they acquire the verbal scripts for various language functions.

Competence The idea of competence has both theoretical and practical implications. To Chomsky, competence is the human capability of generating language. However, to other psycholinguists, competence refers to more than an innate sense of language. To them, competence is knowing how to use language as a tool in everyday situations (Wood, 1981). It is a totality that includes an individual's ability and skill to know the social/communication rules and to be able to perform accordingly. These abilities and skills include both cognitive and performance processes interdependently (Wiemann & Backlund, 1980). Therefore, children can be considered competent users of language if their language seems appropriate to the goals of the message, the participants, and the situation. It is usually the gross deviations from the generally recognized developmental patterns that are labeled either "immature" or "so grown up!"

IMPLICATIONS FOR EDUCATION

A few important implications of the research on the thinking process and the development of language presented in the above sections will be mentioned here, and others will be cited throughout the remainder of the text.

One important conclusion of Piaget's theory is that development affects learning. How children learn will change as they mature. Children's thinking is different from that of adults. Children's world views are not "wrong," but they are different.

In addition, some things cannot be taught to children in the usual sense. They must experience objects and activities in order to acquire new cognitive structures. Children are constantly learning regardless of their activity, albeit not always what we wish to be learned. School-age children are involved with their world, and even apparent daydreaming contains some aspects of learning.

The results of research based on Piagetian theory have some relevance to the practices of beginning reading instruction. Children in the later stages of the preoperational period—corresponding to the kindergarten and first-grade years—may not have developed "conservation." Such children are characterized by their inability to undo a task they have performed. They cannot deal with a slightly changed situation without thinking it is a new situation. This implies that the use of a code-emphasis, rule-oriented phonics program in the beginning stages of reading is not consistent with the abilities of "nonconserving" children. In addition, Piaget's work points out the importance of curricula in which activities, including reading, are "carried out in social situations where children are working together, sharing information, and learning to take into account another person's point of view" (Raven & Salzer, 1971).

When something has been learned, whether it is a mathematical concept, a grammatical rule, or the names of various objects, that information has been committed to a child's long-term memory. That which is transferred into long-term memory is under the control of the individual. The control is not actually conscious. It is rather a "predisposition" to gain other information and to transfer information from the sensor register through the short-term memory into the long-term memory.

In the classroom, the predisposition for learning can be facilitated by developing appropriate cognitive readiness. One procedure is to use "advance organizers," which are questions or directions focusing on features of the information that should be retained. This allows the child to attend to the particular information, or a particular aspect of the information, that is to be learned. Most important, the teacher should help the child develop general advance organizers so that self-learning strategies can be developed. It is also wise to promote the use of rehearsal or practice. Greater rehearsal is needed for new or different information. Old or additional information added to an already learned body of information needs much less rehearsal. A final procedure is to guide children in developing information-processing strategies, that is, encoding procedures. Since information is encoded into long-term memory in its deep structure form, children need training in processing information according to the nature of the information. Different strategies are needed depending on

1. The difficulty level of the information
2. The importance of the information to the individual
3. The interest of the information to the individual
4. The amount of information to be acquired
5. The organization of the material (Kumar, 1971).

The teacher must be committed to understanding the child and the content of instruction. The teacher must devise instructional procedures to join the two. Then the desired learning will ensue.

Discussion Questions and Activities

1. What does the following statement by George Miller (1973) mean to you?

    Not all physical features of speech are significant for vocal communication, and not all significant features of speech have a physical representation.

2. Observe a group of people in different situations—waiting in a line, eating in a restaurant and so forth. What are their attitudes and feelings? What gives you this impression?
3. Collect a series of advertisements for some product. For example, collect ads for a particular car or television set. What message is directly stated in the written copy of the ads? What messages are implied in both the physical appearance of the ad and in the copy?
4. Examine a series of elementary school reading or language arts texts. What information does the series contain about the history and structure of the English language? How is it presented and what should the pupil do with the information?

5. A parent comes to you and says she has heard about the "linguistic" method of teaching reading. From the discussion, you realize she means a program that emphasizes the one-to-one correspondence between letters and sounds. She wants her child taught by this method. How will you answer her?
6. The following statement was made by Andreas Feininger (1966), a well-known and highly successful color photographer and author. In what way is his statement substantiated by current research on the thinking process? In what way does his statement help to explain the reading process?

[The phenomenon of color memory] of the eye-brain combine causes us to *see color as we think it should look,* not as it *actually is.*

7. Observe individual and small groups of children of different ages at play. For example, observe children of ages two, five, and eight. Note the language they use when playing alone or with other children. (If possible, tape record about five minutes of their playtime conversations.) How do the children use language in relating to their play objects? How do the children use language in relating to themselves or to the other children?

Further Readings

Those who wish to learn more about the history of the English language in order to understand current trends will find the following quite useful:

Meyers, L. M., and R. L. Hoffman, *Roots of Modern English,* 2nd ed. (Boston: Little, Brown, 1979).

Much that is now being written about nonverbal communication you may already know intuitively. The following is a popular treatment of nonverbal communication and, unlike many other books on the subject, is not intended to be a "code" for you to use to "psyche out" someone's intentions through nonverbal behavior.

Davis, Flora, *Inside Intuition: What We Know About Nonverbal Communication* (New York: McGraw-Hill, 1973).

The following two books, although slightly more scholarly, are still popular presentations of nonverbal communication. Their subjects are the unstated aspects of language.

Hall, Edward T., *The Silent Language* (New York: Doubleday, 1959).
Hall, Edward T., *The Hidden Dimension* (New York: Doubleday, 1966).

In the following popular book on the nature of language and communication, the author tries to answer basic questions about what happens when people talk.

Farb, Peter, *Word Play,* (New York: Knopf, 1974).

Slightly more technical than Farb's book, the following are excellent summaries of recent research on the nature of language and how it develops in children:

Dale, Philip S., *Language Development: Structure and Function* 2nd ed. (New York: Holt, Rinehart & Winston, 1976).
Menyuk, Paula, *Language and Maturation* (Cambridge, MA: MIT Press, 1977).

Piaget's books are sometimes very difficult for the neophyte to read. Nonetheless, every teacher should know his ideas. The following clearly delineate Piaget's theory and positions on education.

Elkind, David, *A Sympathetic Understanding of the Child: Birth to Sixteen* (Boston: Allyn & Bacon, 1975).
Elkind, David, *Child Development and Education: A Piagetian Perspective* (New York: Oxford University Press, 1976).
Furth, Hans G., *Piaget for Teachers* (Englewood Cliffs, NJ: Prentice-Hall, 1970).

This highly readable book on thinking explains the mental process that children undergo during learning.

Smith, Frank, *Comprehension and Learning: A Conceptual Framework for Teachers* (New York: Holt, Rinehart & Winston, 1975).

Chapter 3

THE READING PROCESS

Focus   Questions

1. In what way is the reading process really a thinking process?

2. What factors are involved in any reading situation?

3. In what ways are the act of reading and the reading process different?

The process of reading must be distinguished from the act of reading. Every time we read a book, magazine, or newspaper, we are engaging in an act of reading. We are undertaking the action, the doing, of reading. Our days are filled with many acts of reading, and our purposes for reading may or may not change with each act of reading. But the act of reading is not the process of reading. Rather the process of reading is one component of the act of reading. Examining the *process* of reading focuses on the linguistic, physiological, and psychological factors and their interaction in creating meaning from a text. The *act* of reading includes these features—as the process of reading—and the complex interaction of reader, text, and environment.

In this chapter we examine both the process of reading and the act of reading. After offering some ideas about the general significance of psycholinguistic models of reading and a brief history of their development, we will look at three models of the reading process. (Each model is based on the principles of language and learning given in Chapter 2. The models are complementary in that each explains the reading process in the same theoretical framework but from slightly different perspectives.) Then we will consider a model of the reading act to show how the process models of reading fit into actual reading situations. Finally, we will argue for teaching writing as a means of contributing to the development of reading skills and comprehension abilities in students.

SIGNIFICANCE OF A PSYCHOLINGUISTIC MODEL OF READING

In order to explain the process of reading, educators have created models of reading—theoretical frameworks designed to clarify what happens when we read. Even though the models are usually based on supportable research, they still are hypotheses, and their usefulness depends on the clarity with which they explain our reading behaviors. Any model, useful as it is in decision making, should not be thought complete. It must be continuously modified or even discarded as new evidence accumulates. A model of reading should be capable of serving three general purposes:

1. It should explain the complex phenomenon of reading.
2. It should describe how the phenomenon of reading operates.
3. It should provide a basis for predicting changes that will occur in one aspect of reading when changes are made in other aspects (Geyer, 1972).

With the emergence of a psycholinguistics based on the insights of cognitive psychologists and transformational linguists, educators began to change their interpretation of the reading process. Before the 1960s and 1970s, reading was viewed by most reading educators as an accumulation of discrete skills. More recent models attempt to explain reading as a continuous process. The difference is that a skills model tries to explain what specific discrete skills are involved in reading, and a process model shows not only the skills involved but also how the reader uses those skills and strategies interdependently.

All reading models, whether skills or process, can be classified according to the psychological orientation of the model maker: behaviorist, natavist (biological factors), cognitivist, or theories drawn from psycholinguistics, information processing, or developmentalism. Since it is difficult to find a model that is based on only one psychological school, it has recently become popular to classify models as "bottom up," "top down," or "interactive." *Bottom up* means that the model maker views reading as starting with the input of some graphic signal or stimulus. These models usually describe reading as beginning with the synthesis of letters into words, words into sentences, and so on until a large enough unit of language is perceived to understand what the author has written. *Top-down* models begin with the reader's cognitive structures. In this view, the reader can understand what is on the page only if the ideas are already present in the reader's mind. Reading, from a top-down view, begins with some prior understanding and proceeds to the reconstruction of the author's message. The *interactive* view describes reading as drawing from the top and the bottom simultaneously. In general, the interactivists and the "top downers" have more in common with each other than with the "bottom uppers." The ideas presented in this text are consonant with the interactive and top-down points of view.

Before the 1970s, most of the attention from the bottom-up perspective was on the "word" as the focus of reading research (Guthrie, 1980). That is where reading was thought to begin—recognizing first a single word, then another, and so on. By the late 1970s, researchers were investigating the cognitive processes in order to explain not what readers do but how they understand. The research revealed that readers are able to understand the structure of a story or to draw inferences from an information passage only when they relate it to their background knowledge and undertake reading as a process of searching for information. Only then are individual words on a page "recognized"—that is, their particular meanings are determined.

Reading has been shown to be a language process, a psychological process, a psycholinguistic process, and a physiological process. Researchers (Ryan & Semmel, 1969; Raven & Slazer, 1971; Stauffer, 1971) concluded that the results of Piaget and other cognitive psychologists have important and direct implications for the instruction of reading. Recently, others (Pezdek, 1980; Linden & Wittrock, 1981) concluded that comprehension during reading is an elaborate process that depends on variables both within and outside sentences. Comprehension is a constructive process that results from an interaction of the material presented, the context of that information, and the reader's existing knowledge schemas. Students learn to comprehend by receiving instruction in attending to the appropriate aspects of the text, relating their knowledge and experiences to the ideas in the text, and building associations from and to the text.

PSYCHOLINGUISTIC MODELS OF READING

The three reading models depicting the interactive nature of reading are the Goodman Model of Reading, the Rumelhart Interactive Model of Reading, and the Kintsch Model of Text Comprehension. The Goodman model is presented first. It has existed the longest and has generated much research to support it theoretically and to demonstrate its practicality in classroom applications. To some, the model is a top-down explanation. Here, however, it is presented as an interactive model because of its feedback, or recursive, aspects. Any model that shows that reading is not a direct, linear application of skills is considered interactive. The model and its research have been one of two strong influences on our ideas about the teaching and assessment of reading. The Rumelhart model is presented because of its growing impact on reading researchers and practitioners. It was developed from Rumelhart's investigations into the nature of schemas and memory. The Kintsch model, also based on schema theory, explains the reading process through an analysis of how written discourse is constructed by a writer.

Each model attempts to demonstrate what occurs for a proficient reader during silent reading. (Less proficient readers are identified not so much by the quantitative count of errors but by the qualitative assessment of where the breakdown occurs in the process.) The models are multidimensional in that reading is not considered a single, linear application of skills. Taken together, they provide a comprehensive view of the reading process.

The Goodman Model of the Reading Process

Goodman (1968) defines reading as a process of selecting graphic cues that signal meaning, much as listening is a process of selecting auditory cues for meaning. Goodman supposed that the experienced reader can derive meaning directly from graphic cues without translating them into phonemic cues.

A distinction is made among the aspects of *decoding* (deriving meaning), *recoding* (translating letter patterns into sound), and *encoding* (oral reading). Decoding occurs only when the writer's meaning is analyzed and understood, in other words, when the reader knows the deep structure of the message as generated by the writer. Encoding can take place only when decoding has preceded it. Recoding is a procedure whereby only the surface structure of the message is perceived and changed into a different form. (In most other sources about the teaching of reading, the term decoding refers to the process of translating the printed symbol into sound, that is, word-attack procedures. Goodman prefers to use the term decoding in referring to the meaningful unlocking of a message.)

A proficient reader does not use all of the signals built into the writing system, just as a proficient listener does not use every facet of the spoken language. The reader anticipates meaning and has it reconfirmed. The less often one's thoughts about the message have to change during reading and the fewer cues from the page one needs for arriving at the author's meaning, the more proficient one is as a reader in that reading situation (Goodman, 1967, 1968, 1969; Ryan & Semmel, 1969).

According to Goodman, the process of reading can be compared with information processing. Long-term memory holds those learned responses that have become automatic or habitual. Medium memory[1] holds those learnings and responses based on the particular reading act. They are the "guesses" (predictions) and confirmations made during reading. Short-term memory holds immediate images and signals needed during reading.

Prior to an act of reading, the reader has three sets of information stored in long-term memory:

1. Procedures for regulating the physical aspects of reading.

---

1. In the Goodman model *short-term* and *medium-term* memory refer to the *sensory register* and *short-term* memory discussed previously.

PSYCHOLINGUISTIC MODELS OF READING 69

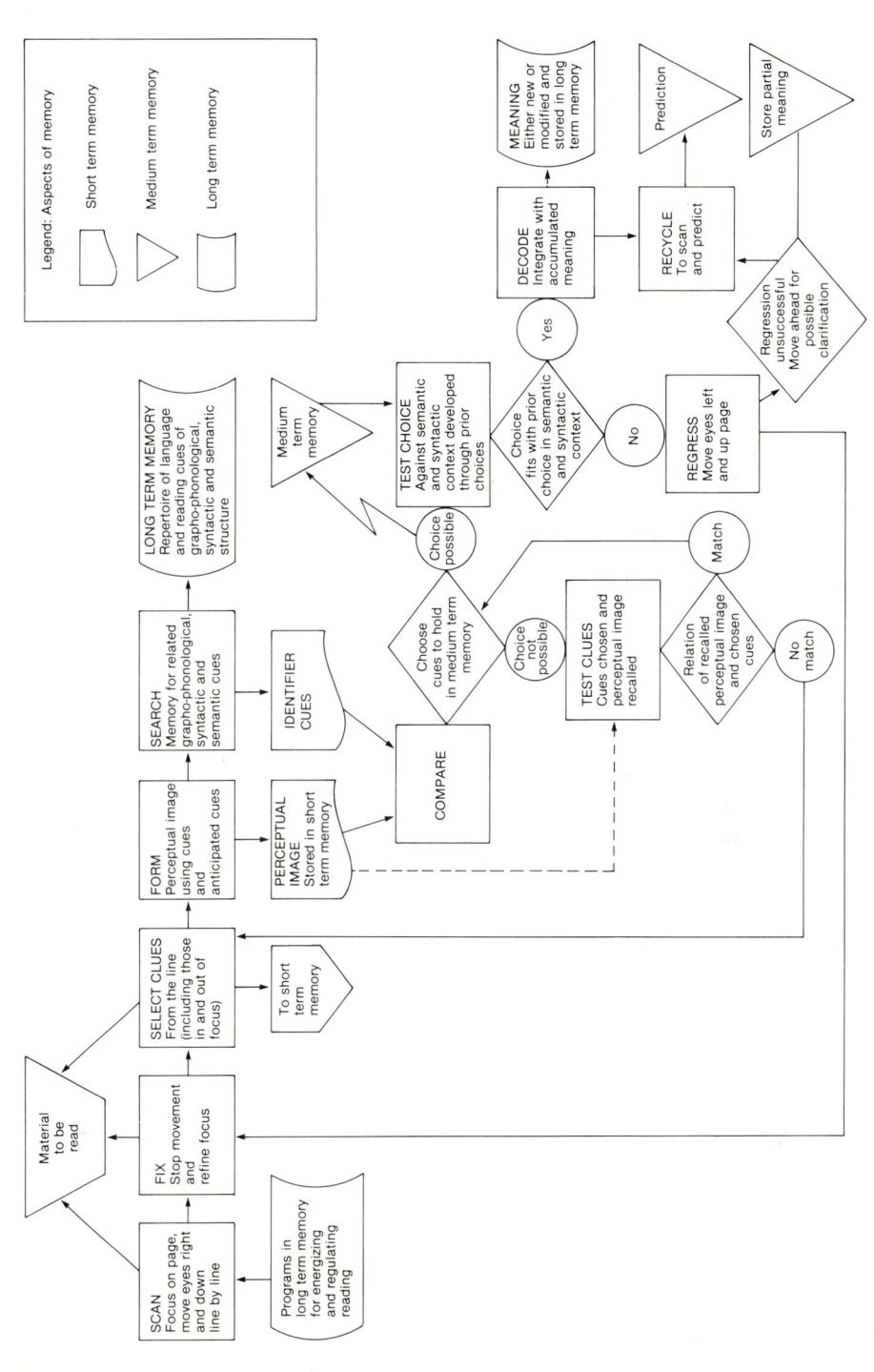

Figure 3-1 A Flow Chart of Goodman's Model of Reading

2. A language repertoire containing all the rules and cues of spoken and written language.
3. Acquired meanings and concepts.

At the onset of a reading act, the regulating programs direct the eyes to move and focus on the material.

Printed language cues in and around the word are selected for making guesses and then are stored in the short-term memory. Prior predictions from the medium-term memory aid in the selection of cues only after the initial instance of reading.

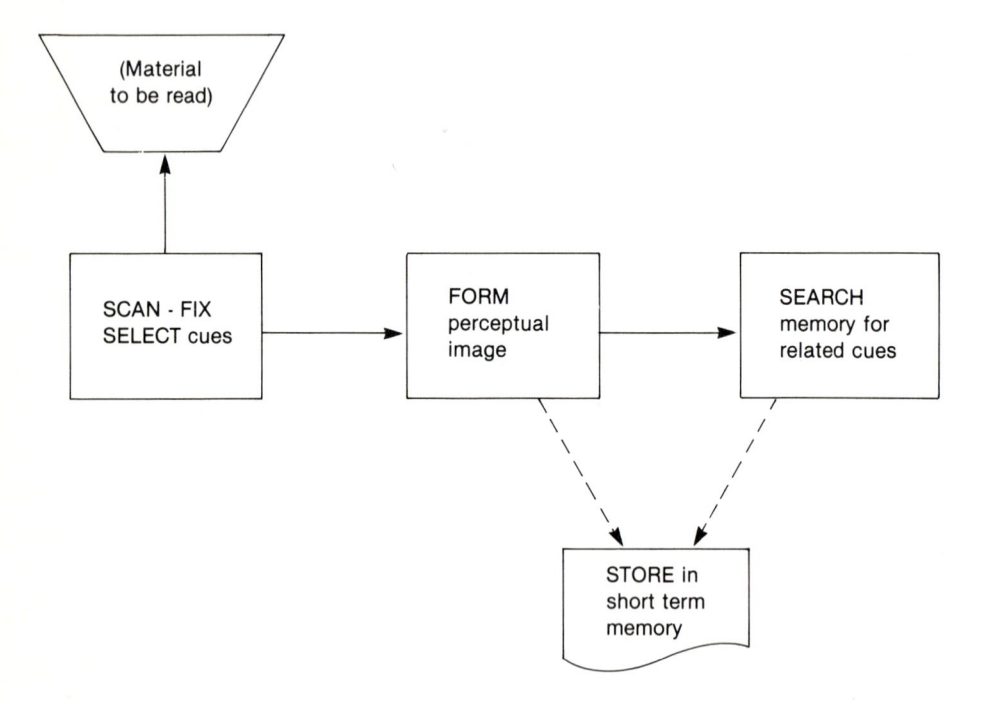

```
(Material to be read)
   ↑
   |
[SCAN - FIX SELECT cues] → [FORM perceptual image] → [SEARCH memory for related cues]
                                    ↘           ↙
                              [STORE in short term memory]
```

The selected cues are used to form perceptual images that are also stored in the short-term memory. The perceptual cues formed may be anticipatory rather than actual. The proficient reader does not use every cue available because then the act of reading would be slow and laborious. Some images formed, therefore, may be anticipations of actual cues that will be substantiated at a later time. There is a search through the language repertoire for known cues (grapheme-phoneme relationships, sentence structures, and meaning structures) that might be related to the present situation. When these cues are identified, they too are stored in the short-term memory.

The perceptual images and the identified language cues are then compared. A decision is consequently made to hold these cues in the medium-term memory by

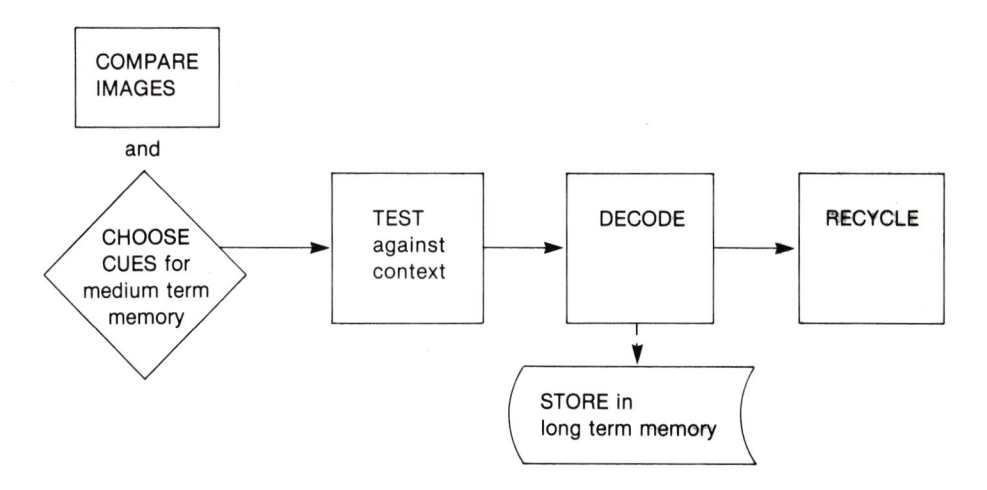

```
        COMPARE
        IMAGES
           |
          and
           |
       CHOOSE          TEST              DECODE           RECYCLE
       CUES for   →    against     →                →
      medium term      context
        memory
                                            |
                                            ▼
                                       STORE in
                                    long term memory
```

testing them to see if they fit with prior information (confirmed predictions and stored partial meanings). If they do fit, the message has been decoded. At this point the meaning (deep structure) is integrated with other meanings, predictions are confirmed, and the process is recycled.

There are two placed in the process where a decision may be made that the perceived cues do not fit and that the message cannot be decoded. The first occurs after the perceptual image and the identified related language cues are compared.

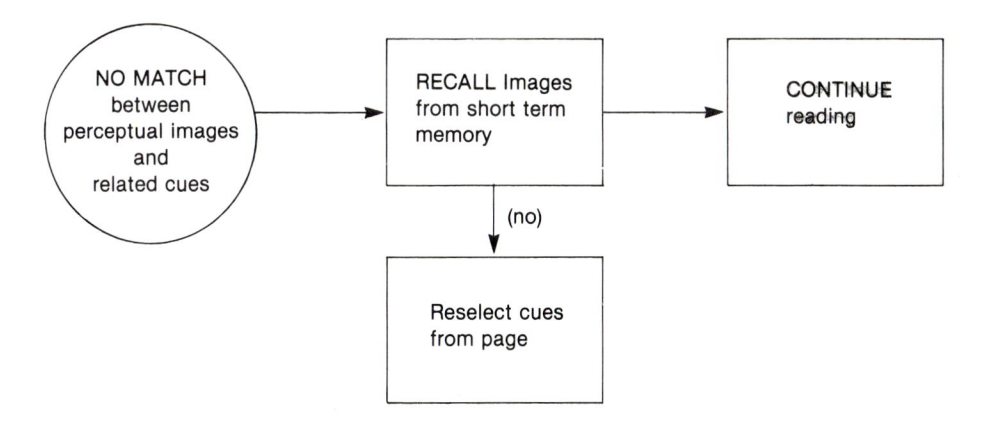

```
      NO MATCH              RECALL Images              CONTINUE
      between           →   from short term       →    reading
  perceptual images          memory
        and                      |
    related cues                (no)
                                 ▼
                          Reselect cues
                          from page
```

At this point, the perceptual image and the chosen cues are recalled. If there is no match, cues are reselected from the line on the page and the process is repeated. If there is a match now, then the cues are held in short-term memory and a second test is made.

The second decision is made when the cues are tested against the semantic and syntactic context developed through prior choices. If there still is no fit, the decision is made to regress and to seek the point of inconsistency. If the regression does not produce decoding, the partial meaning, if any, is stored in the medium-term memory. The reader moves on with the possibility that additional cues will lead to complete decoding of the message.

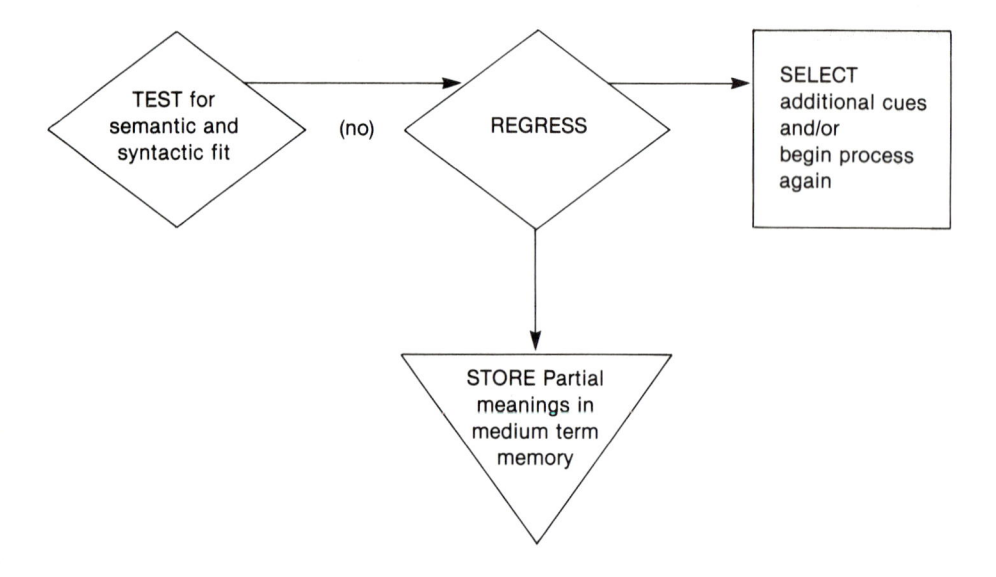

```
    TEST for                              SELECT
  semantic and  ──(no)──▶  REGRESS  ──▶  additional cues
   syntactic fit                          and/or
                                          begin process
                              │           again
                              ▼
                        STORE Partial
                         meanings in
                         medium term
                           memory
```

Goodman analyzed the responses of pupils reading orally and hypothesized the reasons for readers' deviations from the printed text. He does not call these deviations "errors" because the term implies something intrinsically bad or avoidable. He prefers to call them *miscues* because an analysis of them reveals the reader's use and misuse of available language cues. In addition, the analysis reveals the process by which the reader utilizes the available cues to reconstruct the author's message. Chapter 5 contains a discussion of how an analysis of a reader's miscues can be made and used in formulating an instructional program.

The Interactive Model of Reading

Rumelhart (1976) proposed an interactive model of reading to explain how a mature reader interacts with print. The model attempts to explain and illustrate the interactive aspects of the reading process more fully than other models do. The model is created on the plan of "parallel processing" in computer science. In parallel processing, more than one level of information can be acted on at any one time. That is, the information flow is not direct and linear; the information can be acted on by two or more types of processing, and the different types of processing can interact with one another. Rumelhart was not the first to explain reading as an interactive process, but he was the first to introduce parallel processing.

According to Rumelhart, reading involves perceptual and cognitive processes in obtaining meaning from print. The purpose of reading is to produce meaning, and the meaning produced depends in part on the meanings already stored in the reader's schemas. Information is taken in from various sources, and these sources act together to produce meaning. Any one source can be primary at any one time, but utilizing information from one source often depends on utilizing information from the others (see Figure 3-2).

The model has six sources of information input. Each contains specialized knowledge about some aspect of the reading process. These sources of knowledge, stored as schemas, are (1) the semantic, (2) the syntactic, (3) the lexical, (4) the letter cluster, (5) the letter, and (6) the letter features. These are hierarchically arranged with the semantic level being the "highest."

Information from a page can be processed by features of the individual letters (a bottom-up processing task) or by information from the semantic source about some general meaning category of the word(s) (a top-down processing task). For example, on seeing the words "the green house" the reader might input this information:

by examining the individual letter features—the lines and curves that make up individual letter features such as in *h* and *o*
by examining clusters of those letters—*gr, ee,* or *ouse*
by analyzing the input from its syntactic relationships—"noun phrase in the object position of a sentence"
by analyzing the input from its semantic relationships—"colored domicile" or "a place where someone lives"

A second important part of the model is the "message center" or "pattern synthesizer." This center is a highly structured, global storage unit that examines, interrelates, and interprets the information received from any and all of the knowledge sources. Each source generates one or more hypotheses about the incoming information. The message center keeps track of all the hypotheses as well as their origins. It then formulates the most probable interpretation of what is being read. The knowledge sources, in turn, continually scan the message center for a hypothesis relevant to its sphere of knowledge and then evaluates it in light of its own specialized domain.

During reading, hypotheses may be confirmed or disproved by a knowledge source; if disproved, they may be removed from the message center. Or a knowledge source may create a new hypothesis to alter or replace the old one. This process continues until a decision is made about the meaning of the information from the page. At the end, the most probable hypothesis is considered to be the correct one.

The model is consistent with the information presented in Chapter 2 about the nature of language and the development of thinking. It demonstrates the importance of schemas in the reading process and the simultaneous interacting of information from both internal and external sources. Most importantly, it confirms what Goodman argued, that reading is not a precise, accuracy-driven activity or process. Yet Rumelhart seems to have presented his model as a compromise between pure bottom-up and top-down models, (assuming that "pure" models truly exist). Although the model is still incomplete, it shows the need for an explanation of how semantic and syntactic information interacts with graphophonemic information.

The weaknesses and limitations of the model can be traced in part from the direct link of Rumelhart's research to simulating the reading process through computer programming. He seems locked into hypothesizing about only that part of the reading process that can be programmed into a computer. He primarily stresses information from two extremes, the top and the bottom. The model explains fairly well how semantic information (schemas) and letter information (features and clusters) are utilized. But it does not fully demonstrate how syntactic information is used (Diehl, 1978; Harste, 1978). These weaknesses can be attributed to Rumelhart's research being mostly in the areas of letter feature recognition and the development of schemas.

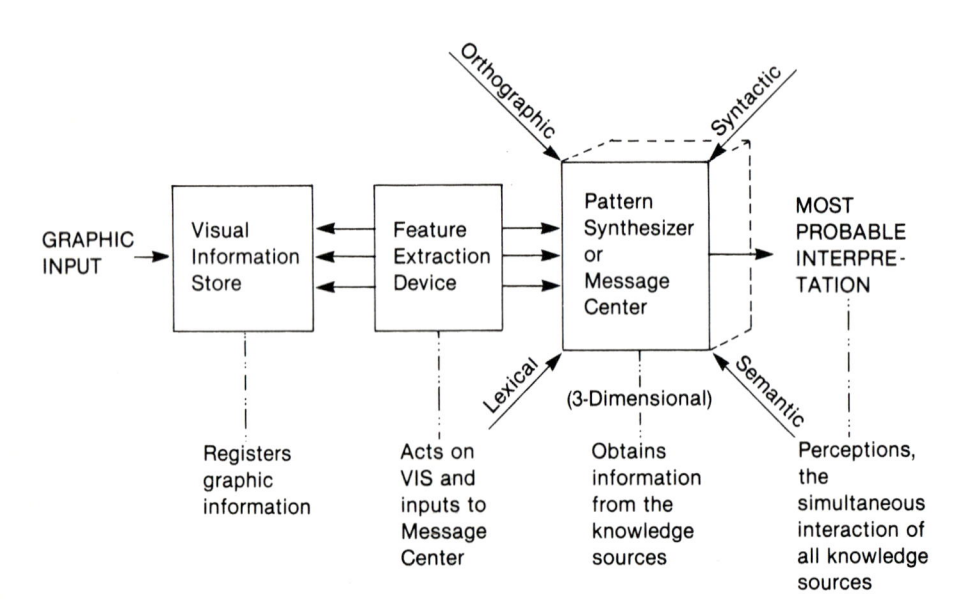

Figure 3-2   The Rumelhart Interactive Model of Reading

A Model of Text Comprehension

Kintsch (1978, 1979, 1980) explains the mental operations that occur during the comprehension of a text and in the recall of information from that text. (Text is any written message and may be a passage in a fictional narrative or an expository, informational passage.) The model focuses on the inferences that a reader makes in comprehending the text and assumes that the more inferences a text requires a reader to make, the harder it is to read. The purposes of the model are (1) to explain how a text is understood and (2) to make predictions about the possible readability of a text by examining the number of "interactions" a reader might have with the text. These interactions are the inferences that require a search of one's schemas. The more searches required of the reader, the less the text's readability.

Kintsch's model grew from his analysis of actual texts. An understanding of Kintsch's theory of the nature and structure of written messages, then, forms the first step in understanding his model. According to Kintsch, a text's surface structure is interpreted as a group of statements or propositions. Propositions have several aspects: they (1) contain one or more arguments, (2) indicate a statement or event, (3) provide facts in relation to other propositions, and (4) qualify other propositions. The propositions, in turn, are organized according to different semantic relationships, some of which are explicit, others implicit.

The semantic structure of the text has two levels. One, the *microstructure,* represents the individual sentences and their intrasentence relationships—letters, syllables, words, word order. The *macrostructure* of the text is more global in nature and represents intersentence information—the "gist" or main idea of the text, the familiarity of the text style and genre to the reader, the presentation of arguments or ideas new to the reader, and the text's placement on a narrative-expository scale. The ways in which a text is structured according to its macrorules are relative to the topic or theme of the text. These "rules" determine how the propositions are systematically arranged. In this model, information can be presented on more than one macrolevel and may be presented on several levels simultaneously. The microstructures, that is, letters, words, sentences, are linked to form a coherent (connected and related) text. By processing these links, the reader may infer the macrostructure(s).

All texts are constructed to conform to certain schematic structures. These are typical ways in which an author develops a text, the rules governing the characteristics and conventions of writing. For example, a story conforms to certain rules depending on whether it is an adventure story, a mystery, or a comedy. The schematic structure is the logic in which propositions are placed. The macrostructure is the broader issue to which the text is addressed: love, triumph of humans over nature, retribution.

The second major aspect of the Kintsch model is the actual process of reading. Through a recall procedure, the way in which a reader processes information is examined. This examination reveals the types of information "understood" in relation to the microstructures and macrostructures. To Kintsch, comprehension is a "search" of one's schemas—cognitive, informational, linguistic—in order to find a match with the proposition in the text. If there is a match, that is, if the text proposition is accepted, the process continues. If there is no match, the reader initiates a process of inferring. These inferences, which are searches of long-term memories, are time consuming. The longer the search takes, the more difficult the reading task (or process) will be, a situation more commonly referred to as "difficulty with comprehension."

The extensive time needed for the search can result from factors in the text or in the reader. For example, the microstructure can be so complex the reader cannot make a match. In this case, the reader has the schema for the information in some form other than that presented by the author: the text is written in a style and maturity of thought inappropriate for the reader, or the text may not be comprehended because the reader has no, or a partial or incorrect, schema for the information. In this case, the reader is not "ready" to read the material.

Through the construction of what Kintsch calls a "coherence graph," the reader's recall of information is matched with how the information is structured in the text. The coherence graph shows the hierarchy of the interrelationships

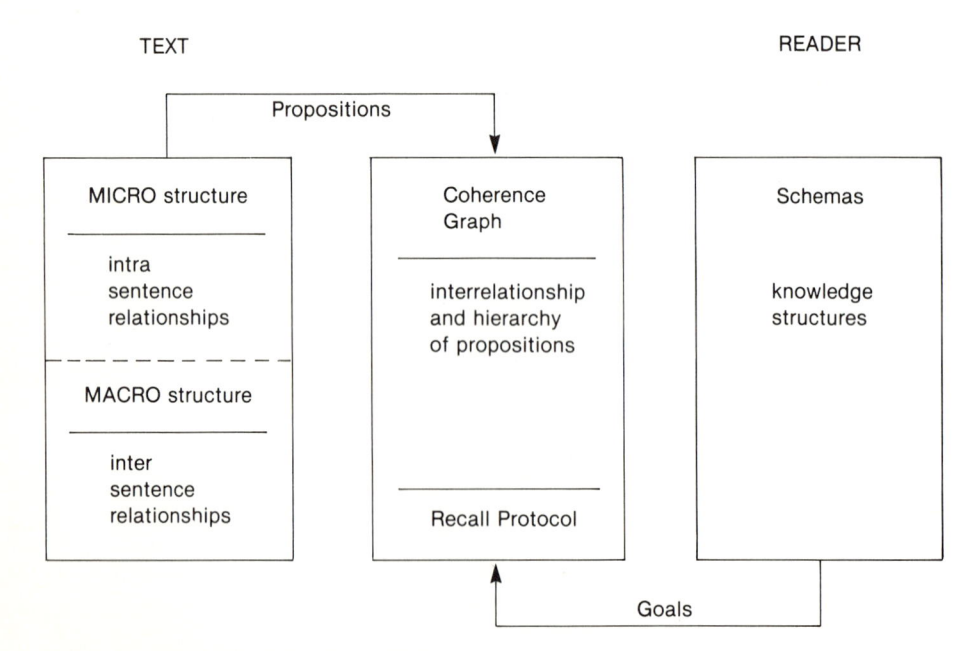

Figure 3-3 The Kintsch Model of Text Comprehension
A coherence graph, constructed for a text to show the structure & interrelationships of its features is used to analyze the information comprehended by a reader.

between the propositions (information) in the text and their pattern of interconnections; each text produces a unique graph structure.

The coherence graph is also intended to illustrate the reader's schemas. By the type of information recalled, Kintsch examines what connections the reader makes and thereby gains a picture of the reader's comprehension strategies. When used in this way, the coherence graphs are known as "recall or summarization protocols." They include the reader's direct remembrances and those reconstructed through inferring.

Kintsch assumes that text comprehension is always controlled by specific schemas, singly or in combination. They set the reader's goal(s) or purpose(s) for reading. There are different control schemas for different levels (specific or general) of comprehension. According to Kintsch's definition of reading, it is impossible to read for absolutely no purpose at all. The schema, which may be complete and detailed or incomplete and unpredicatable, controls what features of the microstructures and macrostructures the reader attends to. An example of a highly predictable text structure is a fairy tale: the actual story may be new, but the reader possesses a complete schema for "fairy tales." The reading is easy because the story is predictable. But the reader may be forced into conflicting purposes when a controlling schema is imposed by a teacher or a situationally specific task. In this case, a reader may start to read a passage for pleasure only to encounter a detailed test after completing it. Or the reader may choose to read a text for purposes very different from those intended by the author. One well-known psychologist interprets fairy tales not for their plot, sequence of events, and unique language, but for their possible implications for interpreting children's behavior according to Freudian psychoanalytic principles. At other times, people may read highly structured texts without clear purposes or loosely structured texts with definite purposes.

Kintsch defines comprehension as learning, stating that comprehension is the "assimilation of a text into a particular knowledge structure, which through this process itself undergoes change. It is this change that is the learning" (1980). Important throughout his theory is the function of the reader's goals as set by the controlling schemas. Although Kintsch recognizes the importance of emotional interest during the reading of a text, his model focuses on what he calls its "cognitive interest." A text has cognitive interest because of its unique pattern and structure of ideas and events determined by an interaction of (1) how much the reader knows about the topic, (2) how much uncertainty the text produces in the reader, and (3) how much sense the text has made to the reader. The last factor, a text's "postdictability," is the process through which a reader goes in order to explain how and why all the parts of the text (microstructures and macrostructures) fit together.

The three factors are another way of indicating that a reader must possess readiness for what is going to be or is being read. Without knowing the appropriate knowledge structures, a reader cannot think and learn. When there is a deviance, when the incoming information does not fit the existing expectations, then the reader undergoes change (learning) as existing knowledge structures, both the permanent ones and those in working memory, have information added and/or deleted.

THE READING ACT: A CONTINUUM OF MOMENTS

The act of reading is a complex interaction of multiple variables, the result of which is understanding and/or learning. The components of the reading act are (1) the reader, (2) the text, (3) the environment, and (4) the process of reading. Each component, in turn, is multifaceted, and these subcomponents interact with and influence one another as well as the other components. Although none of the components exists in isolation—that is, a *reader* entails a *text* being *read* in a given *environment*—we will discuss each separately before examining the interaction among them. (See Figure 3-4).

The model proposed here is called a "continuum of moments" because of two factors. Any reading act is not reducible to a single event or component. It is instead an ongoing interaction of events and the above components, resulting in constant changes in the reader. The reader's approach to the next moment of the reading act is immediately changed as the result (understanding) of the previous moment is accomodated or assimilated. Second, the only way in which the reading act can be studied is by examining what occurs at any one moment. There is no way to measure or determine *all* the ongoing interactions among the variables at any one moment. Only interactions of one or two variables can be examined at any one moment. In physics and molecular biology, this principle is well documented and is recognized as a valid analytical method. Therefore, although there is a wide range of research—each study revealing the presence and influence of one or two particular sets of variables—it may be impossible to study the totality of a reading act or of the reading process. Studying reading may be analogous to studying a cell—analyzing its parts results in a destruction of that essence that enables the cell to live. But we can observe reading in action and describe the products of the process while at the same time formulating ideas about the variables at work.

The model proposed here is the result of a synthesis and expansion of the specific ideas of a few researchers and educators and the general influence of scholars in education, cognitive psychology, language development, social psychology, sociology, and linguistics. Specifically, the model is influenced by Brown's (1981) tetrahedral model for learning from texts; Graesser's (1981) ideas about schema theory and text structures and patterns; Combs's (1958, 1959) ideas about the influence of perception of the context of a communication on behavior; Goodman's (1969) psycholinguistic "guessing game" model of the reading process; Guilford's (1967) concept of intellect; Hittleman's (1973) concept of the

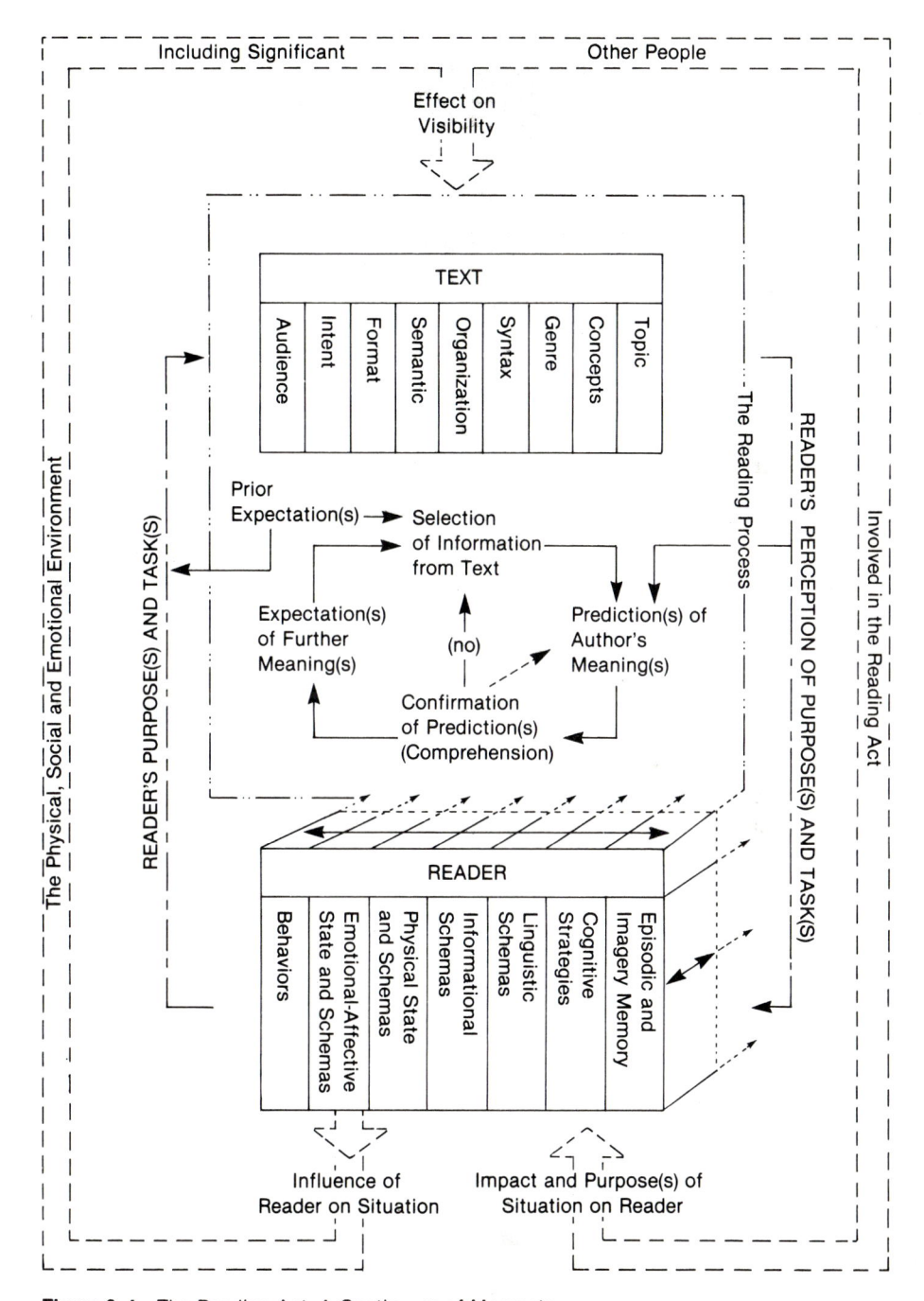

Figure 3-4 The Reading Act: A Continuum of Moments

moment of readability; Kintsch's (1979) concepts of reading comprehension and readability; Robinson's (1978) phases of reading before, during, and after the eye meets the page; and Rumelhart's (1976) interactive model of reading.

The Reader

The reader approaches a reading act as an interconnected, interrelating bundle of energies and energy flows. These energy masses are (1) the physical state and schemas, (2) the affective-emotional state and schemas, (3) the cognitive strategies, (4) the linguistic schema, (5) the information schemas, (6) the behaviors, and (7) the episodic and imagery memories.

The reader has a physical condition as well as schemas for the control and use of his or her body. Their relative maturity and health determine the rate of response. Since thinking has a biological and chemical basis, variables such as rate of synapse, metabolism, chemical composition of the blood stream, muscular coordination, degree of fatigue or stimulation all influence the reading act. The affective-emotional state and schemas consist of attitudes, general personality factors, and "mood." These are not static but fluctuate daily and even throughout the day. They are the ways people have learned to deal with various psychological conditions in regard to themselves and others. The cognitive schemas are the various skills, strategies, and processes for thinking through a problem. The linguistic schemas are based on knowledge of language, language usage and function, forms, and vocabulary. The informational schemas are all the ideas, facts, concepts, and generalizations accumulated through life experiences and schooling. The episodic memories are the storages of thoughts consisting of dated events and the temporal-spatial relationships relating to those events. Imagery memory contains representations, both concrete and referential, not stored in a verbal code. They are images but can be activated by associations from other schemas. The behaviors are all the paralinguistic and nonverbal associations, actions, gestures, expressions, body postures, and use of space that have been acquired through acculturation.

The Text

The text is a fixed entity containing several interrelated sets of variables. It is a product of an author's "bundle of energies." The sets of variables in a text are its topic, concepts, genre, syntax, organization of information, semantic presentation, and format. The topic and subject are the broad area and specific topic about which the author wrote. For example, the author could have written specifically about a barometer, which is part of the larger ideas of weather and climatology. These are related to the second set of variables, the genre—the literary form selected for setting out ideas: short story, exposition, poem. Included is the author's intent. From among many syntactic patterns and organizational features, the author has selected specific sentences. The vocabulary and other semantic forms are chosen in relation to the intent, audience, and topic. The ideas and concepts and how these are spaced in the text (idea density) as well as in what manner they are ordered have been considered together with how they will be supported by illustrations and expanded explanations. Finally, when the text is "put to press," it is placed in some format—size of type, color, quality of paper, binding, and size of page.

The Environment

The reading situation comprises three subenvironments: physical, social, and emotional. The physical setting is the location, time, and position of the reading act. For example, the reading might occur sitting or standing, at a desk or on a bench, indoors or outdoors, in the morning or the evening. The temperature might be hot, cool, or moderate. There may be glaring lights, loud noises, or semi-darkness and absolute quiet.

The social setting consists of other individuals or groups of individuals with whom the reader has contact during the reading act. Each of these social settings has a protocol and each individual involved has a schema, partial or complete, for that situation. For example, school classrooms have a set of rules governing how one is to read in the library corner or at one's desk. There are also rules for reading on a public transport (such as folding a newspaper so that it will be contained in one's body field and reading silently rather than out loud), and reading as part of a public performance.

The emotional climate is influenced by both the physical and social settings. The climate can be humorous, sorrowful, tense, or a generally pleasant ambiance.

These environmental factors create demands on the reader—purposes for reading and specific or general tasks to be performed during or after the reading. For example, the social setting may demand oral reading with accuracy (no deviations from a transposition of print into sound) or for testing (seeking out specific information). These may be actual demands in that a teacher or peer gives the reader the goal, or they may be "perceived" in that the reader infers a task or purpose different from that given in spoken or written directives. An example of this occurs when a student thinks the task is a test of oral accuracy, even though the teacher has stated that the task is to determine the author's meaning. Or the reader perceives that a text is to be read for enjoyment when in reality it is intended to persuade the reader to engage in a particular behavior.

As part of the total context, the reader exerts an influence on the environment. There may be a dislike for the setting, and an attempt is made to change it—to move to another chair or location or to turn on a brighter light. There may be an attempt to read with friends and share the information or a desire to read alone in a secluded location. The reader may also influence the emotional climate by releasing feelings of frustration that have resulted from an interpretion of the purpose(s) for the reading act.

The Process of Reading

The interactions between the reader and the text in a constructive process (as depicted by the previously reported psycholinguistic models of reading) constitute the reading process. It is what Robinson (1978) stated that the reader does before, during, and after the graphic imprint is perceived and evaluated.

The Interaction

None of the variables at work in each of the four components functions alone. Each variable interacts with the variables in its own component and with the many variables of the other components. There is a continual interchange among the reader, the text, the environment, and the process of reading. Any change in one creates a change in the others. The changes occurring to the text, however, are limited—lighting effects on visibility or physical changes to the text made by pulling pages from it, xeroxing it, altering the color presentations, or reprinting it on a different quality of paper. Or the reader may become a coauthor and alter the text—underlining, writing in substituted vocabulary, or cross-referencing. The interactions are continuous in both a circular and spiraling manner. The flow lines in Figure 3-4 show the major directions of influence, but these move in varying degrees and with varying influences throughout the continuum of moments. All may be at work at any one time, or some might be in abeyance. Each, though, is never totally inactive.

THE RELATIONSHIP OF WRITING TO READING

A basic premise of this text is that students of all ages gain immeasurably in their reading proficiency if they are actively engaged in making their own "text." The first chapter contains a number of assumptions about reading programs, one of which is: "Instruction in composing messages accompanies instruction in reading messages. By creating their own texts students learn how to reconstruct the intended meaning of others."

The process of composing allows students to learn how a text "works," how to organize information, how to present ideas clearly and to reduce ambiguity, and how to establish purposes for communicating. The current research and thinking on the integration of reading and writing programs support this conclusion.

From her study of beginning readers, C. Chomsky (1971) reports how they learned to read by creating their own spellings for familiar words. They became active participants in teaching themselves to read. Introducing children to writing their own words makes them aware that the messages belong to them and have grown out of their own consciousness. As she put it, the "word" is "born of the creative effort of the learner."

Elkind, who has long been associated with the interpretation of Piagetian principles and the cognitive development of children, indicated that "comprehension, or the construction of meaning, is also helped by the child's own efforts at giving meaning (i.e., representing) his own experiences " (1976). He proposed that the more oportunities and experiences children have to represent thoughts verbally, the better prepared they will be to interpret others' representations. Since reading and writing are reciprocal processes of meaning construction, "the more children write, the more they will get from reading."

An extensive body of research reveals the strong interrelationship among the language skills of speaking, listening, reading, and writing (Lehr, 1981; Wilson, 1981). The evidence indicates that combining instruction in reading and writing leads to greater proficiency in both. It does not matter whether reading or writing is presented first; each has a positive influence on the development of the other. Both structure meaning, and both develop as natural extensions of children's desire to communicate. So students with the opportunity to experience the trials and satisfactions of structuring their own language (writing) will be better prepared for interpreting the structuring of others.

In sum, what seems to happen when students learn to write in that they learn to "invent reading for themselves" (Guthrie, 1978). This is true for students of all ages as they learn to compose different prose styles for a variety of purposes and for a wide range of audiences. Teaching students how to write their own reading material results in better comprehension of material written by others (Maya, 1979).

IMPLICATIONS

As psycholinguistic models of reading and our model of the reading act point out, reading is an interactive process. Reading is not just the interplay of factors inherent in the reader. Rather, reading at any moment results from the interaction among sets of variables, including the purposes for reading, the types and structures of the reading material, the situations in which reading occurs, the way understanding is measured, and the characteristics of the reader.

Through direct instruction in classrooms, students need to learn strategies that will foster their awareness of those variables and procedures. This means students should be engaged in active learning, which promotes such an awareness.

Both students and teachers should understand that:

1. During reading, information should be actively related to prior knowledge, and new information should be integrated with that prior knowledge through elaboration schemas involving both further reading and writing tasks.

2. Reading for one specific purpose or attention to one specific feature or aspect of a text may impede students' understanding of other features, aspects, or information regarding that text.
3. The level and kind of reader's understanding are affected by their perception of the author's purposes as well as the purpose(s) for reading the material during an instructional activity.
4. Different types of content, stylistic patterns, and organizational structures represent different levels of understanding for readers of different backgrounds, abilities, ages, and interests.
5. The products of all instruction should be independent readers who can apply several strategies in different situations to many types of textural material in a manner so the author's message can be reconstructed as nearly as originally intended. Only then will students have full responsibility for their own learning.

Discussion Questions and Activities

1. Prepare a short statement for a parents' newsletter intepreting this statement by Cambourne (1981):

   Psycholinguistic research clearly shows that everything which has been claimed about comprehending spoken language also applies to the comprehension of written language.

2. Yetta Goodman, among others, encourages us to "kid watch." Try to observe students of different ages reading in all sorts of places, not just classrooms. Talk to them after they have finished reading about what they were doing. How do their actions and comments reveal the process they are undergoing?

3. Select two reading passages on different topics that contain information not generally known by a particular group of pupils. Then:
   a. Ask the pupils to read the first passage as they normally would read something. After the reading, test their retention of the main idea and major details of the passage (1) immediately after the reading, (2) one hour later, and (3) one day later. Determine the type of information that is not retained by the pupils (that is, main ideas or major details).
   b. Plan a lesson so that the type of information not retained in the first reading will be remembered after the reading of the second passage. Again test their retention (1) immediately after the reading (2) one hour later, and (3) one day later. Was there greater retention after the second reading?

4. From at least three other texts on reading instruction, obtain definitions of reading. How are they similar to or different from the one presented in this text?

5. The verb *to read* is defined in the dictionary as both a transitive and an intransitive verb. Explain the confusion that may arise between two speakers who are using different sets of definitions in talking about reading.

Further Readings

The following two books by Frank Smith offer scholarly yet highly readable examinations of the psycholinguistic principles of the learning of reading. They present in greater depth many of the insights according to which the three models of reading have been constructed.

Smith, Frank, *Understanding Reading,* 2nd ed. (New York: Holt, Rinehard & Winston, 1978).

Smith, Frank, *Psycholinguistics and Reading* (New York: Holt, Rinehart & Winston, 1973).

The following contains explanations of a number of different theoretical models of the reading process:

Singer, Harry, and Robert B. Ruddell, eds, *Theoretical Models and Processes of Reading,* 2nd ed. (Newark, DE: International Reading Association, 1976).

The following short but extremely insightful book relates the way in which reading and writing codevelop in children:

Clay, Marie M., *What Did I Write?* (Exeter, NH: Heinemann Education Books, 1979).

For those interested in understanding the composing process the following books are recommended. The first is a theoretical presentation of the composing process, and the second is a collection of interviews with authors of children's literature about their own feelings about writing.

Smith, Frank, *Writing and the Writer* (New York: Holt, Rinehart & Winston, 1982).

Weiss, M. Jerry, ed., *From Writers to Students: The Pleasures and Pains of Writing* (Newark, DE: International Reading Association, 1979).

Chapter 4

PRINCIPLES OF ANALYTICAL TEACHING THROUGH STANDARDIZED TESTS

Focus Questions

1. What is analytical teaching?

2. What are the characteristics of standardized tests?

3. What are the effective uses of standardized tests?

4. What limitations do standardized tests have in analytical teaching?

Many teachers view testing and measuring as postinstructional activities. This kind of testing and measuring, however, is only one kind of assessment. Another kind—one that occurs continuously during instruction—is a check to ensure that teaching and learning are progressing in the desired direction. Both kinds of assessment are important to the overall instructional program, but the second kind is more important to the classroom teacher. The first type of assessment is *summative assessment.* Examples are the end-of-course final examinations and comparisons of two or more different types of instructional procedures after they have been in operation for a period of time.

Formative assessment, the other kind, evaluates an instructional procedure while it is in progress. It looks at the procedures to determine how many of the instructional goals have been accomplished and how well they have been accomplished according to an established standard. Formative assessment, by providing feedback to the teacher, helps the teacher decide how to proceed. It is formative assessment that is referred to in this book as *analytical teaching.*

ANALYTICAL TEACHING

The term analytical teaching has been selected over the more common one, diagnostic teaching, because the term analytical expresses more of the purposes of what school assessment should be. The term diagnostic reflects a medical origin and implies a search for factors of failure. It implies, when applied to reading instruction, a search mainly for reasons why an individual is not reading well. It seems to exclude assessing a reading performance that is not marked by failure.

Analytical teaching as a rule consists of five steps that the teacher undertakes, not sporadically, but as a continuous classroom activity. All five steps of analytical teaching may be undertaken one or more times a day, or over a period of days.

Analytical teaching consists of

Describing: Noting the performance of students without using any qualitative or judgmental statements.
Classifying: Placing students' reading performances in some schema of the reading process.
Inferring: Judging the quality of a student's reading performance by a set of standards. The standards can be applied to individuals or groups and should be consistent with the schema of the reading process.
Predicting: Deciding whether a student's observed reading performance needs to be modified and planning the teaching and learning that will follow.
Verifying: Deciding whether or not the plan instituted was effective. Verification occurs by describing, classifying, and inferring the reading performance subsequent to the planned instruction and learning.

This chapter is concerned with using standardized tests for teaching analytically. In order to make insightful assessments that can be a basis for an instructional program, one should (1) know something about the principles of testing, (2) know the purposes of schoolwide testing programs, and (3) understand the uses and limitations of standardized tests.

OBJECTIVES OF ASSESSMENT

Reading assessment, whether schoolwide or in a single classroom, should be guided by certain objectives. Assessment of programs should:

1. Be directed toward formulating methods of instruction.
2. Attempt to place reading performance and reading instruction in relation to the school's or class's educational program.
3. Be purposeful in that it has a place in the particular philosophy of education according to which the class is conducted.
4. Be efficient so that the greatest amount of pertinent and useful information is collected and analyzed in the least amount of time.
5. Be continuous.

An assessment program begins with the selection of a test, or series of tests, that will allow useful information to be collected. Yet tests describe only the performance of an individual or group; they in and of themselves do not assess someone's performance. For example, if a test shows that a student has answered 16 to 25 questions correctly, all one has is a description of that child's performance. But what is needed is some mearure of the child's reading performance. This is obtained by comparing the difference between the results of two or more tests or by measuring the results of a single test against some predetermined standard of performance. Still, this record of change or lack of change in reading performance is not yet assessment. Assessment is the application of criteria for judging or evaluating the worth of the performance in a qualitative or quantitative manner. The process of assessing reading performance, then, is the deliberate act of testing, measuring, and evaluating reading performance.

Analytical teaching, the conscious application of the principles of assessment, is really a matter of degree. The depth and thoroughness of analysis will depend on the teacher's purpose. A full analysis of different students' reading performances one or more times a year may be desired. On the other hand, a briefer, more frequent analysis of different aspects of the reading process may satisfy the teacher's plan. The amount and type of information collected should be consistent with one's idea of the reading process and fulfill an instructional purpose.

Information is collected about students' reading performance for the purposes of instruction and administration. Information is gathered for instructional purposes when the effectiveness of the teacher's teaching or the students' learning or a combination of the two needs to be determined. Administrative decisions are usually out of the realm of the classroom teacher and concern (1) the volatile issue of accountability, (2) schoolwide effectiveness in comparison with other schools, and (3) the prediction of long-range results of a project or experiment. But for the classroom teacher, the selection and use of tests should help answer instructional questions such as

What has the student done in the past?
What can the student do right now?
What can be expected of the student in the future?

STANDARDIZED TESTS

A standardized test is one that has been experimentally constructed. The test author has followed some commonly accepted procedures and has researched (1) the content of the test, (2) the procedures for administering the test, (3) the system for recording and scoring answers, and (4) the method by which results can be turned into a usable form. Everything about the test has been standardized so that if all the directions are correctly followed, the results will be interpreted in the same manner, regardless of where in the country the test is given. The results should mean the same thing to different people. A common misconception is that the word *standard* represents a goal to be attained. Standardized means that the methods of administering, recording, scoring, and interpreting have been made uniform.

Characteristics of Standardized Tests

There are two main types of standardized reading tests, norm-referenced tests and criterion-referenced tests.

Norm-referenced tests are used to compare the relative position of individuals in different groups. The test is constructed and then given to a large number of students. The average score (or median) is found by noting the raw score for which 50 percent of the scores were higher and 50 percent were lower. This score is then designated as the average for the group. As an example, a hypothetical group of fourth-grade students are given a newly constructed test in the second month of the fourth grade. The middle score of that group represents a grade equivalent of 4.2. Now, if the test is given to other groups, say of third graders or fifth graders, average scores can be obtained for those grade levels as well. The differences among the average scores for the different grade levels—the difference between 3.2 and 4.2, and 5.2 and 4.2—are determined through a mathematical procedure called *extrapolation*. It is also possible to obtain average scores for different periods of time during the school year. Many standardized test publishers provide different sets of scores or norms for the beginning, middle, and end of each grade level.

A norm-referenced test is used to measure the performance of a student in relation to the norming, or standardizing, group. If a student in fourth grade achieves a grade equivalent of 4.5 during the month of February, then that student has achieved a score equal to the average score in the fourth-grade norming group, and the score can then be interpreted as meaning that the student scored better than 50 percent of the norming population did. A score of 5.5 would mean the student achieved a score equal to that of the average fifth grader in the norming group. It does not mean that the student should be in the fifth grade or "is doing" fifth-grade work.

The fact that norm-referenced tests are useful primarily to indicate how a student performs in relation to other children becomes even clearer when two other types of norms, the percentile and the stanine, are considered.

The percentile indicates how a student performed relative to all the students in the norming group. For example, students with a score at the sixtieth percentile scored better than 60 percent of the norming group, and 40 percent of the norming group scored better than that student did.

It is possible to create local percentile norms based on the scores made by the students in a particular class, school, or school district. In these cases, a percentile would show a student's performance in relation to his or her immediate peers. It is possible that local norms will not exactly match the national norms provided by the test publisher. A local norm may be higher or lower than the national norm. Consider, for example, the following hypothetical percentiles:

	National Norm Percentiles	Local Norm Percentiles
Vocabulary	45	55
Comprehension	45	40

These would be interpreted as meaning that for the vocabulary test, a student who scores better than 45 percent of the national group, in comparison, scores better than 55 percent of the other students at that grade level in the local school or school district.

The stanine scores are digits that range from one to nine. Like percentiles, their interpretation is based on a relationship to a particular group. The fifth stanine is considered average, and the stanines on either side of the fifth are equally distant from the average. For instance, a student who scores in stanine 3 stands the same relative distance from the average as someone who scores in stanine 7. An advantage of using stanines rather than grade equivalents and the percentile ranks is that stanines represent a range of scores rather than one particular score. Three students in the fourth grade with different raw scores could have different grade equivalents and percentile ranks; yet their stanine scores might not differ. If their scores were within the same stanine unit, they would be considered to have performed equally well on the test. The following scores of three students on an actual test (Karlsen, Madden, & Gardner, 1976) illustrate this:

Table 4-1 Reading Comprehension, Total

	Raw Score	Scaled Score	Grade Equivalent	Percentile	Stanine
Martha	48	446	3.8	41	5
Marc	51	460	4.1	49	5
Myra	52	472	4.5	56	5

In many schools, Martha and Myra would not be considered to be performing about equally. The use of the stanine scores, despite the seemingly wide grade-equivalent spread, makes it more apparent that all three students performed, in comparison to the norming group, in the average range.

Stanines, like percentiles, are relative scores indicating performance relative to the group. Myra and Martha performed (from an absolute point of view) differently, but relative to the group of their peers who took the test, they performed about the same. (A note of caution: although stanines will classify two different scores as similar, they will also classify two similar scores as different if those scores fall close to one boundary between two stanines.)

Another example of using stanines to interpret scores can be seen in the scores of two sixth-grade students on another actual test (Balow et al., 1979). One student obtained a raw score of 49 on the reading subtest at the beginning of sixth grade (fall norms). The other achieved the same number of correct answers, but near the end of sixth grade (spring norms). As can be seen, they both have identical grade equivalents, though the scores mean very different things.

Table 4-2 Reading

	Raw Score	Scaled Score	Percentile	Grade Equivalent	Stanine
Harriett (fall norms)	49	753	65	7.8	6
Henry (spring norms)	49	753	58	7.8	5

Harriett, who received a grade score of 7.8 at the beginning of the year, would be considered high average in comparison to the norming group. But Henry, who received a grade score of 7.8 at the end of the year, would be considered average in relation to the norming group.

Local school districts have begun to report the results of standardized tests in a form called "normal curve equivalents (NCE)." NCEs are similar to percentiles in that they range from 1 to 99. However, they differ in that NCEs are equally spaced units that can be used to compute averages and make comparisons. Percentiles cannot be added or subtracted from each other, as NCEs can. Changes in percentile ranks at different points on the scale cannot be compared. For example, a student who performs at the fortieth percentile at the begin- ning of the year and at the fiftieth percentile at the end has not made the same change as someone has who performs first at the tenth and then at the twentieth percentile. but any student who shows a change of ten NCE units has made an equivalent change of performance, whether it has been from the tenth to the twentieth or the sixtieth to the seventieth NCE.

Criterion-referenced tests determine whether an individual or group has achieved a certain level of mastery. A criterion-referenced test is a set of standards or goals representing a group of tasks that the students are supposed to master. Scores on this test, rather than showing placement in relation to a group, show the students' placement in relation to a set of goals.

To construct a criterion-referenced reading test, the test writer assumes a hierarchy of skills necessary to the reading process. The successful completion of certain tasks is presumed to evidence such skills. If a student can perform the task, then that student is said to have mastered a particular aspect of reading. For example, an item may ask the student to match the letter *b* with the appropriate picture of an object whose name begins with /b/, or the student may be asked to read two paragraphs and mark the one that is ordered in a time sequence. For each task there may be one or more items. When the student can mark the appropriate answers for a particular task, then mastery of that task is assumed. Like norm-referenced tests, criterion-referenced tests can be made appropriate for different maturity levels of reading performance.

Whether a standardized test is norm referenced or criterion referenced, it should have validity and reliability.

A valid test measures what it says it measures. A reading test should indicate something about reading performance, and the tasks should relate to some aspects of reading. Of course, a test may be valid according to the test writer's definition of reading but not according to the definition assumed by the test user. Within the definition of reading set forth in this book, a test of reading composed entirely of lists of words would not be considered as valid. Such a test is in no way concerned with testing the child's ability to reconstruct an author's message.

Reliability refers to the consistency with which a test produces its results. Think of an individual who never is able to keep appointments or is constantly disappointing others by failing to follow through with promises. That person lacks reliability. When a reading test cannot be trusted to give consistent, reliable results, then to classroom teachers the test is worthless. The reliability of a test can be determined from statistical information generally provided by the publisher of the test. If a publisher reports a "coefficient of reliability" somewhere between .90 and .99, then the test can be accepted as being fairly reliable. A test, however, can have a high degree of reliability but not have validity: whatever it may test—which may or may not be part of the reading process—it tests it consistently.

Standardized tests are usually accompanied by a manual of directions that contains a variety of information about the test. This manual should be read carefully in order to find out (1) the intended purposes of the test, (2) the content of the test, (3) the manner in which the test is organized, (4) the recommended procedures for administering the test, (5) the publisher's estimate of its validity and reliability, (6) the various tables of norms (not included in criterion-referenced tests), (7) an explanation of how to interpret the scores, and (8) a discussion of some uses of the test results.

The manuals accompanying norm-referenced tests also contain another bit of information that is often overlooked—the standard error of measurement. This number, which is usually but not necessarily expressed in grade-level equivalents, is an indication of how much the particular test could be wrong. No test can produce completely accurate estimates of a student's actual performance. The standard error of measurement should be used to estimate how much a student's score can differ from the one produced on the test. If a student scores a grade equivalent of 5.3 on a test with a four-month (.4 year) standard error of measurement, it can be assumed about 68 percent of the time that the student's real score is between the grade equivalents of 4.9 and 5.7 (obtained by adding and subtracting 1 standard error of measurement from the student's score). It could be assumed about 95 percent of the time that the student's score is really between the grade equivalents of 4.5 and 6.4 (obtained by adding and subtracting the doubled standard error of measurement).

Standardized Reading Tests

Norm-referenced reading tests usually contain two sections, a vocabulary subtest and a paragraph reading subtest. Separate scores are obtained for each subtest, and some tests have a composite score. The vocabulary sections attempt to test a student's knowledge of specific words by matching the word to its pictorial representation or to an appropriate synonym. The student's comprehension is tested by a series of questions about different paragraphs or short selections. Figure 4-1 contains sample vocabulary and comprehension questions from a standardized norm-referenced reading test.

The following are representative of some widely used norm-referenced reading tests:

Comprehensive Tests of Basic Skills: Reading. 1981. Monterey, CA: CTB/McGraw-Hill. Intended grades: 1-12. Subtests: oral vocabulary, oral sentence and story comprehension, visual and sound recognition (lowest level), word-attack skills, reading vocabulary, and reading comprehension of sentences and passages (primary and intermediate levels).

Gates-MacGinitie Reading Tests, 2nd ed. 1978. Lombard, IL: Riverside. Intended grades: 1-12. Subtests: vocabulary and comprehension.

Iowa Tests of Basic Skills: Reading. 1979. Lombard, IL: Riverside. Intended grades: 1-9. Subtests: reading comprehension and word analysis.

Metropolitan Achievement Tests, 5th ed. 1979. New York: Psychological Corporation. *Survey Battery: Reading Comprehension.* Intended grades: 1-12. Subtests: reading comprehension and word meaning in context. *Instructional Tests: Reading.* Intended grades: 1-9. Subtests: reading comprehension, word-part clues, word attack, and vocabulary in context.

Sequential Tests of Educational Progress: Reading. 1979. Menlo Park, CA: Addison-Wesley. Intended grades: *1-12. Subtests: vocabulary and literal and inferential comprehension.*

Although the surface appearance of the criterion-referenced test looks similar to that of a norm-referenced test, the difference is greater than their layout and format suggest. The criterion-referenced test measures the students' mastery of certain specific objectives. Whereas a norm-referenced test cannot be used to pinpoint strengths and deficiencies, the criterion-referenced tests can do just that without any reference to a norm group.

The following is a representative published criterion-referenced test:

PRI/Reading Systems. 1980. Monterey, CA: CTB/McGraw-Hill. Intended grades: K-9+. Subtests: oral language, word attack and usage, comprehension, and applications.

1. A large **boat**
   1) car
   2) house
   3) animal
   4) ship

4. He **speaks** fast
   1) drives
   2) talks
   3) runs
   4) eats

7. **Yell** for help
   1) ask
   2) beg
   3) look
   4) shout

> Do you know the shape of a sign tells what it means?
> A sign with three sides means to let the other car go first. A sign with four sides means to be careful. A sign with an X on it means that there are trains crossing ahead. A stop sign has eight sides.
> Know your signs and play it safe!

11. Where would there be a sign with an X on it?
    1) At a bus stop
    2) At a railroad crossing
    3) At a hosptial
    4) At a gas station

12. What should drivers do when they see a sign with four sides?
    1) Slow down
    2) Watch for trains
    3) Stop quickly
    4) Pull off the road

13. What should drivers do when they see a sign with more than four sides?
    1) Look back
    2) Turn to the right
    3) Slow down
    4) Stop

14. What does a round sign mean?
    1) Stop
    2) Slow down
    3) Keep going
    4) The story does not say.

Figure 4-1 Sample Questions from a Norm Referenced Test
Source: *Iowa Tests of Basic Skills, Practice Test Booklet for Levels 9-14, Forms 7/8.* Copyright 1978 by the University of Iowa. Published by Houghton Mifflin Co., Boston; distributed by Riverside Publishing Co.

Some publishers try to combine the features of norm-referenced and criterion-referenced tests. A feature indicated for the *Metropolitan Achievement Tests* is that an "instructional reading level" can be obtained from either the reading survey or the reading instructional tests. The score represents the reading levels in current basal reading series and attempts to show an appropriate level of mastery at which instruction may be started. The *PRI/Reading Systems* has also correlated scores so that norm-referenced information may be estimated from criterion-referenced performance.

Another type of criterion-referenced test is the functional literacy, or life skills, test. (For a discussion of functional literacy, see Chapter 10.) A life skills test assesses students' performance in reading nonacademic materials in school, at home, and in the community. The items include reading and interpreting signs, street maps, advertisements, shopping catalogs, schedules, and directories. Figure 4-2 contains sample questions from a test of functional literacy.

The following are representative published tests of functional literacy:

Life Skills: Tests of Functional Competencies in Reading and Math. 1980. Lombard, IL: Riverside. Intended grades: 5–12.
Performance Assessment in Reading (PAIR). 1978. Monterey, CA: CTB/McGraw-Hill. Intended grades: 5–9. Subtests: two.

One test totally different from all others is the *Degrees of Reading Power* test (DRP). The test consists of series of prose passages on a variety of nonfiction topics. Each test passage is formed by the deletion of seven words with five possible responses for each deleted item. (Since the test is constructed on the principle of a modified cloze procedure, you may wish at this time to read the section in Chapter 5 about the cloze procedure.) Figure 4-3 contains sample questions from the DRP. The students' responses depend directly on their ability to comprehend the syntactic and semantic relationships in the passage. Their scores are reported in DRP units, which represent "readability levels," or predictions of the readability of prose they should be able to read. The publisher also offers readability estimates in DRP units for some commonly used instructional texts in various curricular areas so that the results of the test can be used for placement purposes. The Department of Education of New York State, which codeveloped the test, uses various forms of it to measure students' progress in the third, sixth, and ninth grades and to determine whether the reading competence of high school students qualifies them to receive diplomas.

Degrees of Reading Power (DRP). 1980. New York: College Entrance Examination Board. Intended grades: 3–12.

Limitations of Standardized Tests

Both types of standardized test—norm-referenced and criterion-referenced—have limitations and should be used judiciously with these in mind. Some of these limitations derive from inherent qualities in the tests themselves and some derive from misunderstandings about the capabilities of the tests and what they represent.

Some of the limitations of norm-referenced reading tests are

1. Some tests overestimate an individual's reading performance.
2. The supposedly comparable forms of a test may not in fact be so.

OPERATING INSTRUCTIONS FOR PERFECTION OVEN

Checking Dial:
The reading on the oven thermostat dial shows that the BAKE area is from 150° to 500° and the BROIL area is from 375° to "Broil."

Baking:
Turn oven dial to on and then set at desired temperature. If the dial is set above 300°, both broil and bake elements stay on until desired temperature is reached, then the broil element goes off. You will know when the desired temperature is reached, since the indicator light will go off.

11. What is the minimum temperature that may be used for broiling?

   A. 375°
   B. 350°
   C. 300°
   D. 150°

12. According to these instructions, what is the proper oven temperature for backing potatoes?

   A. 500°
   B. Not given
   C. 300°
   D. 375°

Oven Pot Roast

2-3 lb. Chuck Roast
1 tsp. salt
1 cup water
1 bay leaf

3 large potatoes, peeled and quartered
4 peeled carrots
1 medium onion, quartered

Sprinkle salt over both sides of the roast. Place in roasting pan with 1 cup of water and 1 bay leaf. Cover pan and place in oven preheated to 325°. After 45 minutes add vegetables. Then allow to roast another 45 minutes or until vegetables are done. Serves 4.

78. From the recipe shown above, if you put the roast in the oven at 10:10 AM, at what time should you add the vegetables?

Figure 4-2 Sample Questions from a Functional Literacy Test
Source: *Life Skills: Tests of Functional Competencies in Reading and Math.* Copyright 1980 by the Riverside Publishing Co.

3. Speediness—how much time is allowed for different parts of the test—influences the results.
4. The validity of tests may differ or be lost at different age levels.
5. The scores may be influenced by guessing.

It was sunny and hot for days. Then the __S-1__ changed. It turned cloudy and cool.	S-1	a) price b) road c) job d) weather e) size
it isn't safe to go out today. There was too much __S-2__ yesterday. Many streets are flooded with water.	S-2	a) rain b) food c) mail d) noise e) work

Figure 4-3 Sample Questions from the Degrees of Reading Power (DRP).
Source: The Degrees of Reading Power, Form PX-1. Copyright 1979 by the University of the State of New York and 1980 by the College Entrance Examination Board.

6. The interpretation of scores may be misleading if the norming population differs from the users' student population.
7. The revisions made on tests sometimes result in different forms of the test not being comparable.
8. The test results do not always correlate with actual classroom performance.
9. The reading abilities sampled by some of the tests seemed to be limited (Strang, 1969).

Some of the above conclusions warrant further comment. First, in regard to the validity of any particular test, a number of researchers have questioned what it actually is that publishers say a reading achievement test measures. According to one test manual,

[The reading comprehension questions of the test intended for use from the middle of grade four to the middle of grade five] sample these skills: 1) comprehension of global meaning, 2) comprehension of the meaning of detailed information, 3) comprehension of implied meaning, 4) use of context for word and paragraph meaning, and 5) drawing inferences from what has been read (Madden et al., 1973).

The manual adds in another place that reading ability "is measured by a comprehension test which involves reading in context." In other words, the test measures whether students can read and understand this material. A number of researchers, however, have found some evidence to contradict such claims.

A set of five different standardized tests were administered, and the results were compared with the results of a test consisting of the questions only of these same tests (Tuinman, 1973). If the questions really measured a student's ability to read and understand the paragraphs, then the questions should not be able to be answered by any student who did not read the paragraphs. That is not what was found. On three of the tests, the subjects of the research who did not read the paragraph were able to get 70 percent as many answers correct as did those subjects who did have the paragraphs to read. This study concluded that the questions on the reading tests did not depend on the paragraphs and that students can answer correctly a surprisingly large number of questions without ever reading the passages. This seemed to be increasingly true at the higher grade levels.

The results of this study are consistent with other studies. Pyrczak (1972) found that a substantial number of the subjects knew the point being tested before they even read the paragraph. Weaver and Bickley (1967) found that at least two distinct sources of information existed for completing multiple choice questions (the kind found on most reading achievement tests). The first was the student's existing concept information about one or more of the topics on the test samples. The other was a cue in the question itself or a cue in a previous question. In other words, the test itself revealed many of the answers to the questions. The researchers concluded that some reading comprehension tests are highly dependent on various reader characteristics and often have little to do with the reading tasks assumed by the tester.

MacGinitie (1973), a test writer himself, found that as much difference exists between different edition levels of the same subtest as between differently named tests on the same level. What this means is that a vocabulary test on the primary level may differ from a vocabulary test on the intermediate level as much as it differs from an arithmetic test. MacGinitie pointed out how many vocabulary tests on the primary level test students' ability to recognize in print a number of well-known words generally found in their auditory vocabularies. On the other hand, the vocabulary test on an intermediate level requires students to recognize less well known words and uses minimum contrast clues (distinguishing between two graphically similar words) to measure their knowledge of a variety of words. The titles of the tests remain the same, but the tasks required of the pupils differ radically.

In a comparison of the vocabulary subtests on a reading achievement test and on a test of intelligence MacGinitie (1973) discovered an indication that by the end of third grade the two are indistinguishable. They are the same test—requiring very similar tests—yet they are interpreted differently by educators.

In a study of nine popular published reading tests intended for group and/or individual administration Winkley (1971) found that

1. The tests have a wide range of purposes.
2. Most of the tests could not be used to determine a student's chief skill deficiency.
3. Most of the subtests of word recognition evaluate spelling ability rather than reading ability.
4. The skills sampled usually require decoding single syllable words more frequently than multisyllabic words.
5. Errors existed in many of the tests.

In regard to validity, then, a reading achievement test may measure something entirely different from reading. It may also test specific aspects of reading that are limited and provide only a partial picture of how a student actually functions.

Another limitation of standardized tests is how the scores may be interpreted and used for instructional purposes. The following considerations should affect the use of standardized tests in classrooms:

1. A *score is not a judgment*. Judgments must be made by teachers and reflect the value they place on any score.
2. A *score is not high or low; it is only higher or lower than some other score or scores*. This means that any individual score is meaningless unless it is compared with some other score. Most commonly, the other scores are the national norms. It is inappropriate, then, to compare any scores unless the group from which they were obtained have the same characteristics as the norming group. The manual must be carefully examined to ensure that the national norm group contains students with characteristics similar to those being tested.
3. *Grade-equivalent scores from one subtest are not comparable to those from another subtest*. In order to determine whether or not two grade-equivalent scores differ, one of two things must be done: (1) the stanine table must be checked to determine if the scores fall within the same stanine. If they do, then no matter how large the difference between the two scores seems, they mean

relatively the same thing; (2) the standard error of measurement for each subtest must be added to or subtracted from the obtained score. If the range of the two sets of scores overlaps, they mean relatively the same thing.
4. *The grade-equivalent scores on tests administered at different times of the year represent different performance levels.*

If the results from an achievement test are used to compile a student's profile—a graphic representation of relative performance on a series of tests—then stanine scores may be the most useful. They are useful because they provide the same kind of information—the student's performance on the various tests relative to the performance of a peer group.

Criterion-referenced tests, too, have certain limitations. In regard to the validity of the test items, the comments made above hold for criterion-referenced tests as well as norm-referenced tests. The classroom teacher should be sure that the tasks represent some aspects of reading. Other limitations of criterion-referenced tests are a lack of empirical justification for the number of items to be used for measuring an ability to perform a task, the percentage of correct items needed for mastery to be demonstrated, or the length of time allowed for administering the test.

When criterion-referenced tests are constructed, the question usually arises as to whether it is necessary to include items that test mastery of every identified skill of reading. Depending on how narrowly the skills are differentiated, this might result in an unwieldy test. Researchers do, of course, attempt to determine how many of the individual skills to test and the number of items for each skill to include. Since they are interested in determining student flow from performance level to performance level and not in comparing individuals with one another, more criterion-referenced test makers are reluctant to use other test makers' normative procedures. Therefore, when teachers consider using criterion-referenced tests, the following should be kept in mind: the criterion-referenced items should represent skills essential to learning to read, and the tasks must be evaluated in the context of a normal reading situation (Pikulski, 1974).

The second point is more important. Quite often a student is asked to perform a task, perhaps to match words that contain a similar final consonant cluster. Yet this task rarely occurs in an actual reading situation. The matching task might be appropriate for a spelling situation, but it has limited utility in an act of reading.

A caution about the "effect of examinations" is offered as a final word about all standardized tests (Bloom, 1969). Students, teachers, and administrators are affected by what each perceives to be the purpose of a test or testing situation. There may be, then, either positive or negative effects from the assessment depending on the attitudes of those involved. If the test is viewed as punitive—as they are in some schools in which the results of achievement tests are used for student promotion or retention or for the evaluation of teachers—the entire learning process may be viewed as punitive as well.

Effective Use of Standardized Reading Test Results

Certain information is necessary for a teacher to be able to administer and interpret standardized tests in a classroom. A wise user of tests knows (1) the scope of the school testing program, (2) its relationship to the entire school educational program, and (3) the uses to which test results will be put.

The classroom teacher should know

1. The objectives of the school testing program. What are the administration's purposes for all testing that occurs in the school? How have these objectives been developed, and when was the last time they were reviewed?
2. The content of the tests. What is the relationship between the content of the tests and the objectives of the instructional and testing programs? Who examined the tests to make this decision, and when was the test last reviewed?
3. The pretesting arrangements. What information about the testing has been given to the students, parents, and teachers? What attitudes toward testing are implicitly and explicitly expressed in this information?
4. The testing schedule. What advance information has been given to the teachers, students, and parents about who will administer the tests and when and where the testing will occur?
5. The scoring of the tests. How will the tests be marked—by the teacher, auxiliary staff, secretaries, or machine? In what kind of scores will the results be expressed—grade equivalents, percentiles, or stanines?
6. The recording of the results. What test data are to be recorded? What forms will be used for recording the results? Which of the derived tests scores will be recorded?
7. The meaning of the scores. What interpretation of the scores will be given to the teachers, students, and parents? What is the relation between the test scores obtained and other data available about the students?
8. The reporting of scores. How will the test results be reported to the students and parents? When will the reporting take place and in what form?
9. The use of the tests in the school. How will the test results be used by the administration, teachers, school psychologists, and guidance counselors? In what way do these uses conform to the objectives of the testing program?

OBTAINING INFORMATION ABOUT ACADEMIC POTENTIAL

The process of reading is closely related to the entire process of thinking. The analytic teacher attempts to determine whether or not students' reading performances are commensurate with their maturity of thinking. To many, this may immediately bring to mind "intelligence"; however, the use of the term intelligence has led to many misconceptions about students' performance in school. There are different types of intelligence, and in school there is concern with only one of them. For this reason, the term *academic potential* is used rather than intelligence. Academic potential draws attention to specific abilities that directly influence a student's school performance. As stated in the discussion of Guilford's structure-of-intellect model, there are different types of intelligence for different types of tasks.

An estimate of a student's academic potential may be made from the results of a standardized individual or group test. Individual tests, which should be administered by a psychologist, psychometrician, guidance counselor, or another qualified person, require a great deal of time. Therefore, many schools regularly administer some type of standardized group intelligence, mental maturity, or academic potential test.

The following are representative of some widely used standardized group measures of academic potential:

Cognitive Abilities Test. 1978. Lombard, IL: Riverside. Intended grades:K-12. Subtests: verbal, quantitative, and nonverbal.

Otis-Lennon School Ability Test. 1979. New York: Psychological Corporation. Intended grades: 1-12.

Test of Cognitive Skills. 1981. Monterey, CA: CTB/McGraw-Hill. Intended grades: 1-12. Subtests: sequences, analogies, memory, and verbal reasoning.

The academic potential, or mental maturity, tests usually contain a nonverbal, or nonlanguage, subtest and a language, or verbal, subtest. Careful examination of the tests themselves indicates that these terms do not accurately describe the tasks included on the tests. The subsections are tests of nonwritten and written language. In fact, since reading is required on all the language, or verbal, sections of these tests, one can ask whether the test measures academic potential or reading achievement.

Since the results of the verbal forms of group intelligence tests have such a high correlation with performance on reading achievement tests, the differences seem to arise primarily because of the two tests' errors of measurement (Strang, 1969). It would seem wise, then, when estimating a student's potential for doing academic work, to select a test that requires little or no reading or to use the results from the subtests that require no reading.

Classroom teachers should be alert to any discrepency between a test result and the student's observed performance in actual class settings. When there is a question, the student should be referred for further appraisal by the appropriate school personnel.

Some cautionary words about using group tests of academic potential to predict student's reading potential:

1. Intelligence tests are not a sure measure of innate ability to learn. They represent "developed ability."

2. Intelligence tests show how an individual is functioning at the time the test is taken.
3. Intelligence scores for a student fluctuate from test to test.
4. Intelligence tests may lack validity.
5. Intelligence tests should be interpreted according to the student's cultural background and home environment.
6. Intelligence test scores should be interpreted in accordance with the student's proficiency in language.
7. Intelligence test scores may be raised by practice and coaching (Strang, 1969).

The group tests of academic potential should be used guardedly as part of analytical teaching. If the tests are administered, the results should be used as only one means for comparing a student's cognitive maturity with that of the students the same age. A student who matures at a slower rate or who has not had an equal opportunity to learn cannot be expected to perform in the same manner as the other students do. Using group tests of academic potential allows for the identification of those students whose performance is markedly different from the others but it will not disclose the cause for the difference. For this, further analysis is necessary.

Discussion Questions and Activities

1. In order for a test to be valid it must first be reliable. Why isn't the converse of this statement true?
2. Examine a standardized reading test and its accompanying manuals. From your examination of the test items, does the test seem to measure what the author states it is supposed to measure? How many of the questions in the comprehension subsection can be answered from information contained in other questions and answers? Are there features in the layout of the test and its answer sheet that might confuse pupils and cause them to answer the test items incorrectly?
3. Prepare a statement for a parents' group, explaining in nontechnical language (1) the characteristics of a good standardized test and (2) some of the advantages of using standardized reading tests.
4. If there is no single standardized reading test that is best for all student populations, all instructional programs, and all school settings, how then should school personnel select a standardized test that is "best" for their situation?
5. Explain what the following statement means to you: A school instructional program is no better than the means by which it is assessed.
6. The meaning of grade equivalent is often misunderstood by many parents and teachers. Explain how the terms grade equivalent, as used on standardized

tests, and grade level, as used on instructional materials may be confused. How might school personnel clarify the meaning of these terms for both parents and teachers?

Further Readings

Three short books, addressed to teachers' concerns about problems of assessment in reading instruction are

Blanton, William E., Roger Farr, and J. Japp Tuinman, eds, *Measuring Reading Performance* (Newark, DE: International Reading Association, 1974).

MacGinitie, Walter, ed., *Assessment Problems in Reading* (Newark, DE: International Reading Association, 1973).

Scheiner, Robert, *Reading Tests and Teachers: A Practical Guide* (Newark, DE: International Reading Association, 1979).

The following is a series of yearbooks with which teachers should be familiar, even though the books may not be immediately needed. They contain critical reviews and descriptions of standardized tests in all subject areas. They can be of immense help to teachers wishing to select tests for particular purposes.

Buros, O.K., *The Mental Measurement Yearbooks.* Highland Park, NJ: Gryphon Press.

The issue of preparing students for taking standardized tests is a controversial one. The following, all available through the ERIC system, were written on the premise that students's full performance can be measured only when they know what is expected of them and have a set of procedures for effectively dealing with the directions and format of tests.

Jongsma, Eugene A., and Elaine Warshauer, *The Effects of Instruction in Test-Taking Skills upon Student Performance on Standardized Achievement Tests. Final Report* (New Orleans: University of New Orleans, Department of Elementary Education, ED 114 408, 1975).

Maryland State Department of Education, *Improving Student Attitudes and Skills for Taking Tests* (Baltimore: Maryland State Department of Education, ED 128 352, 1975).

Sabers, Darrell, *Test-Taking Skills* (Tucson: Arizona Center for Educational Research and Development, ED 133 341, 1975).

Chapter 5

STRATEGIES FOR ANALYTICAL TEACHING THROUGH INFORMAL TESTS

Focus Questions

1. What information about a student's background and physical condition is relevant to instruction?

2. How can a teacher informally estimate a student's potential for doing academic work?

3. How can a teacher analyze a student's oral and silent reading performances?

4. What can be discovered about a student's reading performance by analyzing a writing task?

Analytical teaching is not prolonged assessment. It is an ongoing activity in which the teacher constantly watches for the emergence of patterns in the students' reading or writing performance. Analytic teaching activities include the selection and recording of information during instances of the student's oral and silent reading and writing tasks.

Assessment is only as effective as the individual performing evaluation. Teachers should be able to devise and administer informal instruments and make the necessary instructional judgments that lead to appropriate programs for all students.

Although useful information about students' performance may be obtained through group comparisons, the analytical teacher tries to identify individual needs and progress as well. Elementary and intermediate students might pass through the same developmental stages in their acquisition of reading and writing tasks. But, no two students will pass through the stages in exactly the same manner, using the exact same pattern of strategies or the same language cues. Analytical teaching attempts to relate the developmental growth characteristics of all children and the individual needs of each student.

Analytical assessment begins with an examination of the total reading and writing situations. The model of a reading act described in Chapter 3 should be used so that assessment is focused on an individual and a situationally specific task. Reading and writing are examined during the acts of reading and writing at different stages of development with different types of materials. The individual informal assessment procedures are used to answer these questions:

What is the student doing?
Is what the student is doing appropriate for his or her age and/or grade?
Are there factors other than those directly related to the actual reading and writing processes that could cause the students response and/or behavior?

After examining the procedures for obtaining information about students' academic potential, we will discuss ways of obtaining information about oral and silent reading performance. Finally, we will consider ways of assessing students' writing performance and its relationship to their reading performance.

USEFUL BACKGROUND INFORMATION

Often information about the students' home situations, prior school and nonschool experiences, and attitudes toward reading and other activities gives the teacher insights about students' school behavior and, in particular, their reading and writing performances. Although this information in itself may not explain why students read and write the way they do, it may help explain why they do or do not respond to certain instructional activities and learning situations.

One source of information is students' school records. They often contain notations about previous achievement and home-school interaction, specialized reports or tests on record, and general impressions and evaluations. If school records are incomplete or unavailable, it might be beneficial to interview the students and their parents, being sure to make it quite clear that the information obtained will be used only to help formulate programs geared to the students' needs.

Sometimes students will reveal their attitudes toward reading and their preferences in story content during discussions with the teacher or with other students. Teachers can be guided by these attitudes and preferences when forming instructional programs with students who show reluctance to read independently or who resist conventional instructional materials.

Classroom teachers should observe students' behavior for signs of certain physical conditions that may impede school performance. In general, one should particularly look for general coordination problems, possible visual defects, or possible auditory deficiencies. Students who demonstrate speech problems also need special attention. (Speech in this case refers to the physical production of oral communication.) At no time should an attempt be made to correct those deficiencies without proper guidance. It is a fallacy that children normally outgrow speech defects; they must in general be corrected by knowledgeable personnel.

By noticing deviations from the behavior of the other students in the class, teachers can identify those who need further examination by an appropriate specialist. It is good educational policy to bring to the attention of the school nurse-teacher, psychologist, speech teacher, guidance counselor, or principal any observations of deviancy. After consulting with the appropriate school personnel, teachers may make a general recommendation to the parents about seeking further professional assistance.

Information About Academic Potential

When formal measures of academic potential are not available, a student's cognitive maturity and potential for academic performance can still be estimated. Listening comprehension seems to be directly related to reading. Listening comprehension is a reflection, among other things, of student's language development and knowledge of spoken words and sentences (F. Smith, 1975a). Since the cognitive processing of written language seems to be the same as the processing of spoken language, a listening comprehension test can be a good estimate of reading potential.

Informal tests can be devised for particular classroom situations. All that is needed is a passage representative of the material with which the students are expected to work. After reading the passage aloud to the students, the teacher asks them about it to determine how well the material was understood. If the students understand the material as it is read to them, then they can be judged to have the potential for reading similar material.

In order to devise listening comprehension tests, the procedures discussed in the next section for developing informal tests of reading comprehension may be followed by substituting "listening" for "reading."

Be aware, however, that attempts to measure comprehension may instead measure memory. The student who "understands" but does not retain that understanding over a period of time should be identified. This issue is further discussed in a later section. In addition, be sure students' reading and listening performances are compared using materials of similar types and difficulties. Reading and listening comprehension often vary from one type of material to another.

OBTAINING INFORMATION ABOUT READING PERFORMANCE

The discussion now focuses on techniques for obtaining and analyzing samples of students' oral and silent reading. These assessments are made to determine the strategies the students are using while reading. As noted previously, these are analytic assessments that should be made throughout the school year. From these assessments, teachers can determine the specific lessons that should be included in the instructional program for particular students as well as keep track of the progress they are making in using their reading strategies.

The Bell of Atri

Atri is the name of a little town in Italy. It is a very old town and is built halfway up a steep hillside.

Years ago, the King of Atri bought a huge brass bell and had it hung in a tower in the marketplace. A length of rope reaching almost to the ground was fastened to the bell so that even a small child could ring it by pulling the rope.

Figure 5-1
Source: Fay, Leo, Ross, Ramon Royal, and La Pray, Margaret. *The Rand McNally Reading Program,* Level 10, Telephones and Tangerines. Copyright 1981 by The Riverside Publishing Company.

Assessing Oral Reading Performance

Researchers indicate that both proficient and less proficient readers of all ages produce miscues (Goodman, 1969a; Hittleman & Robinson, 1975; Page, 1976). In assessing oral reading performance, it is not the quantity but the quality of the miscues that is important to the reader's understanding.

A miscue is an actual response in oral reading that does not match the expected response—that is, the reader orally produces a message that is not an exact reproduction of the message on the page. Teachers can analyze the miscues in students' oral reading by asking them a series of questions about the miscues. The answers to the questions are then tabulated and summarized, and the pattern of the miscues is evaluated (Burke, 1973, 1975; Goodman, 1969a).

Obtaining the Miscues The analysis of miscues is made from the oral reading of an unfamiliar story. The story should be moderately challenging but not so difficult that it will frustrate the student. The story should be challenging enough that the student will make at least twenty-five miscues. The story should be selected from material intended for use one year above the grade level at which the student is reading. In reading a challenging but not frustrating story, the schemes a student uses to read are revealed. The miscues produced under frustration usually do not indicate the student's normal approach to reading.

The exact number of miscues per hundred words that indicate "challenging" or "frustrating" cannot be determined through a formula. Only through the process of doing miscue analyses can a teacher decide what material is too easy or too difficult for a student. The factors that make a story difficult for one student are not the same ones that make another story difficult for another student.

The oral reading of each student should be recorded on an audio tape or cassette recorder. This will allow the teacher to replay the student's responses at a later time. For the novice in miscue analysis, a recorder is almost a necessity. Quite often, miscues are missed or need to be reconfirmed. Intonational miscues also are sometimes difficult to judge without a second or third listening.

Place the recorder in a position that is not distracting to the student. Explain to the student why the recording is being made but do not overemphasize this. Ask the student to read the story aloud. Indicate that no assistance will be offered during the reading and that at the end the student will be asked to retell the story. Directions can be similar to the following:

Please read this story to me. Read it out loud. While you are reading, I will not help you in any way. If you come to a word you do not know, try to do the best you can. You may skip the word if you cannot figure it out. However, I would like you to try to guess the word. When you are all finished reading, I will ask you to tell me about the story in your own words.

Tabulating the Miscues All miscues are written on worksheets which are copies of the story being read. The copies should faithfully maintain the line length of the story. On the worksheet each line is numbered for reference. Figure 5–2 shows how a worksheet is prepared for use in a miscue analysis from the original story and how the miscues are recorded on the worksheet.

CHAPTER 5/ANALYTICAL TEACHING THROUGH INFORMAL TESTING

Edward, 3rd grade

```
         The bell ⓒ Antarg
              (of) Atri
                Anter  Ⓝ
101    Atri is the name of a little town in Italy.
                              it        well ⓒ
102    It is a very old town and is built halfway
          ⓒ    the
           s
103    up ˄ the side of a steep hill.
                                         artery
104       A long time ago, the King of Atri bought
                               Ⓐ     fine large bell
105    a fine large bell and had it hung up in a
              ⓒ       Ⓐ
106    tower in the marketplace. A long rope that
                                   ↰He↲
107    reached almost to the ground. was tied ;
                                 ˄        ˄
        T
108    (to) the bell. Even the smallest child could
                                    his ⓒ
109    ring the bell by pulling upon this rope.
                       Ⓐ just
201       "It is the bell of justice," said the King.
                                       re  Ⓐ
202    When at last everything was ready, the
             artery
203    people of Atri had a great holiday. All the
204    men and women and children came down
                Ⓐ       L          ↓It
205    to the marketplace to look at the bell, of ⓒ Ⓘ
                        t   ⓒ
206    justice. It was a very pretty bell and was ⓒ
207    polished until it looked almost as bright
       as ⓒ    ¡A      →
208    and yellow as the sun
             Ⓘ      look ⓒ    the bell
209       "How we should like to hear it ring!"
210    they said.
                  ⓒ
211    Then the King came down the street.
                     ⓒ
212       "Perhaps he will ring the bell," said the
213    people. And everybody stood very still
214    and waited to see what he would do.
215       But he did not ring the bell. He did not
216    even take the rope in his hands. When he
```

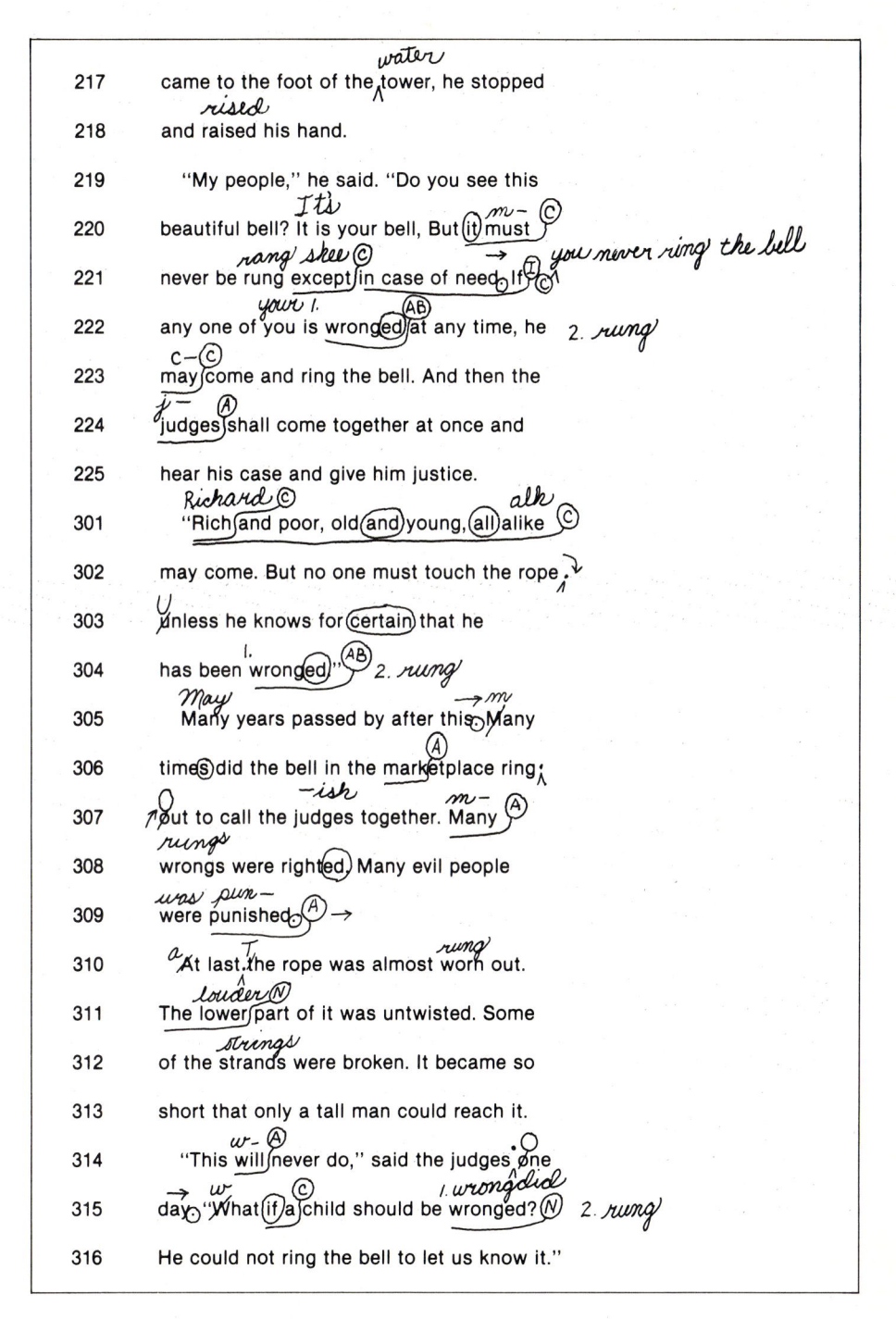

OBTAINING INFORMATION ABOUT READING PERFORMANCE   **113**

217   came to the foot of the tower, he stopped [*water*]

218   and raised his hand. [*rised*]

219   "My people," he said. "Do you see this

220   beautiful bell? It is your bell. But (it) must [*It's*] [m—©]

221   never be rung except in case of need. If [*rang skee* ©] [→] [*you never ring the bell* ©] [L]

222   any one of you is wronged at any time, he [*your 1.*] [AB] [2. *rung*]

223   may come and ring the bell. And then the [c—©]

224   judges shall come together at once and [j—] [A]

225   hear his case and give him justice.

301   "Rich and poor, old and young, all alike [*Richard* ©] [*alk* ©]

302   may come. But no one must touch the rope. [↓]

303   unless he knows for certain that he [U]

304   has been wronged." [1.] [AB] [2. *rung*]

305   Many years passed by after this. Many [*May*] [→ m]

306   times did the bell in the marketplace ring; [A]

307   out to call the judges together. Many [O] [—*ish*] [m—] [A]

308   wrongs were righted. Many evil people [*rungs*]

309   were punished. [*was pun—*] [A] [→]

310   At last the rope was almost worn out. [*a*] [T,] [*rung*]

311   The lower part of it was untwisted. Some [*louder* N]

312   of the strands were broken. It became so [*strings*]

313   short that only a tall man could reach it.

314   "This will never do," said the judges one [*w—* A] [O]

315   day. "What if a child should be wronged? [→] [*w*] [C] [*1. wrongdid* N] [2. *rung*]

316   He could not ring the bell to let us know it."

Figure 5-2   Miscue Worksheet

Each miscue is indicated on the worksheet by means of some commonly accepted markings:

1. The *substitution of a word:* Write the substituted word above the word in the text. Spell nonsense words phonetically. A partial substitution of a word correct to the stopping point and then repeated is not considered as a miscue; however, it is marked on the worksheet.

    look
    He would like to put it
    in the art contest.

    whee—
    I don't want it if it won't whistle.

2. An *insertion of a word:* Indicate the placement of the inserted word by means of a caret.

    fine
    "My prince," said the queen one ^ day.

3. An *omission of a word:* Circle the omitted word or word part.

    All day (long) the rain fell.   It did(n't) whistle.

4. A *reversal of two or more words:* Draw a z-shaped figure between the words reversed. If more than two words are reversed, extend the horizontal lines to the end of the words.

    Once upon a time there lived a prince.

    (Read by the student as: One upon a time a prince lived there.)

5. A *repetition of one or more words* (to correct a miscue, to change a correct response, or to maintain continuity of thought): Underline the repeated word or words. Place a symbol in a circle to show the type of repetition.

    A correction:
    house ©
    All day long the prince rode his horse.

    A repetition of a miscue, but the miscue is not corrected:
    pasting (H)
    He is painting a picture.

    A repetition that changes or abandons a correct response:

Jack ran~~/~~to Pat's house. *runs* (AB)

A repetition to maintain continuity:

And you know~~/~~that a prince must marry a princess. (A)

6. *Intonation miscue:* Indicate the student's intonation by means of punctuation or by means of arrows.

"Now why don't you get on your horse ?

and go looking?";

Tabulating the Retelling At the completion of the oral reading, the student is asked to retell the story. At first, provide the student with no assistance. On an outline of the story (see Figure 5-3), record the information the student freely recalls. When additional information cannot be provided unaided, guide the student through the use of some general questions. The following guidelines should be followed:

1. Questions should not contain any information from the story that the pupil has not already given.
2. Questions should be general. The questions should not be so specific as to lead the pupil to conclusions that would not have been formed from the reading of the story.
3. Questions should retain any mispronunciations made by the pupil (Y. Goodman and Burke, 1972).

Some general questions should be prepared before the student retells the story (Y. Goodman & Burke, 1972). These questions should be appropriate to a variety of situations and story plots, yet they can be just the encouragement a student needs for retelling the story. The following are sample questions for guiding a student's retelling:

Tell me more about ... (Use information already offered by the student.)
Who was in the story? or Who else was in the story?
What did (he, she, they) do?
What kind of person was ... ? (Use characters student offers.)
What else happened in the story?
Where did the story take place?
When did the story take place?
What was the whole story about? or What kind of problem was the story about?
Why do you think the story was written? or What did the author want you to know when he (she) wrote the story?

116 CHAPTER 5/ANALYTICAL TEACHING THROUGH INFORMAL TESTING

Edward, 3rd grade

Characterizations (30 Points)

Identification (15) *9* Traits (15) 3

King of Atri	Hung the bell of justice
Men and women *people*	Curious about the bell
Judges	Heard cases of wronged; gave order for new bell rope
Man	Volunteered to fix rope
Knight *minister/master*	Once brave; now a miser
Horse	Mistreated; became lame and sick
Boys	Threw rocks at horse

Theme of Story (20 Points) *5*

Justice applies to all creatures: animal and human. *Not to be bad.*

Plot of the Story (20 Points) *10*

How a faithful horse that is wronged brought retribution to his unkind master. *about a King and a horse   someone was mean to*

Main Event of the Story (30 Points) *14*

The King of Atri provided the town with a bell that had a long rope so even a child could ring it. *Took place in Italy*

The King declared it is the bell of justice and proclaimed that anyone who was wronged should come and ring the bell. The bell would summon the judges to hear the case of the wronged. *king would punish*

The people of Atri had a holiday when the bell was finished.

Years passed and many cases were heard and settled. Finally the rope became worn *short* and no longer reached the ground. Only a tall person could reach the bell rope to ring the bell.

Since there was no rope in the town long enough to hang to the ground, someone climbed up and tied a long grapevine to the bell, instead. *King said to leave it.*

OBTAINING INFORMATION ABOUT READING PERFORMANCE 117

A knight who was once brave had grown old and become a miser thinking only of his gold.
the master was mean to
All day the miser sat and counted his gold. He neglected <u>his horse who</u> had been his best friend and had carried him safely through many dangers. The knight could only think of how
someone wanted to be minister
much the horse would cost him so he left the horse to starve. *minister wanted to get the master's gold.*

The horse, grown lame and sick, was chased by the boys of the town and barked at by the dogs.

One day, the horse wandered into the town when everybody was indoors. He came upon the grapevine connected to the bell. The hungry horse begin to eat the leaves on the vine.

<u>As the horse ate the leaves</u>, the bell was rung calling the townspeople and <u>judges</u>.
at the bell
When they <u>saw the horse</u>, <u>they knew he had been wronged</u>. They realized that the horse had called for justice against his master because of the way he had been treated. All the townspeople explained how they had seen the horse mistreated.

master
<u>The miser was called for</u>. He was told that he must pay half of his gold to provide the once faithful horse with food and shelter.

The miser grieved for his gold, and the townspeople were happy.
the people put
<u>The horse</u> was led to his new shelter and food.   *Total = 41*

Figure 5-3 Retelling Outline for "The Bell of Atri"

The following conversation shows how a teacher guided a student in the retelling of the story, "The Bell of Atri." From the retelling, the story outline in Figure 5-3 was marked and scored.

Teacher: Can you tell me what you remember about the story?
  Child: I don't remember too much.
 T: Well, tell me what you remember.
Ch: A king put up a bell. If someone was being bad they would ring it. And everyone would come and the bell ... the rope got too short. And then the man, another man got another rope and put a vine on it. And the the king said leave it the way it is. And then the other guy wanted to be the minister. And he got gold and he was mean to his horse. He didn't feed him. The

horse ate the leaves off the bell and he rang it and all the judges came. And they brought his master. And then they put him in a stall at the end. And one day there was a ... The bell string got short and only a tall man could ring it. And then they made a new one. That's all I remember.

T: Can you tell me more about the horse?
Ch: He was starved. And he had nothing to eat and to drink so they put him in a stable and he began to eat. He had a lot of dinner.
T: Who put the horse in the stable?
Ch: The people after they found him.
T: Where did the people find him?
Ch: At the bell.
T: What was he doing there?
Ch: Eating the vine.
T: What happened when he ate the vine?
Ch: He rang the bell.
T: Why did the people think he rang the bell?
Ch: Because someone was being bad.
T: Who was that?
Ch: The master.
T: How was the master being bad?
Ch: By not feeding the horse. And not giving him shelter.
T: Can you tell me more about the judges?
Ch: I don't know. I forgot.
T: Why did the king put up the bell?
Ch: So if there were any person who was bad, another person would ring the bell and everyone would come.
T: And then what would happen?
Ch: They would punish him.
T: Who would they punish?
Ch: The person who did the thing bad.
T: Who would decide if the person was bad?
Ch: The king.
T: Can you tell me more about the minister and the master?
Ch: The minister wanted to get the master's gold, but he wouldn't let him. He wanted to keep it himself. That's why he wouldn't feed the horse.
T: What happened when the bell string got short?
Ch: They fixed it.
T: How?
Ch: With the pine ivory. No, a grapevine.
T: Do you remember where the story took place?
Ch: No.
T: Can you remember what kind of place it was?
Ch: In Italy.
T: Can you tell me what the whole story was about?

Ch: About a king and a horse someone was mean to.
T: What do you call it when people who are bad get punished?
Ch: Judges.
T: Can you tell me why this story was written? What message did the author want to give you? Can you think of it?
Ch: To not be bad.
T: Is there anything else you an tell me about the story?
Ch: No.

Although miscue analysis has been used most often with stories, it also can be used to assess students' understanding of informational material (Hittleman, 1980). The procedure for obtaining, recording, and analyzing the miscues remains the same. What changes is the form of the retelling outline. The categories of information listed on an informational retelling outline are (1) the major concepts or ideas, (2) the important supporting concepts or ideas, and (3) the specific details and examples used to explain or expand the major and supporting ideas. The scoring can be apportioned: twenty-five points for major concepts, twenty-five points for supporting concepts, and fifty points for details and examples.

Some general questions should be prepared before the students retell the ideas from an informational passage. Like the questions prepared for encouraging the retelling of a story, they should be appropriate to a variety of informational passages. The following are sample questions:

Tell me more about ... (use information the student has already offered).
What did the author think was most important?
What are some more ideas about (examples of) ... ? (use information the student has already offered).
What specific things are discussed in the passage?
What do you think is the most important idea?

Analyzing the Miscues The student's miscues are analyzed by asking three groups of questions (Burke, 1975) about each miscue:

How effective are the student's strategies for recognizing words in context?
How effective are the student's strategies for using his or her knowledge of language?
How much do the student's miscues change the author's intended meaning?

Word recognition questions are asked only when the student substitutes one word for another. Answers to these questions indicate the extent of the student's use of graphophonological cues and knowledge of grammatical functions.

Q-1. Does the miscue look like the word in the text?
   High: There is a high degree of similarity.
   Some: There is some degree of similarity.
   None: There is no similarity in any part of the word.

   (Note: In determining the difference between high similarity and some similarity, teachers may find the following useful: high similarity exists when two of a word's three parts generally look like the other words and some similarity exists when one of the word's parts is similar to that of the other word.)

Q-2. Does the miscue sound like the word in the text?
   High: There is a high degree of similarity.
   Some: There is some degree of similarity.
   None: There is no similarity in any part of the word.

Q-3. Does the miscue retain the same grammatical function as the word in the text?
   Same: The miscue is the same part of speech.
   Questionable: It is difficult to tell whether there is a change in the part of speech.
   Different: There is a change in the part of speech.

Knowledge-of-language questions are asked of every sentence in which a miscue has occurred. Each sentence with one or more miscues—not just substitution miscues but all types of miscues—is examined. Answers to the following questions give some indication as to whether the student is concerned with producing acceptable language during oral reading. The final sentence, with all of the student's attempts at correction, is evaluated. The criterion for judging acceptability is whether or not the student would produce such a sentence in spoken language. (Chapter 12 contains a discussion about judging the acceptability of the spoken language of students who speak divergent dialects of American English. The general rule is: If the sentence the student reads aloud contains elements of speech and lanaguage found in the normal, everyday speech of the student, the sentence and its miscues should be judged acceptable.)

If a miscue extends across a sentence boundary, judge the acceptability of both sentences together in order to maintain the relationship of that miscue to all the others in the sentences.

Q-4. Is the sentence as finally produced an acceptable and grammatical sentence?
   Yes: The sentence as finally read by the student is an acceptable sentence that could stand by itself as grammatically correct.

No: The sentence as finally read by the student is not acceptable and could not stand by itself as grammatically correct.

Q-5. Does the sentence as finally produced have an acceptable meaning?
Yes: The sentence as finally read by the student can stand by itself as a meaningful sentence.
No: The sentence as finally read by the student cannot stand by itself as a meaningful sentence.

A comprehension question is asked of every sentence in which a miscue has occurred. The answer to this question indicates the student has changed the author's intended meaning.

Q-6. Does the sentence as finally produced change the meaning of the story in relation to its plot and theme?
No: The sentence as finally read by the student does not change the intended meaning of the author.
Minimal: The sentence as finally read by the student moderately changes minor incidents, characters, or sequences in the story.
Yes: The sentence as finally read by the student greatly changes major incidents, characters, sequences, or themes in the story.

After the student's miscues have been fully transcribed from the recording onto the copy of the story, the first twenty-five substitution miscues are written on the evaluation form. Then the word recognition questions are asked of them. Figure 5-4 contains a sample completed evaluation form. In the first column of the form write the line number on which the miscue occurred, and in the second column write the student's response. In the third column, write the word as it appears in the text, and then place a check in the appropriate column for answering the word recognition-in-context questions, Q-1, Q-2, and Q-3. When the three questions have been answered for the first twenty-five substitution miscues, calculate the column totals and percentages.

The second part of the evaluation form is completed by answering the two knowledge-of-language questions and the comprehension question for the first twenty-five sentences containing miscues. In the first column of the second part, write the number of the line on which the sentence begins. In the second column indicate the total number of miscues in the sentence. This number represents the sum of all miscues (not just the substitution miscues). In the last column, complete the appropriate answers to the knowledge-of-language questions, Q-4 and Q-5, and the comprehension question, Q-6. When you have answered the three questions for the first twenty-five sentences containing miscues, calculate the column totals and percentages.

The percentages from the two parts of the evaluation form are summarized and compared. The result is a profile of reading strategies indicating the student's

CHAPTER 5/ANALYTICAL TEACHING THROUGH INFORMAL TESTING

Edward, 3rd grade

No.	Reader	Text	Graphic Q-1 High	Graphic Q-1 Some	Graphic Q-1 None	Sound Q-2 High	Sound Q-2 Some	Sound Q-2 None	Grammatical Function Q-3 Same	Grammatical Function Q-3 Questionable	Grammatical Function Q-3 Different
101	arter	atri		✓			✓		✓		
102	it	is		✓			✓				✓
102	halfwee	halfway	✓			✓				✓	
103	ups	up	✓			✓				✓	
103	the	a			✓			✓	✓		
104	artery	atri		✓			✓		✓		
109	his	this	✓				✓				✓
201	juist	justice		✓			✓			✓	
205	It	of			✓			✓			✓
208	as	and		✓			✓				✓
209	look	like		✓		✓			✓		
209	the bell	it			✓			✓	✓		
212	Peerhaps	Perhaps	✓			✓			✓		
220	It's	It is	✓			✓			✓		
221	rang	rung	✓			✓			✓		
222	your	yore	✓			✓					✓
222	rung	wronged		✓			✓		✓		
301	Richard	Rich and	✓			✓					✓
301	alk	alike		✓		✓				✓	
305	May	Many	✓			✓					✓
306	time	times	✓			✓			✓		
308	rungs	wrongs		✓		✓				✓	
308	right	righted	✓			✓			✓		
309	was	were		✓			✓		✓		
310	rung	worn			✓			✓	✓		
		Column Total	11	10	4	11	10	4	13	5	7
		Question Total		25			25			25	
		Column Percentage	44	40	16	44	40	16	52	20	28

Figure 5-4 Miscue Evaluation, Part I

OBTAINING INFORMATION ABOUT READING PERFORMANCE 123

Edward, 3rd grade

Sentence or Line Number	Number of Miscues	Syntactic Acceptability Q-4	Semantic Acceptability Q-5	Meaning Change Q-6 No	Meaning Change Q-6 Minimal	Meaning Change Q-6 Yes
101	1	Yes	Yes	✓		
102	4	No	No	✓		
104	2	Yes	Yes	✓		
106	2	No	No			✓
108	1	Yes	Yes			✓
201	1	Yes	No			✓
202	1	Yes	Yes	✓		
203	3	Yes	Yes		✓	
206	3	Yes	Yes	✓		
209	2	Yes	Yes	✓		
211	1	Yes	Yes	✓		
212	1	Yes	Yes	✓		
216	2	Yes	No	✓		
220	1	Yes	Yes	✓		
220	3	Yes	No		✓	
221	3	No	No			✓
301	4	Yes	Yes	✓		
302	3	No	No			✓
305	1	No	No			✓
305	1	No	No			✓
307	2	Yes	No			✓
308	2	Yes	No	✓		
310	1	Yes	No		✓	
311	1	Yes	No			✓
311	1	Yes	Yes	✓		
Total Miscues 47		Total Y 19 / 76	Total Y 12 / 48	13 / 52%	3 / 12%	9 / 36%

Figure 5-4 Miscue Evaluation, Part II

strengths and weaknesses. From the individual profiles you can construct a composite class profile to use in planning instructional procedures and class groupings. Figure 5-5 is an example of a class summary and profile sheet.

Evaluating the Pupil Profiles   All miscues are analyzed in relation to their impact on the story's intended meaning as determined by the comprehension question, Q-6, and the retelling score. The first evaluation of the student's profile is of the strategies used for word recognition in context. Clues to the strategies the student uses are obtained from the answers to questions about the degree the miscue (1) looks like the original word, (2) sounds like the original word, and (3) retains the same part of speech. Answers to the these questions do not themselves indicate the student's proficiencies as a reader. They only provide some insight into the manner in which the student's attempts at reading may affect the interpretation of the story. Miscues that have a low degree of sound or graphic similarity but that do not change the meaning of the story, are not considered as miscues of prime importance. A miscue that does change the meaning of the story as intended by the author on the other hand is of some concern.

The second evaluation of the student's profile is of the student's strategies for using knowledge of language. In reconstructing an author's message, some students change the part of speech of some words. Again, if the miscues change the meaning of the story, then there is evidence of a deficiency. However, some miscues result in a change in a part of speech without major change in the meaning of the story. This is possible because the student's miscues result in other miscues, and the sentence is adjusted grammatically. For example, notice that the miscues in the following sentence resulted in a grammatically and semantically acceptable response:

By the time Niko was part way home, he had overcome some

of his disappointment.

On the class summary and profile sheet, enter:

1. The combined percentage of each student's *high* and *some* sound similarity totals.
2. The combined percentage of each student's *high* and *some* graphic similarity totals.
3. The percentage of miscues that retained the same part of speech.
4. The percentage of the sentence that were grammatically acceptable.
5. The percentage of the sentences that had acceptable meanings.
6. The percentage of sentences that resulted in no change of the meaning in the story.

OBTAINING INFORMATION ABOUT READING PERFORMANCE   125

3rd grade "The Bell of Atri" Pupil's Name	Q-1 (High + Some %) Graphic Similarity	Q-2 (High + Some %) Sound Similarity	Q-3 (Yes %) Retained Part of Speech	Q-4 (Yes %) Grammatical Acceptability	Q-5 (Yes %) Meaning Acceptability	Q-6 (No %) No Meaning Change	Retelling Score	Effective Strategies
Alfred	90	90	85	65	60	45	40	sound and graphic cues, some language sense
Betty	60	95	80	80	75	80	75	sound cues, language and meaning sense
Charles	65	50	60	40	35	15	30	some sound and graphic cues
Diane	100	95	95	90	90	85	90	all
Edward	84	84	52	76	48	52	41	*

* What effective strategies does Edward have?

Figure 5-5 Miscue Analysis—Class Summary Sheet

7. The score of the student's retelling.
8. The strategies each student uses effectively.

The class profile sheet should contain information about each student's reading of the same story. If this is not possible, be sure the stories read by the students do not differ in style, length, and difficulty of concepts.

You should make the following comparisons to determine the students' effective reading strategieis. You may have to refer to the evaluation form and the story worksheet for additional information while making these comparisons.

1. Compare the word recognition scores with the knowledge-of-language scores. Does the student use strategies mainly for recognizing individual words without using knowledge of language for deriving meaning from the sentences? Which seems to influence the student's use of strategies most: the sound relationships in the word, the graphic structures in the word, or the function of the word in the sentence?

2. Compare the grammatical acceptability and meaning acceptability scores. Is the student creating sentences that are grammatically correct as sentences but that do not have any meaning? Is this due to a large number of gross mispronunciations or substitutions that, while maintaining a grammatically correct form, distort the author's meaning?

3. Compare the grammatical function and grammatical acceptability scores. Is the student correcting miscues that change the grammatical function of a word so that the final sentence is grammatically acceptable? Does the student make other alterations in the sentence so that a miscue that changes the grammatical function of a word still results in a grammatically acceptable sentence?

4. Compare the meaning acceptability scores and the meaning change scores. Is the student producing sentences that are meaningful by themselves but that change the intended meaning of the entire story?

5. Compare the meaning change and effective retelling scores. Does the student's retelling reflect the quality of the miscues made on the story? Does the retelling score seem to be affected by memory factors?

6. Compare the miscues per hundred words with the comprehension scores. Are the miscues so spread out over the story that any apparent change in meaning is offset by the sparseness of the miscues? Is the student maintaining understanding because the distance between the miscues allows meaning to be gained from the intervening passages?

The final step in miscue analysis is using the results of the profile sheet for formulating classroom instruction. From the class analysis, it is possible to identify some individuals or groups of students who need instruction in developing and/or reinforcing strategies.

Students who show a need for developing word recognition strategies might benefit from those strategies for using graphophonological information discussed in Chapter 9. If their need is in correctly identifying the grammatical functions of words, they might benefit from lessons constructed from the information on sentence-reading strategies in Chapter 8 or that on contextual signals of word meanings in Chapter 9. For those who oral reading responses are not syntactically or semantically acceptable, the strategies on sentence reading in Chapter 8 might be helpful. Those students who make many changes in meaning while reading orally, might receive instruction on the prediction strategies and the paragraph- and longer discourse–reading strategies discussed in Chapter 8. Those who have difficulty in retelling a story after oral reading might benefit from the guided reading and questioning strategies in Chapter 7 and the prediction strategies discussed in Chapter 8.

Assessing Silent Reading Performance

Students' silent reading performance can be assessed through (1) the oral retelling of a story or information passage read silently, and (2) a cloze procedure silent reading test.

Oral Retelling A student's silent reading comprehension is analyzed in a manner similar to that of assessing the oral reading retelling. After the silent reading, the student is asked to retell the story or information. You should offer no help and record the information the student recalls on an outline. The guidelines and types of questions used to encourage or guide the student are similar to those used for the oral reading retelling.

The student's performance on the oral reading retelling and the silent reading retelling can be compared to see if there is a pattern of similarity in the types of responses given. The following questions can assist the teacher in determining the degree of difference between recalling stories after oral and silent reading:

Is there a difference in the recall of the main characters in the stories?
Is there a difference in the recall of information about the appearance, feelings, actions, and relationships of the main characters?
Is there a difference in the recall of events in the stories?
Is there a difference in the recall of the plots of the stories?
Is there a difference in the recall of the themes of the stories?
Is there a difference in the recall of major concepts, supporting concepts, and details or examples?

The comparison of a student's recall from oral and silent reading gives one indication as to whether the estimate of a pupil's reading performance provided by the miscue analysis can be assumed for silent reading as well. Some of the common patterns emerging from the above comparisons are:

Pattern 1: *The silent reading recall score is greater than that of the oral reading recall score.* Possible reasons for this are that the student during oral reading is attending primarily to the pronunciation of words. Prior experience may have taught the student that correct pronunciation, or at least attempts at such, are the important aspects of reading. Often a student is judged in reading ability not by a comprehension check, but by the ability to accurately recode the printed symbol into sound. During silent reading, the student can attend to the development of the story without undue concern for the accurate pronunciation of the words printed on the page.

Pattern 2: *The silent reading recall score is less than that of the oral reading recall score.* A student displaying this pattern may need the conscious effort applied in reading aloud in order to maintain involvement with the story. Such a student may only be an active reader when forced to recode the written story into sound. The overt involvement may be keeping the student's attention directed at reconstructing the author's message. During silent reading, this student may experience difficulty in the selection of cues for reconstructing meaning.

Pattern 3: *Both the oral reading and silent reading retelling scores are much below the meaning change score from the miscue analysis.* In this case, the student may be processing the story information with meaning at the instant of reading. However, the retention and/or recall of this information may be hindered. A student understands a story when miscues do not change the meaning of a story or miscues that do change the meaning are corrected. The problem may lie in the lack of strategies for adequately storing the information. The problem may also lie with a lack of adequate strategies for producing an effective association among the bits of information so that recall is facilitated. As another possibility, a student displaying this pattern could have facility in reconstructing surface features; the student may not have strategies for reconstructing the author's deep structure meaning.

When the student's oral and silent recall scores both fall below the meaning change score of the miscue analysis, one further step may be taken to determine the student's ability to understand the material. Keep the story passage open and allow the student to refer to it during the retelling. This procedure is not effective with materials in which the entire story plot is carried in pictures. However, most materials above the beginning reading levels have pictures that correspond to the story, but do not reveal the entire plot and theme. If the student can produce a greater portion of the story information after referring to the text, then this may be further evidence that the student's ability to recall is interfering with the story retelling. Such a student may need instruction in developing schemas and strategies for retaining and recalling information such as those based on the information in Chapter 2 and expanded upon in Chapters 7 and 8. Recall is a desired trait to develop in students, but the ability to recognize information is also a vital comprehension task. A student should not be deemed deficient in comprehension strategies because of a limitation in recall strategies.

Cloze Procedure A means of measuring students' comprehension that has been gaining popularity is the cloze procedure. The cloze procedure is a technique in which words are systematically deleted from a passage and the reader is expected to replace the deleted word while reading. It is a comprehension test that is easy to construct and score and it also can provide teachers with insights into how students "think through" material as they read. Figure 5-6 shows an abbreviated sample cloze procedure comprehension test.

The cloze procedure test is a quick and efficient way for a classroom teacher to estimate the appropriateness or "readability" of any book for use with particular pupils (Hittleman, 1978). It can be used to estimate the appropriate level of a basal reading series into which students should be placed. The cloze procedure test can also be used to determine whether particular material can be read independently, whether it can be read only with the teacher's guidance, or whether it will be too frustrating for the students.

For example, a teacher could create a series of cloze tests to cover a fairly wide range of texts in a basal series or a content area series. The easiest level test can be administered to the whole class. If the students' responses indicate that a harder level is inappropriate, they are assigned to a text, and the remaining tests are administered to the other students. Additional testing might be required for those for whom the first test is too difficult or the last test too easy. Thus, in a few days a teacher can place students into texts that are commensurate with their ability to read.

> My uncle is an anthropologist. That (1) _____ he studies all about (2) _____ kinds of people and (3) _____ they act. He travels (4) _____ over the world to (5) _____ people and to learn (6) _____ about them.
>
> My uncle (7) _____ me that one of (8) _____ most important things an (9) _____ does is talk with (10) _____ That isn't as easy as it sounds, since that means he has to know how to speak many different languages.
>
> Answers: 1. means   2. different   3. how   4. all
>   5. meet   6. all   7. tells   8. the
>   9. anthropologist   10. people

Figure 5-6 Sample Cloze Comprehension Test
Source: Leo Fay, Ramon Royal Ross and Margaret La Pray, *The Rand McNally Reading Program*, Level 10, *Telephones and Tangerines*. Copyright 1981 by Riverside Publishing Company.

Much research has been done in an attempt to substantiate that the cloze procedure measures an individual's ability to comprehend a written message. First, it seems that the cloze procedure measures the reader's ability to deal with the linguistic structure of the language. Accordingly, it is related to a reader's ability to understand the relationship between words and ideas (Horton, 1972). Second, since the cloze procedure requires the reader to predict the exact word that was deleted and replace it, the cloze procedure measures the reader's ability to perform comprehension processes. Research based on psycholinguistic principles has consistently shown that a reader's comprehension is measured by how well the information surrounding the blank is used and how well the information taken from the text is employed to obtain additional information. Also, studies show that a reader's performance on a traditional comprehension test (questions) cannot be distinguished from that person's performance on a cloze comprehension test (Bormuth, 1975). Hence, the cloze procedure measures the mental processes during reading that are commonly called *comprehension*.

The procedures for creating cloze tests have become fairly standardized (Bormuth, 1975). For the third grade and higher, the procedure is to:

1. Select a 250-word passage.
2. Beginning with any one of the first five words of the second sentence of the passage, delete every fifth word until fifty words are deleted. The first and last sentence are always left intact. Punctuation and hyphens are never deleted, and numerals, such as 1975, are deleted as if they are whole words. Apostrophes are deleted along with the words they appear in.

3. Type the passage on a master, double spacing between lines. For each deleted word, type a line fifteen spaces long. The spaces should be uniform in length, regardless of the length of the original word.
4. Provide the students instructions and a sample test before giving them the actual cloze tests. The instructions may be similar to the following:

> At the bottom of this page is a sample of a new kind of test. Your job will be to guess what word was left out of each space and to write that word in that space.
> Remember: Write only one word in each space. Try to fill every blank, and don't be afraid to guess.
> You may skip hard blanks and come back to them later. Wrong spellings will not count against you (Bormuth, 1975).

This untimed test is scored by counting every response that correctly replaces the exact word deleted from the original passage. Research has shown that when the cloze procedure is used to measure students' comprehension, the most efficient means is to use the exact word as the standard for marking (Bormuth, 1975). In Chapter 8 we will discuss the cloze procedure as an instructional procedure. In such circumstances, deviations that retain the intended meaning of the passage are acceptable. However, in order to maintain some consistency in interpreting the cloze procedure as a comprehension test, only exact reconstructions are counted as correct.

After the number of the student's correct responses has been determined, convert that number into a percentage. Research has shown that a student's ability to obtain a score of approximately 40 percent indicates that the material is appropriate for instructional purposes. When a student receives a score of approximately 60 percent or greater, the material can generally be read independently. Scores below 40 percent indicate that the material may be too frustrating (Jones & Pikulski, 1974; Bormuth, 1968). Thus, when groups of students are tested for placement in any series of texts, they are given higher-level materials whenever they score 60 percent or greater. Those who score below 40 percent are assigned to the last level at which they scored 40 percent or greater.

Additional insight may be obtained into how students process information in a passage. Simply point to each cloze item and ask the student why the word was selected to complete the cloze item. When using this informal procedure, it is not necessary to have the student read the entire passage aloud. In fact, it is preferable not even to ask the student to pronounce the answer word. Just ask the student to explain why the word was selected and note the types of clues the student indicates were used to determine the answer.

Although the cloze procedure test seems to be a valid and reliable measure of comprehension, there are certain limitations which should be noted (Hittleman, 1978). Some cloze tests may contain many deletions for which there are not contextual clues. Certain children, particularly those in the primary grades, should not be given cloze tests without some modification. These modifications will be discussed in Chapter 8. Also, major emphasis should not be placed on the written response but rather on the comprehension of the given passage. In cases in which the student is reluctant to write, the teacher may accept an oral response. In such cases the teacher still can obtain some indication of the student's ability to read and understand the passage. Finally, the cloze tests measure global aspects of comprehension and not specific substrategies. Therefore, the test cannot be used to analyze specific diagnostic information about a student's strategies and skills.

OBTAINING INFORMATION ABOUT WRITING PERFORMANCE

We have established that both reading and writing use the same cognitive processes of knowing, reasoning, and inferring. Writing is the language production facility corresponding to the receptive processing of reading. Additional information about students' knowledge of and competence in using print can be gained through an analysis of what and how they write.

Informal writing assessments of products composed by students are made after they have had at least one opportunity to review and revise their product. The composing process consists of (1) prewriting, (2) writing/drafting, (3) revising, and (4) editing. These phases are not discrete. They may, in fact, occur simultaneously and recursively. Only for our purposes here are they treated as interrelated but distinguishable phases.

In addition to its cognitive and psychological aspects, learning to write is a social process. Writing is learned most effectively in the community of a classroom where students and teacher interact and give feedback. Learning to write results from students' listening and responding to one another rather than working alone or with only the teacher. As a teacher you will need to create an environment for students learning from all in that writing community.

The prewriting phase includes any and all activities that precede the actual writing of a first draft. Such activities allow students to "brainstorm" ideas with themselves, their peers, or their teacher and to clarify why, what, how and to whom they will write. During prewriting, students' ideas may be generated by means of an experience (group or personal), a story, a picture, research, a discussion, or as the result of sheer fantisizing.

The writing-drafting phase is when the first draft is written. Depending on the age, cognitive maturity, and proficiency of the students, as well as the purpose and context of the passage, the first draft may contain a single sentence or many paragraphs.

The revising phase is the time when the first draft is revised. Changes may be made in the content, the organization of ideas, the sentence structures, and vocabulary, or in all apsects of the passage. These changes may be made any time after the writing-drafting phase is completed—one hour, one day, or a few days. The students make these changes after rereading their compositions and deciding what aspects need to be revised, from reading their work to others and responding to questions about the need for clarification, or from feedback the teacher provides about the manner in which their ideas are communicated.

The last phase, editing, is not necessarily for the informal assessment. This is a time for "polishing," a time when the conventions of mechanics, spelling, and grammer are adhered to and a final copy is made.

After a piece of written work is produced, either through a direct assignment or as a result of a spontaneous act, it is analyzed to gain insights about pupils' understanding of the various schemas for communicating ideas.

Again, these schemas include the four factors of a communication situation: participants, setting, topic, and task. A student's competence in language is judged by the appropriateness of what is written in relation to these factors. The schemas also include competence depending on the developmental stage of writing. The four stages of acquiring facility with written language are: recording, reporting, generalizing, and hypothesizing. This information is used with the rating scale in Figure 5-7 to judge the student's writing performance.

When examining students' writing as communication, remember that there is no direct way to use writing as sources of insights to reading comprehension. But when students demonstrate that they can produce a particular language pattern,

---

Directions:

Use the information in Chapters 2, 8, and 10 on sentence patterns, paragraph structures, and the cohesiveness of longer passages to judge the characteristics of students' writing.
Establish the characteristics of the writing task to be assessed before assigning the writing.
Analyze a variety of writing samples in relation to the students' stages of development in writing.

1. Little or no presence of the characteristic(s).
2. Some presence of the characteristic(s), but communication of the idea(s) or story (stories) is impeded by incomplete schemas or is inappropriate to the participants, setting, topic, or task.
3. Fairly successful communication of idea(s) or story (stories) through detailed and consistent presence of characteristic(s).
4. Highly inventive and mature presence of the characteristic(s) in communicating idea(s) or story (stories) and in relation to the developmental stage of the pupils and their development of schemas.

Figure 5-7 Assessing Students' Writing Performance

you can assume that they have competence to use it in all language forms. Nonetheless, an inability to write or speak a language pattern does not indicate that a student does not have receptive competence.

For example, a student who is just beginning to produce one-sentence compositions about a class trip would be given a rating of at least 3 for producing:

I wlkd to they zoo to see the amnls.

Here, with a student identified as being in the recording stage of development, there is good communication. The participants, the setting, and the topic are identified. The composition fulfills the task of recording an event.

A task for an older student requiring a product with specific directions in sequence, however, would receive a rating no higher than 2 for producing:

How to make a Swing
furst you need a tire
rope a latter nails and a
hammer. Now find a thick
branch and take the
latter and put it againt
the tree. Then get the rope and
tighe it tight around the
branch and hammer it to
the tree make sure its
sterdy.

Here, with a student identified as being in the reporting stage of development, there is not good communication. Although the student does identify the participant and the topic, the student does not identify the setting and task and has not set the tree and the branch in any context. The sequence of directions is inconsistent, and there are few supporting details. In sum, the report does not give another student explicit directions for creating the swing. In both writing samples, the students would be rated differently if they were identified as being in other developmental stages of writing.

When assessing a student's writing, a single sample should not be used to make judgments about their performance or about the relationship of their writing to reading comprehension. It is only by analyzing patterns of performance revealed in assignments requiring a variety of writing patterns that you can determine a student's language competence. Before making these assignments, teachers must have a clear concept themselves of the characteristics expected in the written message. These expectations are to be based on the knowledge of the nature of written messages, the purposes for which one writes, and the appropriateness of the task to the student's developmental stage.

Discussion Questions and Activities

1. Explain why it may be more practical for a classroom teacher to examine students' performance in classroom situations doing typical classroom work than to examine their performance on standardized tests.
2. Using informal procedures explained in this chapter for assessing oral and silent reading:
   a. Compare the oral and silent reading performance of an elementary-school student.
   b. Compare the oral and silent reading performance of two elementary-school students at same grade levels reading the same story;
   c. Compare the oral and silent reading performance of two elementary-school students at different grade levels reading the same story;
   d. Compare the oral and silent reading performance of an elementary-school student reading a narrative story and a passage from a content area text.
   e. Compare each of the above reading performances with a writing sample based on the written retelling of the reading selections.
3. Explain how to identify the significant characteristics to which Helen M. Robinson (1975) refers in the following statement; explain how a teacher might identify them:

   To study the reading process, two essential ingredients must be examined: the reader and the selection read. If the significant characteristics of each could be identified, then the interaction of the reader and the materials could be interpreted.

4. Construct cloze procedure comprehension tests on three different types of reading materials for use at the same grade level: a narrative story, a social studies passage, and a science passage. Administer the tests to:
   a. a group of students at the same grade level; and/or
   b. students from each of three different grade levels. Identify those students for whom the passages: (1) maybe used for instructional purposes and (2) may be read independently.
5. The following statement by John Bormuth (1975) has implications for classroom teachers when they construct tests to measure students' comprehension. Explain how the procedures for guiding retelling after oral and silent reading, discussed in this chapter may help overcome some of the difficulties to which Bormuth refers:

   Test writers influence the difficulty of tests: two writers making a test over a single passage could produce tests of quite different difficulty, the one writer's test eliciting mostly low scores, and the other's mostly high scores.

Further Readings

For those who wish to investigate in greater detail the administration and interpretation of miscues, the following texts will be helpful. The first is the manual for the full miscue inventory, and the other two contain articles explaining the application of miscue analysis in various educational settings.

Goodman, Yetta M., and Carolyn L. Burke, *Reading Miscue Inventory: Manual, Procedures for Diagnosis and Evaluation* (New York: Macmillan, 1972).

Goodman, Kenneth S., ed., *Miscue Analysis: Applications to Reading Instruction* (Urbana, IL: National Council of Teachers of English and ERIC Clearinghouse on Reading and Communication Skills, 1973).

Page, William D., ed., *Help for the Reading Teacher: New Directions in Research* (Urbana, IL: National Conference on Research in English and ERIC Clearinghouse on Reading and Communication Skills, 1975).

The following book has two purposes: to compile informal instruments that can be used to assess performance in all the language arts and to compile reviews of these instruments. The tests are listed by area, but there is a cross-reference index so that instruments appropriate to a particular age or grade level may be located. It is an excellent source of existing instruments and ideas for teachers to use in constructing their own informal assessment procedures.

Fagan, William T., Charles R. Cooper, and Julie M. Jensen, *Measures for Research and Evaluation in the English Language Arts* (Urbana, IL: ERIC Clearinghouse on Reading and Communication Skills and National Council of Teachers of English, 1975).

In the following article, the authors explain an interesting variation of the cloze procedure that can be used to identify children with comprehension problems and to monitor students' progress in comprehension development:

Guthrie, John T., Mary Seifert, Nancy A. Bumham, and Ronald I. Caplan, "The Maze Technique to Assess, Monitor Reading Comprehension," *The Reading Teacher* 28 (1974): 161–168.

The following two articles contain additional ideas for informally assessing students' language:

Clark, Charles H., "Assessing Free Recall," *The Reading Teacher* 35 (1982): 434–439.

Pickert, Sarah M., and Martha L. Chase, "Story Telling: An Informal Technique for Evaluating Children's Language," *The Reading Teacher* 31 (1978): 528–531.

An expanded discussion of the ideas about assessing students' writing is found in the following:

Greenhalgh, Carol, and Donna Townsend, "Evaluating Students' Writing Holistically—An Alternative Approach," *Language Arts* 58 (1981): 811-822.

The following are detailed discussions about the effect on comprehension of specific types of miscues:

Beebe, Mona J., "The Effect of Different Types of Substitution Miscues on Reading," *Reading Research Quarterly* 15 (1980): 324-336.
Goodman, Kenneth S., and Frederick V. Gollasch, "Word Omissions: Deliberate and Non-Deliberate," *Reading Research Quarterly* 16 (1980): 6-31.

Chapter 6

STRATEGIES FOR DEVELOPING READINESS FOR READING INSTRUCTION

Focus Questions

1. What is "being ready to learn to read", and how does the concept relate to the idea of schemas?

2. What factors affect students' readiness to read and write?

3. What strategies must students be able to use in order to be ready to receive formal reading instruction?

4. How can students' readiness for reading be assessed?

5. How can students be made ready to participate in group activities for reading and writing instruction?

The concept of reading readiness has been the concern of educators for as long as there has been concern about developing reading programs in the elementary schools. Teachers want to know when students can begin to receive reading instruction and often ask, "When are children ready to have a book placed in their hands and to begin reading?" Professional texts and journals contain numerous check lists for identifying those students who are ready to read. These check lists are accompanied by suggestions for prescribing programs of "readiness" training for those who are not ready. The main problem with using extensive and detailed check lists is believing that readiness is represented by a specific collection of subskills that have some demonstrable connection with the process of reading. This thinking also fosters the impression that readiness is a period of time or a specific program that must be completed before reading instruction can begin.

The aim of this chapter is not to present another check list or to list those specific skills required to learning to read. Rather, we will examine what it means to be "ready" to read and produce any type of material at any stage of development. We will be concerned with identifying the general factors that affect readiness to use language in oral and printed form and relating those factors to the initial stage of literacy—commonly called reading readiness. As will be shown in the discussion, although the suggested activities usually occur in school at the kindergarten- or first-grade levels, readiness activities should precede all learning. Therefore, reading readiness, in the broad sense of the term, is the concern of all elementary or intermediate school teachers, regardless of the grade level they teach.

READINESS FOR ALL READING

In a Piagetian sense, readiness means possessing those skills and abilities of a preceding stage of development. Or, simply put, "development determines learning" (Elkind, 1974). Every student in school, regardless of grade level, is ready to learn something about the reading process. What that something is should be selected and prepared in keeping with the student's abilities at the moment. The teacher's responsibility is to identify what the student is to learn and to determine whether the student can learn what is expected.

All of a student's school experiences affect the manner in which any subsequent school task is undertaken. Although no developmental pattern of school tasks has ever been established it does seem logical that positive experiences, which have given the student skills in the various routines of school work, can only aid in learning. Students should have had preschool exposure to language-oriented activities. Those without this exposure will be less likely to undertake the learning of reading and writing with the same facility as those who understand "what school is all about."

Cognitive and linguistic skills, physical-motor abilities, emotional and social development—these constitute what is being called readiness. No sequence of skills is presented here because any such sequence would be purely arbitrary. There is no empirical evidence that justifies the use of one hierarchy of skills over another. Indeed, very little is known about what specific skills should be taught, and very little is known about (1) specific student characteristics required to master a given task, (2) specific characteristics amenable to literacy training, and (3) specific training procedures that can be imposed upon children who lack the prerequisites for learning written language tasks (Blanton, 1972).

We will discuss readiness here because there is evidence that linguistic preparation for reading can be fostered. However, the evidence indicates only the broad kinds of activities with which children should have experience and these will be the focus of our discussion.

Reading readiness seems to be the product of maturation and environmental factors (Durkin, 1968). Readiness seems to depend upon a combination of children's particular capacities and the kind of learning opportunities made available to them. Most important, readiness does not seem to be one particular combination of abilities or circumstances. When a child is ready to begin reading varies as children vary. The time when readiness to read occurs is a reflection of not only a child's capabilities and interests but also the degree to which instruction can accommodate both. A child is never totally ready or unready to learn to read. "Readiness is not all-or-none; it depends on the method and materials that are used and on the level at which instruction begins" (MacGinitie, 1969). Since reading is a thinking process of language, much of what constitutes readiness is the development of schemas and a predisposition for learning.

PARENTS AND READING

Teachers can and should involve parents in the development of their children's reading and writing strategies. To be sure, parents are the children's first teachers, and they should remain involved throughout their children's school education. Parents can reenforce classroom learning through language games and activities.

Teachers can describe to parents the skills and strategies being learned and also encourage them to reenforce and extend learning through easy, fun activities that they and their children can share. These activities should include language games; use of television programs; use of family trips and hobbies; and books, games, and records that the parents might buy as gifts. Teachers can decide how to distribute and use these materials and how to introduce these ideas to the parents. It might be done at a back-to-school night, at a parents' meeting, through a class newsletter, or through a note home. As students begin to understand and use written communications, they might be encouraged to "invite" their parents to become involved in their learning. The activities shared with the parents can be based on the ideas presented in this chapter with, of course, adjustments made for the student's age. The resources section at the end of the chapter has other suggestions and lists books to share with parents.

DEVELOPMENT OF READING READINESS

The reading readiness program should be one of creative problem solving (Lundsteen, 1974b). It should be a program that develops and extends a child's ability to think. In Piagetian terms, the teacher should cause some sort of cognitive conflict (disequilibrium). The conflict, which should be challenging but not excessive, makes it possible to maintain motivation (McDonell, 1975).

Problem solving depends on careful and conscious acts by both the teacher and the student (Using a variety of school problems that are full of unknowns (Lundsteen, 1974b), the teacher can lead students to

1. *Clarify the problem.* During the beginning of the problem-solving process, students are led to recall already known information relevant to the problem.
2. *Generate a hypothesis.* Here students are guided in generating alternative ways of stating the problem. This helps the students to further clarify the problem and put it into some form.
3. *Plan procedures.* The students, with the teacher's guidance, attempt to determine various ways in which the question or hypothesis may be answered. At

this time the teacher helps the students to determine which of the plans seem more workable and to undertake those first.
4. *Evaluate results.* The students are led to examine the various results obtained by working through the procedures used to solve the hypothesis. If the hypothesis cannot be verified at this time, the students are guided in how to deal with an unresolved problem. Plans for suspending judgments for future verification or rejection are developed.

Readiness is the ability and desire to take risks (McDonell, 1975). With the teacher's guidance, the students discover prediction strategies and develop schemas about written language form for selecting, questioning, testing, and generalizing about the information in their world. This, by the way, is how the students learned their language in the first place.

In helping to develop student's cognitive strategies, the teacher has the task of instructing them about their environment. The students' world consists not only of the classroom, but also of home, stores, streets, radio and television programs, and all the people met in these places. To help them to cope with their environment, the teacher can help the students focus attention on the immediate problem, realize how information is searched and evaluated, and find alternatives for searching and evaluating the obtained information (Mishler, 1972). Throughout, the importance of language is underscored. Special or important words relating to the students' environment are given attention and their roles in helping one think are identified.

If the process is to be a true readiness procedure, then the emphasis of the program has to be on language development. "Children become familiar with written language by hearing the language of literature and other print within their environment, just as they learned oral language by listening to complex, but meaningful speech" (Cohn, 1981). An important part of every school program must be the daily oral reading by the teacher to the students of a variety of printed messages, stories, and information. Whenever possible, the students should have a representation of what is being read before them. Children become familiar also with written language by being involved in producing their own texts. They become truly facile with written language as they fulfill their need to produce some form of written communication daily for a variety of purposes and audiences.

A program of readiness, then, that is concerned with preparing students to learn to read effectively and naturally should also be concerned with developing *expectancies* in both the oral and written language systems. In one's language system, the expectancies are both verbal and non-verbal. These expectancies are those referred to in Chapter 3 in the discussion of the representative psycholinguistic models of reading. To review, they consist of

1. Procedures for regulating the physical aspects of reading.

2. A language repertoire containing all rules and cues of spoken and written language.
3. Meanings, concepts, and schemas that have been acquired.

The development of a readiness to read, therefore, consists of providing a chance for students to store in their long-term memories the knowledge, rules, and strategies for reconstructing meaning from language. These are the schemas referred to in Chapter 2. The discussion that follows examines some instructional procedures for readying students for reading.

READINESS FOR FORMAL READING INSTRUCTION

Since most readiness programs occur in elementary schools within the kindergarten and first grade, the following discussions will seem to be more concerned with students of this age range. However, the teacher should be fully cognizant that these procedures are really *readiness for literacy* procedures. Any student, regardless of age or grade level, who does not possess the strategies for using and producing oral and written language needs readiness developed. It is a simple matter for a teacher to take the procedures and adapt them for older students. The question arises among many teachers as to whether the kindergarten is the time for "formal" reading and readiness activities. The question, in many instances, draws attention to the wrong aspect of the problem of readiness instruction. There is no doubt that a carefully planned, systematic readiness program has more positive and lasting effects on later reading achievement than does an incidental readiness program (Blanton, 1972). This means that the teacher who intentionally fosters readiness activities in an organized manner provides a better foundation for reading than does a teacher who haphazardly or infrequently promotes such activities.

In addition, the question of formal or informal readiness activities many times refers to the use of a particular commercial program for developing reading readiness. The answer to such a question depends not so much on whether the materials are teacher made or commercially produced but on the type of activities and the use made of the materials. There is no inherent wrong in commercial readiness materials as long as they are used wisely by teachers. The activities should indeed foster a readiness to read, and they should be appropriate for the students with which they are used. Research indicates that both formal and incidental readiness programs that emphasize language development and experiences appear more successful than those whose use focuses on narrower aspects of readiness (Blanton, 1972). In addition, it appears that language development "is neglected when children are placed in a regimented situation whereby all children merely follow directions" (Church, 1974).

One important misconception about readiness, cited previously, is that readiness is a product that must be acquired before reading can begin. This belief is fostered by those who indicate that there is such a thing as reading readiness which exists independently of the methods and materials used and the pace of instruction instituted by the teacher (Mayer, 1975). This is an oversimplification. When students are made ready, they are made ready for something. Therefore, what the teacher assumes to be the reading process should determine what it is that constitutes readiness for reading. The reading readiness program cannot be considered apart from the kind of reading instruction available (Durkin, 1968).

Learning to use language can occur only in social situations. Since the purpose of language is to facilitate communication, there must be ample opportunity for interaction with other children and adults. The goal of a readiness program is to provide situations that foster cognitive, affective, psychomotor, and linguistic growth in using and producing written language. This is accomplished through experiences in which the students can act on the environment and in turn be acted on by the environment. The linguistic factors are the strand running through all the others and provide for the students' internal manipulation of the environment, their thinking organization, their development of self-expression, and their interrelation of thoughts and action (Foerster, 1975a).

The Place of Writing in Beginning Reading

The study of beginning readers and writers reveals that young children gain their knowledge of print and its functions developmentally. The stages of print awareness can be observed first at about age three or four, and they continue through the child's first year of formal instruction (C. Chomsky, 1971; Clay, 1975, 1982). The growth period includes a wide span of understanding and schema acquisitions. A students' understanding of print begins with their learning that a sign or symbol is a means for delivering a message. Then a complicated period of attempting to relate spoken messages to written ones ensues. As children begin to acquire knowledge of the alphabet, they experiment with and invent words and sentences. Attempts to copy print and to explore various combinations of letters and words (invented spelling—see Chapter 9) lead to an understanding of what they know and their ability to classify that knowledge. When directionality is understood, there may be a period of reversing or mirror imaging. Finally, the child begins to develop a concept of spacing of words and varying arrangements of information on a page.

After students gain an ability to produce written messages, their writing develops in stages that seem to have some theoretical basis in Piaget's stages of cognitive growth. The stages begin with an egocentric (here and now) form and progress to the inclusion of one of hypothesizing and abstracting (there and then) (Moffett, 1968; Britton et al., 1975). The stages do not represent age but, rather, periods of acquiring facility with written language. In the first, *recording*, the student produces an eyewitness account or running commentary. In the second, *reporting*, the student provides a narrative or description of a particular series of events. In the third, *generalizing*, the student provides a more general narrative that detects and demonstrates patterns of repeated events, places, or characters. In the last, *hypothesizing*, the student produces theories, deductions, and hypotheses backed by logical arguments and idea development.

Most important during this development is that students have the opportunity to write, because they will need to. Opportunities to construct texts should grow from a classroom context that helps students extend an effective control of their spoken language to include all sorts of written prose (Clay, 1982).

Strategies for Developing Readiness to Use Print

Concepts are acquired in three ways: (1) through direct experience, (2) through direct verbal explanation, and (3) through conceptual explanation (J. Smith, 1972).

When something is learned through direct experience, there may not be a need for explicit verbalization. A student can observe the teacher performing some task and then, using the teacher's performance as a model, attempt to perform the same task. Or the student can, through several experiences of the situation, form a concept alone. But without associating that experience with a verbal label or description, it will remain locked in a student's imagery memory.

Direct verbal explanation may take the form of a definition, like "This is a hammer," or it may take the form of an explanation of how or why something functions, like

The water comes through the pipe at the top and falls into the little buckets. The buckets are now heavy so they move downwards. The falling buckets are attached to the wheel. The wheel turns as each bucket gets full, falls toward the river, empties into the river, and then rises up to be filled again.

With direct explanation, the situation is generally concrete; that is, the situation is within the sight, sound, smell, or touch of the pupil. The success of a verbal explanation depends on the speaker's and hearer's having had experiences that match; that is, the speaker and hearer assign the same meanings to the same words because they have had similar experiences.

However, in the case of conceptual explanation, verbal message and reality may not be directly connected. Conceptual explanation is abstract; the student must have made long term memory storage of other experiences to which the new experience can be related. The success of learning by conceptual explanation requires that the speaker and hearer share a total experience.

In the development of reading readiness with young students, the sequence of instruction should move from direct experience to direct verbal explanation to conceptual explanation. If teaching begins at the conceptual explanation level without a base of experience, learning is hindered. When a student is able to deal with some experience or concept abstractly (developed as schemas) then the student is ready to read about that particular topic.

This last point is most important. For every thing about which one can read, there must be a readiness. No singular general skill can account for an individual's ability to read. For example, a reader's strategies that are limited to dealing with the grapho-phonological cues in language cannot be expected to fully reconstruct an author's message. Therefore, initial reading materials should be those which deal with experiences and concepts familiar to the reader. Chapter 7 contains strategies for formally introducing students to the reading process through the Language Experience Approach. Here, emphasis is placed on those activities that allow students to develop facility with the oral language system so that functioning in the written language system becomes an extension of it. Reading and writing should become as natural and easy as listening and speaking.

The readiness program outlined below consists of a variety of activities with differing purposes. Individual activities do not develop single skills, strategies, or schemas, and so there will be no attempt to classify them as if they do. The classifications presented, therefore, should not be construed as hierarchical or absolute; rather, they are tentative and heuristic—a means for initiating and stimulating investigation into the nature of readiness to use written language.

Activities for Developing Readiness

Cognitive Factors Some teachers refer to cognitive factors as "comprehension skills." Many of the activities below will seem like "play"; but it should be remembered that play is an integral part of preschool and kindergarten programs. Play is important to the development of the thinking process (Anastasiow, 1979). These cognitive factors represent the knowledge domains referred to in Chapter 2. They conclude specific information and the "scripts" for creating statements about that information in oral and written form.

Classifying and patterning

☐ Show pictures or objects of a general category. Once the objects and the categories have been learned, mix up the items of two or three categories and have the students sort them. Some classifications that might be used are

zoo	farm	street
ride on	ride in	jobs
wear	outdoors	indoors
eat	furniture	containers
things used to eat, work, or write with		

☐ Provide a series of items. From additional items, many of which are not related to the items in the series, have the students select an item or group of items that will continue the series. *It is important always to ask the students why they selected an item. Sometimes they will "see" a pattern that was not intended by the teacher but that is logical.* Some series that might be used are given in Figures 6-1 and 6-2.

☐ After the students understand how to detect series of items, provide them a matrix. The dimensions of the matrix represent two different series. After they have discovered how the matrix works, they should be asked to complete partial matrices. Two sample matrices that can be constructed are shown in Figure 6-3.

☐ Provide the students with objects, or with pictures of objects, placed to show the various relationships that are expressed by the prepositions of our language: *in, on, under, over, behind,* etc. The students should be able to create a

Figure 6-1

Figure 6-2

statement that indicates the relationship between two or more objects. Or, they should be able to place the objects in a relationship expressed by the teacher. For example, have the students identify "The car is next to the tree," or "Put the block under the ruler."

The above activity can be carried out using the adverbial relationship *how*. For example, "The catsup comes slowly out of the bottle."

☐ Provide the students with various objects having different characteristics that can be identified by different senses. Have the students classify the items according to the sense(s) that provides them with the most information about the item. This activity works well with items that share characteristics. For example, use items that look somewhat alike (sugar-salt), feel somewhat alike (sand-sugar), smell somewhat alike (flower-perfume), etc.

☐ Provide the students with samples of various sounds found in their environment. Have them match the sound to the appropiate object by either having the object or a realistic representation of the object at hand. The sounds can be prerecorded so that home and street sounds can be included.

Also, have the students compare sounds of objects placed in closed cannisters (for example, plastic film containers). Use objects such as seeds, pebbles, sand, flour, nails, money, or water. Have the pupils classify the sounds by intensity and descriptive qualities—"clinky," "rattley," "swishy."

The above activities can be extended into other modalities. Have the pupils taste or touch an object and attempt to name the object and/or match the taste or feel to the real object.

☐ Present the students with a group of objects that have one or more characteristics in common. Ask them to indicate what the items have in common. The activity can be extended by using items that have one or more characteristics which are different. For very young children, the characteristics must be observable. As the students mature, more abstract qualities can be used to group the

A series of geometric shapes

△ ○ □ ◇ △ ?   △ △ □ □ ○ ?

A pattern of dots

• •• •ː ːː ːˑ ?

A pattern of sounds

♫♫ ♫♫ ?   ♫♩ ♫♩ ?

A pattern of colors

◉ ○ ◎ ◉ ?

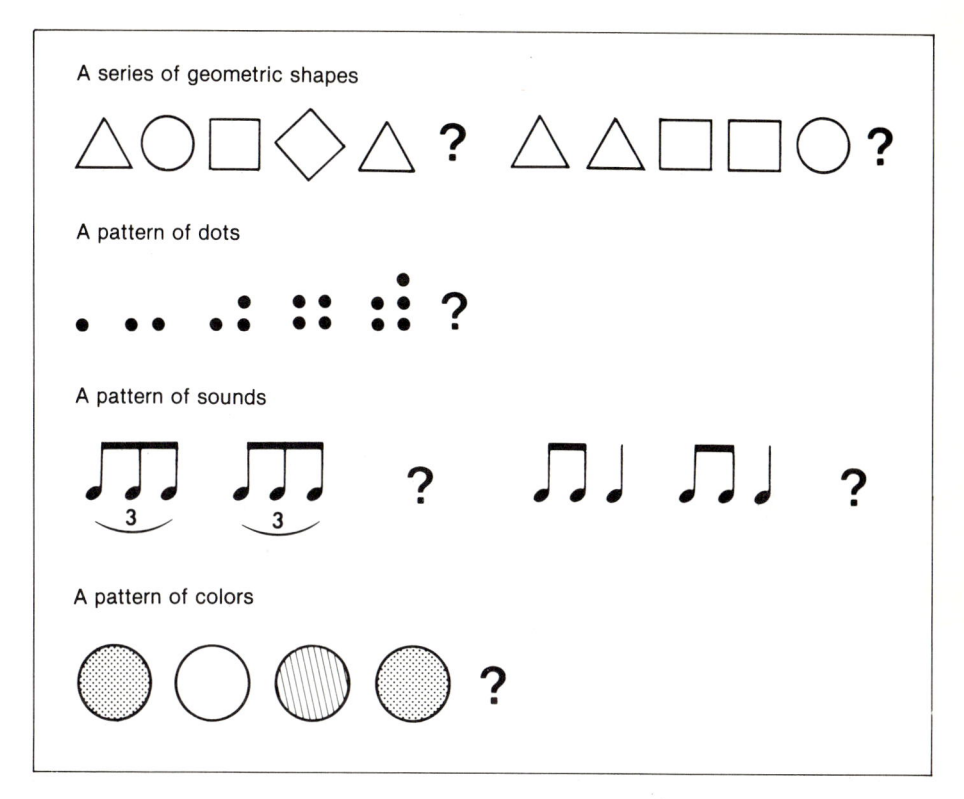

Figure 6-3

objects. For example, young children may be asked how objects that are all blue are the same. As the children mature, the objects may be classified by function ("used in cooking"), or higher order quality ("all made of metal"). *It is most important that the teacher constantly ask the students for their reasons in classifying distinguishing features.*

☐ Provide the students with a sequence of pictures that tell a story. Mix up the pictures and have the students rearrange them to tell the story. As students gain facility in this task, provide them with a sequence of pictures, but do not show them the completed story beforehand.

☐ Provide the students with a problem. Have them generate as many solutions to the problem as possible and then test out each to determine which are the more workable. The alternative solutions do not always have to be workable. Allow the students to determine whether a solution is workable or not after it has been tried.

☐ Provide the students with various illustrations of completed events and have them indicate what could be possible causes of the activity or incident. The situations can be given to the students pictorially or verbally. For example, show the students a picture showing the results of a storm, or tell them that a baseball player is being congratulated at home plate. Allow the students to generate as many possible causes as they can.

Understanding

☐ Let the students listen to a story. When the story is completed, ask them what the story was about. Discuss the details or major events of the story, the general plot, and the theme of the story. Students who experience difficulty in remembering the events of a story should be allowed to develop strategies for remembering. One such device is to allow the students to make simple drawings while listening. Then in the retelling, they may use their simple sketches as "notes."

In order to facilitate remembering, students can also develop techniques for ordering the events. As they listen, have them apply sequence cues—first, second, third, etc.—to the events.

☐ Remembering can also be developed through variations of the game of "concentration." This game is played by constructing a deck of playing cards that consists of paired items the same shape, color, use, etc. The deck is dealt out face down in rows. When a student turns over two paired cards, they are kept. Unsuccessful matches are turned face down again, and the next student takes a turn. Encourage the students to develop "tricks" for remembering where the various cards are after they have been returned to the field of play.

☐ To develop an understanding of *plot,* provide the students with some sample story outlines. The students then try to match the story outline to stories they know or have heard. For example, the students should be able to recognize some of the more common fairy tales from outlines such as:

A little girl takes some food to a sick relative.
A girl finds an empty house and tries out the family's food and furniture.
Three young animals try to set up homes but run into trouble from another
    animal.

☐ To develop an understanding of theme, have the students listen to stories, poems, plays, etc., which are all examples of a particular theme. Start with themes within the students' experiences and to which they can easily relate. As they hear stories, encourage them to state the theme of the story and classify it with other known stories of the same theme. Some themes around which many stories appropriate for young elementary students are written are:

We cannot always do everything we want to do.
Family and close friends can be of great help sometimes.
Some people have different ways of doing things.
We have different feelings when we are personally rejected or accepted.
Things aren't always what they appear to be.

☐ Provide the students with opportunities to follow and demonstrate they understand different types of directions. Beginning with simple, one-step directions, have them carry out the instructions. Then move to more complex directions. Allow the students to discuss among themselves why certain directions are difficult to follow and others are easy. Let the students suggest how directions can be remembered over brief periods of time.

The above activity can be extended to an investigation of the ways people of all ages remember a set of directions. Have the students question their parents, relatives, teachers, and other students in the school, and any other children or adults they have contact with, about ways they remember directions.

☐ Find examples of directions which are given in pictures or in symbols. Have the students translate the directions into verbal directions. (Pictorial directions often accompany toys and games.) Have the students write out directions for an activity of their own choosing.

☐ After hearing a story, have the students listen to a musical version of the story. For example, read or tell the story of *Peter and the Wolf* or the *Sorcerer's Apprentice,* and then play a record of Prokofiev's *Peter and the Wolf* or Dukas's *Sorcerer's Apprentice.* After the children have become familiar with both the story and the musical version, have them narrate the story to the music.

Extend the above activity by having the students create their own musical versions of well-known stories. They can orchestrate the story by using rhythm instruments that are either provided by the school or made by the children. These activities work best with stories in which the number of characters is not too large and each character is repeated in the story at least twice.

☐ Have the students listen to brief vignettes, but do not complete the story. Have them offer possible endings to the stories. This activity can also be done with a long story. At various points in the story, stop reading and ask the children to suggest what they think will happen next. (See Chapter 7, "A Guided Reading-Thinking Lesson." Turn the lesson into a guided *listening*-thinking lesson.)

☐ Read a story about some familiar activity. Include in it some incorrect information. After you have finished, have the children identify the incorrect information. Be sure to tell them before reading the story what you will ask them.

Affective Factors Activities that have as their prime concern the development of attitudes and interests are considered as fostering readiness in affective factors. Included in this area are activities that lead students to make generalizations about themselves as individuals and as members of groups. Language is studied as a key to understanding social relationships (Mishler, 1972). The affective factors represent the schemas of roles, personalities, and objects; the scenarios for the spatial domain; and the goals, plans, and actions of the intentional conceptualization domain.

☐ Provide the students with opportunities to differentiate themselves as physical bodies in space. They should develop a sense of their own bodies as well as a sense of themselves in relation to other individuals and objects.

☐ Play dough or clay can be used to create human and animal shapes. The students are encouraged to examine pictures of animals to discover what body parts animals and humans have in common. They can discover how the shapes of various body parts differ among humans and animals.

☐ Have the students create family portraits through montages of photographs or drawings. Have them pay attention to the physical characteristics that distinguish one individual from another. The students should identify how body parts change as people get older.

☐ Play games that require the identification of body parts and their relative positions in space. Use games such as "Simple Simon" and the dance movements that accompany songs such as "Looby Loo" and "Hokey Pokey."

☐ Read stories to the students which deal with body parts and individual characteristics (hair, skin, and eye color, shape of face, type of hair). Have the children discuss what everyone has in common and how individuals differ.

☐ Play matching games in which the students match a piece of clothing to the part of the body for which it is intended.

☐ Use thumb, hand, or foot prints to create animal characters or abstract designs. Or have the students lie down on a large piece of paper and have other children trace their outline. They can then draw in the facial and clothing features. Those drawings can be incorporated into a "me" book.

☐ Provide the students with opportunities to express their feelings about themselves in different situations. These activities can be combined with stories about how other children and animals feel in different situations. Have the children list words that relate to emotions and words that evoke emotions. In the latter case, connotations of some common words can be explored. For instance, the students can discuss what feelings are evoked by words like *bacon, bath, ice cream, vacation,* and *dentist* (for additional suggestions, see Chapter 9).

☐ Read different types of literature to the students (see Chapter 11). Have them discuss the types of stories they prefer. Extend the discussion to include television programs and movies. Make them aware of the factors that affect their attitudes toward interests in and preferences for such things as choosing a program to watch, selecting a friend, buying dessert in a restaurant, and picking clothes to wear.

☐ Give the students a number of different roles to act out. At first, the activities may require them to go through the motions of a house builder, a baker, or whatever. Then have them act out emotionally charged situations in which they must show fear, happiness, anger, sadness, and the like. Extend the role playing to hypothetical situations. Use open-ended stories to enable the students to explore answers to questions such as: What could you do? What would you do? What should you do?

☐ Have the students survey adults and older children about their attitudes toward reading. Let the class as a whole classify the various feelings about reading and try to hypothesize why people feel differently about it.

☐ Have the students express their feelings and attitudes through art. Have them examine various pictures or reproductions of artists' work grouped according to theme. Have them describe what characteristics of the pictures create different moods. Have them create mood pictures by turning a story or a musical selection into a picture. Encourage them to experiment with realistic and abstract renditions of things, with color, with size, and so forth to create different moods. Let other children try to explain what the pictures mean to them.

Psychomotor Factors The activities included in this section are aimed at helping pupils understand that some body movements relate to the culture or group to which one belongs and that other body movements relate to one's own personality (Foerster, 1975b). Cultural body movements are the conventional body movements that distinguish members of one culture from the members of another culture. Individual body movements distinguish individuals of the same culture and are an expression of personality. These are the paralinguistic aspect of language development.

☐ Using pantomime, have the students communicate an idea to the others. Using facial expressions, convey feelings. Using gestures, convey an idea or mood. Make a study of the body language people use in different situations. Lead the students to notice how most people who grew up in the same area use similar movements with individual variations.

☐ Play games such as "Indian Chief." One child leaves the room and someone from the circle of other students is chosen to be the chief. The child initiates different changes of actions or movments that the other children must follow. The chief must signal changes without any verbal communication. The child who was out of the room returns and tries to figure out who the chief is.

☐ Have the children play games such as "Move as if you ... " in which they must move their bodies as if they were performing some task or as if they were some other person or animal. Some suggested movements are being a baby, walking up (down) the stairs, carrying a heavy load, eating something sticky, being bored, and finding a dollar. Encourage the other children to express verbally the idea or feeling being conveyed by the student's movements.

This activity may be expanded by having the childen move to different rhythms. They also may be asked to do various movements with one or more other children. Have them explain how doing something alone differs from doing it with others.

☐ Have the children lead blindfolded children around the room without any verbal communication between them. They may only touch the other child's arm with one hand. Have them tell how it felt to be totally dependent on the other children.

☐ Watch a movie or television program without the sound. Have the students suggest from the action and body movements of the actors what ideas are being conveyed. Then have them watch a rerun of the same program with the sound turned on. Have them discuss how their interpretation coincided with or differed from the intended meaning.

☐ Have the students make up dances to musical selections that vary in tempo, rhythm, melody, sound, and pitch.

☐ Have the students learn and act the movements to songs such as "If you're happy and you know it." When they become familiar with the song, change *happy* to some other emotion or feeling. Then have the students move a body part and make the appropriate facial expression.

☐ Explore with the students the various sounds it is possible to make with one's body. For instance, they should be able to make sounds represented by *knock, slap, snap, tap, "raspberry,"* as well as various sounds for which there are no words in English.

☐ Have the students learn and act out various work songs. When they understand the idea of work songs, they may be able to create parodies of them to express their own "work" in school.

☐ Have the students play any type of circle game in which the outcome of the game depends on being able to "read" the body movements of the other students. Such games as "dodgeball" and "crows and cranes" are examples.

☐ Have the students create artwork out of materials of various textures. Have them create mood stories that can be "read" only by running their hand over the completed work. Then have other students give their interpretation of the various stories.

☐ Have the students explain to a "Martian" how certain physical activities are performed. During the explanation, the children should not use any physical motions. This can also be done by putting the explainer behind a screen. Explain to the Martian what a telephone is, how to tie a shoelace, and what a knife, fork, and spoon look like.

☐ Have the students repeat various sentences that could be ambiguous except for the intonation and gestures that acompany different meanings. Sentences such as the following can be used:

"That's great." "I like growing children." "I ate the whole thing."

☐ Students are blindfolded and seated in the middle of the room. When sounds are made from different sides of the room, the students have to indicate the direction from which the sound came. They should have ample opportunity to develop eye-hand coordinations and spatial relations. An activity that fosters spatial orientations is block building, especially tall towers!

☐ The students may act out stories with puppets. Let them create their own character puppets and perform with them. Puppets can be easily and inexpensively be made from paper bags, fingers, fists, sticks, socks, toilet paper tubes, and old tennis balls.

A variation of puppet plays is "finger plays" in which a story is dramatized with the hands. In finger plays no additional props or "make-up" is used. In this sense, finger plays become almost a sign language.

Linguistic Factors Linguistic factors permeate all the other factors. However, there are some activities that relate basically to the nature of language itself. To develop linguistic factors children must be able to identify and interpret the oral and written cues of language. Here the student learns how language works, what types of activities or situations may or may not promote effective communication, and the appropriateness of different kinds of language in different situations. (See the nature of language and language development in Chapter 2).

Since most material that is read is prose and not conversation, reading readiness instruction should move from conversation to spoken prose before reading instruction is begun (McDonell, 1975). Part of each day should be devoted to reading aloud to the students. There is support for this suggestion; research shows that a teacher's reading aloud daily is associated with a measurable increase in students' language ability (Cullinan, 1974). Stories read aloud to students help them draw inferences at a higher level than when they read the stories to themselves and they provide models that the students can use for writing their own stories. In addition, a special program in literature using daily oral reading by teachers has been shown to have a significant effect on the students' reading and writing ability.

Traditional readiness programs have often assumed that students hear words as units of sound within sentences. The traditional programs also assume that they can recognize and understand the relationship between letters and their sounds or meaning. However, there is evidence that neither assumption is correct, that these abilities seem to be a function of experience and maturation (Sawyer, 1975). For children under five, the sentence probably is the basic psychological unit of meaning. For adults the smallest unit of speech processed seems to be the syllable. The ability to analyze speech into units of single words does not begin to appear until after the ages of five or six (Sawyer, 1975; Downing & Oliver, 1973). Chapter 9 contains a discussion about "invented spellings" and their relationship to reading readiness, beginning reading, writing, and word recognition. The following activities build on students' linguistic knowledge.

☐ Students may be introduced to the discussion and investigation of linguistic factors by asking "How can we communicate with others when they are not near?" This should help them recognize how newspapers, magazines, letters, and other written material can preserve ideas for others to deal with at a later time. The students should also recognize the function of records and films. Have them try to answer the question: When is writing a better way of saving and communicating ideas then record or film is?

☐ Discuss the use of picture language and sign language. Have the students create their own stories using only picture sequences. Then have them create symbols for many of their activities and their feelings and attitudes. Encourage them to write stories for one another using these symbols. What happens when someone uses a symbol the others do not know? What happens if some of the symbols the students devise are similar to others and seem ambiguous?

☐ Let the students explore the advantages of the telephone, radio, and television for quickly bringing information to people. Discuss the use of the telephone for reporting a fire or accident. Guide the students to an understanding of the techniques for sending and receiving calls on the telephone. (The local business offices of the telephone companies provide many services free to schools, including demonstration telephone kits, films, filmstrips, recordings, and sample telephone information materials.)

☐ Make a collection of words that have multiple meanings. Explore with the students how they can tell what meaning a particular word will have.

☐ Read riddles to the students and provide them with opportunity to solve them. Let the students begin to write their own riddles. For those who do not catch on to the idea, point out how many riddles use words with multiple meanings.

☐ Read or tell the students stories in which confusion occurs between two or more individuals because different meanings are applied to words. From these stories, let the students explore some of the common idioms of our language. Have students draw pictures of the literal and intended meanings of the idioms to show how confusion may arise when one does not know the use of a particular idiom. For instance, let the students illustrate the literal and idiomatic meanings of: They had lunch over my house. We got on the bus.

☐ As an alternative to listening to the teacher, small groups of children or individuals can listen to recordings of the story in the classroom listening center. The recordings can be teacher or commercially produced. This activity works well when copies of the book are available for the students to follow along. Be sure the recordings, whatever their source, clearly identify the page being read and allow enough time for the students to be able to peruse the illustrations.

☐ Using the basic kernel sentences discussed in Chapter 2, provide the students with oral and written models of how these sentences may be transformed or expanded. Let the students make suggestions for transforming and expanding other sentences. Also, provide sentences which are transformations and expansions of kernel sentences and have the students identify the kernel sentences and the embedded sentences. For instance, the activity could start with a sentence like "The player saw the ball." Have the students create a question, a passive, a negative, and a sentence beginning with "there" or "it." Then a sentence such as "The funny clown rode on the brown horse" could be broken down into

The clown is funny.
The clown rode the horse.
The horse is brown.

    This activity will require a great deal of repetition and modeling in oral and written form. The task is not easy for young students and the teacher should not expect all the students to acquire facility in doing the tasks. Many will be able to find only a few sentence patterns, but some will be able to find many. If the teacher constantly asks, "Is there another way to say that?" and "Can we put those two ideas together?" or "Can we take those two ideas and say them separately?" then the students will be alerted to the possibilities for dealing with the syntactic patterns of their language. The results will be that they develop an appreciation of the English language and great facility with language in general.

    □ Read a sentence to the students in which a word has been deleted (an oral cloze exercise). Have them generate words that could complete the sentence and ask them how they selected the word they did. To those who have some difficulty at first, give three alternatives—a possible correct response, a word that is the correct part of speech but semantically incorrect, and a word from another part of speech. Whenever the students give the *correct* response, ask them how they came to select that word.

    □ Play word games in which the students' answer is a word that rhymes with the key word. You might use incomplete rhyming couplets such as

One fine day
We went out to _____.

Or you might use rhyming adjective-noun combinations such as fat/cat, green/bean, mad/Dad.

    □ The students can begin to develop a sight vocabulary from various labels and signs that the teacher or students place around the classroom. In many instances, teachers use single words to label things on bulletin boards as well as things such as doors and windows. However it is a more natural lead-in to reading if these labels contain sentences. Instead of controlling the students vocabulary, the teacher could begin to use sentence patterns that are used in many first-grade readers (not to be confused with preprimers, which often use artificial language). For instance, a bulletin board about community helpers could include captions for pictures that read "This is a fire fighter"; "This is a police officer"; "This is a postal worker." Classroom signs that could be put up are "We go to Art at 9:30 a.m."; "Please close the closet door"; "The coat hooks are in the back of the room."

☐ Students can be introduced to the alphabet through a discussion of how their names are spelled. They can become acquainted with the many alternative forms and shapes in which the letters are drawn by creating montages of words from newspapers, headlines, advertisements, and signs. They can determine how to distinguish the letters when they have various forms.

cat milk TOOTHPASTE

☐ Let the students play games in which they describe a letter to another student who cannot see it. In this game use only basic lowercase or uppercase manuscript letters. For example, one student might say, "I see a letter that has one long line going up with a circle on the left side of the line," and the other students should answer, *d*."

☐ Have the students begin to "read" and construct calendars, maps globes, thermometers, pictures, simple graphs, and the like. On many of these, symbols are used. After the students have become familiar with the symbols, have them read the information to other students. For instance, using some of the common symbols used on television weather programs, have them create weather maps. Other students can then interpret the maps.

☐ Acquaint the students with the different parts of a book. As a story is read to them, demonstrate techniques for the careful handling of the book. In addition, identify the cover, title page with author and publisher, main story part, and table of contents. Have them use these parts when creating their own books.

☐ Sometimes communication among individuals is hindered because the speaker uses many pronouns. Young children will use pronouns so much that the referents of each may become ambiguous. As they engage in various oral activities, be alert to their use of ambiguous pronouns. Also, read or tell stories in which many pronouns have been substituted for the characters' names. Each time a pronoun is said, the students must supply the name of the person to whom the pronoun refers.

☐ Another type of substitution is the use of *this* and *does* for entire ideas, as in: "It's raining; because of this, we won't go to the beach"; "Sometimes Melissa will not help her mother, and sometimes she does." As sentences such as those above are read to the students, ask them to supply the words for which *this* and *does* are substitutes.

☐ Create a "word of the day" display in which a new word is posted each day. To maintain the students' interest, the words may be related to some upcoming school event or public holiday. The display could be changed seasonally—a tree with colors in the fall, a snowman in the winter, children flying kites in the spring. Words may be printed on small signs that fit the decor of the display. A few minutes each day can be spent discussing the word and its meaning or meanings. During the day and succeeding days, the students may be encouraged to use the words as many time as they can in "natural" situations. No word is too big to be learned; that is, the length of the word in no way determines its appropriateness for the students. But the teacher should take care to select words the students can conceptualize. Words with high imagery are good.

☐ Provide opportunities for the students to become familiar with the language's melodic qualities. Use echo activities in which they must repeat a sentence exactly as it is said by the teacher or another student. This "follow the speaker" activity can be used as a lead in to choral speaking. Beginning with short poems or rhymes that can be easily memorized, interpret each differently by changing the rhythm intonation, and accent given to the words and sentences. Then let the students decide which interpretation they prefer. (In using choral speaking, the teacher should assume an active role as leader. The purpose is not to develop individual styles of interpretation but to develop a sense of a number of individuals working together to produce a group result. After the students understand what "leading" and "following" entails in such activities, they may assume the leadership positions.)

DETERMINING READINESS TO READ

As stated previously, many teachers would like a nice, neat way to identify those students who are ready to read. To accommodate individuals with this view, test writers have devised reading readiness tests that are supposed to discriminate between those who are ready to read and those who need additional readiness activities. But there is very strong evidence that reading readiness tests cannot distinguish those who are ready nor are they so precise that they can specify the areas in which a student needs additional instruction (MacGinitie, 1969; Pikulski, 1974a; Rude, 1973; Sawyer, 1975; Vogel & McGrady, 1975).

First, term *readiness* means different things to different people. Whatever one's definition of reading is, there are some factors that make a student ready to read. The question then becomes, What is a definition of readiness that is consistent with what is known about child development in language and thinking? Using a definition of readiness consistent with one's definition of reading, the prerequisites for reading then can be determined. In essence, then, any assessment of students' readiness to read must consider the methods and materials that will be used to teach reading.

Second, reading readiness tests are predictive, not diagnostic. Since there has been little agreement among authorities as to what constitutes reading readiness skills, the tests were designed to predict which students probably would be successful on a reading achievement test after a period of instruction. The discussion in Chapter 4 pointed out how some achievement tests may not measure reading ability. In the same vein, what the readiness tests may be measuring is general potential for doing academic work.

In assessing readiness to read, then, the wrong questions have been asked (MacGinitie, 1969). Instead of asking "Is the student ready to learn to read?" teachers should be asking "*What* and *how* is the student ready to learn?"

The predictive value of any estimation of students' readiness derives from the resemblance of the task to the process of reading. Since reading is a complex interaction of cognitive, affective, psychomotor, and linguistic factors, "there appears to be no nice, clean way to identify children who are likely to encounter difficulty in reading" (Pikulski, 1974).

Readiness assessments should grow out of the classroom activities. Through the application of analytical teaching procedures (Chapter 3), the teacher can assess the students cognitive and linguistic abilities and how these abilities are used in different situations.

Some formal instruments exist that the teacher can employ for determining those abilities that students possess and those for which additional learning is needed. One representative standardized instrument, which measures students mastery of concepts considered necessary for achievement in the first year of school is

The Boehm Test of Basic Concepts. The Psychological Corporation, 1971 edition, Forms A and B. Intended level: kindergarten and grades 1 and 2.

The Boehm Test of Basic Concepts may be used to identify students with deficiencies in concepts used in common curriculum materials and to identify individual concepts for which particular students could profit from additional instruction. The manual of instructions contains information for the teacher on how to use the test for analytical purposes and includes some suggestions for instructional practices.

Another instrument is the *Concepts About Print Test*. The test allows teachers to observe students at the beginning stages of reading and to evaluate their concepts about (1) the orientation of books; (2) whether a message is carried by the print or the pictures; (3) the directionality of the print, the sequence of pages, and the directionality of words; (4) the relationship between printed language and oral language; and (5) words, letters, spacing, and punctuation.

The test is unique and significant in its contribution to the assessment of beginning reading and writing readiness. It does not precisely predict student's behaviors, but with it teachers can analyze what students know about the oral-written language relationships and how they use these schemas. The test can even be used to distinguish the knowledge that students possess after a year of formal instruction (Johns, 1980). The test does have a few limitations that teachers can overcome after gaining familiarity with it (Y. Goodman, 1981). Most importantly, the test is provided with norms of performance that were created on schoolchildren in New Zealand. These norms in other English-speaking countries will need to be used either with caution or be disregarded. This should be no problem because the test can be a good informal means of assessing student behavior. The test books, *Sand* and *Stones*, contain subtests of "upside down print" and "words, letters, and sentences out of order." These may be confusing to readers of all levels of proficiency. Teachers may wish to substitute other picture books for these test books and adapt the testing procedures. This also provides sources of reading with more cultural relevance to their situation. Any use of the test needs to be interpreted cautiously, since an "awareness of concepts about print may interact with the reading acquisition process so that it exists as both a consequence of what has occurred and as a cause of further progress in reading" (Johns, 1980).

In order to use the test, the following are needed:

Clay, Marie M., *The Early Detection of Reading Difficulties: A Diagnostic Survey with Recovery Procedures*, 2nd ed. (Exeter, NH: Heinemann Educational Books, 1980).
Clay, Marie M., *Concepts About Print Test: Sand*, 1972.
Clay, Marie M., *Concepts About Print Test: Stones*, 1979.

Measures for Research and Evaluation in the English Language Arts, by William Fagan and others (cited in Chapter 5, *Further Readings*), can be used or adapted for assessment purposes. The sections on measures for assessing language development and listening should be very helpful. In addition, some of the sources cited in a later section of this chapter, *Resources for the Teacher*, contain suggestions for assessing pupil proficiency in the cognitive, linguistic, psychomotor, and affective areas.

DEVELOPING READINESS FOR PARTICIPATING IN GROUP ACTIVITIES

Bringing a number of students together for a lesson does not mean a "group" has been formed. In the first chapter it was suggested that "flexible" classroom grouping procedures should be used. The intent was to focus on the purposes for forming groups. Teachers should have a variety of reasons for organizing groups, and the requirements for a student to join a group or be included in one after it is formed should be flexible.

However, although a number of students are brought together for a particular purpose, a group still may not have been formed. Quite often so called "groups" are nothing more than aggregations. A real group has an internal interpersonal structure. When a number of students meet with the teacher, and each student communicates solely with the teacher, then the students are not functioning as a group. When each of the students communicates with the others as well as with the teacher, a true group is functioning.

One common misconception about grouping is that grouping only entails organizing students of somewhat equal ability. Usually what is meant is that the students are reading "at the same level," or that they need the same skill development. What results is usually an aggregation in which the teacher is presenting a lesson to a number of individuals simultaneously. Although ability may be, at times, a desired criterion for inclusion in a group, it is not the hub about which a group is formed. The primary purpose for organizing any group is to facilitate learning through joint problem solving ventures.

When a true group exists, there are at least three functioning levels:

Groups function at the task level. This usually represents the original purpose for organizing or designing the group. Most groups to which individuals belong have a conscious task need. Quite often, that is the main level at which the members seem to operate.

Groups function at a maintenance level. Groups function with a constantly changing system of relationships among its members. This is the group personality. The members of a real group are aware that they exist as a group, and they are confronted with the need to maintain the interpersonal relationships so that a working system exists.

Groups function at an individual level. Each group consists of individuals who have their own personal needs. The needs can range from the need to share experiences with others to the need for domineering. Too often, because the individual needs of the group members are masked, the functioning of the group breaks down. When members, consciously or unconsciously, place their needs and goals ahead of the main purpose of the group, the cohesiveness of a group lessens.

The group can be efficient only as the members interact and maintain some balance among the three functioning levels. Learning to be a good group member is important. The group process can facilitate a great deal of the learning that occurs in schools. Therefore, teachers should be sure that their students are ready to participate as members of real groups.

Group Functions

Although students may not overtly identify the three functions of a group, they should have some awareness of a goal and the personal responsibilities of helping the group reach that goal. Below are some of the more common task and maintenance functions that can be carried out by group members (Gorman, 1974). Through guidance and modeling, the teacher can encourage students to assume many of the functions as the group operates.

Task functions
Initiating. Group members propose goals, define a group problem, and suggest ways for solving that problem.
Seeking ideas. Group members request information and seek suggestions and ideas.
Giving information. Group members offer information and ideas and state a belief or opinion.
Clarifying ideas. Group members interpret or reflect on information or ideas already given, give additional information or examples, and suggest alternative solutions.
Summarizing. Group members bring together others' ideas and offer conclusions for the group's acceptance.
Testing. Group members test to see how much agreement exists among the group's members.

Maintenance functions
Encouraging. Group members become responsive to others' ideas, suggestions, and opinions; accept their contributions; and recognize them for their contribution.
Expressing feelings. Group members sense the group's mood and feelings and express this to the other members.
Reducing tension. Group members help individuals in the group explore their differences.
Offering compromises. Group members attempt to resolve conflicts through compromise.

Facilitating communication. Group members make suggestions for sharing and discussing ideas and reconciling differences.

Setting limits. Group members state standards for evaluating the group's functioning and achievements.

In summary, it is not possible to talk about grouping without specifying (1) the group's purpose, (2) the situation in which it will operate, and (3) the learning that is expected to result from the group's efforts. For a group to be productive—to achieve its goal—its members must share concerns and aims, and they should understand how group members constructively work together toward the completion of their goal. With the teacher's guidance and initial leadership, groups can be formed that allow the individual members to function without losing self-respect or experiencing rejection from other group members.

Forming Groups in a Classroom

The nature and size of groups will vary. The duration of a group will depend upon the task and the abilities of the group members. However, before classroom groups can function adequately, the students should be familiar with certain routines which prevent chaos.

Although it may take students varying periods of time to learn to become effective group workers—some students may learn how in a matter of weeks while others may take years—all should be encouraged to participate in the identification of the task and maintenance level functions. At the kindergarten and first grade level this might be accomplished by organizing, at first, interest groups. For example, some students might wish to develop a puppet show from a favorite story, or some students might wish to design and build a class store, or some might wish to collaborate in composing a book for the class library.

Next, students must know some of the techniques that will be the basis for their activity. The students must know

1. How to handle specific materials such as phonographs, woodworking tools, tape recorders, and filmstrip projectors.
2. How to follow the class routines for using supplies such as paper, crayons, paint, and paste.
3. How to seek help from the teacher and from other class members.
4. How to maintain class decorum so that no one is imposing upon the ability of others to perform whatever activity they wish.
5. What to do whenever an activity is complete or cannot be completed at that time.
6. How to work in special learning centers without adult guidance.

Finally, the students must know how to work independently. There will be times when not all the students are working at group activities or under the teacher's direct guidance. At these times, the students must work on individual projects or assignments. The students should understand

1. How to allow others to work without interference.
2. How to stay with a task until it is completed, or at least, to understand how, why, and when a task may be terminated before its completion.
3. How to move from one activity to another without requiring the assistance of others.

When teachers complain that a class is uncontrollable or that the students do not have the maturity to work independently or as effective group members, it usually means that the teachers have not effectively established routines for efficient classroom practices. It is widely accepted that children are self-motivating. Without guidance and limitations, they will seek their own ways to relieve boredom and frustration, the prime causes of most uncontrolled classrooms.

Resources for the Teacher

Any teacher beginning to undertake the development of reading readiness programs is faced with a task of accumulating materials for instruction. When schools have readiness materials from a basal reading program, they too often are only exercises in letter-sound relationships. In such cases, the teacher may wish to supplement the program with activities and materials that will provide a well-rounded program of readiness for reading.

The resources listed below are representative of those that a teacher can use for creating a language-centered readiness program. The first group of materials are commercial programs. When the entire readiness program is not available for instructional purposes, teachers might find it worthwhile to obtain one or more of the manuals as handbooks or guides.

Peabody Language Development Kits (revised), *Manuals for Level P and Level 1* (Circle Pines, MN: American Guidance Service).
Language Experiences in Early Childhood, Teacher's Resource Book (Chicago: Encyclopedia Britannica Press).
Matrix Games Package, Teachers' Guide (New York: Appleton-Century-Crofts).
Ginn Oral Language Development (GOLD), *Teachers' Manual.* (Columbus, OH: Ginn).

The following series, an introduction to reading and to the basic concepts needed for reading, develops young readers' strategies through thematic books: numbers, seasons, shapes, colors, sensory experiences, and communication:

Beginning to Learn About (Milwaukee, WI: Raintree Publishing Group).

The following texts contain suggestions for instructional activities:

Berger, Allen, and Blanch Hope Smith, *Language Activities* (Urbana, IL: National Council of Teachers of English, 1973).

Carin, Arthur, and Robert B. Sund, *Creative Questioning and Sensitive Listening Techniques: A Self-Concept Approach,* 2nd ed. (Columbus, OH: Chas. E. Merrill, 1978).

Gerbrandt, Gary I., *An Idea Book for Acting Out and Writing Out, K-8* (Urbana, IL: National Council of Teachers of English, 1974).

Glazer, Susan M., *Getting Ready to Read: Creating Readers from Birth Through Six* (Englewood Cliffs, NJ: Prentice-Hall, 1980).

Moffett, James, and Betty Jane Wagner, *Student Centered Language Arts and Reading, K-13: A Handbook for Teachers,* 2nd ed. (Boston: Houghton Mifflin, 1976).

Rhodes, Lynn K., *Children's Literature: Activities and Ideas* (Denver: UCD School of Education Publications, 1981).

Sealy, Leonard, Nancy Sealey and Marcia Millore, *Children's Writing: An Approach for the Primary Grades* (Newark, DE: International Reading Association, 1979).

Anthologies can be useful to teachers seeking stories and poems for listening and acting-out activities. Anthologies such as the following provide teachers with a great variety of literature that can be kept conveniently at hand in the classroom:

Arbuthnot, May Hill (revised by Zena Sutherland), *The Arbuthnot Anthology of Children's Literature,* 4th ed. (Glenview, IL: Scott Foresman, 1976).

Johnson, Edna, Evelyn R. Sickels, Francis C. Sayers, and Carolyn Horowitz, *Anthology of Children's Literature,* 5th ed. (Boston: Houghton Mifflin, 1977).

A list of "predictable" books is included in the following article:

Rhodes, Lynn K., "I Can Read! Predictable Books as Resources for Reading and Writing Instruction," *The Reading Teacher* 34 (1981): 511–518.

The following companies produce recordings and filmstrips for all curriculum areas. Teachers developing readiness programs will find them a good source for recordings of songs, games, children's literature, rhythmic activities, and for filmstrips and picture-study-story prints.

Educational Activities, Inc., P.O. Box 392, Freeport, NY 11520
Educational Teaching Aids, 159 West Kinzie Street, Chicago, IL 60619
Good Apple, Box 299, Planview, NY 11803
Incentive Publications, Inc., 2400 Crestmoor Road, Nashville, TN 37215
Raintree Publishing Group, 205 West Highland Avenue, Milwaukee, WI 53203
Troll Associates, 320 Route 17, Mahwah, NJ 07430

Teachers need resources for suggestions to parents about home activities with children. The following short monographs, intended for distribution to parents, are available from the International Reading Association, PO Box 8139, Newark, DE 19711:

Chan, Julie M. T., *Why Read Aloud to Children?* (1974).
Glazer, Susan M., *Who Can I Help My Child Build Positive Attitudes Toward Reading?* (1980).
Ransbury, Milly Kayes, *How Can I Encourage My Primary Grade Child to Read?* (1972).
Rogers, Norma, *What Is Reading Readiness?* (1971).
Rogers, Norma, *How Can I Help My Child Get Ready To Read?* (1972).
Rogers, Norma, *What Books and Records Should I Get for My Preschooler?* (1972).

The following brochure contains twenty suggestions for parents to encourage their children's writing at home and support a school writing program. It is available from the National Council of Teachers of English, 1111 Kenyon Road, Urbana, IL 61801.

How to Help Your Child Become a Better Writer (1980). (One to fourteen copies are free.)

Discussion Questions and Activities

1. Select a basal reading series and examine the teacher's manual for the readiness materials. In what way do the activities foster the development of a readiness to read in light of a psycholinguistic definition of reading? Is the aspect of readiness viewed as a broad, many-faceted process or as a limited, one-dimensional one? How are the teaching and learning of reading and writing integrated (see check list, Chapter 5).
2. Some of the kindergarten teachers in a school wish to implement a reading readiness program that consists primarily of a workbook purporting to teach the letters of the alphabet and their sounds What advice would you offer these teachers to assist them in the selection of a readiness program?
3. A parent of a first-grade student wants to know why the class plays so much of each day. The parent is concerned that the students in the class are not learning and will lose out in learning to read, in comparison with the other first-grade classes. In actuality, the class consists of a large number of immature students. The "games" are activities of the type described in this chapter. What will you answer the parent?
4. How would you support Black's (1980) statement to teachers and parents who feel that uncorrected "errors" only lead to the reenforcement of "bad habits?"

While young children are allowed by parents and preschool teachers to make "mistakes" when learning to talk, most teachers feel they must correct children's "mistakes" when learning to read ... [even though] pointing out "mistakes" seems to do little for children in helping them develop communicative competency.

How would you explain to parents the "errors" students make in learning to write (compose)?
5. Examine several reading readiness tests and their accompanying manuals. In your opinion, what items on each of the test, although they may predict possible reading achievement, do not indicate the strategies used during the reading process?
6. Administer to a child in kindergarten or the beginning of first grade a series of informal language and cognitive tasks like those discussed in this chapter. (In developing these informal language and cognitive tasks, use the information in Chapter 2 about language structure and schemas.) Describe the student's behavior—apparent cognitive strategies, linguistic proficiency, psychomotor activity, and emotional reactions—while undertaking the tasks.

Further Readings

Various issues of *Language Arts* are devoted to theme's dealing with language development and reading and writing readiness. Many articles contain not only theoretical discussions but also suggestions for instructional activities. Of particular interest may be these issues:

May 1979: "Teaching and Learning Language—Naturally"
September 1979: "The Child as Communicator"
November/December 1979: "The Child Learning to Read"
November/December 1980: "Reading"
February 1981: "Listening and Talking"

The following texts deal with the underlying cognitive and language bases of learning to read and write.

Graves, Donald H., *Writing: Teachers and Children at Work* (Exeter, NH: Heinemann Educational Books, 1982).
Hunter-Grundin, Elizabeth, *Literacy: A Systematic Start* (New York: Harper & Row, 1979).
Pinnell, Gay Sue, ed., *Discovering Language with Children* (Urbana, IL: National Council of Teachers of English, 1980).

The following two books deal with behavior in the classroom and the relationship of teachers and pupils as encoders and decoders of language:

Clark, Margaret L., Ella A. Erway, and Lee Beltzer, *The Learning Encounter: The Classroom as a Communication Workshop* (New York: Random House, 1971).

Gorman, Alfred H., *Teachers and Learners: The Interactive Process of Education,* 2nd ed. (Boston: Allyn & Bacon, 1974).

Chapter 7

STRATEGIES FOR GUIDED READING DEVELOPMENT

Focus Questions

1. How can the language experience approach be used to introduce students to literacy?

2. How can classroom instruction be organized by using thematic units?

3. What are the procedures for developing a guided reading-thinking lesson?

4. What are the different types of questions that can be used to develop and extend students' understanding during guided reading?

A distinction has to be made between reading guided by the teacher and that in which the pupils independently guide themselves. In guided reading, the teacher assumes the responsibility for directing the students in reconstructing the author's message. Just as a safari guide leads the inexperienced hunter to the quarry but leaves the last shot for the novice, the teacher structures a lesson so that the students arrive at a point where they can capture the author's thoughts. In independent reading, the students take full responsibility for initiating and completing a reading act. At such times, they are their own guides.

A reading program that is responsive to the needs of the students provides for both types of activities. The teacher guides the students' reading until they are mature enough for independent reading. Since students are always capable of some independent reading, both types of instruction are generally appropriate. This chapter focuses on those strategies a teacher employs to navigate students through a reading selection. The succeeding chapters focus on strategies that permit the students to be responsible for finding their own way through a story. All include means for using students' writing to increase their understanding of printed messages.

THE LANGUAGE EXPERIENCE APPROACH

The language experience approach to reading deliberately attempts to develop reading skills through the natural relationships among all the language processes. The language experience approach is predicated on the idea that

... reading can be most meaningfully taught when the reading materials accurately reflect the child's own experience as described by his language. The language of instruction then must be that which proceeds from the wealth of linguistic, conceptual, and perceptual experience of the child. A child is more likely to learn to read when the activities associated with the approach have functional relationships with his language, experience, needs and desires (Cramer, 1971).

A common misconception about the language experience approach is that it is an activity normally relegated to the first-grade classroom. Nothing could be further from the truth. The language experience approach to reading is a way to foster literacy in students of any age. Since the difficulty of the material read is controlled by the learner's own language abilities, the material developed by this approach is appropriate for any age.

Hall (1972, 1981) suggested that

1. Beginning readers are users of language. A teacher should accept the students' language as a starting point. (The language of speakers of divergent dialects is taken up in Chapter 12.)
2. Beginning readers should learn to view reading as a communication process.
3. Beginning readers should understand the reading process as the conscious relating of print to oral language.
4. Beginning readers should incorporate the learning of writing with the learning of reading.
5. Beginning readers should learn to read meaningful language units. The minimum meaningful language unit is the sentence.
6. Beginning readers should learn to read with materials written in their own language patterns.

Although the language experience approach to reading has been extensively researched, reviews of the literature show findings reflect a multitude of contrasts (Hall, 1978; Vilscek, 1968). These conflicting findings seem to be due to differences among the studies in how the researchers defined "language experience," selected their subjects, and designed and implemented the research itself. Although there are still some unanswered methodological questions about the procedure, there is growing interest in the approach as a means for introducing students to literacy. The research does substantiate the language experience approach as an effective way to teach reading and related communication skills. Specifically, students taught by the procedure produce satisfactory if not superior results on achievement tests, compared with those of students taught by other procedures. This approach provides learners with meaningful reading and writing vocabularies; it can motivate students with special learning problems; and students' performance in writing is particularly impressive (Hall, 1978).

One complaint about the language experience approach is that it offers too little structure to the teacher. Although it is no panacea and is not necessarily an easy program to implement, through the language experience approach the teacher can provide a rich experimental and activity-oriented program that uses the child's own language and provides for individualized instruction (Schwartz, 1975). Through its use, a teacher can make learning an active, dynamic process.

As one teacher discovered (Gelb, 1975), the language experience approach can bring revelation to the teacher as well as the student. While working with a ten-year-old nonreading child on a series of activities related to "colors," the teacher decided to let the student become physically involved in mixing the creating colors. He concluded:

finally the experience meant something to him. The words were felt because he was living them. That was the key to the whole problem: One must live the words to understand them. I felt I had read this 10 million times, but until this day, they had no meaning because *I had not lived them either.* [Emphasis added.]

Implementing the Language Experience Approach

The language experience approach has as its most important consideration the cultivation of the idea that language communicates meaning. There is no attempt to separate any skill development from the process of thinking. The language experience approach includes planned and continuous activities like the following:

1. Individual- and group-dictated stories.
2. Individual student word banks of known words.
3. Handwriting exercises.
4. Creative writing situations.
5. Daily oral reading of prose and poetry by the teacher to the students.
6. Students' illustrations of dictated stories.
7. Maintaining of a student notebook containing individual- and group-dictated stories.
8. Opportunities for working at learning stations.
9. Teacher-guided reading-thinking lessons.
10. Keeping records of students' progress (Stauffer & Pikulski, 1974).

Many opportunities are structured into the school day so that

1. *The teacher works with the whole class.* The teacher might read aloud to the class from some book or story related to a class activity, read the children's class discussions, show a movie, introduce a new game, sing or perform rhythmic activities, and lead choral reading or speaking.

2. *The teacher works with small groups.* A teacher might follow up a large group lesson, take dictation, listen to students' oral reading, develop a reading skills lesson, lead listening development lessons, and guide the reading of a story.

3. *A teacher works with individuals.* A teacher might engage in many of those same activities carried out with the whole class or small groups.

4. *The teacher works as a resource person.* A teacher might suggest ideas for students' creative writing or drawings, help them explore and think out an activity, assist those who need help, and be a sounding board for their ideas.

The learning stations within a classroom can consist of library centers, writing resource centers, listening stations, viewing areas, art centers, and game corners. The number and structure of the learning stations will depend on the facilities of the school as well as the ingenuity of the teacher. For example, a writing center can be established by placing on a table in one part of the room some paper, writing instruments (pen, pencils, brush-point pens, crayons, and possibly a typewriter); resources for words such as picture dictionaries; and story motivators such as story beginnings, pictures, and comic strips with the "talk" cut out. A dictating center can be created by placing a tape recorder and some story starters together. At a later time, the teacher and the student can listen to the story. The teacher can write it out for the student, or in schools where they are available, educational assistants, aides, or volunteer parents can function as transcribers.

In a language experience approach, the planning and selection of topics and activities should take into account the students' experiences with words, their study of the English language, and their experiences with authors' ideas. The activities from each of these three areas of student experiences should be simultaneous and continuous throughout the school year. Never should there be a feeling that learning about something is ever finished. The air of things being a little "unfinished" is a great stimulus for further independent learning.

Allen and Allen (1970) offer a framework for a language experience approach:

Group One: Extending Experiences with Words
1. *Sharing experiences*—the ability to tell, write, or illustrate something on a purely personal basis.
2. *Discussing experiences*—the ability to interact with what other people say and write.
3. *Listening to stories*—the ability to hear what others have to say through books and to relate ideas to one's own experiences.
4. *Telling stories*—the ability to organize one's thinking so that it can be shared orally or in writing in a clear and interesting manner.

5. *Dictating words, sentences, and stories*—the ability to choose from all that might be said orally the most important part for someone else to write and read.
6. *Writing independently*—the ability to record one's own ideas and present them in a form for others to read.
7. *Authoring individual books*—the ability to organize one's ideas into a sequence, illustrate them, and make them into books.

Group Two: Studying the English Language
1. *Conceptualizing the relationship of speaking, writing, and reading*—the ability to conceptualize, through extensive practice, that reading is the interpretation of speech that has been written and then must be reconstructed, orally or silently.
2. *Expanding vocabulary*—the ability to expand one's listening, speaking, reading, and writing (including spelling) vocabulary.
3. *Reading a variety of symbols*—the ability to read in one's environment such things as the clock, calendar, dials, and thermometer.
4. *Developing awareness of common vocabulary*—the ability to recognize that our language contains many common words and patterns of expression that must be mastered for sight reading and correct spelling when expressing one's ideas in writing.
5. *Improving style and form*—the ability to profit from listening to, reading, and studying the style of well-written material.
6. *Studying words*—the ability to pronounce and understand words and to spell them correctly in written activities.

Group Three: Relating Authors' Ideas to Personal Experiences
1. *Reading whole stories and books*—the ability to read books for information, pleasure, and improvement of reading skills on an individual basis.
2. *Using a variety of resources*—the ability to find and use many resources in expanding vocabulary, improving oral and written expression, and sharing ideas.
3. *Comprehending what is read*—the ability, through oral and written activities, to gain skill in following directions, understanding words in the context of sentences and paragraphs, reproducing the thought in a passage, reading for detail, and reading for general significance.
4. *Summarizing*—the ability to get main impressions, outstanding ideas, or some details of what has been read or heard.
5. *Organizing ideas and information*—the ability to restate ideas in the order in which they were written or spoken.
6. *Integrating and assimilating ideas*—the ability to read and listen for personal interpretation and elaboration of concepts.
7. *Reading critically*—the ability to determine the validity and reliability of statements.

In summary, the language experience approach to reading gives students multisensory experiences in observing their world, listening to and reading about what others have observed, experiencing authorship themselves, and understanding the various literary forms.

A specific language experience activity is structured so that the students are led from a concrete experience to the verbalization of that experience and then to the conceptualization of that experience. The sequence of implementing the approach over a few days might be to:

Phase I:
1. Offer a concrete experience as an attention getter and conversation starter. If possible, the experience should allow the students to manipulate objects.

2. Allow the students to talk spontaneously about the experience.
3. Through pertinent questions, guide the students' attention to relevant features of the experience.
4. Solicit from the students some dictation about the experience. In small group settings, allow each student to contribute at least one sentence to the narrative account.
5. Read the completed story to the students.
6. Have the students make a drawing of, or in some other way, illustrate a significant aspect of the experience. On the illustration place a sentence from the dictation that corresponds to the student's illustration.

Phase II:
1. Reread the story or narrative to the students.
2. Have the students read the story as a group.
3. Allow individual members of the group to read the story.
4. Have each student find in the story particular sentences, phrases, and words.

Phase III:
1. Reproduce the story for each student.
2. Provide the students literature related to their experience. After the material has been read to them, allow them to peruse the material individually.
3. Place into the students' word banks all the words that they know. Only those words that a student can read from the dictated story without teacher assistance should be placed in the word bank.
4. Give the students a skills lesson that develops or extends their ability to read independently.

The following account illustrates how this approach was used successfully with three fourth-grade students who were experiencing difficulty acquiring beginning reading strategies (Bercari, 1975). The result was the filmstrip illustrated in Figure 7-1.

The activity was initiated by reading and carrying out with pupils the instructions for making salt dough which was in a supermarket magazine. My aims in getting the girls to produce the filmstrip were to develop a sense of sequence, exercise their memories, develop written expression of their own experiences, and to give each girl a sense of accomplishment.

We developed the strip by: (a) writing individual stories on how we made the salt dough, (b) reading each other's stories and discussing what had been left out of all three, (c) taking the ideas from all three stories and making a master story following the sequence in which the project was carried out, (d) writing sentences on 5 × 7 inch papers for each frame, (e) illustrating those frames in which there was room with ideas that could be drawn, (f) doing a final editing of the story to see what had been left out, and including additional material and frames. When the

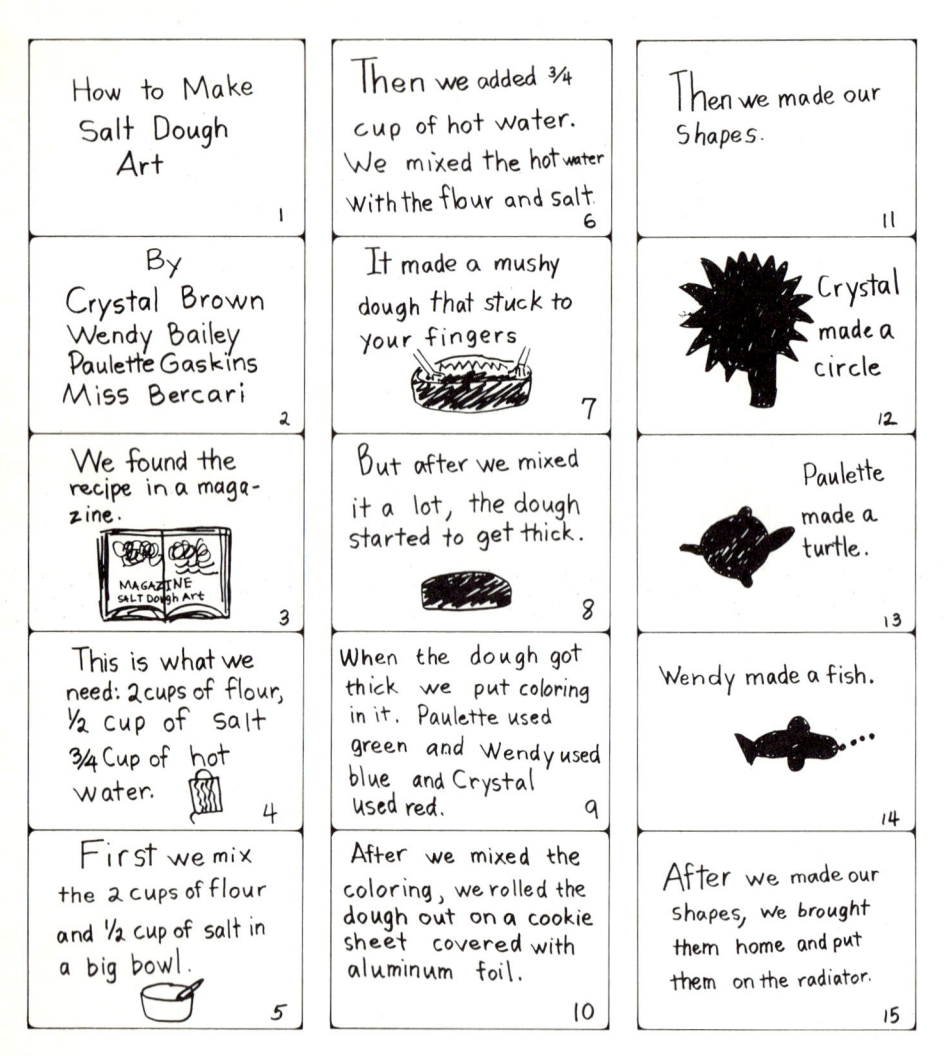

178 CHAPTER 7/STRATEGIES FOR GUIDED READING DEVELOPMENT

How to Make Salt Dough Art `1`	Then we added ¾ cup of hot water. We mixed the hot water with the flour and salt. `6`	Then we made our shapes. `11`
By Crystal Brown Wendy Bailey Paulette Gaskins Miss Bercari `2`	It made a mushy dough that stuck to your fingers `7`	Crystal made a circle `12`
We found the recipe in a magazine. `3`	But after we mixed it a lot, the dough started to get thick. `8`	Paulette made a turtle. `13`
This is what we need: 2 cups of flour, ½ cup of salt ¾ cup of hot water. `4`	When the dough got thick we put coloring in it. Paulette used green and Wendy used blue and Crystal used red. `9`	Wendy made a fish. `14`
First we mix the 2 cups of flour and ½ cup of salt in a big bowl. `5`	After we mixed the coloring, we rolled the dough out on a cookie sheet covered with aluminum foil. `10`	After we made our shapes, we brought them home and put them on the radiator. `15`

Figure 7-1 An LEA Filmstrip

filmstrip came back from the processing lab, the girls discussed what colors should be added to the filmstrip with permanent marking pens.

Finally, the filmstrip was shown to the other pupils. The girls alternated in reading the frames on the filmstrip during the showing.

Individual and small group dictations transcribed on class charts can be one of four types:

1. Personal language charts, which are the student's own dictation in written form.
2. Narrative charts, which are the record of a group's dictation.

When the shapes got dry-on the top side, we turned them over. 16	Don't put too much coloring in, and don't let the dough dry out before you finish. 20	You can make animals 🐟 or flowers 🌷 or bowls ⌣ or what— 24
The dough had to dry for about one week. Thurs. Fri. Sat. Sun. Mon. Tues. Wed. 17	If the shape breaks before you get to varnish it, use white glue to put it back together. 21	ever you want! baskets signs faces things people 25
Then we painted our shapes with varnish and had our salt dough art. 18	If the dough is sticky when you roll it out use a little more flour. 22	Good Luck! 26
Be careful not to roll the dough too thin. 19	Now you know how we made salt dough art. Why don't you try it. 23	

Figure 7-1 (continued)

3. Work charts, which represent the consensus of a class or small group on how something should be organized or directions for using class resources.
4. Skill charts, which are records of or instructions for carrying out strategies in one of the language areas (Lee & Allen, 1963).

When composing the charts for use in the classroom, teachers should follow certain principles of composition:

1. *Make the charts attractive.* Be sure to letter them neatly and clearly. The final chart should be copied from a draft after the teacher and students have made their final editorial changes. Allow the students to decorate the charts with planned illustrations.

2. *Give the charts some measure of literary quality.* Although most of the charts should retain the students' own language, the imaginative and resourceful teacher can lead them, through guided questions, to attempt to emulate the literary forms with which they have become familiar from the teacher's daily readings.

3. *Give consideration to phrasing.* Especially with younger children, the lines should be written to provide the maximum of language redundancy through helpful syntactic and semantic clues.

4. *Compose the charts with consideration for the greatest legibility.* Aside from well-drawn letters, the teacher should consider the spacing of the lines, margins, typographical clues such as numerals or symbols, color, and contrast between the color of the printing and the color of the paper.

Figure 7-2 show some examples of well-planned and well-executed language experience charts.

Implementing a Thematic Unit

One way to organize the language experience approach to reading is by using *thematic units.* The various experiences to which the students are exposed are related to a theme, a problem, or an area of interest. The contents of various areas are brought together in a series of lessons. The basic unit, called a *resource unit,* is developed in advance by the teacher and is flexible enough for cooperative planning

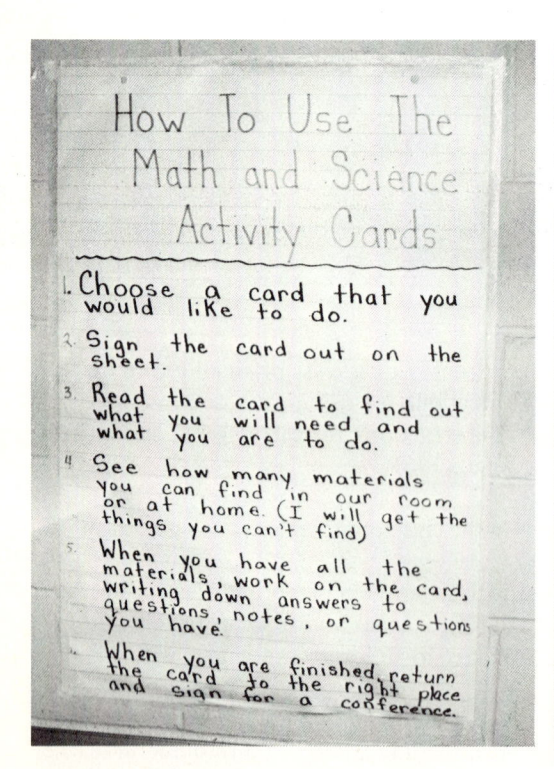

Figure 7-2 Examples of Language Experience Charts

by the teacher and the students. Flexibility also allows changes to be made as conditions in a classroom change.

There is no single pattern for the formal construction and organization of a resource unit. The teacher's preparation may vary according to the students' abilities and needs, the opportunities in the school and community, and the amount of time available for carrying out the unit. In addition, the selection of a theme will depend on the cognitive and affective needs of the class members, the school and community resources available for developing experiences, and the availability in the school of instructional materials such as textbooks, records, audio-visual aids, maps, reference books, and library facilities. The source of the themes may come from one of the content areas or from the students' interests. The teacher's methods of instruction should vary depending upon the teaching objectives, the students' needs, and the materials available. Some of the more common methods used by teachers include whole class and small group discussions, trips, dramatizations, audio-visual materials, and individual and small group research projects.

The resource unit contains suggestions for activities, materials, and concepts to be learned. It contains information for both the teacher and the students. The activities, resources, and instructional plans are detailed, with specific reference to titles of books, films, and records as well as to the materials that may be needed to carry out a project. The thematic unit is introduced to the students through a stimulating activity that focuses their attention on the topic. Motivation is usually fairly easy when the teacher capitalizes on children's natural curiosity.

Resources for the Teacher

Some teachers may feel that they lack the background, insights, and resources for implementing thematic units and a language experience approach to reading. This is understandable. However, a teacher who hesitates to use a completely original, language-based program can use commercial materials to foster language experiences for reading and writing. The following are selected resources, with brief notations about their contents:

Allen, Roach Van, and Claryce Allen, *Language Experiences in Reading. Teacher's Resource Guides, Levels* I, II, III (Chicago: Encyclopedia Britannica Press, 1970).

Each resource book contains five or six thematic units. Although the material is geared toward the primary grades, a creative teacher, using the formats of the units, can adjust the themes for use with older students.

Two important complements to the above resource are the following:

Allen, Roach Van, *Language Experiences in Communication* (Boston: Houghton Mifflin, 1976).

Allen, Roach Van, and Claryce Allen, *Language Experience Activities* 3rd ed. (Boston: Houghton Mifflin, 1982).

The kits listed below, mentioned previously, contain detailed lesson plans, picture cards, story posters, recorded stories, puppets, and manipulative materials.

Peabody Language Development Kits, Levels I, II, III. Revised ed. (Circle Pines, MN: American Guidance Service).

Teachers who wish to find existing publications of thematic units should refer to the following sources:

1. State and city education departments and boards of education.
2. Specialized groups and societies such as natural history and ecology societies, the various associations of manufacturers and industrial groups, and historical and scientific societies.
3. The major encyclopedia publishers, who often provide supplementary educational materials.
4. The files in public libraries and in university curriculum centers.

The following publications offer teachers free materials. The information is listed by subject for easy reference.

Educator's Guide to Free Films. Educator's Guide to Free Filmstrips (Randolph, WI: Educator's Program Service, annual).

The following text is a guide for providing and coordinating the educational activities that will help young children develop self-confidence, individuality, and creative freedom. The book consists of a series of unit plans organized around major themes appropriate to young children.

Taylor, Barbara J., *When I Do, I Learn* (Provo, UT. Brigham Young University Press, 1974).

The authors of some basal reading series are beginning to integrate the teaching of reading, writing, and spelling in order to emphasize the development of comprehension strategies (rather than the testing of comprehension as explained in this text) and to select stories and informational articles representative of quality literature by award-winning authors of children's literature. The following basal series are examples of such attempts:

The Ginn Reading Program, K-8 (Columbus, OH: Ginn, 1982).
The Houghton Mifflin Reading Program, K-8 (Boston: Houghton Mifflin, 1983).

STRATEGIES FOR GUIDING STUDENT'S LEARNING

Basal reading series are used extensively in reading and language arts classrooms. Each series has teachers' manuals or guidebooks which detail lesson plans. For each story, teachers are given summaries, objectives, lists of materials, vocabulary to be developed, teaching strategies and activities, questions for directing silent and oral reading, specific skills, and enrichment activities. All this seems well and good. But there is evidence that manuals and guidebooks do not help teachers develop the types of strategies that lead to effective, independent readers.

The teachers' manuals and guidebooks of five major basal reading series were examined to identify the procedures used to teach comprehension strategies (Durkin, 1981). An important distinction is made between comprehension tasks that deal with the process of comprehending and those pertaining to the assessment comprehension. The manuals were examined for information and activities provided to teachers for (1) instructional purposes, (2) review purposes, (3) application purposes (transfer of learning), (4) practice purposes, and (5) prereading or preparation purposes.

The results of the study led to these conclusions. First, there are numerous application and practice activities but little explicit instruction in comprehension strategies. Second, when instruction does exist, it does not link those individual skill activities with direct applications to reading. Rather, they seem to exist totally for their own sake. Third, there is little attention to the schemas of writers and what writers do to help or hinder a reader's comprehension. Fourth, there is little assistance to either teachers or students in explaining what it means to answer a question and what strategies are used to answer different types of questions.

Another analysis of the questions contained in some basal series' manuals reveals that the questions are not consistent in their development (Beck & McKeown, 1981). Some of the questions seem to be adequate for developing comprehension, but many others are not. The questions are not central to the comprehension of the story: tangential questions that may deal with the topic but not with the ideas in the specific story; a sequence of questions that violates the natural progression of the story ideas and irrelevant questions that included trivial literal details and pointless inferences.

Our position is that the basal readers themselves are convenient anthologies of stories and informational selections. There may be teacher's manuals and guidebooks for some series which develop instructional activities based on psycholinguistic principles similar to those for the activities presented here, and these activities may be structured in ways that lead students to become independent thinkers and learners. Therefore, as the students' instructional guide, you must assess the appropriateness of the lesson plans in a basal series and when they are found lacking, develop lessons based on the principles and models demonstrated throughout the text. The guided reading lesson is built on the premise that reading material communicates directly to the reader. "It is through pupils' actions upon material and their interaction with each other that sound intellectual reading skills and appropriate emotional dispositions are best acquired" (Stauffer, 1975). The guided lesson is a procedure for use with almost any type of reading material.

Since reading is a thinking activity, the guided reading lesson is in reality a guided thinking lesson. It is adaptable for use as guided-listening lessons as well. Some authorities consider what is here called "guided reading" to be critical reading. All reading, however, is critical thinking.

The three stages of the guided reading-thinking lesson are (1) the act of inquiry, (2) the processing of information, and (3) the validating of answers (Stauffer, 1975). During the lessons, the students and the teacher both have active roles (Burrows et al., 1972).

Pupil Actions
Predicting (setting purposes)
Reading (processing ideas)
Proving (testing answers)

Teacher Actions
Activate thought (What do you think?)
Agitate thought (Why do you think so?)
Require evidence (Prove it!)

The strategies that students learn through use of the guided reading-thinking lesson are (1) examining information, (2) hypothesizing, (3) finding proof, (4) suspending judgment, and (5) making decisions (Stauffer, 1975). These strategies are applied in four steps:

1. Predicting from title and picture clues.
2. Predicting from first-page clues.
3. Predicting from one or more subsequent pages.
4. Predicting from the point just prior to the story climax.

The exact number of lines, paragraphs, or pages that a teacher expects the student to read will vary in accordance with (1) the students' cognitive maturity, (2) the amount of data they are capable of processing, (3) the type of information contained in the story, and (4) the purposes for reading the selection (Burrows et al., 1972).

For example, some teachers may find they have to let the students read the story one paragraph at a time. In such cases the students may have limited experience with making predictions or processing the information. There may be so many concepts in the reading material that they strain the students' memory. However, other teachers may find that the reading material is so familiar that the students can process as a unit the information given on two, three, or more pages.

The guided reading-thinking lesson differs from the typical "directed reading lesson" advocated by many reading authorities and found in many basal readers. One major difference is that the responsibility for establishing a purpose for reading the story is shifted from the teacher to the students. With the teacher's guidance they identify a purpose or set of purposes for reading the story based on what they perceive to be the author's purpose for writing the story.

Another difference is that so-called new words are not presented to the students prior to the reading of the story. Only by meeting unfamiliar words in the natural context of a story can the students use their word recognition strategies. Teachers often have a mistaken notion about how students should be prepared for reading. The teachers selectively present the new and unfamiliar words before the reading of a story and lead a discussion about their meaning and pronunciation. By doing this, the teacher prevents the students from learning through application the purpose of word recognition strategies. Also, what is new to one student may not be new to another. No basal series author, and few classroom teachers, can accurately predict those words that will be unfamiliar to each student. Since the lesson is *guided* by the teacher, whenever a student fails to use word recognition strategies successfully, the teacher and the student together can explore why the word was not understood and how it may be processed in the future.

The Lion and the Mouse

One day a big lion was walking in the woods.
He sat down by a tree, and before long he went to sleep.

Just then a little mouse came by.
The little mouse didn't look where he was going.
He walked right up the lion's back.
He walked right into the lion's ear!

Figure 7-3
Source: Fay, Leo, Ross, Ramon Royal, and La Pray, Margaret, *The Reading Program*, Level 6.

The following two lessons, one constructed on a story from a first grade basal reader and the other from a fourth-grade reader, illustrate the initial preparation a teacher should undertake for a guided reading-thinking lesson.

During the guided reading-thinking lesson the teacher guides the students through the reading of a story to help them reconstruct the author's meaning. The guided reading-thinking lesson is a time when the student can demonstrate their mastery of various reading strategies. When mastery is not evident, the teacher should be prepared to assume the role of guide and assist the students in the process of reading and thinking. The teacher should be alert to signs that the students may not be able to apply their reading-thinking strategies to new situa-

STRATEGIES FOR QUESTIONING   **187**

Figure 7-3 Continued

tions or particular types of material. In the guided reading-thinking lesson the teacher should be aware of both the reading tasks the students are to perform and the significance of the students behavior in the performance of these tasks. The analytic teacher observes their application of various reading strategies during silent and oral readings. Based on these observations, follow-up lessons on specific strategies for making the students independent readers can be planned and implemented.

Analytic teaching is a process whereby the teacher continually adjusts the teaching, learning pace, and methods to meet the students' needs. The guided reading-thinking lesson provides an opportunity for students to be observed and assessed in actual reading situations.

STRATEGIES FOR QUESTIONING

The thought-provoking questions of the guided reading-thinking lesson are only one kind of question that teachers should use to generate the students' thinking strategies. In addition, the teachers should tap different thought processes through the use of questions that require different cognitive operations. (Some may find it useful to review the Guilford structure-of-intellect model described in Chapter 3.)

> One day when the lion was looking for food, he walked into a trap.
> The trap was made of strong rope, and the lion couldn't get out.
> The lion jumped this way and that way.
> He tried and tried.
> All day long, the lion worked to get out of the trap.
> But he couldn't get out.

> When night came, the lion began to cry.
> "Help! Help!" he called.
> "Help me get out of this trap."
>
> Many animals heard the lion.
> They went to look at him.
> But they couldn't help him.
> The little animals were scared of him.
> And the big animals didn't know how to help him.
> "We've never helped a lion before," they said.
> "We don't know what to do."

Figure 7-3 Continued

The following types of questions are suggested (Torrence & Myers, 1972):

1. Recognition Questions—
   a. Multiple choice:
      In the story, Chun Toy was allowed to
      build the boat
      paint the boat
      row the boat
   b. Matching:
      Match the character in the story with a word that describes the person
      Li Lun   ashamed
      Teng Lun   wise
      Sun Ling   afraid
2. Analysis Questions—
   a. Interpretive:
      What did Sun Ling mean when he said: "There are other things than fishing?"
   b. Comparison:
      In what ways was the kitten like the tiger?

> The lion began to cry again, "Won't someone please help me get out of this trap!"
>
> This time the mouse heard the lion. The mouse came up to him.
>
> "Don't cry," said the mouse. "I'll get you out of the trap. One time you let me go. I told you that I would help you someday. Now I can help."

> Then the little mouse sat down and chewed one of the big ropes.
> Then he chewed another rope.
> He chewed and chewed.
> Soon he had chewed all the ropes.
> The lion was free!
>
> "Thank you, little mouse," he said. "You are a good friend. Never again will I say that anyone is too little to help!"

Figure 7-3 Continued

    c. Analysis of series or process:
        How do the animals and insects in the story get ready for winter?
3. Synthesis or Hypothesis Formation Questions—
        Based on how Josie felt about her brother, what might you expect her to do?
4. Convergent Thinking or Redefinition Questions—
        Which of solutions offered by Pierre would be acceptable in our school?
5. Open-ended or Divergent Thinking Questions—
        What are some other ways Chun Toy could have helped his brothers as they worked on the boat?
6. Evaluation Questions—
    a. Judgmental:
        In this story, do you think that the grasshoppers are thieves?
    b. True-false:
        Is the following statement true or false? "Megan's actions in the story were more because of fear than of love."
    c. Provocative or extension of thinking:
        If an earthquake were to hit this school five minutes from now, what things would we do?

> Guided Reading-Thinking Lesson for "The Mouse and the Lion"
>
> Story Theme: No one is too little to help.
>
> Story Plot and Summary: A rather pompous lion catches a mouse. The little creature begs for mercy, appealing to the lion's common sense by pointing out that he, the mouse, would hardly be much of a meal. When the mouse is free, he expresses his gratitude, vowing to help the lion someday. The lion is amused by such a promise and laughs. But it is the mouse who has the last laugh when he rescues the lion from a trap by chewing through the binding ropes (Fay, Ross, & LaPray, 1974).
>
> Guiding Questions:
> 1. Title and picture, first page of story
>   Do you think this is a real story?
>   Does the title give you any idea as to what may happen in the story?
>   What do you think may happen?
> 2. First page
>   What has happened?
>   Do you have any idea from this part of the story as to what may happen next?
> 3. Second and third pages
>   Were any of you correct in what you thought?
>   If the lion was talking, what kind of voice would he have? What about the mouse?
>   What do you now think the rest of the story will be about?
> 4. Fourth page
>   Were any of you right? What do you now think will happen?
>   Do you want to change your ideas about what will happen?
> 5. Fifth, sixth, and seventh pages
>   Why did the author write this story? What message did he want to give you?
>   Why couldn't any other animal help the lion?
>   Were there any words you didn't know and couldn't figure out from the story? What information on the page let you understand the story without knowing what those words were?

Figure 7-4

How teachers use questions has an impact upon how students understand. Not only the type of question asked but also the way that the students' responses are interpreted create impressions of what and how students are learning. In addition to classifying questions by the thinking processes tapped, questions can be classified by (1) the type of answer expected and (2) the relation between the questions and the responses.

> ### Guided Reading-Thinking Lesson for "Miss Esta Maude's Secret"
>
> Story Theme: Outward appearances do not necessarily indicate a person's true interests and personality. Even very staid and quiet people may secretly long for excitement in their lives.
>
> Story Plot and Summary: Esta Maude Hay, a school teacher for twenty years, leads what the townspeople think is a pitifully dull and ordered life. Nobody knows that locked in Miss Esta Maude's barn is a powerful red racing car, with which she tinkers every night. On Friday nights, dressed in helmet and goggles, she speeds down the highway and often meets with adventure. She saves a stray flock of lambs, brings a sleepwalking boy home, and successfully races the stork to the hospital.
>
> Central to the story is the contrast between Miss Esta Maude's outwardly quiet life and her secret love of speed. However, the car is not her only source of happiness. Miss Esta Maude enjoys teaching and likes to help people: the car merely adds a note of excitement and adventure to her life (Fay & Anderson, 1974).
>
> Guiding Questions:
> 1. Title and pictures on first and second pages
>   What do you think this story is about?
>   What kinds of feelings do the pictures give you?
> 2. First and second pages
>   What do you think now?
>   What have you learned about Esta Maude?
>   Are there any clues as to what her secret might be?
>   Are there any words you could not figure out from the story? Was the word important to understanding the story?
> 3. Third and fourth pages
>   Were you right about her secret?
>   What have you learned about Esta Maude?
>   Which description shows the "real" Miss Maude?
>   What type of adventures might she have?
>   Why wouldn't people know who she is while riding in the sports car?
> 4. Fifth, sixth, and seventh pages
>   Do you think people will ever find out about Esta Maude's secret?
>   What might happen if many people started talking about a "stranger in a sports car"?
>   What message did the author want to get across to the reader of this story?

Figure 7-5

The type of answer expected, or the product of the questions, is the particular information that teachers want from their students. The information could be in the form of a concept definition, a generalization, or an application of a rule. In each case, if provided with a different purpose for reading, the students will not accurately produce the product intended. For example, one may read an account of a native American legend about the creation of corn with the focus of attention during reading on applying cause-and-affect relationships. A question directed at specific details or one directed at asking students to compare that legend with a science article about agriculture will require the students to produce information different from that of the original focus. Learning outcomes are going to be related to the goals given to the readers and to the purposes set for their attention or action. The goals may fail because they imprecisely or indirectly define what it is they are to learn (Frase, 1977).

The relation between the questions and the responses deals with the source of the information for the answer. Three sources of information for questions have been identified (Pearson & Johnson, 1978): (1) text explicit, (2) text implicit, and (3) script or schema implicit. Text explicit information is found directly in the passage being read.

For a passage such as

As Paul came into the apartment, Pee Wee flew from its cage and landed on his hand, unbalanced for a moment then righting itself. It opened its beak and gave out a tiny squawk for food.

a *text explicit* question might be "What did Pee Wee do when Paul entered the apartment?" A *text implicit* question deals with information that requires a less obvious answer, but the source is information in the reading passage. Such a question might be "What type of a creature is Pee Wee? To answer script implicit questions, readers need to use information stored in their schemas, or scripts. Such a question might be "What will Paul feed Pee Wee?"

Teachers should be aware of some of the positive and negative features of the above question patterns:

1. Questions that focus on remembering may be of limited value in that (a) no further learning is compelled (b) answering them may be interpreted by the student as either a punishment or a reward, and (c) the information received by the student is only as accurate or complete as that provided by the teacher.

2. Recognition questions are popular and can be used to identify incorrect thinking. However they may foster unstructured guessing.

3. Analysis questions may have limited use if the students do not have enough background information to make interpretations or comparisons. Too many of these questions also may become tedious.

4. Synthesis questions are good in that they can lead students to discover generalizations. But they are limited in that the responsibility lies with the students to select the significant details. Therefore, students may never arrive at a generalization.

5. Convergent thinking questions require that students already know what would be "best" or "acceptable" in a given situation.

6. Open-ended, or divergent thinking, questions provide students with the opportunity to give a number of responses. They may be of limited value for

immature students who may be unable to generate alternatives. Some also may become upset or frustrated by questions that do not have a "right" answer.

7. Evaluation questions are good in that they stimulate rational thinking. They are limited to the degree that (a) students have been given appropriate criteria for forming judgments, (b) they have had experience in decision making, and (c) pupils have the ability to do extended thinking activities (Torrence & Myers, 1972).

8. Questions classified by the type of answer expected and by the relation between the question and answer can result in miscomprehension. The student might not have a schema, or have a naive or incomplete schema, about the topic, and so the scriptually implicit questions will be missed. Sometimes, when students have incomplete schemas, there are "intrusions" from other, also incomplete but related, schemas. The student might then create far-fetched answers that result in a change of meaning. Or the question may not be clearly or precisely stated, and more than one schema or script is appropriate as a source of the answer (Strange, 1980).

Many of these limitiations can be overcome. Over a period of time, a variety of questions can be developed which foster different thinking operations. Not all stories lend themselves to all types of questions; yet a good teacher, when possible, directs students through a variety of questions about a variety of reading materials.

Good instructional questions can be constructed by using the following guidelines. (The answer, of course, to each of the guideline questions should be yes.)

Do the questions tap more than a limited number of thought processes?
Do the questions focus on information significant to the general plot and theme of the story?
Do the questions imply that there is no "right" answer all the time, and do they allow for possible alternative responses?
Do the questions require the students to use a type of thinking for which they are cognitively ready?
Do the questions challenge, but not frustrate, the students so that information is obtained as to how they perform in problem-solving situations?

WRITING AS A STRATEGY FOR COMPREHENSION

In this section we will consider the place of writing in the language experience approach. As writers, students create texts for themselves and for others. Even first-grade students can share their works. In one school, first graders wrote books, stocked the shelves of their class libraries, and then invited their parents, older students, and other members of the school community to use the library and share their books (Powers, 1981).

Writing has a part in guided reading-thinking lessons. In establishing purposes and testing answers, students can use writing as a means for organizing and expressing their ideas. Many teachers and basal series authors assume that guided lessons will be conducted orally, but there is no valid reason why students must "think on their feet" all the time, responding orally to their teacher's questions. Predictions and confirmations of those predictions often take time, and students who are asked to write out their responses have the opportunity to mull over, reexamine, and elaborate on their initial responses and actively interact with the ideas and information of the reading passage.

Comprehension is also facilitated when students create their own questions. Using their teacher's questions as models, students can write questions for other students who are reading the same book or will read it at another time. The interaction among the students as they respond to their peers' probes leads to a greater understanding of the organization and development of the authors' ideas and the purposes and themes of their works. In addition, the students gain greater insight into their own roles as the author's audience.

These ideas about integrating writing activities into the development of reading comprehension are exemplified in an article by Hennings. In it, she concisely describes strategies through which "oral interaction leads into writing and writing in turn helps students build schemata for comprehending textual material they read."

Hennings, Dorothy G., "A Writing Approach to Reading Comprehension—Schema Theory in Action," *Language Arts* 59 (1982): 8-17.

Discussion Questions and Activities

1. Prepare a teacher's resource unit on a particular theme. Be sure the unit contains the age or grade level for which it is intended; the major skills that will be developed, stated in terms of instructional objectives; the period of time the unit will cover; the particular experiences and activities in which the students will be engaged; the school and community resources that are available; and examples of the books, records, and films that will be available for the teacher and students.
2. Present an argument that either supports or refutes the following statement by Idella Lohmann (1968): "The teacher who is unfamiliar with the relationships in language, unfamiliar with concept development, and unfamiliar with ways to assess growth in language might find [the language experience] approach, in total, beyond her [or his] capacity to use."
3. Examine a basal reading series to see (a) how it presents a guided reading activity and (b) what types of questions it suggests for comprehension develop-

ment. Are the lessons and questions constructed according to the guidelines presented in this chapter? Do the criticisms of Durkin (1981) and Beck and McKeown (1981) apply to the series you examined?
4. Select a story from a magazine or book and create two sets of comprehension questions. The first should attempt to tap different thinking processes, and the second should be a combination of questions. If possible, try out these questions with a group of students. How do their responses give you insight into how well they understand the story?

For students who are currently teaching:
5. Select a story and prepare a guided reading-thinking lesson for a group of students. Use the lesson. In what ways did you have to modify your original plans because of the students' responses?
6. Create a language experience lesson and use it with two groups of students of different age and grade levels. How did you have to modify the lesson to meet the cognitive, affective, and instructional needs of each group? How did the groups's language performances differ?

Further Readings

The following three books give detailed instructions on how to use a language experience approach to reading:

Dunne, Hope W., *The Art of Teaching Reading: A Language and Self-Concept Approach* (Columbus, OH: Chas. E. Merrill, 1972).

Hall, Mary Anne, *Teaching Reading as a Language Experience* 3rd ed. (Columbus, OH: Chas. E. Merrill, 1981).

Veatch, Jeannette, et al., *Key Words to Reading: The Language Experience Approach Begins* (Columbus, OH: Chas. E. Merrill, 1973).

For the teacher who desires help in developing activities and techniques for constructing with the students instructional materials as part of thematic units, the following book is recommended:

Calder, Clarence R., Jr., and Eleanor M. Antan, *Techniques and Activities to Stimulate Verbal Learning* (New York: Macmillan, 1970).

The following text provides teachers with a discussion of the rationale for using thematic units as well as explicit instructions for creating series of learning experiences:

Hanna, Lavone A., Gladys L., Potter, and Robert W. Reynolds, *Dynamic Elementary Social Studies: Unit Teaching,* 3rd ed. (New York: Holt, Rinehart and Winston, 1973).

Chapter 8

STRATEGIES FOR RECONSTRUCTING AND CONSTRUCTING MEANING

Focus Questions

1. What is the function of prediction strategies in understanding an author's message?

2. What typical sentence constructions do authors use?

3. How can knowledge of the structures and functions of paragraphs increase one's understanding of an author's message?

4. What are the steps in developing a reading strategy lesson?

5. How does the construction of sentences and paragraphs aid students' reconstruction of authors' messages?

When an author constructs a message, a communication with a reader or group of readers is initiated. The author usually has some intended audience in mind, though, of course, there can never be total assurance that the message will reach the intended audience. The author builds a message using knowledge of

1. The subject area and topic to be discussed.
2. How much the intended audience knows about the subject area and the topic.
3. The style of language in which the message is to be written and the manner in which the ideas are to be organized.
4. The language maturity of the intended audience.

Once the message is formed, the author's meaning lies in strings of words. Whether the message is meaningful to the reader depends on factors residing within the reader. A message is potentially meaningful when the reader's knowledge of the subject area and topic, the reader's language maturity, and the reader's familiarity with language styles are at least equal to the author's.

Traditionally, the process of dealing with an author's message has been called *comprehension,* which is conceived to be a set of skills the reader must possess in order to understand the author. It is traditionally assumed that these comprehension skills can be separately defined, sequentially developed, and generally applied to any and all reading situations (Harker, 1973a).

PEANUTS

NINE IN A ROW! THAT'S A NEW RECORD!

WHAT'S A NEW RECORD, SIR?

THIS IS MY SUMMER READING PROGRAM...

I'VE READ NINE BOOKS IN A ROW WITHOUT UNDERSTANDING ANY OF THEM!

Copyright © 1974 by United Feature Syndicate, Inc.

These skills are usually identified as the abilities to grasp the main idea, understand stated and implied details, follow a sequence of events, make inferences, and understand vocabulary in context. Through the application of these so called skills, the reader is supposed to be able to know what the author is talking about.

However, research on the development of comprehension seems to indicate that the traditional view of comprehension is in error (Harker, 1973a). The research suggests that comprehension is a multidimensional process involving the cognitive processing of language. The traditional comprehension skills do not refer directly to language but, rather, are concerned with how people classify information (Bormuth, 1969b); the skills themselves are just a manifestation of the inner cognitive processing of language (Harker, 1973a). But from a psycholinguistic viewpoint, *"the features of language provide the information upon which the comprehension processes operate"* (Bormuth, 1969b). These features of language are the syntactic and semantic features of language and the linguistic knowledge domain discussed in Chapter 2. They are represented in the psycholinguistic models of reading (Chapter 3) by the selected semantic and syntactic clues of the Goodman model, the semantic and syntactic levels of the Rumelhart model, and the microstructures of the Kintsch model.

The comprehension processes are mental operations that occur while an individual is reading. The so called traditional comprehension skills (getting the main idea, sequence, details, etc.) are really products of the comprehension process. They represent what is produced after comprehension has taken place (Simons, 1971). The traditional skills explanation of comprehension fails (1) to specify those skills unique to reading and those found in general mental processes and (2) to distinguish between the how and the what of something that is comprehended.

Instructional programs, then, are inadequate if reading comprehension skills are considered reading specific and do not treat the ends of comprehension differently from the processes of comprehension.

In this chapter, we will present strategies to help students understand the process by which authors construct messages. By analyzing various sentence, paragraph, and longer passage patterns and by constructing their own messages in sentences, paragraphs, and whole passages, students gain the ability to become independent processors of language and information. (Chapter 10 contains additional ideas about reading and writing expository prose.)

The strategies for reconstructing an author's meaning and for constructing one's own messages presented in this chapter are based on the following:

1. Information is more easily gained when it is learned as a process rather than as a collection of facts.
2. Comprehending involves the cognitive processing of language and language cues.
3. Understanding oral language and oral language cues is preparatory to understanding written language and written language cues.

THE READER RECONSTRUCTS THE AUTHOR'S MESSAGE

The strategies suggested in this chapter are those that a teacher helps develop in students so that they may function as independent readers. We will examine (1) techniques for fostering student's prediction strategies; (2) students' strategies for understanding sentences, paragraphs, and longer pieces; and (3) students' strategies for answering questions that appear in instructional materials. On pages 219-224 is a model for preparing and implementing strategy reading lessons to develop these techniques and strategies.

Writing as a Strategy for Reconstructing Meaning

"Children learning the written form of language ought to be producing it as well as reading it" (Holt & Vacca, 1981). In learning to understand various ways authors construct meaning through a variety of sentence structures, paragraph structures, and longer discourse organizational patterns, no greater insight is gained than in being an author oneself. Having students learn how a text is constructed and relate their own knowledge and experience to building associations, abstractions, and inferences will facilitate the development of their reading comprehension (Linden & Wittrock, 1981). To do this, the teacher can have the students generate summary sentences or paragraphs about stories they have read, produce critical comments about or reviews of the stories, and construct expansions of some character, place, or event in the story. To expand on a character, the students can write what happens to that person either the week before or the week after the story occurs, or write what happens when two characters meet in a different location at a different time.

Specific lessons to develop in the students the ability to create sentences containing the various sentence information or to write the same information in different ways provides them with insight into how ideas can be transmitted in more than one form. You can expand on this by discussing how the ideas might take on a new or different meaning in the transposed form and enhance those insights. For example, the students might try to take a paragraph describing an object and turn it into a dialogue between two people, one teaching the other about the object. The students' aim should be to make the dialogue informative yet natural. Or the emotions and emphasis that is provided by specific words might be rewritten so as to convey the same meaning through graphic cues: bold print, italics, exclamations.

In sum, writing activities which place the students in the position of thinking through the decisions that authors must make allows them to appreciate, as both sender and receiver, the totality of the in-print communicative process. The techniques and strategies discussed in this chapter and based on the structures of language and the reading process explained in Chapters 2 and 3 should be learned by students simultaneously as reading and writing processes.

Prediction Strategies

Often teachers' attempts at encouraging the development of prediction strategies are dismissed as the encouraging of guessing. The negative connotation of the term *guessing* is unfortunate here. To some, the term implies a random attempt to hit upon the correct answer. Yet, guessing is in fact an important strategy that people use constantly throughout their lives. When viewed as a proper activity, it is usually referred to as *hypothesizing* or *predicting*. Individuals who spend much of their lifetime trying to guess the outcome of sporting events rarely refer to their endeavors as guessing; rather, they state that they are making predictions based on the best, currently available information.

In school, students should be encouraged not to guess but to test hypotheses or to predict. Activities should direct the students' attention to the information that language provides so that they can accurately make predictions about the meaning of a particular word in a context or the overall meaning of a story as the author intended it.

Setting Purposes An important aspect of prediction strategies is the setting of purposes. As stated previously, authors have very definite purposes when they write something. On the other hand, many readers undertake reading acts without a purpose of their own. If they do have one, it often is not consistent with the author's purpose. "When students are encouraged, indeed required, to set logical purposes for reading non-fiction and to make predicitions when they are reading fiction, they soon discover that the ideas and sense of form of the author are frequently different from their own" (Cramer, 1970). Thus, it is important for students to make predictions about and set purposes for any reading they undertake.

Predicting requires the use of prior knowledge relevant to the material being read (F. Smith, 1975b). Individual words have many possible meanings out of context so that a reader must have had some experience with the topic and its related vocabulary in order to come up with a meaning consistent with the author's. Often the spelling of a word does not give any clues to how it should be pronounced, and so the reader must already know what the word should be. (More on this subject will be found in Chapter 9.) Since there is a limit to how much visual information the brain can process during reading, the reader must have some prior knowledge so that the author's ideas can be associated with known information and stored more readily in memory. This schema matching is described in Chapter 2.

Simply, the act of making predictions is the act of eliminating unlikely alternatives (F. Smith, 1975b). When considered as such, predicting is not wild guessing but is systematicaly evaluating alternatives and selecting those that seem to match the reader's expectations of the author's meaning. It should be evident, then, that predictions are most difficult and are likely to be incorrect when the reader has had limited experience with the topic and is unfamiliar with or cognitively not ready to process the language and stylistic features used by the author.

There are advantages to having the reader regularly make decisions to accept, modify, or reject assumptions about the author's meaning. The reader will be working at a level of meaning and does not have to worry about loading short-term memory with a great deal of visual and auditory information. It is when teachers stress the "accurate" processing of every visual clue provided by the author that many readers attend to only the surface features of a passage instead of being concerned with the message at its meaning level.

Students can develop prediction strategies just by being encouraged to predict. Some students have an intuitive sense of prediction, but others have learned not to predict. Their instruction has instilled in them a sense that only accuracy should be valued; they withhold any attempt at predictions making for fear of being considered "wrong."

In order to make predictions, students must know what information to select and how to confirm their predictions. In this entire chapter we will discuss some of the types of information students should use in making their predictions. In this section, we will be concerned with a general prediction strategy, that is, one that is used for getting the overall message of the author.

The type of information used for prediction making will differ among students. We know that children at different stages of development differ in how they think and use language. For example, in one research study, third-grade students showed a different cognitive style by selecting a more concrete "best" answer compared with sixth graders who selected a more abstract choice (Lundsteen, 1974a). Therefore, teachers must be aware of the level of thinking that each student is capable of doing.

Self-guided Reading-Thinking Lesson One method for fostering prediction strategies for the general meaning of a story is to use a technique similar to the one described in Chapter 7 for a guided reading-thinking lesson. The involvement

The Eagle and the Boy

One day the Indian boy, Waukewa, was hunting along the mountainside. He saw a young eagle with a broken wing. It was lying at the base of a cliff.

The bird had fallen from its nest high above. It was too young to fly and had fluttered down the cliff. Now it was so badly hurt that it was likely to die.

Figure 8-1
Source: Fay, Leo, Ross, Ramon Royal, and La Pray, Margaret.
The Rand McNally Reading Program, Level 6, Red Rock Ranch.
Copyright 1981 by the Riverside Publishing Company.

level of the teacher makes the difference between a guided lesson and one in which the student develops a sense of creating predictions. When the teachers' actions totally structure the students' actions, the lesson is a guided one. When the teacher places the greater responsibility for selecting information and creating purposeful questions on the students, they are then moving toward becoming independent readers. For example, the introductory sequence of questions for a guided lesson of "The Eagle and The Boy" might be

Title and picture, first page of story—
What do you think the story is about?
Where do you think the story took place?
Have you ever read any other story about a human and an animal?
Based on the title, what do you think the story will be about?

After the students have been guided through a number of stories in which the teacher has used the principles of a guided reading-thinking lesson, they will be ready to begin making their own predictions about a story. The teacher's repetitive use of the guiding questions should have established a pattern for the students to follow. The introductory sequence of questions for a lesson that fosters the student's independent prediction strategies might be

Title and picture, first page of story—
Looking only at the picture and title of the story, what questions can you ask about it?
After reading the first page of the story, what questions can you now ask about the story?
Do you want to change any of the questions you asked before you read the page?

The above sequence of questions illustrates how the responsibility for setting purposes for reading the story can be shifted to the students. The following responses show how students with different levels of thinking and language maturity react:

I bet this story is just like the one I saw on television where the boy helps the eagle and then later when the boy's in trouble, the eagle helps him.

We could probably ask, "What's going to happen between the Indian boy and the eagle?" Usually when a story has two people in the title, the story is about what happens to them. What's going to happen to the Eagle? The eagle probably won't die because they wouldn't have put him in the title if he did. The story's probably about how the Indian and eagle become friends and help each other.

For anyone who knows the story, the above predictions, although produced by students of different maturity levels, are quite accurate. Both students have definite, self-created purposes for reading the story. How well the students are able to predict depends on the pattern of questions the teacher asked in earlier lessons.

Unless confirmation is expected, asking students to make predictions is not effective for developing an understanding of the relationship between reading and thinking. They should be asked whether their predictions were accurate and their responses can be justified. In this way, reading is not just reading and answering questions. It becomes an active, purposeful endeavor. The students are made conscious of reading as an attempt to match the purpose of the reader to that of the author so the latter's message can be understood.

Deletion Procedures A second procedure for developing a sense of prediction is the cloze procedure. We examined in Chapter 5 use of the cloze procedure as a silent reading test. Here we will discuss its use as a means for developing students' prediction strategies.

A cloze passage constructed for teaching differs in two ways from one constructed for testing. First, the systematic deletion is not limited to every fifth word. The cloze procedure can be used to teach first- and second-grade students with as few deletions as every tenth word. In the other grades, passages with deletions over every seventh word can be used.

To introduce your students to the use of cloze, you may want to use this criterion: The words used to fill the slot must make sense and they must be located somewhere in the passage. This first step creates text explicit responses (see Chapter 7, "Strategies for Questioning.") For example:

Huge crowds gathered at the _____ to watch the boat race on the Charles River. The most daring of the spectators climbed high on the bridge cables to see better. To others, this was more interesting to _____ than the boat race.

The second difference is that synonyms are accepted, since the purpose is to foster a sense of anticipating what the author intended. When introducing the procedure, use short passages with a total of about five deleted words. As the students become more adept at predicting, you can use longer passages with more deletions. After the students can independently complete as many items as they can have them discuss the reasons for their choices. This activity is most effective when the students question one another and give reasons for their selections.

When using synonyms, you should not emphasize attaining the "correct" answer but should guide the students with questions like: Does the word keep the meaning that the author wanted?

An analysis of the research on the cloze procedure as an instructional technique found that it is most effective (1) when developing reading comprehension or at least some of the skills involved in the comprehension process; (2) when discussion is focused on clues that signal responses and on the appropriateness of the students' responses; (3) when materials are carefully sequenced according to difficulty, length, or purpose; and (4) when selective deletion systems aimed at particular contextual relationships are used instead of semirandom deletions. The cloze procedure is least effective when developing or improving word knowledge or vocabulary (Jongsma, 1980).

Another procedure for developing students' sense of predicting is somewhat similar to the cloze procedure (Pehrsson, 1975). But unlike the cloze procedure, in which only single words are systematically deleted, this procedure deletes more than one word at a time. Instructional material is prepared by deleting in every other sentence the main verb phrase and all the information following that verb. For example, a prepared passage might look like this:

By now the entire city was awake. Buses _____,
and trucks _____.
Paula had never seen such confusion as this, and she could not understand why everyone rushed so. She _____.
Seeing a number of people coming at her like a herd of stampeding cattle, she jumped into the doorway of the drugstore on the corner.

The materials should be selected from any reading matter appropriate for any independent or instructional level. The passage may be read orally or silently, and the student may be asked to write all responses or tell them to the teacher. The student's responses are then used as the basis for discussing the use of semantic clues in the story.

The instruction associated with this procedure of developing anticipatory thinking involves an examination of three types of information: (1) grammatical acceptability, (2) semantic acceptability, and (3) contextual acceptability. In response to the passage above about Paula, one student replied:

1. Buses jammed the traffic and trucks blew their horns very loud.
2. She yelled at them to stop.

The responses are grammatically acceptable as independent sentences. The first is also semantically and contextually acceptable. The second, though semantically acceptable as a sentence, does alter the context somewhat.

However, the following responses by another student are not contextually appropriate, although they may be grammatically and semantically acceptable:

1. Buses picked up the people and trucks made deliveries.
2. She got on the bus.

In these responses, the student did not relate appropriately to the information in the surrounding sentences. The first answer does not indicate that the buses and trucks were the sources of some of the confusion as the city awoke. The second answer seems to indicate that the student was responding to the prior knowledge that one can board a bus. This response is not acceptable according to the information in this passage.

Practice and instruction in anticipatory thinking should help focus students' attention on acceptable sentence patterns and appropriate meanings.

Inquiry Lesson Another activity that shifts the responsibility for asking questions to the students and away from the teacher is the use of "inquiry lessons" (Olmo, 1975), This activity aims at increasing student involvement in a lesson, thereby decreasing the amount of teacher talk, and increasing the level of the students' thinking from fact stating to problem solving.

An inquiry lesson is devised as follows:

1. The students, who have been randomly divided into four to six groups, are provided with packets containing different material about the same general theme. The material can be in a variety of forms: textual material (books, magazine articles, etc.), pictures, recordings, and graphics.
2. As a group, the students examine, read, and analyze the material in the packet and begin to prepare answers to questions the other students will ask them.
3. In turn, based on the type of information in their folder, the students should begin to develop questions they will ask the other students. (The type of information in each folder is the same; only the particulars differ.)
4. As a group, the students attempt to find a solution to the common problem that ties together the information in all the packets.

In a third- or fourth-grade classroom, the teacher might ask the students the following question: What problems do people who live in desert areas have? Four packets might then be prepared, each of which illustrates the life and problems of people in four desert regions—the Sahara, the Gobi, the Australian desert, and the American Southwest. The folders might contain information about the problems desert dwellers have in getting water, food, shelter, and clothing. For sources the students can use library books, newspaper articles, magazines and children's school newspapers, films, records, maps, encyclopedia articles, and large pictures or study prints.

As the above lesson unfolds, the students are given an opportunity to simultaneously gather information for questions that might be asked of them and to prepare questions to ask other students.

Throughout this activity, which might last from one to five days, the teacher acts as a resource, providing additional information or suggesting where the students might find it on their own, and as an interpreter, clarifying anything that the students do not fully understand.

Strategies for Understanding Textual Material

As students are developing a sense of predicting and confirming, they should work on strategies to reconstruct the author's meaning. These strategies fall into three catagories: (1) sentence-reading strategies, (2) paragraph-reading strategies, and (3) longer selection-reading strategies. A study of language cues will reveal how authors have built their messages. By recognizing, responding to, and creating these signals, students can become independent readers.

To reiterate a point made previously, these strategies do not have the traditional names usually associated with comprehension skills. These strategies should, however, increase students' understanding (as revealed by their "getting the main idea," "following directions," and so forth).

The idea of having students take cues from language structure is not new. What is new in this approach is that the structures are not treated in isolation, but in a manner that allows the students to realize that comprehension is a set of processes operating on specific features of language (Bormuth, 1969a). These specific features are visual presentations of language signals to which the students generally respond in oral language. They can learn to respond correctly to the language signals without having a conscious knowledge of formal grammar and rhetoric (Bormuth, 1969a). Therefore, the study of the language signals can lead students to be able to answer the following questions (Christapherson, 1974) without their knowing the correct grammatical terminology:

Who or *what* caused an event?
Who or *what* was directly affected by the event?
What was used to perform the event?
Where did the event take place?
Who or *what* benefited or suffered from the event?
What was the outcome of the event?
What descriptions and identifications were given about the event?

According to Bormuth (1969a), some of the general signaling systems of which elementary students can develop an awareness are

The meaning of words.
The ways word affixes affect meaning and syntactic function.
The ways deep structures are assigned to sentences.
The ways surface and deep structures of sentences govern word and phrase meanings.
The ways structures are assigned to paragraphs and larger units of discourse and how those structures are used to modify sentences, paragraphs, and section meanings.
The identification of antecendents of pronouns and other referring words.

Identifying what certain words refer to often poses problems for students. For example:

Pronouns
Some spiders are hairy all over. *They* are called wolf spiders.

Deleted nouns
Then the cloth is put into different liquids. *One* cleans the cloth. *Another* makes the cloth stronger.

Proverbials
He was not very smart, but he knew he could not stop. If he were to *do so,* the tiger would eat him up. So he continued.

Synonymous terms
The horse arrived at the barn door just before feeding time. *The building,* however, was locked up.
The pin was set with precious jewels. Each *gem* glistened in the sunlight.

Arithmetic pronouns
As the group approached, Bill could recognize the *three* who had visited him last night—Mr. Watkins, Mr. Stevens, and Mr. Olivera. The latter seemed to be the leader of the group.

Prosentences
When you talk or sing or shout, the air passing between your vocal cords make them vibrate. *This* is what makes the sound of your voice.

The strategies that follow are not hierarchical. Although it may be logical to begin with sentence-reading strategies before dealing with paragraph-reading strategies, there is no need to limit instruction only to sentence reading and writing until all these strategies are mastered. The result would be unnatural. It is rare to find sentences isolated from paragraphs and paragraphs isolated from longer discourse. Thus, the specific strategies in which students receive instruction will depend on their capabilities of processing units of language. The strategies should be learned cyclically rather than hierarchically. The students are alternately exposed to sentence- and paragraph-reading and writing strategies until as they are able to deal with more mature discourse.

Sentence reading strategies   The specific strategies students need in order to understand sentences are

1. Recognizing and using who or what the sentence is about.
   Felice got into the blue truck.
   The animals in the zoo stared back at the children.
2. Recognizing and using what is being done by the who or what of the sentence.
   Raymond *hugged his aunt and uncle.*
   More and more people *are interested in how to protect wild birds and animals.*
3. Recognizing and using the signals for information that indicates where something is or is done. The signals for where information are *under, over, in, on, at, to, between, among, behind, in front of,* and *through.*
   The class had its morning recess *in the school gym.*
   Jocie took careful aim and shot the ball *right through the hoop.*

4. Recognizing and using the signals for information that indicates when something is done or happens. The signals for when information are *before, after, later, while, as, now,* and *then.*
Frank was able to get inside his house *before the thunder and lightning started.*
After breakfast, we all started to clean up the yard.
5. Recognizing and using the signals for information that indicates how something is done. The signals for how information are the adverbial endings *-ly, like,* and *as.*
They walked *quietly* up the steps.
Like safari hunters, the children crept through the weeds stalking their older brothers.
6. Recognizing and using the signals for information that indicates how long or how much something is. The signals for how long and how much information are *for, about, almost, as long (much) as,* and *until* (and any sort of measurement).
The cat sat *for hours* waiting for the canary to leave its cage.
The teacher gave Alice *until Monday* to finish her project.
7. Recognizing and using the signals for information that indicates a condition exists. The signals for condition information are *is, seems,* and *appears.*
Harry *is* the name of my pet cat.
Nobody *seems* happy with my answer!
8. Recognizing and using information that indicates what kind of thing something is. The clues for what kind of information are the possible transforms of the condition sentences.
The *tired* quarterback looked at the clock and wished the game as over. (The quarterback is tired.)
High in the tree sat a *reddish* bird I had not seen before. (The bird is reddish. The bird appears red.)
9. Understanding how some information in a sentence can be moved without changing the meaning of the sentence.
The architect skillfully drew the lines of the house.
Skillfully, the architect drew the lines of the house.
Once in a while we like to bring pizza home for supper.
We like to bring pizza home for supper once in a while.
10. Understanding that different sentences can have practically the same meaning.
Sandra painted the furniture to match the drapes her mother made.
The furniture was painted by Sandra to match the drapes made by her mother.
11. Recognizing and using the signals for information that indicates that the sentence contains information about someone or something. The clues to this extra, descriptive information are *who, which,* and *that.*

Once there was a little gray mouse *who* lived with his mother.
Since everyone *who* wanted to help had arrived, it was now time to think of some way to get the skunk out.
All of a sudden, Jean remembered the cows *that* were waiting to be milked.
The test questions, *which* seemed unanswerable by all the students, covered everything *that* they had learned about the geography of Asia.

12. Recognizing and using the signals for information that indicates that certain information has been replaced. The clues to the replaced information are *I, you, he, she, it, they, we, us, them, their, his, her, your, our, him, this,* and *these.*
    As the young mouse grew, *he* became more curious about the world.
    Aunt Harriet landed the plane on *her* ranch.
    Fran liked to tease *her* cat, but Sally thought it was a silly thing to do.
    "Wait until you see *this*," shouted Randy, running to the other kids with *his* stamp collection.

The teacher should note that *it, this,* and *these* many times do not replace just one word. Often these pronouns replace groups of words or entire ideas.

13. Understanding that words are often left out of a sentence and that the reader has to replace the omitted information mentally. The clue that information has been omitted is that questions beginning with *what* or *did what* can be asked at the point the information was omitted.
    While everybody was eating the hot pancakes, Leslie made some more. (More *what?*)
    When the coach shouted, "Run!" all the players began. (Began doing *what?*)
14. Understanding how different sentences can be connected together, and conversely, how sentences can be separated into other sentences. The signals to understanding the connecting of sentences are a variety of conjunctions that seem to signal four types of relationships:
    a. Joining. The relationship is one of bringing together ideas that are similar. The common signals to joined information are: *and, moreover, furthermore, in addition, too, also.*
    b. Excluding. The relationship is one of discriminating, negating, or rejecting ideas. The common signals are: *not, this ... not this,* and *neither ... nor, but, except.*
    c. Selecting. The relationship is one of taking from a larger category a subset of items. The common signals to selected information are: *one, the other, both, some, part, a few, either ... or,* and the quantitative pronouns.
    d. Implying. The relationship is one of effect/cause, result, necessity, proof, or condition. The common signals are: *if ... then, if not this .. then that, although, though, because, since, so, in order, as, unless, before, where, when, how, why, however, therefore, nevertheless,* and *hence* (Henry, 1974).

In addition to instruction about various sentence strategies, students should receive instruction in recognizing, using, and understanding these strategies as they apply to groups of two or more sentences. Quite often, authors place additional information (of, say, the *when* or *where* type) in a subsequent sentence. Students must be taught to recognize the signals that indicate the additional information and to understand the relationships among the sentences. They need to have opportunities to construct these relationships in their own sentences. In the examples below, additional information, or the referent of replaced information, is in a previous sentence. The signals are in italics.

They all tried to lift the first bar. *But* only Stan Mojeski, Pete Pussick, and a stranger from Johnstown could lift *it*.

Then Pete and Stan and the stranger moved on to the next bar. Pete and Stan each got *her* off the ground, but the stranger from Johnstown had to give up.

So Esther filled the big jug again and hurried home. *Her* mother was awake when *she* got there.

That's what people all over the world do. *They* wear what the people around them wear.

Another young woman from a different tribe in South Africa wears a blanket of wool. *She* folds *it* into a cape around her shoulders.[1]

Paragraph Strategies   Paragraphs are more than just individual sentences that have been grouped together. A paragraph is a set of relationships among the sentences it contains. The teaching of paragraph reading and writing strategies focuses on how paragraphs are structured as well as the function they perform in longer discourse. We will first discuss how to follow the flow of an author's ideas through a paragraph and the various structures authors use in constructing paragraphs.

To understand and to construct paragraphs, students must be able to recognize who or what a paragraph is about. The normal signals for determining who or what a paragraph may be about are repeated and replaced words.

Repeated words are content words found in practically all of the sentences of the paragraph. By noting these words, a reader is able to follow or construct a flow of ideas and determine the agent of the paragraph. It is not too often that paragraphs with the same word or words repeated throughout are found in literature. The following paragraph as been constructed for illustration and would be used only to introduce students to the concept of a paragraph agent.

There are many kinds of storms. Some of the most common storms are rain storms, ice storms, blizzards, and snow storms. Hurricanes are another kind of storm that are known for their strong winds. Another type of wind storm is called a typhoon. Storms of different kinds occur all over the world.

1. These examples and those following in this chapter—except where otherwise noted—are from Fay et al., 1981.

More often, authors use various words to substitute for words that would be repeated throughout a paragraph. The most common category of substitute words is pronouns: *he, she, him, her, his, hers, it, its, their, them, they.* By mentally replacing the substitute word with its referent, students can follow the author's flow of ideas as above.

A dolphin cannot live out of the water. Its whole life is in the ocean. It is born in the ocean. The dolphin's mother teaches it how to stay alive in the ocean. It eats nothing but fish from the ocean.

It is commonly held that all paragraphs have a "main idea." This does not seem, in fact, to be the case (Robinson, 1982). All paragraphs have a topic, but not all paragraphs have a single "main" point. Some paragraphs do. For example, the following paragraph has a main point, or generalization, that is stated in its first sentence.

A dolphin is among the fastest swimmers in the ocean. It can swim faster than the fastest person, and faster than many fish. Often it follows ships. It can keep right up with a ship, swimming and jumping and playing.

However, the following paragraph, while it has a topic, cannot be considered to have a specific "main idea." Rather, it is part of a larger main idea and only serves to add more information in a descriptive form.

Now the monkey knew the name of the older sister too. He waited until they had left the tree, and then he climbed down and went home.

The topic has to do with some action of the monkey, which is part of the larger idea of the monkey employing various schemes to obtain information and pass it on to another animal.

Readers have to realize that authors organize ideas about a topic in various ways. The notion of "main idea" is only one of the major organizational writing patterns an author may use (Robinson, 1982). Readers need to learn the various patterns and the signals that help them to recognize these patterns. The various writing patterns are not unique to one particular level of reading material. They are found at all levels and in all subject areas. The differences that will be found between the same pattern at different levels are in the concepts, sentence patterns, and vocabulary that an author uses. By creating these patterns in their own writing students more fully understand and appreciate an author's task and purpose. There are six main paragraph patterns (Robinson, 1982).

1. *Enumeration.* The enumeration pattern is one of the easiest to recognize. It usually consists of a statement and then a number of other subordinate

statements that list subtopics of the major topic. The common signals of the enumeration pattern are:

one, two, three, etc.
another, more, also
one kind, another kind, etc.

The following paragraphs illustrate an enumeration pattern.

Musical instruments are often played together in an orchestra. There are four main kinds of instruments used: strings, woodwinds, brass, and percussion.

There are many different sounds. There is the sound of the wind rushing through the trees. There is the sound of raindrops hitting against your window. There is the sound of a train whistle, of a door closing, of footsteps, of a cat's meow. There are the sounds of birds singing, of a baseball when it is hit by a bat, of your mother calling you home from playing, of chalk on a chalkboard.

Sometimes the enumeration pattern spans a number of paragraphs. Signals within the title, topic heading, or one of the paragraphs indicate the use of this pattern. In the example below, the story title along with the signals in the first two sentences indicate that the enumeration pattern will be used in succeeding paragraphs.

All Kinds of Spiders, All Kinds of Places

There are many different kinds of spiders. Spiders live in almost every part of the world. They live in dry places. They live in the far north and in the highest places in the world.

Sometimes the enumeration pattern is introduced in a longer selection. The following paragraph introduces the enumeration pattern, and subsequent paragraphs complete the pattern by listing other kinds of horses.

To us, probably the most familiar work animal is the horse. There are many different kinds of horses. One kind is the *draft horse.* It was bred in England and France hundreds of years ago.

2. *Generalization.* The generalization pattern is the closest to what traditionally is referred to as the main idea. In the generalization pattern, authors usually make some broad statement and then provide supporting evidence for this statement. The supporting evidence may be examples, explanation, or reasons. The generalization pattern can be distinguished from the enumeration pattern in that

the generalization is some statement containing an idea or belief. The enumeration pattern indicates only that there are various types or kinds of a particular thing. The generalization can usually stand alone without the supporting ideas, whereas the enumeration statement is incomplete without any additional information.

In the following paragraph, the generalization is found in the first sentence. Notice that the words *for example* can be included after the first sentence to introduce the other sentences.

With his hands the conductor tells the players just what kind of sound he wants. He may want the violins to be the loudest and the timpani to be very soft. Or maybe he wants the trombones to be the loudest with no violins playing at all. Maybe he wants everyone to play softly, or slowly, or as fast as possible.

In the following paragraph, the generalization is found by combining the information found in the first two sentences. The other sentences provide information illustrating the generalization.

Some very small spiders live on flowers and leaves. They change color to look just like the flowers they are sitting on. On red flowers, the spiders are red. On sunflowers, they are yellow. On leaves, they are green.

3. *Comparison and contrast.* In this pattern, two related ideas are compared and/or contrasted. Sometimes the two contrasting ideas are signaled by *but, however, although, yet,* and *even though,* as in the following paragraphs:

Even though burros look sad and sleepy, they are very intelligent animals. People are always surprised at the clever tricks burros think up to get out of working.

Ned thought that his father looked both funny and sad as a clown. The white and red and black pants made his father look funny. So did the bits of red hair stuck on all over his head. But the black rings around his eyes and the big white mouth he painted made the face seem sad.

4. *Sequence.* At first, sequence pattern may seem similar to the enumeration pattern. But, in the sequence pattern the order in which the ideas are presented is more important. In the enumeration pattern, the order of the ideas can be changed without substantially altering the author's intended meaning. There is no way to reorder a sequence pattern without changing the author's meaning. The common signals of a sequence pattern are *first, second, third, last; before, after, while;* and *then, later.*

The following sequence of paragraphs illustrates the sequence pattern:

After the cotton is dried and cleaned at the gin, the workers put the cotton onto trucks, and the trucks take it to cotton mills.

At the cotton mills, the cotton goes through many machines. Some machines clean the cotton. Other machines make it into thread. Other machines make the thread into cloth.

(Notice that the enumeration pattern is also a part of the paragraph development of the second paragraph. These paragraphs were taken from a selection in which the main pattern is sequencing. However, one step in the sequence is further explained by the enumeration of examples.)

5. *Effect/cause.* The effect/cause pattern is really one of implication. One idea is subordinated to another in a relationship to show that it is dependent on that idea. Commonly the effect/cause relationship is signaled by *if ... then.* Other signals also show this pattern: *because, so, in order that, unless, as a result of, since, so that, where,* and *when.*

The following paragraph illustrates an effect/cause pattern. Notice the absence of signal words that forces the reader to supply the relational signals.

Frogs and toads go deep under the water and into the mud. The mud keeps them warm, and they can sleep all winter.

In the following paragraphs, the effects and causes are in separate paragraphs:

Trash and garbage cause other problems. Garbage dumps made fine homes for rats, flies, and other pests. These pests were often the cause of sickness.
So garbage men tried digging deep pits in the ground for the trash and garbage. But trash and garbage sometimes made drinking water bad.
Drinking water comes from the ground. When underground water ran through the trash and garbage pits, the water became bad.

Notice how the first paragraph above contains an effect/cause relationship signaled by *cause.*

6. *Question and answer.* In the question-and-answer pattern, both parts are needed to complete the idea of the author. Too often, either the question or the answer is thought to be the "main idea" of the paragraph.

In the following paragraph, the kind of information needed to answer the question is signaled by the word *why.* The information should be a "reason." In other paragraphs, the type of information required to complete the pattern may be signaled by words such as *how, when, where,* and *what.*

But why doesn't the spider stick to its own web? For one thing, the spider knows which threads are sticky and which threads are not sticky. And the spider has a special oil on its feet. If the spider has to walk on a sticky thread, the oil keeps it from getting caught.

(Notice how the signals "for one thing," and "and" signal that two answers will be enumerated for the question.)

Longer Discourse Rarely does a reader meet individual paragraphs that stand alone. The paragraphs are generally part of a longer discourse. Within these longer selections, the paragraphs serve some function. Each paragraph is not autonomous; rather, each serves to expand, clarify, or change in some way the main concept the author wishes to convey to the reader.

According to Robinson (1982), the reader can follow the flow of an author's ideas in longer discourse when the reader can recognize the following paragraph functions: (1) introductory, (2) explanatory, (3) narrative, (4) descriptive, (5) definitional, (6) transitional, and (7) concluding.

1. *Introductory paragraphs* can begin a whole selection or they can begin a new idea within a selection. The following paragraphs contain common signals that inform the reader that a story is beginning. Some of the signals are figures of speech. Students acquire the ability to recognize these signals through being made aware of them and experiencing them as often as possible in their textbooks and in their own writings.

A long time ago, at the edge of a dark and gloomy forest, there lived an old man and his wife. They were very poor, and their only pleasure lay in eight beautiful children. Even though they loved all eight of their children dearly, their favorite was the youngest, Erendel.

Maybe I should tell you a little bit about Caeser before I begin my story. Caesar was a big, dapple-gray horse. He and I used to work for the fire department. You see, a long time ago the fire wagons were pulled by very big, fast horses.

I had heard a lot about a young dolphin that spent a summer with the people of Opononi. I thought it would make a good story for my newspaper. So I went to Opononi to talk with the people there.

When a paragraph introduces a new idea within a longer selection, it often follows a transitional paragraph. Therefore, the recognition of introductory paragraphs within longer selections is dependent to some degree upon the reader recognizing that the author has changed the flow of his ideas and has introduced another idea or set of ideas.

2. *Explanatory paragraphs* explain, inform, tell about, or provide some factual support to an author's idea. The internal organization of the paragraph may take the form of one of the paragraph patterns discussed earlier. This category encompasses most paragraphs in a long selection. Quite often, the paragraph has a signal that relates it to the ideas in a previous paragraph.

In the following paragraph, the first sentence ties the paragraph to a preceding paragraph and continues the explanation of an idea:

Not too many years ago, it was simple. Garbage men took trash and garbage far outside of town to dump it. The garbage dumps and trash heaps were ugly and smelly. But they were far from town so people did not see them or smell them.

The following paragraph is signaled to be an explanatory one through the use of *the oxen* rather than just *oxen*.

In America, the oxen helped settle the western part of the country. They pulled settlers' large, heavy wagons thousands of miles across the country. In India they pull big, clumsy carts filled with grain. In Portugal they plow the muddy fields in the spring, and they pull carts loaded with wine barrels and other goods.

The word *too* in the first sentence of the next paragraph signals that the paragraph continues to explain an idea introduced elsewhere.

Some kinds of butterflies fly south, too. One kind is a big orange and black butterfly. Every year, on the same day, these butterflies begin their trip. It takes them a long time to get where they are going.

3. *Narrative paragraphs* are usually found in story type selections and are used to advance the story line or explain the actions of a character. The following paragraphs are examples of paragraphs that continue the narration of a story:

Lee ran back through the MAIL ROOM door. She saw another door marked OUT. She pushed the OUT door, but on the other side was a door marked IN. People came and went through both doors.

Mr. Pepperkorn whistled the song all the way to the hospital. He wanted to whistle it there, too. But there were signs everywhere that said QUIET PLEASE. So Mr. Pepperkorn walked quietly up the steps and into Ruthie's room. Then he hugged Ruthie and she hugged him right back. Ruthie loved her grandfather very much. She thought she had the nicest grandfather in the world.

He went on for miles and miles. Sand was getting in his shoes. The hat made his head hot. The trunk was beginning to hurt his back. Even the boxes he had carried for his master had never hurt his back. And he still didn't know what was over yonder. It seemed as far away as ever.

4. *Descriptive paragraphs* describe an event, person, or thing. These paragraphs do not usually advance the story line. They usually provide descriptive information in the explanation of an author's story.

One music box had a golden bird. The bird sat on top of a tree. On another box girls and boys danced up and down. On another, Goldilocks ran around the three bears.

Draft horses have large bones and heavy, strong muscles, especially in the chest and legs. The are usually over five feet tall at the shoulder. They are gentle and patient, and they can work long, hard hours without getting tired.

5. *Definitional paragraphs* provide the meaning of some term used by the author. In narratives, these paragraphs usually do not advance the story line or add information about the authors main concept. They often can be omitted from the selection without breaking the flow of the author's ideas.

The smallest particle of mercuric oxide that you can see is still much larger than the smallest particle of a compound, called a molecule. A molecule is the smallest particle into which a compound can be divided and still have the properties of the compound (Brewer et al., 1972).

6. *Transitional paragraphs* indicate that the author is changing the flow of ideas. Besides signaling a change of ideas, some transitional paragraphs introduce a new idea. The following paragraph makes a transition to a story that has its own introductory paragraph:

Can you guess what happens to a landfill? Here is a story about what one town did with a landfill.

The following paragraph makes a transition and introduces a new idea:

But there are some parts of the world where a horse cannot go. A horse cannot live where the weather is very cold and cannot run through deep snow. So people in very cold countries have found other animals to work for them.

7. *Concluding paragraphs* close the story or the author's ideas. Readers can learn to recognize the various signals that authors use to indicate the conclusion of their selection. The following paragraph has the traditional signals ending a fairy tale:

The enchantment was broken. Erendel and the Prince returned to their palace where they lived happily ever after. And Erendel was always very kind to bears.

The following paragraphs contain signals that the author is concluding a discussion or explanation. One signal that authors often use is to relate to some idea introduced at the beginning of the selection or to give some sort of brief summary or restatement of the important ideas presented in the selection.

And now we begin our long swim up to the top of the ocean. Back we climb toward the sun and sky and trees and people and animals that we know. But we shall never forget, you and I, the wonderful watery world that lies deep within the Atlantic Ocean. And we shall never forget our sea monster, the octopus.

All over the world animals are moving loads for people. In some places machines are doing the jobs animals used to do. But there are some places in the world where machines cannot go.

And some people may never want to use a machine instead of an animal. After all, you can't pet an airplane or milk a tractor or whisper into a truck's ear.

Although the seven paragraph functions enumerated above have been illustrated with isolated paragraphs, the teaching and learning of the paragraph functions should not occur in isolation. Students should be given the opportunity to examine and make generalizations about the various paragraph functions only during the reading and writing of longer selections.

DEVELOPING STRATEGY LEARNING LESSONS

In order for the students to make good predictions about an author's message, they must possess information. One kind of information (that discussed in this chapter) is contained in the various signals to meaning we have in our language. When students can recognize and use these signals, then it is more likely that they can reconstruct an author's message and construct their own. The language signals in sentences and paragraphs can be learned intuitively by the students. However, a much more expedient procedure is for the teacher to teach them.

When a teacher has determined that a student, or group of students, cannot consciously use the language signals to reconstruct an author's message, lessons should be developed to have the students learn strategies for recognizing and using those signals. The lesson below uses five steps to develop a reading strategy: (1) the identification of a situation, (2) an example of the situation, (3) the strategy for recognizing the situation, (4) guided application of the strategy, and (5) independent practice in using of the strategy.

The first four steps in the strategy-learning lesson are under the teacher's direct supervision. The final step allows the student to work out some problems independently and to gain facility in using the strategy.

The identification step establishes the point of the lesson. During this step, the teacher gives the students information about what signals, patterns, or organization the author uses. They are not asked to identify the signal or pattern. (If they could identify it, there would be no point in having them complete the lesson.) The identification step usually ends with a paraphrase of the strategy that will be stated in step 3.

The example step is, again, a teacher directed step in which another instance of the situation is provided for the students. In the lesson below, the example step provides an opportunity to demonstrate a second and third signal. The teacher should decide how many examples will be provided during this step.

The third step, the strategy, is where the students are given the statement of the strategy and all of the signals that are to be learned with the strategy. The signals for the strategy should be placed on poster paper and hung in the room for the students' reference during the guided application and practice portions of the lesson. The poster can remain hanging until the students are completely familiar with the signals and no longer need to refer to it.

In the guided application step, the teacher provides extensive guidance during the first example. Less guidance is provided for the second example, and practically no direct guidance is provided for the last. This procedure—almost a weaning from teacher direction—lets the teacher observe the students in situations of increasing independence. The last part of this step should be identical to the practice step. Therefore, if the students are observed to experience difficulty, the teacher can repeat the first four steps using other sentences. Some students may need more than one "step through" before they are ready to do independent practice.

The sample lesson deals with the strategy for recognizing and using signals for a *cause* and a *result*. The material was prepared for use with students in the fourth grade. The students are provided with a worksheet containing all of the example sentences. Although this exercise could be done by writing the examples on a chalkboard, teachers' experiences have shown certain drawbacks to this practice. First, if the related activities are done on the chalkboard, not all of the students receive a chance to perform all of the tasks. Second, if the students are required to copy the example sentences onto paper at their desks, the task could be tedious for many students and could direct their attention away from the main purpose of the lesson. Therefore, two worksheets are recommended: one containing the examples of steps one to four, and one containing the practice sentences of step five.

(Note: Prior instruction was undertaken to ensure that the student understood the concepts *cause* and *result*.)

I. Identification of Situation

Teacher: In the first sentence, the writer has given two ideas. One is a cause, and one is a result. The sentence has a signal to help you see which idea is the cause and which idea is the result. The signal word, *so*, is circled. *So* tells you that the cause comes first. Going out in the rain without an umbrella caused Sara to get wet. The result is that Sara got wet.

cause
Sara went out into the rain without an umbrella

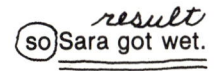

result
(so) Sara got wet.

The signal word *so* tells you that the cause comes first in the sentence. The result comes after *so*.

Writers sometimes use other words to signal cause and result.

II. Example

Teacher: For example, in the next sentence,

result
Mrs. Polansky's class could not go on their

cause
picnic (because) the bus broke down.

the word *because* is circled. It is a signal that the result comes first in the sentence and that the cause comes second. The bus's breakdown was the cause of the class's not going on its picnic. The idea after the word *because* is the cause. Another signal writers use is *as a result of*. In the next sentence,

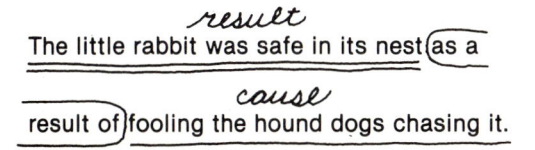

result
The little rabbit was safe in its nest (as a

cause
result of) fooling the hound dogs chasing it.

the cause of the rabbit's being safe was fooling the dogs. The words *as a result of* signal that the idea following them are the cause.

III. Guided Application

Teacher: Look at the next sentence. This sentence has a cause-and-result signal in it.

The dog hid under the bed because it was afraid of the lightning.

Find the cause and result signal and draw a circle around it. *(Pause)* What word did you circle?

   Students: Because.
   Teacher: What does the word *because* signal, a cause or a result?
   Students: A cause.
   Teacher: Draw a line under the words that show the cause. Write the word *cause* above the part of the sentence with the cause in it. *(Pause)* What words did you underline?
   Students: It was afraid of the lightning.
   Teacher: What is in the other part of the sentence?
   Students: The result.
   Teacher: Draw to lines under that part and write the word result over it *(Check students' work.)*

Look at the next sentence. It also has a cause and result. Find the signal word and circle it. Then draw a line under the cause and two lines under the result. Write *cause* and *result* above the correct parts of the sentence. (Pause) Look at the answer. (Write the correct answer on a chalkboard or poster.) Does your answer look like this?

   cause   *result*
   I was hungry (so) I bought two pretzels.

If the students have incorrect answers, discuss their answers to discover why. Some students may need continued guidance, such as was given on the first sentence. Such students may need more than three applications to be able to do the task independently. Others may not understand the concept and may need to repeat the identification and example steps with additional sentences. since the final sentence in the guided application is a test to see whether or not the students can do the task independently, do not move on until you are sure that they understand the concept and the task.)

Teacher: Do the next sentence the same way. (Pause) Does your sentence look like this?

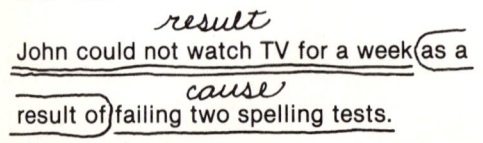

   result
   John could not watch TV for a week (as a
             cause
   result of) failing two spelling tests.

(Discuss any different answers with the students. Then decide which students are ready for the practice and which may need additional guided instruction.)

IV. Practice Sheet

Teacher: Each sentence below has a cause and result. Each sentence also has a signal word that can help you find the cause and the result.

Draw a circle around each signal word. Then draw one line under the cause and two lines under the result. Write *cause* and *result* above the correct part of each sentence.

The coyote was eating the farmer's chickens so the farmer shot it.

My tooth ached because I ate two pieces of candy.

He put water on the flower seeds so they would grow.

Saul had two broken legs as a result of his skiing accident.

Everyone on the street stopped to look because the girl in the window was waving.

Teacher: When you are finished, take the answer sheet and mark your work. After you have marked your work, take your paper to the teacher.

This five-step lesson can be used to teach any of the sentence- and paragraph-reading strategies. Once you are sure that the students understand the concept and can recognize and use the signals, you can prepare lessons that focus on the authors' ideas. For example, the following exercise can be used after the students are able to recognize and use the signals for *cause* and *result*:

Teacher: Read the sentence and answer the question after it.

The pitcher's wild throw went over the second baseman's glove into center field. So Carlos was able to run to third base.

Which of these statements is true?
1. Carlos went to third base because of the pitcher's wild throw.
2. Carlos's run to third base was the cause of the pitcher's wild throw.
3. The pitcher's wild throw was the result of Carlos's run to third base.

Exercises such as the above one do not teach students how to reconstruct an author's ideas. But they do place the students in situations in which the strategy must be used and in which their ability to use the strategy is tested.

An activity which supports the learning of the strategy is to have the students construct sentences using the signals of the strategy. For example, you may have the students combine the following sentences in a way that shows that the first is the result of the second.

1. (result) The dish fell and broke.
2. (cause) Phil ran through the kitchen and bumped into the table.
   Signal: because

After doing this and similar sentence-combining exercises using the different signals for the strategy, the students should create their own sentences.

IMPLEMENTING READING STRATEGIES

A technique for making students aware that authors use plans for organizing their ideas is to provide the pupils with a "map" of the flow of ideas of the author. This map can be duplicated so that it fits alongside the pages of the selection being read. On the map, the various paragraph functions found within the selection are identified. In addition, various paragraph structures may be identified. In this manner, the students gain insight as to how an author constructed a particular piece of reading matter. Most importantly the students may come to see that authors have definite plans for organizing their ideas when they write and that ideas are not just haphazardly or randomly placed on the paper.

The development of the author-idea map can begin as soon as students are reading selections of any length. The maps can be made to fit a typical story type selection or they can be constructed to follow the ideas in informational, nonfiction type selections. To illustrate that this technique can be used with young readers, the following example was taken from material originally prepared for use at the first grade level. Too often, comprehension development is left until after the students have learned "basic word recognition" strategies. It should be obvious after reading this far in the text that understanding must precede the recognition of individual words. That is why the chapter on vocabulary and word recognition strategies follows rather than precedes the chapters on comprehension.

No student is too young to begin understanding the strategies authors use for writing selections. What has to be varied with students differing in cognitive and linguistic maturity is the language the teacher will use for explaining the ideas to the students.

The author-idea maps are constructed by dividing a duplicating master into columns to correspond to the pages of the selection. The idea map is aligned with the page and each column is identified by its corresponding page in the selection. Some selections, such as the one in the example, may need more than one duplicating master. The less mature the reader, the more there is a need to write out complete sentences on the idea map. As the reader gains maturity, sentence fragments, phrases, and single words can be used to identify the author's organization and development of ideas.

The idea map in Figure 8-2 identifies the patterns used by the author. The map does not explain the author's ideas; it merely points out how the author put the ideas together. Whether the students understand the author's ideas can be determined through the guided thinking strategies and the questioning techniques discussed in the previous chapter. Remember, however, that the prime purpose of the strategies discussed in the present chapter is to develop in the students a sense of independence. Therefore, this portion of the reading instruction should emphasize techniques the reader can use to recognize the organizational and writing patterns of the author as a means of locating what it is the author is saying.

Although the story, "The Terrible Lizzards," does not contain paragraphing in the usual sense, typographical features are used to differentiate between ideas. Notice the use of double spacing between certain groups of sentences. Examination of the entire piece reveals that these spacings correspond to paragraphing. All the sentences between such double spacing are intended, it appears, to be read as a unit.

The use of the author-idea map, then, allows teacher and student to identify the various writing patterns used by authors. By recognizing these patterns, students can more easily locate what it is authors wish to communicate about a topic. However, the mere location of an author's ideas does not mean that there will be understanding. Whether students understand these ideas depends on their knowledge of the concepts presented and their understanding of the relationships established between these ideas.

Students' proficiency in reading longer selections can also be aided by developing a sense of story organization. Narrative stories are generally constructed with five main elements:

1. *Characterization.* Every story has a cast of characters. Some are important to the main story line while others play incidental or minor parts. In addition, each character can be identified by some distinguishable, identifying trait.
2. *Plot.* Every story is constructed around some general outline or problem. The plot is the basic framework within which the story unfolds and the characters operate. Quite often the plot takes the form of a problem that provides the impetus for the characters to act. Many stories can be recognized as having similar plot structures; they differ, however, in the characters and specific events.
3. *Events.* The events of the story are the specific, sequential happenings that provide the flow of the story. The events can be recognized as those things the characters do, or as those things that happen to the characters.
4. *Other information.* Stories often contain information that cannot be considered as "an event." This information may take the form of explanations about what or why something is happening or happened. It might also take the form of description. Although this other information may be important to the overall understanding of the story, it does not convey the story action.
5. *Theme.* Most stories have a theme or message. The message relates to one of the moral issues humans face during a lifetime. In the case of expository or informative writing the message is the main thesis of the author. The theme in

> # The Terrible Lizards
>
> ### Long Ago
>
> Dinosaurs were huge animals.
> ❶ They lived a long time before people lived.
>
> They have been gone for a long, long time.

Figure 8-2 A Sample Idea Map
Source: Fay, Leo, Ross, Ramon Royal, and La Pray, Margaret. *The Rand McNally Reading Program,* Level 6, Red Rock Ranch. Copyright 1981 by Riverside Publishing Company.

1. This tells <u>when</u>.

narratives should not be confused with the statement of the plot. A statement such as, "A young girl seeks the help of her brother in finding out what a 'shadow' is only to find out what a 'silhouette' is," states the plot of a story. This story outline could be developed to exemplify various themes, one of which is, "Sometimes it's hard to get answers to your questions."

Thunder Lizard

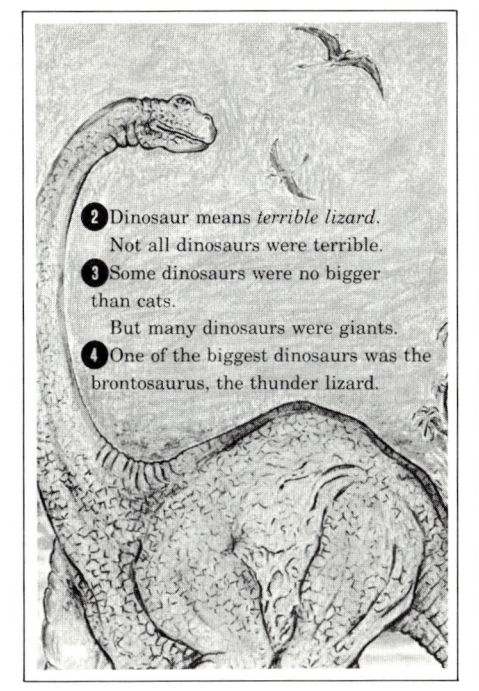

2 Dinosaur means *terrible lizard*.
Not all dinosaurs were terrible.
3 Some dinosaurs were no bigger than cats.
But many dinosaurs were giants.
4 One of the biggest dinosaurs was the brontosaurus, the thunder lizard.

5 Picture a lizard as long as ten cars.
Picture a lizard as big as a house.
Picture a lizard as tall as a giant tree.

That's how big the brontosaurus was.
When the brontosaurus walked, it made a sound like thunder.
That's how it got the name, brontosaurus, which means *thunder lizard*.

Figure 8-2 Continued

2. This gives a meaning.

3. This tells what they were like.

4. This tells what will come next.

5. This describes, or tells about, one kind of dinosaur.

    Students can be introduced to these five elements of a story as soon as they are confronted with their first story, either oral or written. Once students understand these five aspects of stories, they can begin to identify them in the stories they read or hear. Also, they can begin to use the story elements as a basis for reconstructing an author's idea and as a scheme for recalling the story. During lessons, an author-idea map can be used to identify the different aspects of the story.

> **❻** It was hard to be a giant.
> A thunder lizard was so big that it
> could not run.
> It was so big that it had
> a hard time walking.
>
> The brontosaurus was so big that
> it had to eat a lot.
> It ate plants.
> **❼** In the water, there were many plants.
> So the thunder lizard lived
> in the water.
> The brontosaurus needed the water
> for other things, too.
> The water helped hold the big
> lizard up.

> The water helped keep enemies away.
> Some of these enemies were
> meat-eating dinosaurs.
> The meat-eating dinosaurs wouldn't go
> into the water.
>
> **❽** But the thunder lizard had other
> enemies.
> Time was one of them.
> Time changed everything.
> Time changed the land.
> The land changed from hot to cold.
> The land wasn't wet anymore.

Figure 8-2 Continued

6. This tells more about it.

7. There is a cause and result here.

8. This gives a list. What is it a list of?

    Another means for developing pupils' understanding of complete stories is through the use of semantic maps and semantic webs. Semantic maps are created to establish relationships among an event's components (Pearson & Johnson, 1978). When students understand these maps and begin to make their own, they become actively involved in the reconstruction of the authors' messages. Semantic maps are constructed by linking an action with the agent of that action, with the instrument of the action, and so on. These can be reduced to questions such as: What happens? Who causes it to happen? To whom or what does it happen? With what is it done? Where? When? How? These are then linked as additional actions are linked with other agents until a map of the story is formed. Semantic webs organize a story in one of three ways: episodically, inductively (drawing

IMPLEMENTING READING STRATEGIES   229

> **9** When the land changed, the plants changed.
>
> But the brontosaurus did not change.
>
> **10** The brontosaurus couldn't eat the new plants.
>
> It couldn't find food.
>
> And where there was no food, the brontosaurus couldn't live.
>
> After a long, long time, all the thunder lizards were gone.
>
> **11** Today we find these things that the brontosaurus and other dinosaurs left.
>
> **12** Lizards are still around today. Dinosaurs are the great-great-great-granddaddies of these lizards.
>
> But the great-great-great-granddaddies, the terrible lizards, are gone.

Figure 8-2 Continued

9. There are two different ideas here.

10. This information is given in an order.

11. The last sentence tells about the picture.

12. There are two different ideas here.

conclusions), or emotionally (Cleland, 1981). An episodal web organizes the story information according to its actions and events. An inductive web organizes the information by generalizations or conclusions pertaining to the characters and their interactions with other characters. An emotional web organizes the story information by the attitudes, feelings, or impressions of the characters for each other. Figure 8-3 contains a semantic map and a semantic web.

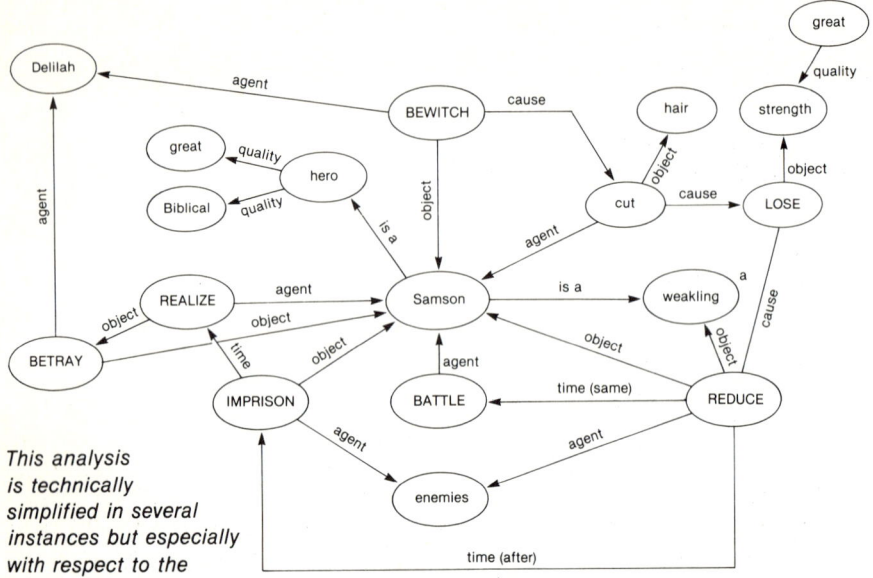

230 CHAPTER 8/RECONSTRUCTING AND CONSTRUCTING MEANING

This analysis is technically simplified in several instances but especially with respect to the treatment of weakling. Even so, the interrelationship of the events in the scenario can be captured without the technical detail.

Source: P. David Pearson and Dale Johnson. *Teaching Reading Comprehension*. New York: Holt, Rinehart and Winston, 1978.

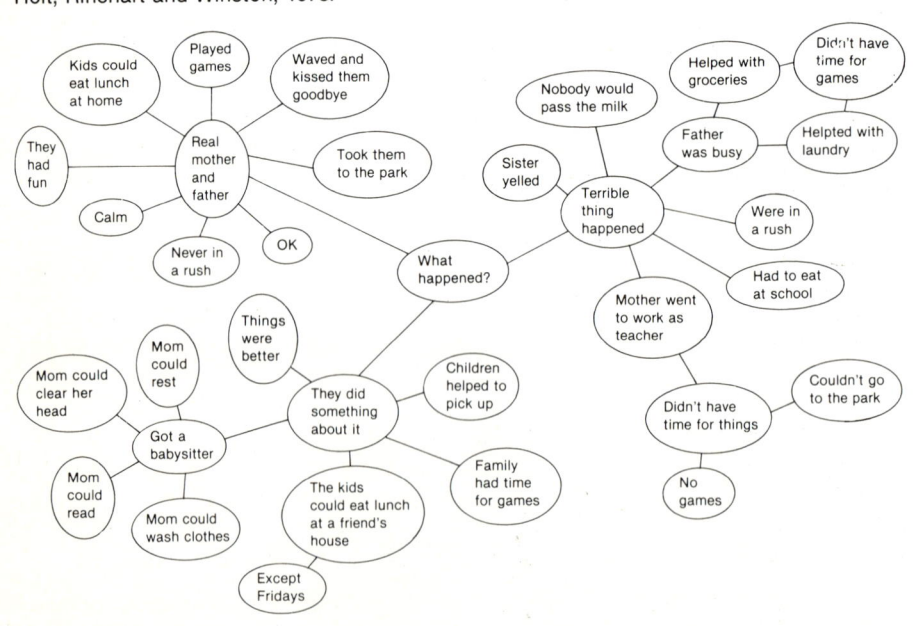

Source: C. J. Cleland, "Highlighting Issues in Children's Literature Through Semantic Webbing," *The Reading Teacher* 34:6 (March 1981).

Figure 8-3 Semantic Maps and Semantic Webs

Activities for Reconstructing Meaning

The following activites illustrate the many types of activites that can be used to improve proficiency in using strategies to reconstruct an author's meaning, and to construct one's own messages. With slight modification, each of the following can become writing activities.

☐ Provide the students with pictures and sentences and have them read the sentences and match them correctly with the appropriate picture. This task can be made more difficult by using pictures that have similar scenes or activities. Only by using the information in the sentences can the students distinguish among the pictures. The length and complexity of the identifying sentences can be adjusted to meet the students' reading and language maturity.

This activity can be used with paragraphs. Instead of limiting the paragraphs to descriptions of the pictures, paragraphs can be written or selected from other sources that relate to, but do not fully describe, the information in the picture. For example, a series of pictures may be used that shows a scientist in a laboratory, someone preparing a meal, and a mechanic working on a car. The paragraphs could be a recipe, steps in an experiment, and directions for repairing a flat. Or, using the generalization paragraph organization: a reason for safety in the laboratory, the need for cleanliness in the kitchen, and an appeal for wearing safety clothes while using tools.

☐ Provide the students with opportunities to read the directions of real situations. Many students do not have the opportunity to play certain games at home. They can learn to play these games by reading the directions. Other sources for learning to read and follow directions are in the constructing of model planes or cars, and the learning of card games. Many books exist which explain card games of varying complexities for various ages. The reading of directions such as these should not be considered as a frivolous activity. Board games and card games provide many of us with enjoyable, challenging recreational activities. Model building is not an activity engaged in by the young alone. Many adults have as their hobby the building of model railroad cars and the constructing of model aircraft. Since the formats of the directions are generally the same within each of the three categories mentioned, students can begin to learn about them and acquire the necessary vocabulary as part of their school learning.

☐ Provide students with sentences that contain the same words but different punctuation. The students read the sentences orally using the correct intonation to convey the intended meaning. For example, one group of sentences might be:

"Frank," said Marty, "Let Jimmy do it!"
Frank said, "Marty, let Jimmy do it?"

Or, let the students read sentences such as the following to show, through different intonations, what may be the meaning of the sentence.

I like boxing bears.
He can't imagine flying fish.

☐ Provide the students with an opportunity to expand basic sentence patterns through the addition of different information. For example, information such as *where, when, how,* and *why* can be added to:

The puppy cried.
The teacher gave everyone a book.

Another activity is to give the students sentences with one type of information omitted. They have to complete the sentence with the appropriate type of information.

The cat sat_____watching the birds at the bird feeder.
         (where)
_____gave me a new pen for my birthday.
 (who)

This activity can be extended to paragraphs. A paragraph is constructed in which different types of information are omitted. The teacher, or another student, asks for the information. The first student supplies answers without knowing the story. After the students' answers have been added to the paragraph, the paragraph is read in its entirety.

☐ Provide the students with sentences in which some information has been moved to other parts of the sentence. They are to determine whether the meaning has been changed by the shift of information. *Ask the students to justify their decisions.* For example:

The cow ate the apples behind the barn.
The cow behind the barn ate the apples.
Behind the barn, the cow ate the apples.

Slowly, Jaye opened her eyes and got out of bed.
Jaye slowly opened her eyes and got out of bed.
Jaye opened her eyes slowly and got out of bed.
Jaye opened her eyes and slowly got out of bed.
Jaye opened her eyes and got out of bed slowly.

☐ Provide the students with a sentence and have them select from a group of other sentences which of the sentences indicate accurate information about the sentences. For example:

Atri is a very old town and is built halfway up the side of a steep hill.
1. Atri is a very old town.
2. Atri is the side of a steep hill.
3. The hill is built on the old town.
4. Atri is built half-way up the side of a steep hill.

> One hot afternoon when no one was on the street, the old horse chanced to wander into the marketplace. He saw the grapevine rope that hung from the bell of justice.

1. He saw the bell of justice.
2. He hung the rope on the bell of justice.
3. The grapevine rope hung from the bell of justice.
4. He hung the bell of justice.
5. He saw the rope hanging from the bell.

The complexity of the sentences—that is, the number and types of transformations that the sentences have undergone—should fit the students' language and reading maturity. *Always discuss with the students why they selected the answers they did.*

☐ Provide the students with a basic sentence and other information that should be added to it (Peltz, 1975). Have them place the information in different places and then discuss with them any changes this makes in the meaning of the original sentence. For example:

Mother planted five new rosebushes in the garden.

Add *only*. Some possible constructions:

Only Mother planted five new rosebushes in the garden.
Mother only planted five new rosebushes in the garden.
Mother planted only five new rosebushes in the garden.
Mother planted five new rosebushes only in the garden.
Mother planted five new rosebushes in the garden only.

Or again,

My brother plays with the toy duck.

Add *in the bathtub*. Some possible constructions:

In the bathtub, my brother plays with the toy duck.
My brother in the bathtub plays with the toy duck.
My brother plays in the bathtub with the toy duck.
My brother plays with the toy duck in the bathtub.

□ Provide the students with cut-up sentences. First, type the sentence on construction paper or oaktag. Then cut up the sentences into word groups or individual words. Have the students arrange the parts of the sentence to make a logical statement. For example, the sentence parts could be

the	we	check	landlord
rent	the	for	the gave

in the race	this Saturday
will be running	Harold

This can be extended by typing out the sentences of a paragraph and giving the students clues to what type of paragraph organization they should construct from the sentences.

□ Provide the students with a variety of puns, jokes, and riddles. Examine cartoons and comic strips to identify how meanings are conveyed through dialectal writing and typographical features. Have the students explain what in the joke or cartoon creates the humorous situation. What creates the humor in the following?

Why is the letter *f* like Paris?
(Because it is the *capital* of *France*.)

Discuss what a reader must know before a joke, pun, or riddle seems humorous.

□ Provide the students with domino type cards. On the cards write the words *who, what, when, where,* or *how* or words that provide similar information. Sample dominoes are

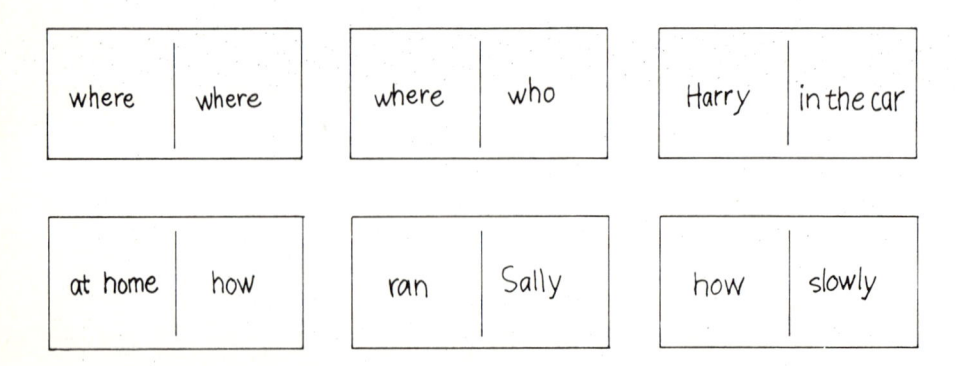

where	where		where	who		Harry	in the car

at home	how		ran	Sally		how	slowly

□ The game is played following typical domino rules. For example, a domino with *where* and *where* can be matched at either end to a domino with *where* or one with *at home*. A domino with *Harry* and *in the car* can be matched at one end to a domino with *Sally* or *who* and at the other end to a domino with *where* or *at home*.

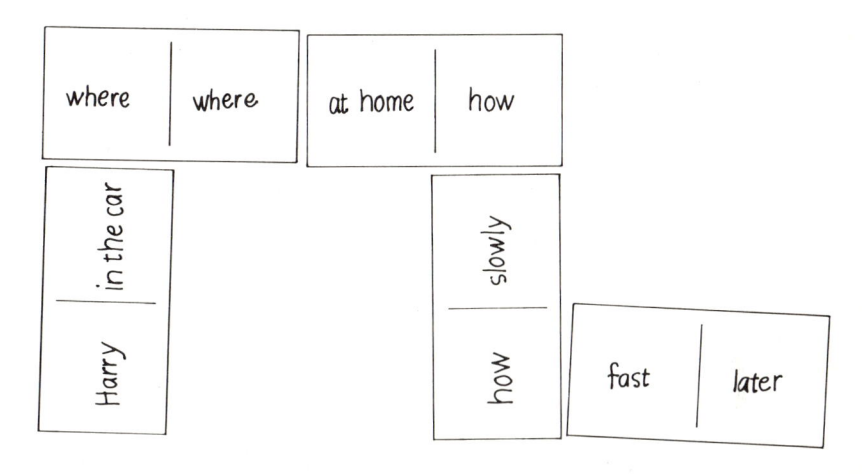

where	where		at home	how			
Harry	in the car		how	slowly		fast	later

☐ Provide the students with a story that has many simultaneous or overlapping actions. Have them identify the signals for actions using *as soon as, meanwhile, at the same time, while* and the like. On a time line, have them map out the time relationship among the various events.

☐ Provide the students with sentences or short paragraphs that describe a situation. They must act out the situation as it appears on the paper, and other students must determine what is being enacted.

☐ Provide the students with a story that has accompanying illustrations. Have them decide which sentences in the story relate specifically to the pictures and whether the pictures provide the information needed for understanding the story that is not provided in any of the sentences or paragraphs.

Resources for the Teacher

The following resources were selected because they contain exercises that relate specifically to the strategies discussed in this chapter. Many basal reading series contain lessons and exercises that correspond to the reading strategies for reconstructing meaning previously discussed. However, the following were selected because they have easily identifiable components relating to one or more strategies. The exercises in these components often are at varying levels of difficulty or maturity.

Teachers should not expect these materials to teach, but they are excellent sources of examples for teachers to use in a lesson. As with all instructional materials, teachers should select only those that are appropriate for the age, language development and reading maturity of their students.

CROFT Skillpacks: Reading Comprehension (Old Greenwich, CT: Croft).

Separate skillpacks, primary and intermediate, offer classroom practice in selecting details, translating details, identifying signal words, selecting the main idea, determining implied details, identifying organizational patterns, and inferring the main idea.

Specific Skill Series (Baldwin, NY: Barnell Loft).
Supportive Reading Skills (Baldwin, NY: Dexter and Westbrook).

Two series have multileveled sets of booklets of exercises in several areas. Titles in the *Specific Skill Series* that complement the strategies in this chapter are Detecting the Sequence, "Using the Context," "Drawing Conclusions," "Getting the Main Idea," "Following Directions," and "Cloze Connections." Appropriate titles in the *Supportive Reading Skills* series are "Understanding Word Groups" and "Understanding Questions."

New Practice Readers. 2nd ed. New York: Webster Division/McGraw-Hill
Reading for Concepts. 2nd ed. New York: Webster Division/McGraw-Hill, 1970).

These multileveled series contain stories about many topics. Each story is followed by a series of questions that require a different type of thinking strategy.

The Thinking Lab Series: Junior Thinking Lab, grades 2-4; *Think Lab,* grades 3-adult; *Think Lab 2,* grades 5-adult (Chicago: Science Research Associates [SRA]).

This series contains activity cards, puzzles, and worksheets to develop creativity and reasoning abilities.

The Thinking Skills Development Program: Primary Thinking Box, grades K-3; *Thinking Box I,* grades 3-5; *Thinking Box II,* grades 6-9 (Westchester, IL: Benefic Press).

This program consists of activity cards, filmstrips, and cassettes. The activities are structured around various thinking operations and draw their content from a variety of subject areas.

Reading, Thinking, and Reasoning Skills Program, grades 1-8 (Austin, TX: Steck Vaughn).

This is a series of fourteen books containing various categories of thinking strategies: categorizing, analogies, sequencing, implying, judging, synthesis, evaluating, comparing and contrasting, and restructuring.

Strategies for Reading: Sentences; Words in context; Paragraphs; Longer Selections, grades 6-8 (Boston: Allyn & Bacon).

These are four books for developing comprehension strategies similar to those presented in this text. Each lesson is constructed according to the format for developing strategies for learning lessons suggested in this chapter.

The Specific Skillbooster Series, grades 2-6 (Cleveland: Modern Curriculum Press.
This series of books is divided into six areas: following directions, increasing comprehension, organizing information, building word power, working with facts and details, and using references.

Spectrum of Skills: Reading Comprehension Booklets, grades 4-8 (New York: Macmillan).
This is a set of multileveled booklets intended for the intermediate and upper elementary grades.

Activity Cards, grade 2-6; and *Basic Skills Activities Cards,* grades K-3 Palos Verde, CA: Frank Schaffer Publications).
These are sets of index-size activity cards that require the students to read, solve problems and riddles, create things, work out relationships, and use their imagination.

TODAY Reading Comprehension Tactics, Cloze Power, grades 3-8 (Huntington Station, NY: Instructional/Communications Technology).
These three workbooks that provide students with instruction in how to make predictions for the completion of cloze procedure (maze technique) in informational passages.

Thinking Skills (Pacific Grove, CA: Midwest Publishing).
These are several books dealing with critical thinking, analogies, puzzles, logic in easy steps, and inductive thinking.

SRA Schoolhouse: Comprehension Patterns (Chicago: Science Research Associates).
This kit contains multileveled exercises to help determine the meaning of words, sentences, and paragraphs. The exercises, on individual activity cards arranged in units, provide practice with a variety of sentence and paragraph patterns.

The following is a text containing sample lessons that are models for many of the strategies highlighted throughout this chapter. It is a practical book in which the authors present sample lessons and also explain why and how they work.

Goodman, Yetta M., Carolyn Burke, and Barry Sherman, *Reading Strategies: Focus on Comprehension* (New York: Holt, Rinehart & Winston, 1980).

The following monograph provides specific examples of ways to implement lessons with semantic mapping and webbing:

Buckley, Marilyn H. and Owen Boyle *Mapping the Writing Journey* (Berkeley, CA: University of California, Bay Area Writing Project, 1981).

Discussion Questions and Activities

1. Rewrite the following statement by Ronald E. Johnson (1975) so that it would be understandable to a group of teachers who do not understand psycholinguistic principles:

   Whether a concept is meaningful thus depends upon the associational background of the learner and also the semantic structure of the concept within the linguistic community.

2. The following statement by Frank Smith (1971) has implications for teachers whenever they give students reading or writing assignments. Does Smith mean that students should never be asked questions?

   The more a reader expects to be asked questions on what he reads the more he will rely on visual information, and the more difficult will reading become.

3. Construct a series of lessons to demonstrate to a group of students the following principle as stated by John W. Miller (1974):

   Certain words place restrictions on the meaningful occurrence of other words within a sentence.

4. Select a story appropriate for primary-grade children. Construct an author-idea map that
   a. Identifies the main characters of the story.
   b. Shows the flow of the main events of the story.
   c. Identifies information that is important to the story but that does not carry the main action.
   d. Points out where the theme or moral of the story is stated (or implied).
   Use the map as the basis for a lesson in which the students are to recall the story's major information.

5. Select two stories—one appropriate for primary-grade children and the other appropriate for upper-grade students,—and analyze the sentence and paragraph patterns used in each. How do they differ in construction? Use the patterns that occur most frequently as the basis for as an informal test to determine whether the pupils can recognize and understand those structures.

6. Review current reading instructional materials to determine whether their authors would agree with the following statement by W. John Harker (1973b).

   Comprehension results from a dynamic cognitive process and not from the rigid application of a set of predetermined skills.

7. Select some current and popular reading instruction materials. From them select sentences that show description, attitude, or mood. Devise a lesson using those sentences to develop the concept that sentences do not necessarily show action.
8. Create different deletion procedure exercises from the same passage for the following purposes:
   a. To improve predicting and confirming.
   b. To understand a particular syntactic structure of English.

Further Readings

For those who feel the need to obtain additional information about the construction of English sentences, the following two small books present this idea clearly and concisely:

Waddell, Marie L., Robert M. Esch, and Roberta R. Walker, *The Art of Styling Sentences: 20 Patterns to Success* (Woodbury, NY: Barron's Educational Series, 1972).

Elgin, Suzette Haden, *A Primer of Transformational Grammar for Rank Beginners* (Urbana, IL: National Council of Teachers of English, 1975).

The following monograph contains an explanation of the general nature of syntactic complexity and some questions about the nature of the readiability of materials:

Dawkins, John, *Syntax and Readability* (Neward, DE: International Reading Association, 1975).

In order to better understand the structure and function of paragraphs, teacher might find it helpful to consult references on rhetoric and style.

Teachers often want to improve their own reading procedures. One popular book that does not follow the traditional "how-to-do-it" format is the following:

Adler, Morimer J., and Charles Van Doren, *How to Read a Book: The Classic Guide to Intelligent Reading* (New York: Simon & Schuster, 1972).

Many of our ideas about teaching paragraph structures were drawn from the following text. Although it is written primarily with examples from high school materials, elementary teachers also can use it to learn how authors construct textual materials at all levels from reading the book in its entirety. It is one of the few books that provide specific techniques for strategy lessons on the structures of English.

Robinson, H. Alan *Teaching Reading, Writing and Study Strategies: The Content Areas* 3rd ed. (Boston: Allyn & Bacon, 1982).

Chapter 9

STRATEGIES FOR DEVELOPMENT AND WORD RECOGNITION

Focus Questions

1. How can students' knowledge of concepts and words be developed and extended?

2. How can students use context as an aid to word recognition?

3. What strategies should students have for recognizing an unfamiliar word in print?

4. How should students use dictionaries?

Our discussion of vocabulary development and word recognition is purposely placed after our discussion of recovering an author's meaning. Psycholinguistic investigations suggest that individual word recognition occurs after the reader understands the author's message. Meaning is not derived from the synthesis of identified and understood words. Rather, psycholinguists have discovered that the opposite is true, that the sentence supplies the context for determining the meaning of the words.

Our examination in this chapter is based on the assumption that students come to school with a basic speaking and listening vocabulary. In previous chapters we demonstrated that a student's vocabulary, no matter how limited, can form the basis for literacy through a language experience approach. Strategies for understanding can then be developed for all levels of language maturity.

This chapter will present ideas for (1) extending students' word knowledge, (2) developing students' strategies for determining the meanings of unknown words in context, (3) teaching students' to use graphophonological information with sentence and other meaning signals for recognizing and writing words, and (4) developing students' strategies for using the dictionary.

One clarification should be made first. The term *word recognition* is used vaguely in the professional literature. In fact, it is used interchangeably with at least five other terms: decoding, word perception, word identification, word analysis, and word attack. In this text, *word recognition* indicates the processes by which a reader realizes what word an author has used and the meaning intended for it. A word is recognized in various ways: the reader already knows the word; the reader surmises what word is intended because the general meaning of the passage is understood; the reader translates an unknown graphic form into a recognizable oral form; or the reader relies on some other source—for example, a dictionary.

STRATEGIES FOR DEVELOPING AND EXTENDING WORD KNOWLEDGE

Every child comes to school with a listening vocabulary and a speaking vocabulary. As the child becomes educated two other vocabularies are acquired—a reading vocabulary and a writing vocabulary. For most people, the listening vocabulary is usually the largest because it has been developing for the longest time. The size of one's listening and speaking vocabularies when entering school is in large part determined by the individual's prior language environment. The more restricted one's language background is, the less extensive one's vocabulary and language patterns will be. All students, however, are capable of increasing their vocabularies by acquiring new concepts and their labels or additional labels for already known concepts.

A significant factor for developing and extending students' vocabularies seems to be the excitement about words that a teacher can generate. An extensive review of research on the teaching of vocabulary (Manzo & Sherk, 1971) revealed that many different activities can successfully lead to increased vocabularies; yet unless the teachers demonstrated enthusiasm for words and were able to transfer this excitement to their students, no instructional activity was any better than any other. Assuming that the teacher can convey this positive attitude, the following are features of a successful vocabulary development program:

1. The teacher's attitude toward vocabulary development is contagious and is rapidly acquired by the students.
2. The program provides continued and systematic attention to words and word acquisition.
3. Almost any technique that draws attention to word parts and/or word meanings can positively influence word acquisition.
4. A gamelike atmosphere, which fosters incidental learning, can often be a major source of vocabulary stimulation.
5. The teacher should guide the development of contextual awareness, dictionary strategies, word derivations, and structural elements.
6. Words are encountered in many different contexts.
7. The study of a few words in depth results in greater usage than does exposure to a large number of words.
8. Although it may be possible, it is not practical to teach words that are not part of the student's verbal community.

Increasing General Vocabularies

Too often, vocabulary development procedures encourage students to memorize lists of words. Learning individual words is no help unless the concept for the word is also learned. Vocabulary development, then, should be concerned with teaching and learning a variety of conceptual relationships (Williamson, 1974). The student must be able to recognize (1) members of the concept, (2) what is not a member of the concept, (3) unique characteristics that place members in a concept, (4) the range of sizes of members in a concept, (5) an act or activity peculiar to members of the concept, (6) the effect one concept has on another, (7) the cause-and-effect relationship between two or more concepts, and (8) what members of a concept depend on for continued existence. For example, developing the concept *mammal* through an exploration of these relationships will result in greater understanding by the students than if they are required merely to learn the label and memorize a definition. Some concepts, of course, such as *possessing aspects of a color* (bluish, greenish) do not require exploration in all of the above relationships.

Vocabularies can be developed and extended through the systematic study of semantics (Burns & Broman, 1983). Throughout the school year, meanings should be identified and used as follows:

1. *Understanding symbols:* Symbols may be nonlinguistic: expressive gestures, traffic lights, road signs, flags, emblems. Language itself is a symbol, along with its derivatives: shorthand, Morse and other codes, Braille alphabets, mathematical symbols, and so on.

2. *Understanding referents:* A *referent* is something that refers or is referred to. For communication to occur, there must be an agreed-upon meaning for the referent—an accepted meaning for both the sender and receiver. It is at this point that much of the confusion of communication can be traced, particularly of multireferent words. For example, what different meanings might *run* have for a baseball player, a stocking salesperson, a playwright? Understanding a referent often requires drawing meaning from the context—verbal, social, emotional, or historical.

In addition to these problems, there are terms without tangible means of referential support: *generosity, patriotism, truth, happiness, goodness, democracy, justice, cooperation.* What such a term means will depend on who uses the word, what this person values, his or her purpose for using the word, and his or her definition of the word. When a writer or speaker uses such terms, it is necessary to pause and think: "Here is a word worth examining. What does this person mean? Is it used to stir emotion or express opinion? Does the word mean to him or her what it seems to mean to me? Do I really understand what this person is saying?"

3. *Understanding the denotative meaning of a word:* This appears to be a fairly straightforward concept, but dictionaries are not published frequently enough

to keep up with all the new words (or new meanings of words)—particularly technical words—nor do they generally contain slang expressions.

4. *Understanding the connotative meaning of a word: connotation* refers to suggested or implied meaning associated with a word apart from the thing it explicitly names. This is one of the more difficult aspects of understanding words, for there are so many words that have multiple and/or changing connotations. For example, a generation or so ago the word *square* carried the connotation of true, honest, and forthright when used in describing a person; today, the same word is used to describe a person who is socially inept and out of touch.

5. *Understanding euphemisms:* A *euphemism* is the substitution of an agreeable expression for one that may offend or be unpleasant: for example, *mortician* for *undertaker*. The word *plump* is less offensive than *fat,* and *slender* is more pleasing than *skinny*. Euphemisms require constant updating, as they occur in usage long before they appear in dictionaries.

6. *Understanding functional shift: Functional shift* requires an understanding not only of connotative shifts but also of shifts in parts of speech, like a change from a verb to a noun; for example: *They* walk *to the bus stand each day* or *Joe went for a* walk.

7. *Understanding the purposes of slang and various groups who use slang:* An activity in this area could be compiling the slang words and expressions used by class members and defining the slang words in standard language. Then the class could discuss who uses these expressions, when they are appropriate, and special slang used by different groups—ethnic, geographical, age, occupational.

8. *Understanding technical language:* Technical terms are important, for people are increasingly exposed to technical fields such as space, medicine, and ecology.

9. *Understanding all forms of affective language:* Social adjustment and consumer wisdom are vital to everyone, as they affect every aspect of life. It is important to realize that every form of communication contains a bias because the sender is expressing the concept from one subjective viewpoint and the receiver is accepting it from another subjective viewpoint. When the two viewpoints are not clearly understood, confusion and/or propagandizing results. Children should know that catchwords and slogans, such as *brotherhood of man,* and *good citizen,* can produce stock reactions.[1]

Developing General Vocabularies

For students to acquire new words—new concepts and labels and new labels for already known concepts—they must be actively involved intellectually, emotionally, and physically (Donlan, 1975). This means that hearing a word or being given a word and its meaning or finding the meaning of a word in a dictionary may not result in actual vocabulary growth. Students should be totally involved

---

1. From Burns, Paul C., and Betty L. Broman, *The Language Arts in Childhood Education,* 5th ed. (Boston: Houghton Mifflin, 1983).

so that the new words and concepts will be assimilated. Once learned, these words will remain part of the student throughout life.

In general, the factors that seem to affect the acquisition of new vocabulary items are utility, application, and memory load (Bruland, 1974). Without some purpose for using new words, students will discard them in a shorter time than it took to learn them. They should be able to use new vocabulary in their daily lives, both in and out of school. Without some opportunity to use the new words, the students will forget them. Once words are learned, there should be planned times for them to practice the words as part of their daily assignments. If too many words are studied at any one time, however, only a few of them will be learned.

Activities for Developing General Vocabularies

In order to develop and extend students' vocabularies, teachers should

☐ Develop action-packed vocabularies (Toothaker, 1974). Over an extended period of time, words that suggest actions, conduct, motions, responses, or behavior can be introduced. The advantage of this approach is that it promotes physical experiences. Two categories of words can be used:

Muscular action words are included in classifications such as traveling, driving reactions, motion with object in front (behind), contracting, facial, eating, rubbing, upward (downward), leaping, to and fro, circular, irregular, fast (slow), exertion.

Mental action words are included in classifications such as memorization, language response, dramatic, musical, artistic, social, creative, mathematical, scientific and analytical, discriminatory.

The difference between the two classifications is that the first pertains to those actions that are more automatic or habitual than the actions in the second.

☐ Provide ample opportunities for new and interesting experiences. New concepts and words can be introduced during field trips, movies, classroom demonstrations, classroom visitors, and seasons and holidays.

☐ Provide opportunities for different social experiences. Use situations in which the students have limited experiences, such as using the telephone to seek information or order something, seeking advice or help from an adult not well known, reporting emergencies to the police or fire departments, or visiting the home of a new friend who belongs to a different ethnic or cultural group.

The activity can be extended to cover other topics such as developing a sense of social responsibility. Role playing provides controlled opportunities for students to practice various roles: givers of orders or information, receivers of orders or information, questioners, mediators. In each situation there is the need for a careful examination of words that increase rather than hinder communication.

☐ Develop an interest in the natural environment. There is an almost universal concern with conserving resources and lessening pollution. The outdoors allows many opportunities for physical as well as emotional involvement as students learn to appreciate the beauty of nature. When it is not feasible to explore natural environments, articles or specimens can be brought to the classroom and set up in "hands-on" exhibits.

☐ Encourage the study of a hobby. Displays of the work of students or teachers who already have hobbies can stimulate many students to undertake one of their own. Even though some may never have hobbies of their own, they can develop an appreciation of others' hobbies. These activities offer many opportunities for vocabulary development through labeling, organizing, and classifying.

I think that English is sickly.
Words change their meanings so quickly.
"Time goes *fast*," simply means that time's fleeting.
When you *fast*, it just means you're not eating.
And "stuck *fast*" means you're glued to the spot.
So if you go *fast*, you will never be *last*,
If you *fast*, you may *last*, or may not.

Source: From *Would You Put Your Money in a Sand Bank?* by Harold Longman, illustrated by Abner Graboff. Copyright 1968 by Harold S. Longman. Used by permission of Rand McNally.

☐ Develop words around a theme. School events, special studies, literary units, and holidays provide students with opportunities to acquire words and concepts related to the theme. Sometimes the theme can be more general, such as friendship, humor, or moods.

☐ Develop an understanding of the figurative and idiomatic expressions in our language (Foerster, 1974a). Idioms—expressions that convey meanings other than the literal one—necessitate a degree of language sophistication in order to be understood and appreciated. Idioms can be analyzed by illustrating both their literal and figurative meanings and pantomiming their meaning. Idioms can also be categorized according to their main source of metaphor: color, parts of the body, animals, food, clothing, solar system, plants, and marine life.

☐ Provide opportunities to explore the meanings of familiar words in new contexts (Deighton, 1959). In addition to the figures of speech mentioned above, students should be allowed to develop an extended understanding of: (1) words frequently used figuratively such as ear, eye, face, foot, head, river, mountain, and road; (2) relationship words with close meanings, such as over/above, across/over, near/by/at/in, along/with/among/together, lower/under, and still/yet; (3) judgment words that can be used in a variety of situations but that may change in meaning because of their usage, such as cold, bad, beautiful, better, best, big, dark, deep, far, fast, fine, good, great, hard, heavy, high, hot, long, new, old, poor, rich, short, strong, and sweet; (4) synonyms such as stay/remain, sure/certain, small/little, glad/happy, and build/make; (5) indefinite words that change in meaning according to the situation in which they are used, such as all, always, certain, every, sure, never, right, true, and whole; and (6) idioms constructed from words such as hold, bring, buy, clear, come, cut, put, make, get, go, in, down, up, and around.

☐ Develop a sense that the vocabulary of our language is constantly changing. The students should be aware of words that are used now but were not a few years ago. Science and technology provide numerous examples of newly created words. Students with more mature language skills may also be able to undertake a study of words that are no longer in current usage.

The changes in our vocabulary can also be noted in the changing meanings of known words. As words are used more and more frequently, new meanings become attached to them. Although many professional writers contend that words are being used "incorrectly," the final judge of the acceptability or correctness of a word in any given context is whether or not it is so used by a significant portion of the population.

☐ Provide the students with a vocabulary "capsule" (Crist, 1975), The capsule is comprised of a list of words related to a specific topic that has been identified through a survey of the students interest. The new words are introduced by the teacher, and the students then talk among themselves using the words. The students judge whether the others are using the words in the same manner as the teacher is. At another time, the students can use the new words in writing activities.

To recapitulate, students' general vocabularies—spoken, listening, writing, and reading—can be built through planned activies that involve direct teaching as well as incidental learnings. The enthusiasm of the teacher appears to be a key ingredient to a successful vocabulary development program. The students are sure to respond to new words that are useful to their everyday lives and schoolwork, if they are introduced in pleasant and pleasurable circumstances.

USING CONTEXT TO DETERMINE UNKNOWN WORDS

As students acquire new vocabulary and extend their understanding of already familiar words, they should be developing strategies for determining the possible meaning of an unfamiliar word met in context. In order to use context clues effectively, students should be aware of the various language patterns and signals from which information concerning the author's intended meaning of the word can be obtained. In context, a number of textual constraint variables are in operation. These variables point out the segments of the printed language that the reader is likely to use in determining word meanings at the sentence level (Aulls, 1970). These variables are (1) the position of the word in the sentence, (2) the grammatical class of the word, and (3) the types of grammatical structures in which the word is found.

The use of context for determining word recognition has some limitations. The results of a study of words and their use in contexts (Deighton, 1959) show

1. Context *reveals* meaning far less frequently than is normally supposed. Although it is true that context determines meaning, it does not always *reveal* it.
2. Context reveals only one of a word's meanings. Since no word has a fixed, unalterable meaning, no one context will suffice for all uses of that word.
3. Context seldom clarifies the whole meaning of a word. At best, context only provides clues from which the reader may infer the meaning of the unfamiliar word.
4. Vocabulary growth and expansion through context revelation is slow and gradual.

Therefore, as strategies for using context clues are developed, teachers should realize that

What a context reveals about the meaning of an unfamiliar or unknown word depends on the reader's past experiences and knowledge (schemas).
The portion of the context revealing, or providing clues to, the meaning of the familiar word must be in relatively close proximity to the word.
There must be a clear connection between the unfamiliar word and the context that clarifies the meaning of that word.

Contextual Signals to Word Meanings

Contextual signals are aids to determining the possible meaning of an unfamiliar word. Contextual signals work partly because of (1) the reader's reasoning ability, (2) the reader's store of possible word meanings, and (3) the extent of the reader's knowledge of the topic (Burns & Schell, 1975). If the reader has the basic prerequisites for determining the possible meaning of an unfamiliar word, the application of strategies for using context consists of hypothesis generating and confirming.

According to Deighton (1959), context may reveal the possible meaning of words through

1. *Definition*. Sentences containing forms of the verb *to be,* alone or in a verb phrase with the word *called,* often give the reader an explicit definition of an unfamiliar word.

   A sculptor is a person who models, carves, or casts a work of art in solid material.

   A person who believes in and campaigns for the careful use and protection of natural resources is called a conservationist.

2. *Example*. Sentences provide clues to possible meaning when they contain expressions such as *for example, such, such as, like, especially, other, this,* and *these.* If the reader has a knowledge of the item used as an example, it may be possible for a meaning of the unfamiliar word to be inferred.

   Many new sporting arenas such as Cobo Hall in Detroit and Madison Square Garden in New York are being built in the form of an amphitheater.

3. *Modifiers*. Sentences often contain unfamiliar words that can be understood because of a modifier used with that word. Modifiers can be single words, phrases, or entire clauses. Two very important modifiers are relative clauses and predicate adjectives.

   My grandfather's chronometer, which had a bright face, glistening black hands, and a loud tick, always brought excitement to all of us when he removed it from his vest pocket.

   Delphinium are beautiful perennials that bed nicely with white lilies.

4. *Restatement*. Sentences containing appositives, the punctuation marks of parenthesis and dashes, and the words *in other words, that is,* and *or* provide numerous signals to unfamiliar words.

   The parcels all were sent down a chute—a kind of slide—into the storeroom below.

   The photograph was finished in sepia, or dark brown, tones.

5. *Inference through established connectives.* Sentences may reveal the possible meaning of an unfamiliar word through various grammatical patterns:
   a. Parallel sentences structure. A series—either in the same sentence or in succeeding sentences—often allows the reader to determine the meaning of unfamiliar words.

Each child brought a favorite musical instrument: Fred, his drums, Mary, her tambourine, and Warren, his horn.

b. Repetition of key words. Often a writer will repeat the unfamiliar word throughout a paragraph. Each time the word is used, more information about its possible meaning is given. Or the writer may restate an idea, thereby giving additional clues to the meaning of an unfamiliar word.
c. Familiar connectives. Sentences containing coordinating and subordinating connectives give the reader various clues to the possible meaning of an unfamiliar word.

Although Frances kept her room immaculate, her twin sister's was always messy.

Other ways readers can unlock the possible meaning of an unfamiliar word are by using the sentence-and paragraph-reading strategies found in Chapter 8. Readers can begin to perceive the meaning intended by an author as they begin to question how the word is used:

Does it seem to be the *who* or *what* of a sentence?
Does it seem to indicate *what is being done*?
Does it seem to mean *what kind of thing something is*?
Does it seem to mean *how, how much,* or *how long* something is happening?
Does it seem to mean something about *where* or *when or why* something is happening?
Can the meaning be derived from other examples or reasons in the paragraph?

As students gain experience in using the sentences and paragraph-reading strategies, they also learn strategies for determining the possible meaning of an unfamiliar word.

Contextual aids can also be found in the illustrations, charts, tables, and maps that often accompany textual material. For example, students may not fully understand the meaning of *pedipalps* in Figure 9-1 until they refer to the drawing in the text. However, teachers should not assume that students can and will use illustrations. Relating visual information to its printed counterpart is a necessary strategy and skill that should be developed in all readers (see Chapter 10 for a further discussion of this).

Using Context Signals

Pupils should be taught not only the various signals but also how these signals may be used to determine an author's intended meaning. The most practical beginning place for obtaining teaching and practice material is the instructional materials. You can decide on the specific contextual strategies and the precise order in which to present them to the students after examining the school texts. When a basal series is used, it is best to follow the sequence of that series. Some basal series, however, do not provide continuous instruction in using contextual signals. When they do offer exercises, often they merely ask the students to "use the context" without specifying what they are to use and how they are to use it.

The format of the strategy lesson explained in Chapter 8 should be used to teach the contextual signals and the strategies for using them. After the students have learned various signals, they should be given opportunities to apply their knowledge and gain proficiency in using the contextual aids. The activites suggested below can be used, with slight modification, for practicing most of the contextual signal strategies.

Activities for Using Context Signals

☐ Provide a modified cloze passage. Instead of deleting every *nth* word, selectively delete one or two words from the paragraph. For each deletion give three or four possible choices that are grammatically correct. By examining the contextual signals, the students should be able to select a meaningful response. Afterward, let them discuss the reasons for their choices. For example:

A cotton gin cleans the seeds from the cotton lint. Lint is the part of the cotton that is made into thread, then woven into cloth. Cleaning the cotton with a gin is called_____.

        linting   ginning   clothing

☐ Provide an opportunity for the students to construct their own sentences or paragraphs that reveal the meaning of an unknown word. Each student should be given a card on which an unfamiliar word is written. The students are to use a particular contextual signal in writing their sentence or paragraph. Afterward their sentences and paragraphs are distributed among the other students, who must indicate the meaning of the unfamiliar word. For example, the students would be given cards similar to those below.

escapade:	a reckless or daring adventure
signal:	restatement using *or*

character:	someone in a story or play
signal:	example

> Let's look at the spider's head. Most spiders have a very strange-looking head.
>
> This is because many spiders have four or six or eight eyes. Even so, a spider cannot see very much. A spider can tell only if it is light or dark or if something is moving.
>
> Most of the other parts of a spider's head help it to catch food. The spider has two small leg-like things, called *pedipalps*. It has one pedipalp on each side of its head. The pedipalps help the spider to hold an insect.
>
> The spider has two jaws just in front of its mouth. These jaws have fangs at the end. When the spider catches something, it bites the insect with these fangs. Poison in the fangs puts the insect to sleep until the spider is ready to eat it.

Figure 9-1
Source: Fay, Leo, Ross, Ramon Royal, and La Pray, Margaret. *The Rand McNaly Reading Program,* Level 7. Copyright 1981 by The Riverside Publishing Co.

☐ Play a variation of the game "Twenty Questions." Select a word that is unfamiliar to the students. They may ask a total of twenty questions about the word: the first ten on how the word can be used in a sentence, the other ten on the meaning of the word. For example, the students can establish the function of the word through questions like: Can it do something? Does it describe or tell what kind of thing something is? Can it be moved around in a sentence without changing the meaning of the sentence? Once its function is known, the students can focus on the meaning of the word. The aim is not necessarily to guess the stimulus word but to determine the function of the word and a possible meaning of that word.

STRATEGIES FOR USING GRAPHOPHONOLOGICAL INFORMATION

One aspect of reading instruction that is often misconceived is that set of word recognition strategies pertaining to graphophonological signals. In most traditional approaches to word recognition, there are three categories of subskills: phonics, structural analysis, and sight vocabulary. Under phonics are the sound-letter relationships and the various rules for translating the printed symbol into a speech symbol. Under structural analysis are the various rules for syllabication and the use of "root" words and affixes. Under sight vocabulary comes any word that cannot be translated through the use of phonic or structural analysis rules or information. A basic sight vocabulary usually refers to the function words that do not have a direct referent, such as *of, from,* or *there.*

The traditional interpretation of reading assumes that reading progresses from "decoding" the word to recognizing that word to creating sentences by reading all the words together. As stated previously, the psycholinguistic interpretation of the reading process has suggested how sentences, instead of being the sum of the words they contain, are rather a major determiner of the words within their boundaries. A reader, therefore, can only "recognize" (that is, place into the appropriate schema) the constituent words when the meaning of an entire statement is known.

This is not to say, however, that graphophonological information is not useful. It is, providing one has a clear understanding of its importance. The main purpose for learning about graphophonological information is that it is a help in turning ideas that are unrecognized in graphic form into sound in order to determine if the ideas are recognized aurally (Durkin, 1974). It is quite possible that certain words will be familiar when they are heard—that is, they may be only in a person's listening vocabulary. By translating the visual form into a sound form, the students might recognize the word. If the word is not in a reader's speaking or listening vocabularies, then no amount of decoding will benefit the reader. In order to reconstruct the author's intended message, the reader must rely on the contextual reading strategies discussed previously.

Clarification of Misunderstandings About Graphophonological Information

Of the three traditional word recognition categories, two, phonics and structural analysis, are of questionable value as they are usually taught. Any examination of instructional materials will reveal that more pages are devoted to phonics than to understanding. This seems a strange phenomenon since often the meaning of a sentence determines its sound representation!

Phonics instruction developed as an attempt to use the characteristics of the English alphabetic writing system. Alphabetic writing developed not for the convenience of the reader but for that of the writer (F. Smith, 1972). Normal reading does not involve decoding; we do not understand words on the basis of their sounds. Rather, we attend to the *meaning of the spelling* patterns of the words. If we did respond to the sounds of the words rather than their spellings, the following sentence (from F. Smith, 1972) would not provide the reader with a modicum of confusion:

The none tolled hymn she had scene a pare of bear feat inn hour rheum.

In addition, the alphabetic system is only partially phonetic. Our written language has two sets of relationships: (1) words that are related should look alike—*medicine, medication,* and (2) words that are not related should look different—*fare, fair.* Obviously, these deviations from the original purpose of alphabetic writing (that is, to maintain a simple letter-to-sound relationship) have aided the reader. The complex sound-spelling system is the basis for an idealized phonics instruction program. There is little relation in much of this phonic instruction to the realities of how beginning readers recognize words. Many of the practice exercises found in reading materials require students to identify phonic principles in already visually recognizable words. An example of this point is found in exercises that ask students to mark the so-called long and short vowel sounds in words given on a list. Experienced teachers will verify that students experience most difficulty in correctly labeling the vowels in those words with which they are unfamiliar.

In many current reading instruction texts, much space is devoted to the teaching of the rules of syllabication. This instruction is based on the misconception that the written form is "language" itself or the primary language form (Zuck, 1974). A careful examination of many of the rules of syllabication reveals that they can be applied only after the pronunciation of the word is known. The reason for that is simple: syllabication was devised for the convenience of the typist and typesetter (Waugh & Howell, 1975). The syllable divisions found in most dictionaries indicate the standard units of word divisions. They are not, however, intended as guides to pronunciation. For many English words, the pronunciation division differs from that of the written division. For example, the words *double, strengthen, pleasing,* and *molding* are just a few of those for which dictionaries show a different syllable division for writing and for pronunciation. Dictionaries divide words in the pronunciation guides only as a visual aid in sounding out the word—these divisions have nothing to do with the various rules found as supposed aids to decoding. Teachers, then, should understand the rationale for various dictionary subdivisions and use them for their intended purposes (Waugh & Howell, 1975).

In summary, the syllable division of the written word often differs from the syllable division of the spoken word. Because of erroneous instruction and because syllable boundaries differ in speech and writing, students may (1) apply syllable rules strictly and mispronounce many words; (2) pronounce words with additional syllables; (3) stress each syllable equally, thereby distorting the word; and (4) introduce additional sounds into the word (Zuck, 1974).

Effective Instruction in Graphophonological Information

In order to teach students how to use graphophonological information, teachers should understand (1) the sound structure of English, (2) the relationship between the sound structure and the written form of English, and (3) the spelling structures of written English.

Teachers are referred to Chapter 2 of this text for a review of the sound structure of English. They can assume that students of all ages are familiar with the sound structure when they come to school. (For a discussion of students who speak divergent dialects, see Chapter 12.) The students must become familiar with the written representations of the sounds they know. Word recognition instruction should be directed toward teaching the written representation of the language and its relationship to the spoken language and, more importantly, its relationship to the meaning of the message. The focus of word recognition instruction, then, is on the spelling structures of written English.

Along with learning these structures, students should understand that the purpose of the written code is to communicate the writer's feeling and ideas (Downing, 1975). The students' first and subsequent experiences with the written language should stress its communicative function. Letter-to-sound relationships should always be taught in genuine context of encoding or decoding the author's thoughts and feeling.

There are two kinds of word recognition, immediate and mediated (F. Smith, 1972). Immediately recognized words are those whose image and semantic features are generically stored in long-term memory and can be rapidly retrieved through either conceptually driven procedures (the context of the sentence) or data driven procedures (the internal features of the word). Mediated word recognition occurs when the schemas for the word's image and semantic features and the procedures for its recall are not fully developed. In this case, a longer process of retrieval is undertaken through a combination of conceptually and data driven procedures.

Immediate Word Recognition

Word recognition begins with the acquisition of a large repertoire of immediately recognized words. These may seem like the traditional "sight vocabulary"; however, instead of learning to recognize large numbers of words in isolation, students learn to recognize the printed form of objects and behaviors with which they are familiar. The relationship words (structure or function words) should be learned as part of sentences or phrases that clearly indicate the meaning they represent. For example, the classroom can be filled with labels containing whole sentences rather than single words. Complete sentences containing function words can also be used with pictures that illustrate their meaning. These activities, though common in primary classrooms, do not need to be considered immature for the upper elementary grades. Teachers of grades 5 and 6 might find labeled illustrations helpful in clarifying the meaning of *before* as the students expand their understanding of its usage—*before* as an adverb, a preposition, and a conjunction. Other opportunities for developing immediate word recognition are classroom displays, bulletin boards, and readings containing many repetitions of the words. The students' immediate word recognition repertoire should be constantly expanding throughout their school years.

Mediated Word Recognition

Most of the exercises found in instructional materials cover information and techniques for mediated word recognition. Much of this instruction (or practice, as is more often the case) attempts to develop in the students an ability to decode, or translate into sound, any unrecognized word. The teacher should not forget that mediated word recognition strategies allow students to recognize words that are in their aural vocabularies but not in their visual vocabularies. If the word is not in the students' hearing vocabularies, they must use the contextual strategies discussed previously. No amount of "sounding out" will help them recognize a word they do not already know by sound. They then must try to approximate the word's meaning by using the surrounding context.

In order for the students to understand mediated word recognition strategies, they should understand how the conventional spelling of words corresponds to meaning rather than some surface feature—that is, rather than to the word's pronunciation (C. Chomsky, 1973). Spellings are related to an underlying abstract level of meaning. The mature reader does not need first to pronounce a written word to recognize what it means. Rather, the reader seeks and recognizes the correspondence of the written symbol to some abstract lexical spelling of words. Lexical items are the meaning-bearing items of language. Therefore, instruction in mediated word recognition strategies should direct the students' attention to features of the written word that, when combined with contextual signals, will allow them to identify the unfamiliar written word.

The acquisition of mediated word recognition strategies depends on the understanding of two sets of information: (1) common letter clusters and (2) morphological units.

Letter Clusters The results of investigations into how students actually translate printed symbols into sound representations indicate that readers seem to use a "structures approach" (Glass & Burton, 1973). Students who were successful readers when asked to read aloud, were not seen to use either rules of syllabication or rules of vowel control when they encountered an unfamiliar word. Rather, they seemed to group sounds according to various letter clusters appearing in the word. Examination of the materials commonly used in the elementary grades revealed that 119 common letter clusters appeared in the materials (see Table 9-1)

Table 9-1 Common Letter Clusters Embedded in Whole Words.

sat	bed	fall	fowl	her
sing	big	saw	bus	h*air*
set	lip	tel(l)	fil(l)	pal
sit	mud	d*eck*	bite	t*ied*
hot	lid	nice	mes(s)	few
him	den	tick	Tom	fire
top	hug	clif(f)	poke	h*ear*
ran	hut	sink	tore	*real*
say	far	cob	tow	*tea*
sad	hem	sod	cast	bee
jam	cup	fog	cane	care
sun	mate	tub	meat	de*af*
tin	tent	cuf(f)	glas(s)	b*oat*
rap	test	rush	Bev	cue
s*and*	rake	table	kind	too
t*ack*	hide	sight	toss	*out*
sum	lock	mis(s)	team	p*ound*
tab	made	Ron	most	cure
bag	came	for	rol(l)	n*ature*
told	cape	ful(l)	bone	fur
rash	face	*fact*	pale	fir
fish	sang	taf(f)y	save	raid
	sank	cook	rove	*auto*
	song	nation	folly	b*oil*
			sage	

Source: Gerald Glass, *Teaching Decoding as Separate from Reading* (Garden City, NY: Adelphi University Press, 1973).

It is possible and natural for three- and four-letter clusters to be learned as easily as single-letter phonic units are. These letter clusters should be learned by examining words in the students' listening vocabularies that are not immediately recognized. This system helps alleviate the problem of teaching vowel sounds. A vowel has a sound as part of a cluster and not because of some rule (Glass, 1965).

The teacher presents the clusters as part of whole words. Through direct teaching, the students learn to recognize the cluster and associate it with a common phonological unit. For example, the letter cluster found in *mate* can be presented to students once they have in their speaking and listening vocabularies such words as *crate, date, fate, gate, plate, rate, state, skate,* and *slate*. As they learn other common clusters, they will be able to recognize such words as *inflate, debate,* and *rebate*. This approach can easily be combined with a program in which the students learn to employ mediated writing strategies.

Morphological Units A practical approach to word recognition uses word parts that have invariant meanings and that, when combined with the reader's topical experience and knowledge of contextual signals, produce enough meaning so that the reader can continue reading (Deighton, 1959). The difference between learning letter clusters and learning morphological units is the amount of information about the meaning of the word contained in the graphic unit. For example, the letter cluster contained in the word *fish,* though it may provide clues to the phonological representation of that word, does not indicate what the word may mean. On the other hand, the morphological unit *equi-* found in the word *equinox* gives the reader some idea of "equal." Table 9-2 contains some of the morphological units that have invariant meanings. Students in grades 4 through 8 should receive specific instruction in recognizing and understanding these units. Those in the primary grades may receive instruction in many of them as the need arises.

In devising teaching lessons, teachers may find it necessary to identify the letter cluster or the morphological unit in words out of the context of a sentence. This may be done during the identification and example stage of the teaching lesson. The teacher, however, should be sure to develop within the guided application portion of the lesson an understanding of how the graphophonological information is combined with contextual information in recognizing unfamiliar words.

SPELLING

The generally accepted definition of spelling or learning to spell is knowing or acquiring the basic correspondences between sounds and letters. To many, that is all that is required, and that belief has brought forth a plethora of programs and systems for teaching students grapheme-phoneme relationships. There is also a commonly held belief that accurate spelling is the sign of an educated person and that the goal of spelling programs should be to create flawless spellers. Psycholinguists have shown that these positions are untenable, that learning to spell means learning the underlying forms of the writing system for word creation and word recognition, and that learning to read and learning to spell are complementary processes (C. Chomsky, 1979; Henderson & Beers, 1980; Moffett & Wagner, 1976; F. Smith, 1982).

These misconceptions of spelling seem to be based on misunderstandings of language in general and of the English language and its orthography in particular. Some of these misunderstandings have already been discussed in relation to ideas about phonics instruction and syllabication. Current research has shown that the acquisition of spelling abilities may be developmental.

In a study of how young children develop the logic of orthography, it was found that beginning spellers go through certain patterns in the acquisition of English orthography (Henderson, 1974). In fact, it appears that the trial-and-error pattern of beginning spellers is similar to the trial and error pattern made by that of beginning speakers. The researcher suggested that instead of forcing children to acquire the graphophonological relationships in a set manner,

Table 9-2 Morphological Units with Invariant Meanings.

Units found at the beginning of words

anthro- (man)	hydro- (water)	phil(o)- (love of)
auto- (self)	iso- (equal)	phono- (sound)
biblio- (book)	lith- (stone)	photo- (light)
bio- (life)	micro- (small)	pneumo- (breath)
centro- (middle)	mono- (one)	poly- (many)
cosmo- (universe)	neuro- (nerve)	proto- (first)
heter(o)- (different)	omni- (everywhere)	pseudo- (false)
homo- (same)	pan- (all)	tele- (far)
	penta- (five)	uni- (one)

Self-explaining compounds (beginning and ends of words)

out	under	self	wise
over	up	way	

(Each of these has two clear meanings except *self*, which has only one.)

Common prefixes with invariant meanings

apo- (different from)	extra- (additional)	mal- (bad)
syn- (same)	circum- (around)	intra- (within)
mis- (not)	com- (with)	equi- (equal)
intro- (within)	non- (not)	
in- (in)	in- (not)	un- (not)

Noun suffixes meaning *agent* or *one who*

-eer	-ess	-grapher	-ier
-ster	-ist	-stress	-trix

Common mount suffixes with invariant meanings

-ana (collection)	-fer (bearing)	-meter (mount)
-archy (rule)	-fication (process of making)	-metry (measuring)
-ard (one who)	-gram (written)	-phobia (fear)
-aster (mimic)	-graph (written)	
-bility (able)	-ics (facts)	-scope (something for viewing)
-chrome (color)	-itis (illness)	
-cide (kill)	-latry (worship)	-ee (one who receives)

Common adjective suffixes with invariant meanings

-est (superlative)	-wards (direction)	-most (superlative)
-ferous (bearing)	-wise (way)	-like (like)
-fic (process)	-less (without)	-ous (full of)
-fold (times)	-able (can)	-ose (sugar)
-form (shape of)		-ful (full of)

teachers should allow them to test what will work best for them. This point has been reiterated throughout this book: Learning to read and write should be as easy for children to learn as it was for them to learn to listen and speak.

This leads to a second point, "invented spellings." The development of written English (Chapter 2) explains many so-called discrepancies between English spelling and English pronunciation. But since English is basically phonetic—or, more precisely, alphabetic—the relationships that do exist between speech and print can be discovered by students as they develop literacy. One way evidenced by psycholinguistic research is to allow students in the beginning and later stages of acquiring the skills and strategies of reading and writing to spell words the way they think they should be spelled. These words are part of the students' knowledge domains and as such provide an important motivation for acquiring accurate representations of them so as to facilitate communication. The students' invented spellings help reveal what they already know about the correspondence between sounds and letters. The patterns of misunderstandings students reveal can form the bases of instruction, as long as the students are encouraged to make educated guesses about spelling without the fear of penalties for errors (Moffett & Wagner, 1976). Spelling improves with constant trying, since

... one of the best ways for the [reader] to gain experience with alphabetic representation and with the phonetic makeup of words is through word compositions, or writing words according to the way they sound. Children should be given much more practice in writing at the start. Writing in one's own invented spellings, according to the way words sound, is excellent experience when one is first starting to read, and many children can do this before they read. The practice that they get in attending to the sounds of words, in translating from pronunciation to print, and in the principles of alphabetic orthography are invaluable. (C. Chomsky, 1979).

The complementary nature of spelling and reading result from the processes by which words are recognized. Reading and spelling both utilize visual memory, and the memory of words seen repeatedly in reading helps to standardize the students' representations of those words. Visualizing words leads to generalizations about the regular patterns of words and letter correspondences. Visualizing words helps identify irregular words (Moffett & Wagner, 1976). Students learn to recognize when a word "looks right." In turn, learning to spell already recognizable words helps readers analyze and remember the internal make-up of those words (Ehri, et al., 1978).

DICTIONARY USAGE STRATEGIES

Dictionaries are books that tell what words often mean; they are not books that tell what words ought to mean (Downing & Sceats, 1974). An individual turns to the dictionary because a word is encountered (1) whose meaning is not revealed through the context, (2) that is not in the reader's oral vocabulary, (3) whose precise meaning needs verification, or (4) whose pronunciation cannot be determined through mediated word recognition strategies. In such cases the reader finds a need to use a dictionary.

Dictionaries often may not be of any help to a student because

1. The demands for skill in using it are too great. Some dictionaries are complicated in their format and presentation of information. Students are required to possess skills for selecting information, but they may not know what to select.
2. The information may be presented in a manner inappropriate for the cognitive level of the students. More recent dictionaries are overcoming this failing through the use of more concrete examples and the elimination of definitions more complicated than the entry word (Downing & Sceats, 1974).
3. The students have no occasion to write their own sentences (Moffett & Wagner, 1976).

In order to use a dictionary successfully, a student needs to know the fundamental skills for using a dictionary:

1. Locating a word. In order to locate an entry word students should understand how to use
    a. Alphabetical order.
    b. Guide words.
    c. An inflected or derived form of a word.
2. Deriving the pronunciation of a word. In order to pronounce an entry word, students should understand and be able to use
    a. The pronunciation key to identify consonant and vowel sounds and associate them with the dictionary symbols.
    b. The pronunciation guide for blending the consonants and vowels into spoken syllables.
    c. Primary and secondary accent marks of the visual syllabic divisions.
3. Deriving the appropriate meaning of a word. In order to determine the meaning of an unfamiliar word in relation to the context in which it is encountered, students should understand and be able to use
    a. The basic dictionary definitions.
    b. Illustrations, diagrams, and example sentences or phrases.
    c. The appropriate meaning when an entry word has multiple entries or multiple meanings.
    d. Strategies for adapting the appropriate definition to the context of the word.

Some dictionaries currently being prepared for the elementary levels are being constructed to overcome the limitations stated previously. One way this is being done is by providing separate dictionaries of differing formats for different maturity levels. The illustrations in Figure 9-2 show two levels of dictionary entries as published by one company. In addition, there are supplementary students guides or exercise booklets on dictionary use and practice that teach the fundamental skills of dictionary usage. Figure 9-3 shows one such practice lesson.

An important adjunct to the dictionary is a thesaurus. A thesaurus is a book of synonyms, antonyms, and related words. Students can begin to use a thesaurus almost as soon as they learn to use a dictionary. A thesaurus helps to develop a sense of words and helps students realize that synonyms do not always mean the same things and that different synonyms may be more appropriate in one situation than in another. Just as dictionaries should be written for the students' cognitive and linguistic maturity, so should thesauri. The illustration in Figure 9-4 is from a beginning thesaurus.

---

game
A **game** is a way to play or have fun. Every **game** has rules. Some **games** are played with cards. All sports are **games.**

game |gām| —*noun, plural* **games** **1.** A way of playing or having fun; an amusement: *As a game, we tried not to step on any of the cracks in the sidewalk. The baby tossed his food around as if eating was just a game.* **2.** A contest with rules and a purpose or goal that each side tries to achieve: *a football game; a game of cards.* **3.** Wild animals, birds, or fish that are hunted for food or sport.
—*adjective* **gamer, gamest** **1.** Full of courage; brave; courageous: *He's a game boxer who'll never give up.* **2.** Ready; willing: *Are you game for a long walk?* **3.** Of or among animals hunted for sport or food: *The pheasant is a game bird.*

Figure 9-2 Entries from Two Levels of Dictionaries
Source: *My First Dictionary,* Copyright 1980 by Houghton Mifflin and *Beginning Dictionary,* Copyright 1979 by Houghton Mifflin.

> **Guide words**
>
> Look at that page.
>
> It is the same as page 183 of **My Second Picture Dictionary**.
>
> All the entry words on page 183 come between **oh** and **onion**.
> They are the guide words.
>
> Look again at that page.
>
> Is the entry word **once** there?
> If it is, draw a circle around it.
>
> ---
>
> Below are some more entry words.
>
> Look for each one on that page.
>
> If you find it there, draw a circle around it.
>
> What if you don't find it there!
> It is on another page, between two other guide words.
>
> ---
>
> | **oil** | **Oklahoma** | **one** |
> |---|---|---|
> | **olive** | **orange** | **old** |

Figure 9-3 A Sample Dictionary Use Exercise
Source: From *My Second Picture Dictionary Exercise Book* by William A. Jenkins and Andrew Schiller. Copyright 1975 by Scott, Foresman. Used by permission.

In order to use a thesaurus successfully, a student needs to understand some of the fundamental skills (in addition to the basic dictionary skills) for using a thesaurus:

1. Locating a word in the index. Since a thesaurus is used for finding related words, the students should first understand the principle of locating the word for which a synonym is desired and identifying the page on which that word and its synonyms are located.

agree	*Agree* means have the same opinion or feeling about something as someone else. At first my idea differed from hers, but finally I *agreed*. If something is pleasing to you or healthful, it can be said to *agree* with you. The weather *agreed* with us.
consent comply	*Consent* and *comply* mean agree to something that someone has asked or may want you to do. We asked if we could stay at Grandpa's, and Mom and Dad *consented*. When the supervisor told the workers to put down their tools, they *complied*. You *consent to* do something, but you *comply with*. Mom and Dad finally *consented to* let me go camping. The class *complied with* the committee's decision.
contract	*Contract* is a stronger word than agree. If you *contract* to do something, your words are usually put in writing. The builders *contracted* to begin the house next month.
admit	When you *admit* to something, you accept or agree that it is either true or false, good or bad. It was not hard to *admit* that the other team had better players.
approve	*Approve* can mean agree, but it also adds the meaning of having a good opinion about someone or something. Usually, *of* follows *approve*. Cindy hoped that the family would *approve of* her new wallpaper.

See also *promise* (v).

It was not hard to **admit** the other team had better players.

Figure 9-4   A Beginning Thesaurus Entry
Source: From *In Other Words, A Junior Thesaurus* by Andrew Schiller and William A. Jenkins. Copyright © 1982, 1977, 1969 by Scott Foresman and Co. Reprinted by permission.

2. Understanding the entries. In order to be able to select an appropriate synonym or antonym for a word, the students should understand the form of a thesaurus entry.
3. Understanding cross references. In order to locate a desired word, the students should understand the various means of cross-referencing to other related terms.

The above skills are the basic requisites for effective dictionary and thesaurus use. Students of all ages and grade levels may acquire them or be deficient in them. Once the teacher has determined the students' performance levels, instruction can be instituted to extend the students' abilities.

Activities for Developing Dictionary Strategies

Once the students know the names and sequence of the twenty-six letters of the alphabet, activities such as the following can be implemented:

▫ Give the students four to six noncontiguous letters. Ask them to arrange them in alphabetical order. For example, they would be required to arrange these letters in order: *y, b, m, d, l, v.*

▫ Provide an interrupted sequence which the students are to complete. The sequence can be of contiguous letters: a____ c, d, _____ , f, or the sequence can contain noncontiguous letters and the students are given items from which to select the correct response: d, _____ , g, l, _____ , o, (z, a, f, h, n).

▫ Provide a list of words that begin with the same letter. The students must then alphabetize them according to the second or third letters of the words.

▫ Provide sample guide words and a list of words that all begin with the same letter. The students should select those words that can be found on the page represented by the guide words. For example, the words *bear* and *began* are indicated as guide words. Which of these words would be on that page in a dictionary: *beat, beach, beg, below, bid, beaver,* and *beef?*

▫ Provide a list containing words with inflected or derived forms. The students are to indicate what the original form of the word is.

The first stage of this activity could have the students match the derived form to the original. As they become familiar with various spelling patterns and changes occurring with the addition of inflected endings, they should be able to supply the original word without assistance.

▫ Provide a list of words spelled phonetically according to a dictionary pronunciation key. Have the students match the phonetic spellings to the original spellings. As they gain proficiency in this task, give only the phonetic spellings and have them pronounce the word.

▫ Give the students a list of dictionary definitions and have them read the definition silently, then explain to another student what the entry word means.

▫ Give the students separate lists of dictionary definitions and illustrations and have them read the definitions and locate the illustration that matches the definition.

▫ Give the students dictionary definitions and example sentences or phrases that help explain the word. They should create their own example phrases and sentences in explaining the word to another student.

☐ Give the students a sentence that contains a word with mutliple meanings. They are to refer to a dictionary and indicate the number of the definition that fits the meaning of the word as used in the stimulus sentence.

☐ Provide two sets of sentences, each containing the same multiple meaning word. If the word has three meanings, each set should contain three sentences. The students are to match the sentences from each set having the same meaning for the word.

☐ Provide sentences in which the definition of the word does not "fit" without some adaption. They are to rephrase the sentence so that the definition fits. For example:

Michael grimaced with pain when the doctor gave him the injection.

grimace: twisting of the face; ugly or funny smile.

☐ Provide the students with a set of riddles. Each riddle is followed by a question containing two dictionary references. The students must solve the riddle after referring to each of the references. For example:

I am a long-armed ape that lives in the trees of Asia. Am I a chimpanzee or a gibbon?

I am sitting on a large porch alongside my house. Am I sitting on a piazza or a plaza?

Resources for the Teacher

Many modern elementary-school dictionaries are written for different cognitive and linguistic maturity levels. The following publisher offers dictionaries and thesauri for all elementary grades through the sixth. Each book begins with a series of lessons directed to the student for developing the fundamental skills for using the particular dictionary or thesaurus. Each also has an accompanying student exercise book.

Scott Foresman, Glenview, IL.
    My Pictionary—for kindergartners and beginning grades.
    My First Picture Dictionary—for first graders
    My Second Picture Dictionary—for second graders
    The Thorndike-Barnhart Beginning Dictionary
    The Thorndike-Barnhart Intermediate Dictionary
    In Other Words: A Beginning Thesaurus
    In Other Words: A Junior Thesaurus

The following is a set of multileveled booklets for the intermediate and upper elementary grades. Students are asked to answer questions, complete statements, supply details, and form generalizations.

Spectrum of Skills: Vocabulary Development (New York: Macmillan).

The following series consist of multileveled sets of booklets of exercises in a number of area. Titles in each series that complement the strategies in this chapter are listed. These materials do not offer direct instruction but are useful for teaching and practice lessons.

Specific Skill Series (Baldwin, NY: Barnell Loft).
Supportive Reading Skills (Baldwin, NY: Dexter & Westbrook). Especially *Rhyme Time, Reading Homonyms, Learning to Alphabetize, Using Guide Words, Reading Homographs, Reading Heteronyms, Mastering Multiple Meanings, Recognizing Word Relationships, Word-O-Rama.*
Picto-cabulary Series, What's in a Name, and *Word Theater* (Baldwin, NY: Barnell Loft). (Booklets of various titles that present vocabulary for a particular theme.)

The following publishers provide various booklets and duplicating masters of word puzzles and games. Teachers should review the materials to determine their appropriateness for a particular student population.

The Continental Press, Elizabethtown, PA 17022.
Milliken Publishing Co., c/o AV Sales & Service, 166 Western Avenue, Albany, NY 12203.
Scholastic Book Service, 904 Sylvan Avenue, Englewood Cliffs, NJ 07632.

The following reference is an excellent source of word games for extending students' vocabulary and understanding of word usage. Activities are graded by difficulty.

Hurwitz, Abraham B., and Arthur Goddard, *Games to Improve Your Child's English* (New York: Simon & Schuster, 1969).

There are many trade books that can be used for stimulating students' interest in words. The following is only a partial list of the many interesting and colorful books available:

Longman, Harold, *Would you Put Your Money in a Sand Bank?* (Fun with Words). Illustrated by Abner Graboff (Chicago: Rand McNally, 1968).
Rothman, Joel, *The Antcyclopedia,* Illustrated by Shelley Freshman (New York: Phinmarc Books, 1974).
Hanson, Joan, *Antonyms: Hot and Cold and Other Words That Are Different as Night and Day* (Minneapolis: Lerner Publications, 1973). (This book is part of a series of books on homonyms, homographs, synonyms, and antonyms.)

Davidson, Jessica, *Is That Mother in the Bottle: Where Language Came From and Where It Is Going* (New York: Franklin Watts, 1972).
Applegate, Maurece, *First Book of Language and How to Use It* (New York: Franklin Watts, 1962).
Kraske, Robert, *Story of the Dictionary* (New York: Harcourt Brace Jovanovich, 1975).
Kohn, Bernice, *What a Funny Thing to Say!* (New York: Dial Press, 1974).
Adelson, Leone, *Dandolions Don't Bite: The Story of Words* (New York: Pantheon, 1972).
Paulson, Russell Soveig, A Is *For Apply and Why: The Story of Our Alphabet* (New York: Abingdon, 1959).
White, Mary Sue, *Word Twins* (New York: Abingdon, 1961).

Teachers may want to refer to the following articles, which are the source of the idea for the development of an action-packed vocabulary discussed in this chapter.

Toothaker, Roy, "Developing an Action-Packed Vocabulary," *Elementary English* 51 (1974): 861–897.
Fraizer, Alexander, "Developing a Vocabulary of the Senses," *Elementary English* 47 (1970): 176–184.

The following text presents word recognition and vocabulary-learning strategies based on the same principles of thinking and learning the reading process as postulated in this text:

Johnson, Dale D., and P. David Pearson, *Teaching Reading Vocabulary* (New York: Holt, Rinehart & Winston, 1978).

Discussion Questions and Activities

1. To what kinds of word recognition instruction is Kenneth Goodman (1972) referring:

   Schools may be teaching kids not to comprehend. They may be teaching them to match oral language with written language, which is very different from comprehending.

   Examine some commercial reading instructional materials and determine to what extent Goodman's statement applies to each.
2. Observe a group of primary-grade students engaged in an activity. Through either note taking or recording, obtain samples of the variety of words they use. From the sample, select those that have multiple meanings. At another

time, question the student to determine whether they understand all the meanings the words may have.

Repeat the above activity using the students' instructional materials as the source of the words.
3. Examine the various reading materials for students in a particular grade for the authors' use of contextual signals for unfamiliar vocabulary and concepts. How often are difficult or abstract concepts introduced without contextual aids to their meaning? Collect samples of good use of context in revealing the meaning of a words that might be unfamiliar to the students in that grade.
4. Examine various dictionaries for elementary grades, paying close attention to the vocabulary used to explain the entry words. How many of the explanations seem confusing because they use abstract language? How many require the students to refer to other possible unfamiliar words in order to understand the meaning of the entry word? How many of the teachers' guides suggest their use as prescribers of usage rather than as tools for learning?
5. Prepare a short talk that might be given at a parent association meeting about the parents' role in developing their child's vocabulary. What suggestions would you make, assuming that the audience contains parents of varying educational background?
6. Plan a bulletin board display for interesting students at a particular grade level in the etymology of words.
7. Make a series of informal tests to determine students' performance in the following areas:
   a. The understanding and use of contextual signals for meaning.
   b. The use of graphophonological information to pronounce unfamiliar written words.
   c. Locating a word in the dictionary.

Further Readings

The following articles will give the teacher additional information about the structure and function of written English:

Hodges, Richard E., "Theoretical Frameworks of English Orthography," *Elementary English* 49 (1972): 1069-1105.

Goodman, Kenneth S., "Orthography in a Theory of Reading Instruction," *Elementary English* 49 (1972): 1254-1261.

The following texts, which have been cited in previous *Further Readings* sections, contain chapters on the lack of effectiveness of traditional phonics instruction:

Smith, Frank, *Psycholinguistics and Reading* (New York: Holt, Rinehart & Winston, 1978).

Smith, Frank, *Understanding Reading,* 3rd ed., (New York: Holt, Rinehart & Winston, 1982).

The following is a useful reference for additional techniques for developing and extending students' vocabulary.

Dale, Edgar, and Joseph O'Rourke, *Techniques of Teacher Vocabulary* Chicago: Field Educational Publications, 1971).

Chapter 10

DEVELOPING STRATEGIES FOR CONTENT AREA READING

Focus Questions

1. What are the reading demands of content area textbooks?

2. What writing patterns, vocabulary, and graphic displays are commonly found in content area texts?

3. How can reading be guided in the content areas?

4. What strategies are needed for locating and using information in reference materials?

5. What strategies are needed for reading newspapers?

6. What strategies are needed for organizing information?

To some degree, a controversy exists among content area specialists in regard to the place of textbooks in content area instruction and learning. The intent here is not to become involved in the controversy. But since there are many content area textbooks currently in use in the elementary schools, teachers should understand how they may be used effectively. If school personnel choose to use a social studies, science, or mathematics textbook, or series of texts, then the teacher should understand the typical reading demands imposed by those textbooks.

Textbooks, can be an important part of classroom instruction. Too often, textbooks are blamed for inadequacies that in reality result from the teacher's misuse of them. In classroom instruction, textbooks can be used effectively for

1. An introduction to or overview of a topic.
2. New terms or concepts.
3. Descriptions of events or processes.
4. Initial background or common experiences.
5. Specific facts.
6. The substantiation of an idea or opinion.
7. A source for instruction in the study skills and for reading graphic materials.
8. The summary of a topic (Michaelis, 1972).

Many authorities in the areas of social studies, science, and mathematics instruction now emphasize a "process" approach to teaching and learning concepts, facts, and generalizations. What they call the process approach has been termed in this book the problem-solving approach. The goal of both is to involve the students in experiences that promote the development of language abilities so that they can communicate their ideas. The process in content area instruction differs little from the creative problem-solving activities suggested in Chapter 6.

In order to help students read content area texts, teachers should know the specialized patterns used in writing and organizing such material (N. Smith, 1964a). The following discussion synthesizes the findings of investigators who have analyzed the questions, directions, explanations, and the various types of exercises used in content area texts. It is through the structures and patterns of those components that the content area specialist indicates how students are expected to think and work in the particular field, (N. Smith, 1964a).

THE STRUCTURE OF CONTENT AREA MATERIALS

Content area materials contain many of the same sentences and paragraph patterns discussed in Chapter 8. What makes content area reading different from direct narrative is that certain patterns show up more often in content area texts. The vocabulary load of content area materials also is generally greater than that found in narration. The vocabulary load of content area texts may produce reading difficulties because of the large number of unfamiliar technical terms, the unusual meanings given to some familiar terms, the many different concepts found in the same paragraph. Each content area, however, has its particular recurring patterns of vocabulary and paragraphs, and each pattern can be found in combination with other patterns.

The patterns that we will describe are most prevalent in texts intended for grades 3 to 8. Texts written for the primary-grade levels usually have a style quite similar to that found in the basal reading instructional materials for that level. Teachers should be aware, however, that specialized information in a narrative style can also present problems for readers. Teachers should examine the texts they use so that they determine which patterns appear and may cause reading difficulties for their students.

WRITING PATTERNS IN CONTENT AREA TEXTS

The writing in content area textbooks can be examined in three ways: (1) vocabulary, (2) paragraph structures, and (3) graphics. Vocabulary includes technical or specialized terms and the concepts they represent, as well as familiar terms and concepts. The paragraph structures are basically those discussed in Chapter 8 with particular attention to how patterns are used in content areas. Each content area has illustrative materials necessitating certain reading strategies.

Vocabulary

Each content area has a highly specialized or technical vocabulary. For example, the following chart has representative vocabulary from three content areas. The terms and the concepts they represent are generally unique to each individual area.

Specialized Vocabulary

Social Studies	Science	Mathematics
coastal	cochlea	parallelogram
mountain	bacteria	numerator
cases	spore	numeral
government	glucose	improper fraction
Tropic of Cancer	cytoplasm	congruent figures
adobe	molecules	divisor
latitude	particle	perpendicular

Students should acquire these concepts and their labels during instruction. In mathematics and science the specialized terms often are composed of morphological units that can facilitate the learning of related terms. For example, psychrometer, thermometer, barometer, and chronometer all can be learned as instruments of measurement. However, scientific and mathematical writing can be difficult to read because of many special symbols and abbreviations that are used.

Common Mathematical and Scientific Symbols and Abbreviations

−	(minus)	9°	(degrees)	kph	(kilometers per hour)
+	(plus)	<	(less than)	C	(Celsius scale)
=	(equals)	>	(more than)	∡	(angle)
×	(times)	÷	(divided by)	+	(positive charge)
cm	(centimeter)	l	(liter)	−	(negative charge)
g	(gram)	mm	(millimeter)	→	(direction of a force)

Mathematics reading may be difficult because much of the writing contains a mixture of words, numerals, letters, symbols, and geometric shapes. The reader is required to shift constantly from one vocabulary to another. In the two mathematics passages in Figure 10-1, typical of those that students encounter in texts, what demands are placed on the reader by the combined use of standard vocabulary and mathematics vocabulary?

Whenever students encounter unfamiliar terms and concepts, they (and their teachers) become aware of the problem almost immediately. But the technical and scientific vocabulary is only one problem. Another is familiar terms that have specialized meanings. Notice that the sentences below contain a generally familiar term used in a special manner.

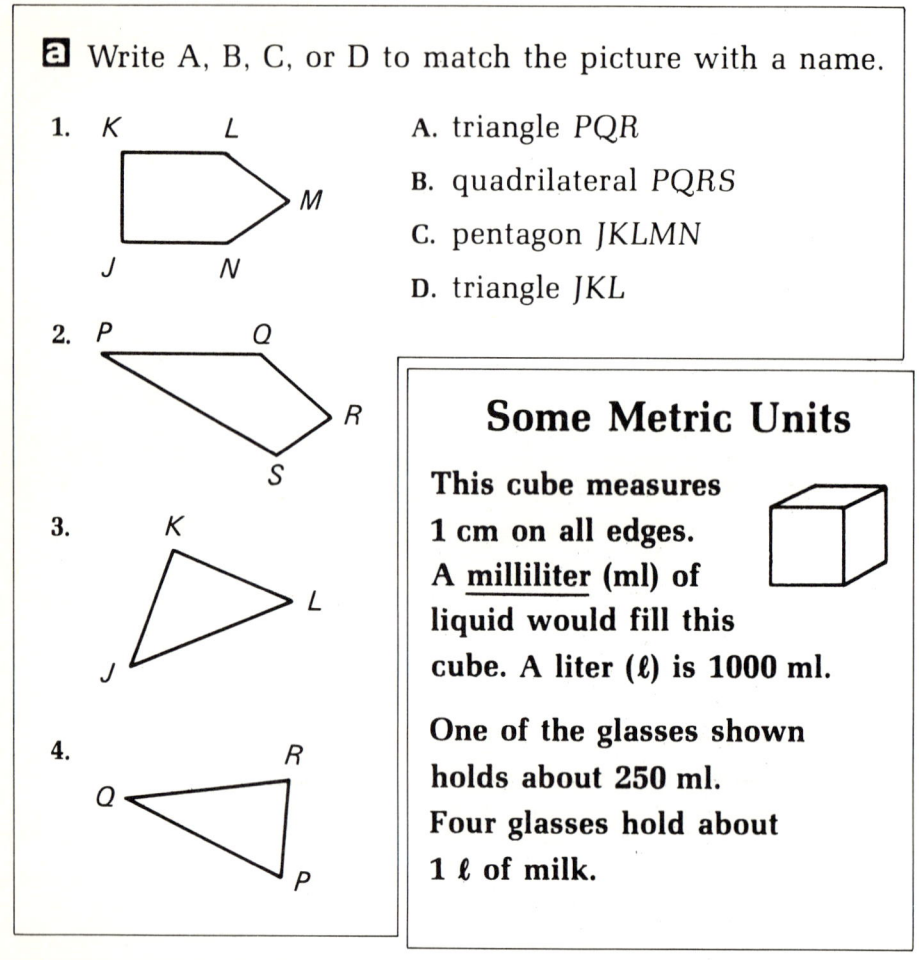

276 CHAPTER 10/DEVELOPING STRATEGIES FOR CONTENT AREA READING

a Write A, B, C, or D to match the picture with a name.

1. [figure: pentagon KLMNJ with point M]
2. [figure: quadrilateral PQRS]
3. [figure: triangle JKL]
4. [figure: triangle QRP]

A. triangle PQR
B. quadrilateral PQRS
C. pentagon JKLMN
D. triangle JKL

Some Metric Units

This cube measures 1 cm on all edges. A <u>milliliter</u> (ml) of liquid would fill this cube. A liter (ℓ) is 1000 ml.

One of the glasses shown holds about 250 ml. Four glasses hold about 1 ℓ of milk.

Figure 10-1 Typical Passages from a Mathematics Text
Source: *Mathematics*, Book 4, by E. R. Duncan et al. Copyright 1981 by Houghton Mifflin.

Look at the vertical section of finely ground material in the *fault* between the layers of rock.

What *forces* made the boat move?

In addition, authors may use terms that have different meanings in the various content areas. The sentences below illustrate this point.

During the long months in prison, Austin's ideas began to *change*.

If I give the salesperson $10, how much *change* would I get back?

The force caused a *change* of state.

Other words that may mean different things in the various content areas are *operation, difference, division, property, product, revolution, planes,* and *positive.* Whenever such words are encountered, teachers should ensure that the students understand the meaning of the word in the context of the content area being read.

Another problem that students may encounter in reading content materials is the use of figurative language. Social studies materials, for instance, contain many concepts stated figuratively. Some of these may be important to the topic, and others may not. In the example below, from a text intended for the fifth-grade level, figurative language is used freely. What kinds of problems may some students have reading this paragraph?

Eager to get rid of Louisiana, Napoleon offered it at a low price which Jefferson delightedly accepted. In a single stroke, the United States expanded from the Mississippi to the Rocky Mountains. Though, at the time, many complained that most of the land seemed worthless and too dry to farm, later it would become the breadbasket of the nation. In making the Louisiana Purchase, Jefferson stretched the constitutional powers of the Presidency to the breaking point. The man who feared a strong central government helped to set a pattern for a long series of strong Presidents. (Davis et al., 1971a).

Paragraph Structures

The writing patterns used in the content areas make certain common demands on the reader (N. Smith, 1964a). Generally, the reader is required to (1) select and evaluate information, (2) organize the information, (3) recall the information at the end of different time periods, (4) locate information, and (5) follow directions. Although these abilities are common to all reading, the reader's success can be assessed only after the act of reading. For example, if students do not know what information to select or how to use the techniques and patterns of organizing the information, they are judged ineffective readers. By teaching students how to recognize and use the structures and patterns in content materials, teachers will prepare them to meet the demands of textbook reading.

In Chapter 8, six paragraph patterns were discussed: enumeration, generalization, comparison and contrast, sequence, cause and result, and question and answer. These patterns appear in general narrative and informational writing and in textbooks. (For a review of these patterns, refer to Chapter 8.) Additional information about the above patterns that is relevant to the structure of content area texts is presented here.

When used in social studies materials, the sequence pattern may be used to present events in a chronological order. The reader is required to understand the particulars of large periods in a specific order. Or the reader has to fix an important date within a large unit. In addition to the time word signals, the reader needs to recognize the sequence of dates. In science writing, the sequence pattern may provide an explanation of a technical process or provide detailed instructions for a demonstration (called experiments in many texts). Intermixed with the sequence may be questions requiring the student to answer an observation of the demonstration. While in the course of reading a sequence pattern in science, students may be expected to follow explicit directions, observe events, explain the results, and draw some conclusions.

In the comparison-and-contrast pattern, an idea, event, person, or process is compared and/or contrasted with another. In some comparisons one whole idea is explained using a closely related, more familiar idea. Or the comparison may be made by detailing the specifics of an idea and comparing them one by one. In another type of comparison, two ideas are given, but the comparison is implied. The reader must match the similar and dissimilar aspects of the two ideas.

In social studies writing, the cause-and-result pattern may consist of a chain of causes and results, especially when the discussion concerns large periods of history.

In addition to these, content area writing may contain other patterns (N. Smith, 1964a, 1964b; Robinson, 1983).

What we shall call *topic development* is not a simple paragraph pattern. A particular idea (topic) is developed in a number of paragraphs. This pattern can be recognized by a title or heading followed by an introductory sentence stating the topic. The complete development of the idea may extend over two or more paragraphs. The paragraphs within the topic development may contain a variety of other patterns. The passage below, from a text intended for use at the third grade, shows how the development of the topic extends over a number of paragraphs. As is the case with many topic developments, the section contains a heading and a general statement about the topic that serves to introduce it.

Puerto Rico

Hola! Welcome to Puerto Rico—one of the most beautiful islands in the Caribbean Sea.

Puerto Rico is a very special place. It has long, white sandy beaches lined with tall, green palm trees.

The middle of the island has high mountains. They are partly covered with a blanket of thick green bushes, trees, and brightly colored flowers.

The weather in Puerto Rico is always warm. People can go swimming all year long. In the mountains, there are often heavy rainfalls, but it rains for just a short time. Soon it is sunny again.

Many different fruits grow well in such warm weather. Bananas, mangos, and pineapples are just some of the delicious fruits that are grown by farmers in the countryside, called *el campo*.

Puerto Rico has small villages, and towns and some very large cities. The largest city is San Juan. It has many tall office buildings and hotels.

Many Puerto Ricans work in offices, stores, and other businesses. The people of Puerto Rico speak and write in Spanish.

Someday you may be able to visit Puerto Rico. Then you can discover for yourself that it is a very special place. (Durr et al., 1983).

A pattern that at first seems to be an enumeration pattern is *classification* and is commonly found in science textbooks. Although the classification pattern may list various subclassifications, it emphasizes the conceptual subdivisions of information rather than the itemization of information. Like other patterns, the classification pattern may span a number of paragraphs.

Energy
Look at the systems on these two pages. In each system, the objects are interacting. It is energy that makes the objects interact. Each system can be called an energy system.

This hitting system is an energy system.
This crashing system is an energy system.
This sliding system is an energy system.

The hitting, crashing, and sliding systems are all energy systems. In each system, objects move. When the objects move, they have energy—motion energy. So all these energy systems can be called moving systems. (Berger et al., 1979).

Another pattern found in elementary content area texts is *problem and solution*. In order to understand the author's entire idea, the reader must understand both the problem and its solution.

Although there are many goods and services to choose from today, some families do not have enough money to buy some of the things they would like to have. Many families want color television sets, but it takes a long time for some people to save enough money to buy one. If they do not want to wait for the set until they save enough money, there is a way they can get it with only a small down payment. It is called installment buying, and it is a form of credit. The family can buy the set with a down payment of they promise to pay a certain amount each month. The set will cost more if it is bought this way, for the store will charge a fee for credit. But the family could be using the set while it is being paid for. (Davis et al., 1971b).

Lastly, a pattern that is not considered a paragraph pattern but does represent a style of writing found in social studies and its related materials is *propaganda*. At all school levels, students should become familiar with the general techniques of propaganda include glad words or glittering generalities, unpleasant words, testimonials, plain-folks implications, and stacking the cards. Although it is rare to find textbook authors using these techniques, sometimes they will let their beliefs or feelings about a topic sway their presentation. For example, in a discussion of desert tribes, the expression "have never even learned to store water" seems to have a connotation that the people of the tribe are incapable of learning. Also, the use of exclamation marks to indiate surprise or emphasis or plain-folks implications and glittering generalities may have connotations of sarcasm or condescension. Finally, some ideas may be presented broadly and loosely, resulting in inaccurate statements. To offset its use, students at all levels should be made aware of both overt and covert propaganda in textbooks and related content area materials.

Graphics

Whenever graphic material appears in content area textbooks, teachers should not assume that students can understand the related concept or process just because it is accompanied by an illustration. Teachers should ensure that students are able to interpret a particular graphic display and alternately read verbal and graphic information.

Various kinds of graphic displays are used in content area textbooks. Depending on the concept and the item to be illustrated, the following types of graphic displays may be found in textbooks (see Figure 10-2):

1. *Photographs.* Science, social studies, and mathematic texts use photographs to support and help explain the textual material. The photographs may be black and white or color.
2. *Realistic illustrations.* Almost all texts use drawings. These are realistic representations, in either black and white or color, of various objects. Some of the drawings may be used directly to support the textual materials. In such cases, the various parts of the drawings may or may not be labeled. In addition, many content area texts contain illustrations that serve only as decoration. In these cases, the illustration may indirectly support the text by showing a related object or event.
3. *Representational illustrations.* Texts may contain drawings in which real objects are recognizable, or the drawing may be stylized in order to highlight various components of the object. Color is sometimes used to differentiate the components.
4. *Diagrammatic illustrations.* When an object or process is shown symbolically, various geometric shapes may be used to represent real objects or events. Diagrams that are used to illustrate a process or a relationship may not show the entire structure of an object or its complete function. In such cases, the diagram directs the viewer's attention to a particular aspect of the process or relationship.
5. *Charts, graphs, and figures.* Some information is represented in a symbolic form that allows the reader to compare or contrast quantities. In such cases, graphs or figures allow the viewer to realize degrees or amounts of difference or similarity without having to process a great deal of numerical information.

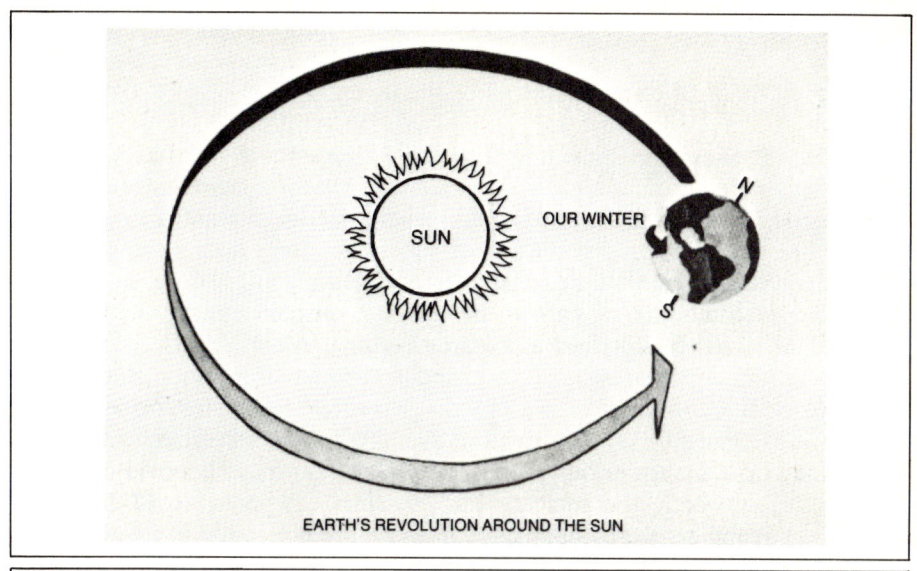

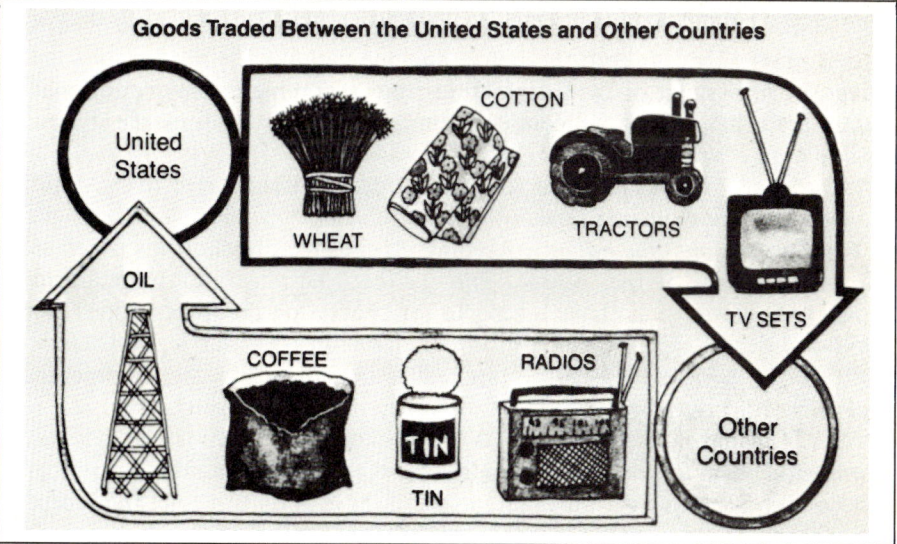

Figure 10-2 Typical Text Graphic Displays
Source: *Ourselves and Others,* Houghton Mifflin Social Studies by S. S. Beattie, Copyright 1980 by Houghton Mifflin.

6. *Maps.* Maps are representations of geographical areas. In order to understand maps, the relationship between the physical word and the symbolic representation must be understood. Maps may be (a) political—showing governmental boundaries of nations, states, cities, or towns; (b) physical—showing land

forms and altitudes; (c) specialized—showing information such as weather patterns, population dispersion, industrial development or natural resources; or (d) a combination of any or all of the three.

The use of graphics in content area textbooks does not always facilitate learning. When readers cannot cope with, or do not possess adequate strategies for, the demands of switching from reading verbal material to reading visuals, then they will be unable to process the author's message. Some authors have referred to reading visuals in textual material as interrupted reading. However, since the visuals are often an integral part of the message, the constant shifting back and forth might be better described as *staccato* reading (Albert, 1971).

The object of any learning is to retain and later recall information, and illustrations are intended to assist in this process. However, many students experience problems in remembering information from graphics unless the images are translated into semantic forms (Berry, 1980). In Chapter 2, a model of human memory shows both the imagery and semantic components of long-term memory. The images stored in imagery memory are not stored in a verbal code, but they can be activated by associations from the semantic memory. For the verbal recall of information stored in the imagery memory, a student must have stored simultaneously both the image and the verbal code (language) for that image. A recounting of the information from a graphic display is not possible unless there has been a concomitant, immediate translation of the illustrated information into words, phrases, and sentences.

In order to help students learn to read graphic displays effectively, teachers should be aware of the confusion that can be caused by visuals.

Photographs and illustrations. Reading pictures requires students to relate the information to what they already know. When the illustrations contain many details, the viewer must have a scheme for processing the information, or else irrelevant details might become distracting. Pictures are not real objects, only abstractions, and so the viewer must realize that they show only a fraction of reality. Further, pictures cannot show something in its totality: pictures depict parts. Drawings and diagrams may oversimplify a continuous process by representing it in stages, thus leaving the viewer with a feeling that the process is not continuous. Nor is it uncommon for an illustration to depict the exception and not the rule.

Estimating size. Photographs, maps, diagrams, and illustrations may not always reveal the scale of objects. The scale from illustration to illustration in the same text also may not be consistent. Small objects may be shown in enlargements, and large objects may be scaled down in order to fit on the page. Close-ups may reveal details that are not always essential to the understanding or recognition of an object. Finally, the perspective of objects may be distorted by the manner in which they are shown.

Color. Color can serve two purposes: functional or decorative. When color is functional, it distinguishes the various components of an object. When it is decorative, it may give the viewer a false impression of the object. In addition, some colors may detract from the illustrator's message. Decorative color may also cause the viewer to focus on unimportant details.

Movement. All illustrations are static, but they are often used to represent movement. Lines and arrows may be used to indicate enlargement, energy release, simultaneous action, movement, and reactions. Since these indicators do not exist in the natural world, the viewer must superimpose them on reality whenever there is to be a transfer of information from the graphic display (Albert, 1971).

GUIDING READING IN THE CONTENT AREAS

The same distinctions made in Chapter 7 between guided reading and independent reading in narrative applies to the reading of content area materials. For the less proficient readers, the teacher should structure the reading activity so that they may more easily determine the meanings intended by the author.

To reiterate, the guided reading-thinking lessons consist of five strategies:

1. Examining information in order to determine what is or is not already known.
2. Hypothesizing about probable meanings based on the information examined.
3. Finding proof of one's hypotheses by reading the text and analyzing the accompanying graphs or illustrations.
4. Suspending judgment whenever information is not available to confirm or reject one's hypotheses.
5. Making decisions whenever the information is available to confirm or reject a hypothesis or deciding to seek additional information elsewhere.

The teacher guides the reading by asking questions that require predictions to be made. For example, using the information contained in a selection entitled "Before History Began" the teacher would ask for predictions about specific segments of the passage. The number of paragraphs that the students read is determined by the amount of information they are capable of processing. Since content area materials are often more demanding, students should not be expected to process the same number of sentences or paragraphs as they might be capable of with narrative material.

The following lesson illustrates how a guided reading-thinking lesson might be structured for reading a sixth-grade social studies text:

Concepts:
1. People have used technology since prehistoric times.
2. Ancient people independently in all parts of the world discovered farming. This might be the most important discovery ever made.
3. Growing crops and domesticating animals changed people's life styles—hunters and gatherers began to live in permanent villages.

Concept: Ancillary
1. Archeologists are scientists who search for traces of ancient people.

Purpose:

To provide pupils with new terms and concepts and specific facts about the impact of the discovery of farming on ancient people's life styles. This is the second lesson in a unit about "People Are Toolmakers."

Guiding Questions
1. Subtitle, "Searching for Beginnings," special subsection on fourth and fifth pages of lesson (pp. 232–233); photograph and drawing of archeological dig. What do you already know about archeologists? What "beginnings" would they be searching for? You sometimes make guesses about things. What kind of guesses do archeologists make?

2. Title page, "Before History Began," first subsection with pictures and time line. What does the picture show you about early humans' life style? When is the period "before history?" What does "history" mean? What information does the time line provide?
3. Second subsection, "The Age of Stone," second and third pages with illustrations. What is the age of stone? Where would it be on the time line on page 239? What questions did the author want you to answer while reading? Did you have an answer for them? What did you do when you couldn't answer the author's questions?

    Were there any words you couldn't figure out from the passage? Was the word important to understanding the author's ideas? What did you do when you couldn't figure out a word? What is important about the Stone Age? How do the pictures on the pages fit in with the information in the text?
4. Third subsection, "Farming in the Fertile Crescent." Before reading this section, read the subsection, "Discovering Farming," on page 234. Why is this section set off from the text by a colored page? (Repeat questions about the author's use of questions and unfamiliar vocabulary here and in the reading of each subsequent subsection.)

    How is the information in this section told differently then the information in the other sections? Why is this information included in the unit? How does the story of the discovery of farming fit in with the information about archeologists' creating hypotheses?

    Subsection, "Farming in the Fertile Crescent," one page with map. What is the Fertile Crescent? In what ways is an understanding of the farming done in the Fertile Crescent linked to the "discovery of farming?" In what ways does an understanding of the discovery of farming help you understand farming in the Fertile Creascent? What part of the world is shown in the map of the Fertile Crescent?
5. Subsection, "Farming in Other Parts of the World," one page with illustration. How does the beginning of farming in other parts of the world compare to that in the Fertile Crescent?
6. Subsections, "Learning to Use Animals," "New Technology for Farming," and "A New Life Style," three pages with illustations. How were ancient people's lives changed because of using animals and the development of new technology? What did their new life style become? (Guided Reading-Thinking Lesson based on Branson [1980] "Before History Began," pp. 229-239).

The guided reading-thinking lesson is an opportunity to direct the students efforts in applying their reading and thinking strategies. All through the lesson, teachers should be conscious of the students efforts to apply their sentence-reading, paragraph-reading, and word recognition strategies in reconstructing the author's ideas. The aim of a guided content reading-thinking lesson is the acquisition of information—that is, the concepts and facts related to the topic—and so the teacher's efforts should always be directed toward that end. The guided reading-thinking lesson is used whenever the students cannot gain that information independently. As they become better at applying reading strategies, teachers can use the lesson to direct their attention to the application of those strategies.

For example, embedded within the text of the sample lesson above are questions or directions for students to provide some information on their own. In the case of this lesson the questions require the students to already know something about the topic. Such questions as "Why do you suppose few bone and wood tools have been discovered? and "How many of the foods discovered by ancient farmers do you eat fairly often?" may interrupt the reading and cause the direct flow of the author's main points to be lost. During the course of the lesson teachers should guide the students around the questions that may interrupt their train of thought. After the entire lesson has been read, you should return to those questions for further discussion. It is quite possible that some students may not be able to answer them. In such instances you should determine whether or not to delay answering these questions until the students have acquired additional information.

The teacher's guidance may also be needed to clarify the referential expressions in this passage, which is quite typical of elementary-school social studies textbooks. Depending on the students' understanding of referential constructions, teachers should guide them in identifying the referents in statements such as

This is just a moment of time compared to prehistory ...
They ate fruit, nuts, roots, seeds ...
That happening has been called perhaps the most important discovery ever made.
Those countries didn't exist when ...
Those broken bones and tools must be made to tell a story.
As you know, that is when history began.

STRATEGIES FOR INDEPENDENT READING IN THE CONTENT AREAS

Students need a system for independently reading textbooks in the content areas. One popular system is known by the acronym SQ3R (Sargent et al., 1970). The SQ3R process consists of five stages: survey, question, read, recite, and review. This technique may be benefit students in that

1. The students are led to an independent approach to reading and using textual materials in the content areas.
2. The students develop procedures for adapting their reading strategies to the reading of an expository style of writing.
3. The students develop strategies for integrating the reading of textual and graphic information.

4. The students extend their understanding of creative problem solving to the acquisition of the specific knowledge and generalizations in the content areas.

The SQ3R technique should be taught to all students. The format of the strategy teaching lesson in Chapter 8 can be modified for presenting the steps to the student. The technique can be introduced to students at any grade level. Although the procedures may be modified to meet the individual proficiencies of each student the SQ3R plan, once learned, can serve students throughout their school years. It provides them with a format into which they can fit their ever-increasing reading strategies and skills.

The steps of the SQ3R plan are:

1. *Survey*. The purpose of the survey stage is to determine what kinds of knowledge or information the author expects the reader to understand. It is a "taking stock" of what one already knows about the topic as well as determining what one does not know. Through a survey of the reading materials, one becomes aware of the reading demands that will be imposed by the materials and what possible difficulties may be encountered in reading the materials.

Specifically, the survey stage consists of examining the heading and subheadings, looking for terms that are written in boldface or italics, examining the graphic displays for the kinds of information they portray, and looking for any signals to the organization of the textual material.

During the survey stage, the reader is to establish an idea about the topic and to determine the reading demands that may have to be met.

2. *Question*. The purpose of the question stage is to set tentative hypotheses about the author's ideas. These hypotheses or predictions become the purposes for which the pupils will read the text. During the questioning stage, pupils should ask themselves what they already know about the topic and what is it the author wishes them to know after they have read it.

Specifically, the question stage consists of establishing questions that may be answered from reading the passage. One source is the list of questions posed by the author at the beginning or end of each subsection. Another source is the collection of subheadings of each section. For example, the subheadings of the passage "You Are Part of the World" (Beattie & Greco, 1980, pp. 184–189), a selection from a third-grade social studies text, are

You Are Part of The World
   Goods Around the World
   Services Around the World
   Cooperation Around the World
   Tools Around the World
   Language Around the World

This is the thirteenth lesson in the unit "What Are Groups?" From a survey, it would be determined that people from all parts of the world share goods, services, tools, and some form of language. (The concepts of goods and services were presented in a previous lesson.) To form specific purposes for reading, students might ask questions such as

How are we part of the world?
What goods are used around the world?
What services are used around the world?
What cooperation takes place around the world?
What kind of tools are used around the world?
What types of languages are used around the world?

In addition, the students could predict from the accompanying illustrations that the passage will contain information to answer questions such as

How are goods traded between the United States and other countries?
What other transporation services do we share with other countries?
How do we help hungry people around the world?
Can all people understand picture signs?

The question and survey stages may be combined so that the information from the photographs, drawings, and diagrams (a representation of different ethnic groups in the world, the flow of goods from the United States to other nations, a bus station, health and food in Asia and Africa, a telecommunications satellite, and international road signs) is used to alter the questions or suggest different ones.

Since textbooks usually contain the same format and structure throughout, the SQ3R procedure is facilitated through continued use of the same texts. Students should be able to acquire easily the strategy of forming predictions about a selection, since they will be able to anticipate the location of cues to the author's message.

3. *Read.* The purpose of the read stage is to locate the information suggested by the questions posed during the previous two stages. Specifically, students should know that they are reading during this stage for two general purposes: (1) to find the answers to the questions they created and (2) find other important information that they did not predict through specific questions. This later aspect of reading is important, since their questions might not have covered all the author's main points. They now should distinguish between information contained in the passage that they predicted would be there and that they did not predict.

Some authors use aspects of the survey and question stages in structuring their textual materials. The passage below gives students a preset question to focus their attention on important ideas. Notice the information and question at the end of the last paragraph of the following selection. This information is indirectly related to the passage's main point, and the final question directs the students' attention away from that point. Only by viewing reading as creative problem solving will they realize this.

What is Culture?
Human beings are different from animals. Our hands are different. The way we stand is different. The way we walk is different. The way we think is different.

Another difference between humans and animals is that humans have culture (KUL-chur). Culture is the human way of living. Tools, language, institutions, and beliefs make up culture.

Human beings use tools for almost everything they do. We use tools to eat. We use tools to work.

Human beings use language (LANG-gwij) to tell others what they are thinking. How are the people in the pictures using language?

Another part of culture is institutions (in sti-TOO-shuns). Institutions are ways people do the same things over and over again.

Holidays are institutions because we celebrate them in the same way each time. Schools are institutions because we do the same kinds of things in all schools.

Beliefs are part of culture too. A belief is something that a person thinks is true. Some people believe that walking under a ladder is bad luck. Do you have this belief? (Beattie & Greco, 1980).

4. *Recite.* The purpose of the recite stage is to answer the questions posed during the survey and question stages. The recitation is actually the immediate recall of information from the portion of the passage just read. Some students will be able to read only one subsection at a time. Others may be able to read the entire section. In either case, they should receive immediate feedback about the success of their reading strategies. It is during the recite stage that decisions are made about what information the author intended to be remembered and what information supports ideas or has an additional, "human interest" effect.

Specifically, the recite stage consists of taking each question and forming an answer to it. The answers may be given in an oral or a written form depending on the purpose of the lesson. After all the questions for a section or subsection have been answered, the students should then identify other information given in the passage. If the information is deemed important to the topic, then a question should be formed for which this additional information is an answer. A discussion should ensue as to why, if the information seems to be important to the author's main idea, its occurrence was not predicted. The answer may be that some clue was missed or, possibly, no clue was provided.

It is during the recite stage that students demonstrate their ability to reconstruct the intended message of the author through a self-guided reading-thinking activity.

5. *Review.* The purpose of the review stage is to answer at a later time the questions formed during the survey and question stages. Since a purpose for studying a content area is to develop a store of information and concepts, remembering is

a desirable characteristic of proficient students. However, understanding an author's message should not be considered synonymous with remembering; one's understanding of a topic does not insure recall of its ideas (Pauk, 1973). Therefore, some additional steps should be taken by students to ensure the retention of learned information. The previous stage, recite, was concerned with the immediate remembering of information. The review stage is concerned with the long term retention of information. The most efficient time to institute this stage is within twenty-four hours of completing the recite stage, and then periodically thereafter.

Specifically, the review stage consists of taking each question created during the survey and question stages, together with those added during the recite stage, and attempting to answer them. At first, no referral is made to the text or to the answers generated during previous stages. Then the new answers are checked against previous answers or the text. This provides immediate feedback to the students about the amount of information that is remembered. Students realize for themselves what information may need additional effort to be retained. Or, they, together with their teachers, may wish to decide whether the information that was forgotten (and there is strong evidence that forgetting is a natural occurrence) is important and should be relearned.

If relearning is needed, there is some evidence that a mere rereading of the text will not result in remembering (Pauk, 1973). What may occur during rereading is the "seeing" of already known information—that is, the eye and mind see learned information and not any unlearned information. What is needed after a first reading may be a different approach to the same information.

The content area text should not be used as the singular source of learning. There are limitations to the effectiveness of texts as informational resources. The technique suggested here, the SQ3R procedure, may assist students become proficient independent readers. Yet, because of factors within the students, the reading materials, or the situations in which the reading acts are undertaken, the technique may not be successful at a particular time. Other learning and teaching procedures should then be sought.

Activities for Content Area Reading

The activities discussed in Chapter 7 for developing questioning strategies, in Chapter 8 for developing sentence- and paragraph-reading strategies, and in Chapter 9 for developing general vocabularies, contextual signals, and dictionary usage should be continued and extended for content area reading. Students should be given extensive opportunities to use their strategies independently in both narrative and expository reading materials. In addition, the teacher can employ any of the following:

☐ Extend the use of the SQ3R procedure to reading word problems in mathematics (Maffei, 1973). The new procedure becomes an SQ4R procedure:

1. Survey. Skim the word problem and locate and list any unknown words.
2. Question. Write a direct question about the problem.
3. Read. Read the problem and list all word facts in a logical order.
4. Reflect. Translate all the word facts into number facts.
5. Rewrite and solve. Write the word problem as a mathematics problem and solve it.
6. Review. Reread the word problem, putting the answer into the correct statement.

☐ Provide an opportunity for the translation of diagrammatic information into standard English sentences. In the beginning phase of this activity, they should match the sentences to the appropriate diagrams. As they become more proficient at interpreting visual displays, they should create their own sentences. For example, give the students an illustration and three sentences from which they are to select the one that matches the drawing according to the ideas being studied.

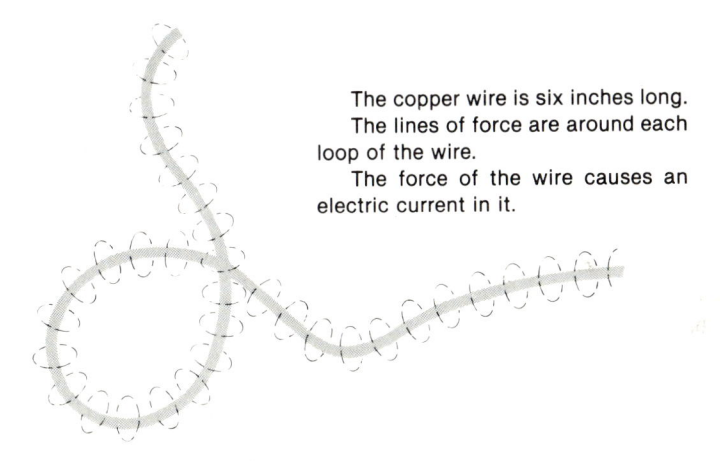

The copper wire is six inches long.
The lines of force are around each loop of the wire.
The force of the wire causes an electric current in it.

This activity can be extended for use with maps or incidental or decorative illustrations. Have the students select information from the passage that comes closest to explaining the illustration. Or have them write a paragraph or explain to another student the information given in the map or illustration.

☐ Provide opportunities for the information learned in the content areas in other situations. Have them create stories, plays, poems, radio broadcasts, or murals in which the information is used. The information may be from any of the content areas. For example, after studying erosion in science, have the students act out situations in which they assume the roles of town engineers planning the construction of a new road in the hilly section of town. Or after studying Latin American customs and cultures, have them play a travel agent preparing a tour group for a visit.

☐ Provide an opportunity to relate the lives of interesting or important individuals to the study of a topic. Have them read and discuss the biographies of individuals who either contributed to the topic or were greatly influenced by it. For example, during the study of plants, the lives of Heinz, Booker T. Washington, Burbank and others can be studied and their contributions explored.

☐ Provide an opportunity to explore the everyday application of content area concepts. For example, during a science unit on machines, they should read repair manuals and "how-to-fix-it" books, or during social studies units, travel books.

☐ Provide simulation strategies that approximate what a reader does when reading independently (Herber & Nelson, 1975). This provides direct instruction in reading with good understanding. It begins with the teacher's reading a passage and asking questions about the author's major ideas. Then, the answers to the questions are used to help make up a set of exercises:

1. The first set provides the students with a number of statements to which they should respond and the pages and paragraphs where information to support or refute those statements can be found. The students should indicate whether they agree or disagree with the exercise statements.
2. The next gives the students a set of statements similar to the preceding, but the teacher does not tell them where additional information may be found.
3. The third provides questions to be answered as well as where pertinent information can be found.
4. In this set of exercises the questions have no references to pages or paragraphs.
5. When the students are able to do the preceding exercise, they are given an assignment to read and are required to create their own questions and answers.
6. Finally, when they are able to read the content area text at their level, they should be able to read a passage and make their own statements of concepts and ideas.

☐ Use children's literature as an aid in content area instruction. Trade books can be effectively used to make complex ideas clear, to illustrate many of the practical ideas of the content areas, to encourage and stimulate expression in speaking and writing, and to foster the growth of vocabulary. There are many informational books on the physical world, people and places, history, and mathematics that can be easily used to extend students' knowledge and understanding. After acquiring the background through class exercises, the students also will have the necessary prerequisites for undertaking the reading of many more books independently.

☐ Provide exercises that lead to the understanding of the relationship between standard English sentences and mathematical sentences. The findings of research on reading in mathematics underscores the importance of a particular language factor. That factor seems to be one of verbal reading ability (Aiken, 1972). The exercises should promote the understanding of the mathematical sentence as an English sentence by means of examples of mathematical structures that parallel English structures (Lacey & Weil, 1975). The first step is to establish that the mathematical sentence is read from left to right. Then basic symbol and word associations should be taught:

and	is synonymous with *plus*
is	is synonymous with *equals*
$=$	is the equivalent of *is;* also, $=$ is the same as *these are the same number of things*
$+$	means *and, increased by, plus*
$-$	means *minus, subtract, decreased by, diminished by*
$\neq$	means *is not equal to*
$>$	means *is greater than*
$<$	means *is less than*
$\times$	means *times, product, multiplied by*
$\div$	means *quotient, divided by, ratio*

Using these symbol and word associations, the students can do the following:

$$\text{seven and four is eleven}$$
$$7 + 4 = 11$$

1. Read the English sentences and write it as a mathematics sentence.
2. Reverse 1.
3. Establish that an addition mathematics sentence may be represented by many English sentences.

Seven added to four equals eleven.

Adding seven and four is eleven.

Follow this with sentences about subtraction, multiplication, and division. compound sentences can be written after some other symbols are learned:

$\vee$	means the conjunction *and*
$\wedge$	means the disjunction *or*
$\geq$	means *is greater than or equal to*
$\leq$	means *is less than or equal to*
$\not<$	means *is not less than*
$\not>$	means *is not greater than*

Sample sentences are

Six plus ten is less than twenty, $6 + 10 < 20$
   and $\vee$
twelve plus ten is greater than four. $12 + 10 > 4$

Nine minus one is not equal to two, $9 - 1 \neq 2$
   or $\wedge$
nine plus two is greater than ten. $9 + 2 > 10$

STRATEGIES FOR LOCATING INFORMATION AND USING REFERENCE MATERIALS

Fully independent readers are able to use almost any type of reading material for obtaining information. The strategies discussed in this section are those needed to locate information (1) in books, (2) in libraries, (3) in encyclopedias, and (4) on maps, globes, and atlases. In some of the literature on reading in the content areas, these strategies are called study skills. In other places they are labeled functional reading skills. it does not matter what name they are given; they are prerequisites for independent, lifelong self-instruction.

The strategies that follow are discussed without reference to a specific grade level. They represent all the locational and reference strategies that should be acquired by the end of elementary school. Instruction should be given after determining the reading demands placed on the students by the instructional materials being used and their abilities to meet those demands.

Locating Information in Books

Beginning with their first contact with books, students should learn the purpose of the various parts of a book as well as procedures for using those parts to locate information. Specifically, students should develop the ability to use

1. The title page to obtain information about the author, illustrator, and publisher of the book.
2. The table of contents to locate topics and general areas of information.
3. The index to locate specific facts or details.
4. The introduction, preface, and foreword to find out both the author's purpose for writing the text and the basic framework of the book.
5. The copyright page to obtain information for estimating the relevance and/or recency of the information in the book.

6. The glossary for the definitions of words as they are used by the author.
7. The bibliography to locate other sources of information on the topic or to check the author's source of information.
8. The appendix to obtain supplementary information about the topic.

In addition, authors use other signaling devices to identify important information. Such signaling devices are italicized words or boldface type, colored type, brackets, underlining, and colored or shaded boxes around sentences or whole paragraphs. A careful analysis of various book formats should reveal other techniques that authors and publishers employ to help readers identify and locate information.

Locating Information in Libraries

Libraries are organized so that information can be conveniently found. Once one knows how to use a library, that knowledge should be useful for a lifetime. Some people erroneously think that the purpose of a library is to store information. Museums are the storehouses of information; libraries are the circulators of information.

In order to effectively locate and use the information in a library, the reader needs strategies for using

1. *The card catalog.* The card catalog contains a listing of all the books in the library. From the catalog it is possible to locate a book if one knows the author, the title, or the subject area. Some libraries use separate file drawers for each of the three references, but most school libraries mix the three types of cards. The strategies needed for using the card catalog are

Identifying the author's name.
Identifying the book's title.
Identifying the subject heading.
Understanding the library classification code.

2. *The library arrangement.* Most school libraries use the Dewey decimal classification scheme to arrange their books. This is only one of a number of ways in which libraries can identify the location of a book. Table 10-1 shows the two most popular classification schemes—the Dewey decimal and the Library of Congress.

Most school and public libraries, however, do not catalog popular fiction or biographies by means of the Dewey decimal system. General fiction is arranged according to the first letter of the author's last name, and biographies are arranged according to the first initial of the subject of the biography, preceded by the letter B.

Table 10-1 Two Popular Libraries Classification Schemes

The Dewey Decimal Classification

000	General Works	500	Pure Science
100	Philosophy	600	Technology
200	Religion	700	The Arts
300	Social Sciences	800	Literature
400	Language	900	History

The Library of Congress Classification

A	General Works—Polygraphy	M	Music
B	Philosophy—Religion	N	Fine Arts
C	History-Auxiliary Sciences	P	Language and Literature
D	History and Topography (except America)	Q	Science
		R	Medicine
E-F	America	S	Agriculture—Plant and Animal Industry
G	Geography—Anthropology		
H	Social Sciences	T	Technology
J	Political Science	U	Military Science
K	Law	V	Naval Science
L	Education	Z	Bibliography and Library Science

3. *Special collections.* Libraries have material in the form of pamphlets and pictures arranged alphabetically according to topic. In addition, libraries may have record and filmstrip collections and magazines. Older pupils may find it convenient to learn to use the *Reader's Guide to Periodical Literature* in order to locate information in the magazine collection.

Strategies for Using the Encyclopedia

The encyclopedia can be an excellent source of information about a wide range of topics. It is sometimes thought that the encyclopedia is an irrefutable source. A commonly heard statement is, "It must be right ... I read it in the encyclopedia" (Wehmeyer, 1975). Although the encyclopedia may look more authoritative than other written works do, it can, of course, be in error. The "facts" about the same event may be recorded differently in different encyclopedias (Wehmeyer, 1975). Students therefore, should be encouraged to note and investigate contradictions whenever encountered, and they should not accept information as true just because it is in the encyclopedia.

Before using an encyclopedia, students should understand (1) the type of information contained in it, (2) the purposes for which the information has been collected, and (3) the relative value of the information.

In order to find and use the information in an encyclopedia, the reader needs strategies for using

1. The encyclopedia index.
2. The information on the spine of each volume.
3. The guide words.
4. The cross-references.
5. The boldface type and parentheses used in the main entries.
6. The bibliographies at the ends of articles.

Although encyclopedias often are scholarly attempts at presenting information concisely, they do have limitations:

1. The size and scope of encyclopedias do not allow them to have current information on all topics. This is especially true in natural and political science, in which essential data may change rapidly.
2. Some encyclopedias are cognitively and linguistically too demanding for children in the lower grades.

These limitations are being overcome by some encyclopedia publishers. Specialized, limited-scope scientific encyclopedias, for example, are available. Many publishers also are producing limited-scope encyclopedia series written especially for young children. These child-oriented encyclopedias are written in a style and format approximating that found in many elementary content area textbooks.

Strategies for Locating Information on Maps

Maps are representations of the earth's physical features. The type of representation that most closely approximates the earth is the globe. However, it may not be practical to use globes for all the different kinds of information that maps can provide. Therefore, a prerequisite for using maps is understanding the element of distortion that occurs when maps are drawn. The distortion affects the size and location of many features of the earth's surface. The greatest distortion occurs on world maps, the least on maps of extremely small areas of the earth.

In order to find and use the information found on maps and globes, the reader needs strategies for using

1. Different map projections. The two most common map projections used in elementary content area texts and school atlases are the mercator projection and the polar projection. In order to develop true perspective of the relative size, shape, and placement of geographical positions, the amount and type of distortion created by each projection should be understood.
2. Different types of maps. The purpose of physical or relief maps, political maps, and certain special maps needs to be understood as well as the features that make each kind of map different.

3. Map symbols. Map makers generally use standard symbols for indicating geographic locations: lakes, cities, rivers, highways, political boundaries, and direction.
4. Map colorations. Understanding the relationship between map color and actual land color is essential to effective map use. Although some colors on physical maps seem to relate to actual land formations—blue for water, green and brown for landforms—the colors on political and special-purpose maps usually have no relationship to the concepts they represent.
5. Scales of distance. Not only are maps not representative of the actual distances found on earth, but the scale of distance and size from one map to another also may differ.
6. Map legends. Most maps provide a legend explaining their symbols, color, and scale.

STRATEGIES FOR READING THE NEWSPAPER

The newspaper generally fits into any school's content area programs. It is a current, constant source of information about events that is relatively inexpensive and easily available. In addition, it can accommodate a wide variation in reading abilities—something in almost every newspaper can be read by children in elementary school.

Any newspaper can be used for instruction, but it is probably best to use one that is familiar to the students and that will be read by them independently. Once the basic strategies for reading newspapers have been acquired, two or more newspapers can be compared in regard to the same information.

The strategies for finding and using the information in newspapers are

1. The content of a newspaper. Every newspaper contains a variety of information. Generally, this information consists of

a. News stories. News stories may be factual, interpretive, or speculative.
b. Human interest stories.
c. Opinion articles. Opinion articles may be either editorials or essays signed by columnists.
d. Sports stories.
e. Business and finance articles.
f. Entertainment articles, news, reviews, time tables.
g. Comics and puzzles.
h. Weather reports and forecasts.
i. Advertisements.
j. Obituaries.

2. The organization of the contents. Each newspaper organizes its contents in a particular manner that remains fairly constant over a period of time. Familiarity with the organization of a newspaper facilitates the locating of information on a particular topic.

3. The organization of news and feature articles. News stories are written so that the most current news is at the beginning of the article. the introductory paragraph usually contains answers to the five W's: who, what, when, where, and why. As one reads further into an article, information that appeared in earlier stories may be found. Feature stories and opinion articles are generally written in a more narrative style.

The newspaper is a source of information that can be used in developing skills and strategies in all of the content areas. Daily, words that are related to social studies and science topics can be found in the newspaper. Most important, these words are available to students in a context that often discloses their meanings. Photographs, maps, charts, and diagrams are used extensively and can be used to supplement the graphic displays used in the content areas textbooks. Human interest stories, reviews, opinion articles, and political cartoons can be used to show how the "facts" found in textbooks and encyclopedias can be used by different people to influence others in their thinking. Finally, advertisements; radio, TV, and movie schedules; the business pages; and the sports sections can provide examples of the utility of arithmetical skills in the students' daily lives.

Activities for Developing Newspaper Reading Strategies

The following strategies for effective newspaper reading can be used in specific units at different grade levels. If funds are available, it is worthwhile to give each student a copy of a newspaper. (This is not unreasonable since every student can receive a newspaper for an entire month for the cost of a typical workbook.)

☐ Develop a sense of the content of a newspaper. Have the students work in small teams to list all the different types of information in a newspaper. This activity can be modified to meet the reading abilities of a wide range of students. Younger children can name the different types of information, and the teacher can record them on the chalkboard or a permanent chart. Older students can make their own lists.

☐ Develop a sense of current events. Each day have the students locate news articles of local, national, and international concern. This activity can done with maps by pointing out on the class map the locale of each story.

☐ Develop a sense of the organization of a news story. Have the students use their knowledge of sentence information to figure out that news writers often use the same signals for the location of that information as do other writers.

☐ Develop a sense of headline writing. Use the headlines of a variety of stories and have the students find the information in the story that was used as the basis for the headline. Extend this activity to develop a sense of figurative language, puns, and connotations in headline writing. Have the students write their own headlines for stories or rewrite the headlines of newspaper stories.

☐ Develop a sense of purposeful letter writing. Have the students elect something from the newspaper—a job advertisement, an editorial, a mail order

300 CHAPTER 10/DEVELOPING STRATEGIES FOR CONTENT AREA READING

Topic: SOCIAL ISSUES   21

COMIC STRIP: ROLE ANALYSIS

Select 4 or 5 comic strips from your local paper. Analyze them according to the criteria below for at least a 4-week period. Write a report which summarizes your findings, indicating what the comic strips are saying about the "American way" of life.

Occupations
1. What occupations do the male characters have?
2. What occupations do the female characters have?
3. Keep a list of the main characters for whom **no** occupation is mentioned.
4. If children or teenagers discuss future occupations, which jobs are boys interested in? girls?

Environment
1. What is the location of the action of each comic strip? (home, office, parks, city streets, etc.)
2. In which of the above settings do women most often appear? In which settings do men most often appear?
3. In "home" or "family" settings, what activities are men engaged in? women?

Dialogue
1. What topics are discussed in each comic strip (politics, education, the home and the family, etc.?)
2. What can you tell about the attitudes of the characters towards each other from the dialogue?
3. Who discusses what? (that is, can you make any generalizations about topics that women discuss? that men discuss? teenagers?)

FIGURE 10-3 Topic Study Sheet: Newspapers
Source: *The Associated Press Newspaper Reading Skills Development Program,* Project File. Copyright 1974 by AP Newsfeatures.

ad—and then write a letter in response to that item. Where it is appropriate have them mail their letters.

☐ Develop a sense of the newspaper as a continuous resource and reference. Give the student a topic study sheet. The topic should be one that is current and that will be reported on almost daily for an extended period, for example, Such topics could deal with politics, social issues, or a sports series. The format and content of the study sheet should help the students make some conclusions about the topic. The guide in Figure 10-3 can be used as a model that may be modified to meet the students' abilities.

☐ Develop an understanding of the use of propaganda techniques. Starting with advertisements and then moving to articles of familiar stories and events, the students can begin to analyze propaganda techniques. They can try to determine by comparing the advertised product (whenever possible) or a number of articles written about the same event or topic whether propaganda techniques were used and the extent to which they might influence an individual's thinking.

☐ Develop an interest in the biographies of interesting or important people. Through the reading newspaper obituaries, students can appreciate the contributions of various people to the topics they are studying in the content areas.

Functional Literacy

Schools have the purpose for preparing young people for survival in the general society. To some people, this means learning the "basics" of the knowledge usually presented in the content areas of science, social studies, and mathematics. Many of these people also believe that the functional skills should be learned by students who do not have the competencies for learning the information presented in the content areas.

However, functional literacy is for all students—those performing in a superior manner in school and those having problems learning. It is not an either/or instructional decision. Functional literacy skills are needed for living and working in our highly industrialized society. Sophisticated technology and complex laws and regulations require us to be able to deal with a large variety of printed matter, not all of which "reads" like a book.

What is meant by functional literacy? A general definition might be the ability to use certain skills and knowledge with the level of competence needed for meeting the requirements of adult living. This means that individuals should be able to cope with their lives. *Functional* means that the ability to read or write is determined in part by what must be read or written. Within this concept, there is no general level of literacy that is to be attained by all people. The level and degree of competence needed in a particular situation may be different for different people, since they may not have the same purpose(s) for performing the reading or writing task.

Functional reading differs from general reading. General reading is what has been described and discussed throughout the major portion of this text and is mainly for informing or entertaining. Although the process of reading is an active search for meaning, the reader's overt response during and after general reading is usually passive. There is no immediate action to be taken because the reader is acquiring information and concepts for a delayed response. Functional reading, on the other hand, is done to do something. There is usually an immediate need for action resulting from an active search for meaning, and the reader will make an active, overt response as the result of the reading situation.

General and functional reading also differ in their organization and format. General reading is usually organized in paragraphs form. On the surface, each piece of general reading appears similar. But functional materials vary noticable in their organization, style, and format. Even in a group or type of material there is great variety, as can be seen in a classified want ad, a telephone directory ad (yellow pages), and a department store advertisement.

As a result of research conducted as part of the Adult Performance Level Project (Northcut et al., 1975) it is evident that there are many kinds of literacy tasks.

Literacy, in its broadest sense, is possessing all the skills needed to perform in all aspects of society. Table 10-2 contains a matrix showing the interaction of society's "skills" and "aspects."

The areas of literacy skills are reading, writing, identification of facts and terms, computation, and problem solving. The first three deal with understanding and using written materials and are of prime concern to us. Writing means the ability to handle everyday writing. Identification of facts and terms is recognizing words in each of the aspects of society. Computation is not just performing the four functions, but it is also understanding problems and manipulating numerical quantities. Problem solving is knowing appropriate and alternative solutions to problems of every day living (schemas).

The aspects of society in which functional tasks are performed are community resources, occupational knowledge, consumer economics, health and government and law. Community resources includes using recreational activities, transportation facilities, obtaining documents, and using informational sources. Occupational knowledge includes knowing job requirements, obtaining vocational counseling, selecting jobs and occupations, and applying for and holding a job.

Table 10-2 Sample Functional Literacy Skills Appropriate for Elementary and Intermediate School Pupils.

Aspects of Society → Skills ↓	Community Resources	Occupational Knowledge	Consumer Economics	Health	Government and Law
Reading	reading a bus or train schedule	reading a poster calling for newspaper deliverers	reading a sales slip	reading a label on a medicine package	reading a ballot in school elections.
Writing	writing a letter for information about recreational facilities	completing an application for a summer camp job	writing for a magazine subscription	answer questions on a medical form	writing rules for a club
Identification of Facts/ Terms	knowing what daylight savings time is	knowing the difference between a job and an occupation	knowing what propaganda is	knowing what the different hospital services are	knowing the meaning of mayor, governor
Computation					
Problem Solving					

Consumer economics includes knowing and demonstrating an understanding of purchasing practices. Health includes understanding the principles and practices that lead to mental and physical health. Government and law includes understanding the structure of government and how the functions of the legal systems delineate the right and obligations of us all.

Specific types of materials requiring functional reading, writing, and identification-of-terms skills are

1. Advertisements. The purposes of these are to identify something that is available: classified ads—a job, product ads—an item or service.
2. Blanks and forms. Their purpose is to file information to be used for obtaining a product or service.
3. Lists. These are sources of information that might be needed to perform another task.
4. Directions. These serve to provide instructions for specific products and services.
5. Legal documents. The purpose of a legal document varies with the specific document. Some are for immediate response—tickets and tax statements—and others are for delayed responses or storing information—wills and birth certificates.
6. Visuals. The purposes of visuals are to clearly identify how information is related and to draw attention to some needed information. These include transit maps, store and office signs, and street and highway designations.
7. Schedules. These put information into time sequence and allow us to plan immediate and future responses or actions.

There are some general guidelines for teaching the reading and writing of functional literacy materials in all classes and at all levels of performance:

1. Use real materials. Students should receive instruction on those materials that will be met in actual life situations. The use of "watered down" or altered materials provides students a false sense of what are the actual demands of life coping or survival reading and writing.
2. Teach the purpose for doing each functional task.
3. Point out the contrasting features of general and functional reading materials.
4. Teach the specialized vocabulary. Each type of functional material has concepts and terms that appear consistently. These should be identified and learned.
5. Base instruction on performance. Performance is the key to instruction and learning to use functional materials.
6. Use problem-solving situations. All communication skills are learned in situations in which individuals have a reason for receiving and sending ideas. These can be role-playing situations in which the students learn the schema of the situation and the verbal skills for acting them out.

7. Extend the activities into real life. Students will be able to recognize their own abilities as they see how they fare in using their skills outside school.

There are many ways that functional tasks can be brought into classrooms—from kindergarten to adult courses. In each case, the type of material, its content, specific tasks, and purposes should be appropriate to the students' age, background, and language and thinking capabilities.

In language arts or English instruction you can be use advertising, legal writing, forms and applications, telephone techniques, resume writing, catalog reading, and order writing.

In social studies instruction you can use immigration documents, transportation, occupations in social fields, contracts, city resources, money and money substitutes, and financial services.

In mathematics instruction you can be use occupations in related fields, time zones, measures, computation of salaries and benefits, budgeting, visuals portraying proportions, and inflation.

In science instruction you can be use consumer products, packaging, applications for medical help, and safety measures.

The idea for all instruction in functional literacy tasks and in developing competence in using real-life materials is to provide the students with real functional situations and give them problems that they can react to. The goal of this instruction is to develop realistic alternatives to real situations.

STRATEGIES FOR ORGANIZING INFORMATION

Once the students have located information, it may become necessary to put that information in a form that can be easily retained for a variety of purposes. When students are working on projects or writing reports, some form of note or outline form may be necessary. The strategies for organizing information should be developed as the students acquire an understanding about different writing patterns. However, unless they have a definite purpose for organizing information, the activities may become meaningless tasks.

The most common form of organizing information is the outline. In elementary-school instruction, the outline may have a variety of forms. Sometimes a simple list is all that is required. At other times a more detailed outline with multiple levels is appropriate. Whatever form is used, the students should realize the relationship between it and the writing patterns from which the information is obtained.

In many instructional materials, outlining is used exclusively with paragraphs written in the generalization pattern discussed in Chapter 8. However, other patterns can, and should, be used to illustrate the uses of outlining. These patterns include topic development, comparison and contract, enumeration, and classification.

The outline is not the only way in which information can be organized. Depending on the purposes for organizing the information, the uses to which the information will be put, and the amounts of information to be recorded, other usable forms of organizing information are charts, graphs, time lines, and diagrams.

For example, if the learner's attention is on the general categories of behavior one can observe in zoo animals, then the outline form may be appropriate.

Some behaviors you may observe in zoo animals are:
the ways they move
the sounds they make
the ways they eat
the ways they protect themselves when they rest and when they move about

But if you want to draw attention to the differences or similarities among the behaviors of the various animals, then a chart may be more appropriate for recording and organizing the information.

Animal	Where it makes its home	What it eats	How it moves	How it protects itself	Other behaviors
Walking stick	twig	insects	crawls jumps	looks like a twig	eats every insect in sight

Strategies for Using Outlines

The concept of outlining can be introduced by listing materials needed to test the properties of various minerals. For example:

Materials needed to test minerals
set of minerals
hand lens
scissors
piece of glass
penny
piece of granite
magnet
steel file
piece of tile

More complex outlines can result from using the paragraph patterns to identify the important ideas of the author. For example, in the paragraphs below, a cause-and-effect relationship is established. A useful outline would emphasize that pattern. See page 307 for an example.

Water Pollution
Many substances are dumped into rivers, lakes, and oceans. Factories are often built near water for just that reason. Most towns dump untreated or only partly treated sewage into the water. Drains and toilets at home and school carry away many different wastes.
   Polluted water affects ecosystems in several ways. Some wastes are poisonous. They kill or injure plants and animals in the water. People and other animals who drink or swim in polluted water can also get sick.
   Some wastes have a different effect. Wastes from food and paper mills, for example, are food for decomposers. The decomposers in the water digest the wastes. The problem is that digesting wastes uses up the oxygen in the water. A polluted river or lake can get very low in oxygen. Then fish and other animals in the water die, just as you would if you could not breathe.
   Sewage is food for decomposers too. It also acts as a fertilizer. It makes plants in the water grow and multiply. A polluted lake can end up looking like a bowl of thick pea soup. As the plants die, they provide more food for the decomposers. The oxygen shortage gets even worse.
   Water pollution problems can be lessened. Wastes can be treated before they enter our waters. Some wastes can be kept entirely out of the water. It costs a lot of money and energy to prevent water pollution. And people have to want to keep the environment as clean and healthy as possible. (Berger et al, 1979).

Only after the students understand the relationships between the major concepts and the supporting concepts should the formal structure of an outline be introduced. The most common outline form is

    Title

  I. Major concept
    A. Supporting concept
    B.

 II.
    A.
    B.

> *Water Pollution*
>
> | Source of pollution | Effect of pollution |
> |---|---|
> | 1. poisonous wastes | 1. kill or injure plants and animals; people and animals get sick |
> | 2. digesting wastes | 2. use up oxygen in the water; fish and other animals die. |
> | 3. sewage | 3. acts as fertilizer; makes plants grow too thickly in water; uses up oxygen. |

Developing Outlining Strategies

The concept of outlining should be introduced in stages. The first stage is concerned with developing a sense of the relationship between the main concept(s) and the supporting concepts. The second stage extends this but requires the students to find the appropriate supporting concepts. In the third stage, the students are given the outline form and must find both the major concept and the supporting concepts.

Stage one. Provide the students with a paragraph and a list of the major and supporting concepts. After reading the paragraph and identifying the paragraph pattern, they should complete the skeleton outline.

Human beings get energy from carbohydrates and fats. When you eat grains such as rice and wheat, you get carbohydrates. Starchy roots like potatoes or cassava also provide carbohydrates. Cassava is the main food in parts of Africa.

Sugar is another source of carbohydrates. The white stuff you sprinkle on cereal comes from sugar cane or sugar beets. But you also get sugar from many other foods. For example, raisins, honey, and even onions give you sugar.

Fats have the highest energy value. Americans get most of their fats from meat, cream, butter, margarine, and nuts. In the body, fats are changed to fatty tissue. About 15 per cent of a healthy body is fatty tissue. It helps keep you warm and protects delicate parts of the body. (Branson, 1980).

    I. _____
       A. _____
       B. _____

Human energy comes from foods with carbohydrates.
Sources of human energy are found in foods.
Human energy comes from foods with fats.

Stage 2. Provide the students with a paragraph and a partially completed outline. After reading the paragraph and identifying its pattern, they should complete the outline.

Nomads depend on their animals for almost everything they need. How does this remind you of the Plains Indians and the buffalo? The animals give good milk, from which tasty cheese can then be made. The desert people shear the hair of their goats and camels. Then they weave clothes or blankets or tents. The nomads sleep on rugs made of sheep wool. When a group of nomads is ready to move, they pack up all their belongings and load them on their camels. Do you think nomads have a lot of things to pack? Could your family pack all their belongings and load them on an animal? Why or why not? (Davis et al., 1971b).

    I. Nomads depend on their animals for their needs.
       A. _____
       B. _____
       C. _____

Stage 3. Provide the students with a paragraph and a skeleton outline of the major and supporting concepts. After reading the paragraph and identifying its pattern, they should complete the outline.

Crabgrass does not need seeds to produce new plants. If you try to pull up crabgrass, some roots break off and stay in the ground. Each piece of root can produce a new plant. When people try to get rid of crabgrass by pulling it up, they often cause more plants to grow. If a lawnmower cuts crabgrass, some of the cut up stems can root and produce more crabgrass plants. (Berger et al., 1979).

    I. _____
       A. _____
       B. _____

You should allow the strategies for organizing information to develop over an extended period of time. You should encourage your students to experiment with different forms of organizing information. Through such opportunities, they will begin to understand, as they develop organizational strategies, what patterns are better suited for use with particular kinds of information. The logic of organizing information can only result from emulating models and attempting—sometimes unsuccessfully—to put information in some sort of rational form.

WRITING AS A STRATEGY FOR CONTENT AREA UNDERSTANDING

Using the ideas from the study of content areas in new and novel forms is a means for building on the concepts and generalizations that students have already learned. All of the ideas from preceding chapters about using writing in the development of understanding are appropriate for the content areas as well. In addition, students can use the information in relevant ways that enhance their understanding of those subjects. Relevancy means using the ideas to solve problems of concern to them or which have an impact on their lives.

Social studies and science textbooks that are fairly high in concept density require active rather than passive reading. Students' attention can be focused on key ideas by using a "dialectical journal." As they read, they write out comments about the author's ideas or questions they have in regard to the author's ideas. These questions differ from those that might be created for the SQ3R technique, in that the journal contains specific questions about the author's key ideas, examples and supporting ideas, and style of writing. They are not created before reading but they are the products of the students' thoughts as they are reading. For example, in response to the reading selection "What Is Culture" (see p. 289), the students' questions or comments might be

How can you live a tool? (paragraph 2)
In two pictures the people are not using language, they are pointing. (paragraph 4)
Do all schools do the same thing? Even this one? (paragraph 6)
It's bad luck to walk on cracks. (paragraph 7)

Other writing activities that help students build appropriate schemas about content area topics are letter writing to real and imaginary people, fictitious journal keeping, and travel brochures. When studying explorers, students can be sailors on the voyage and write home about their adventures. While studying the exploration of the Florida peninsula, they can report in a journal their periodic adventures, musings, and discoveries. The students can also be lab technicians during important discoveries or pilots of the space shuttle. They can demonstrate their understanding of geography, climate, and resources in brochures for attracting tourists or industries to a specific city, state, or nation. Each of these activities requires them to reorganize information and transpose it into another form, adding to their growing schemas of the communicative process.

Resources for the Teacher

Many instructional materials provide exercises in more than one content area. The resources that follow, therefore, are grouped according to format rather than specific area. Teachers should realize that whenever a resource is more extensive in one area than the others, it still has many ideas for creating exercises.

Units. In order to develop content area reading as a language experience, teachers may find it helpful to have a series of prepared thematic units from which they can plan classroom lessons and activities. One source of such units is the cirriculum bulletin prepared and distributed by city and state boards of education and departments of education. Instructional units for newspaper reading in the content areas may be obtained from the educational services departments of many local newspapers.

The first resource is a series of kits that cover three important aspects of content area reading. Each kit provides specific instruction and practice materials, and these same materials also appear in workbook format.

Study Skills Library. Revised ed. Grades 3-9. *Science, Social Studies, Reference* (New York: McGraw-Hill [EDL/Webster Division]).

The next two resources offer instruction and practice in the strategies of organizing information:

Research Lab. Grades 4-8 (Chicago: Science Research Associates).
Organizing and Reporting Skills Kit. Grades 4-6 (Chicago: Science Research Associates).

The following resources offers instruction in reading graphic displays:

Map and Globe Skills, Kit. Grades 4-8 (Chicago: Science Research Associates).
Graph and Picture Study Skills Kit. Grades 4-6 (Chicago: Science Research Associates).

The next resource contains specific instruction in reading and using the newspaper. The kit is to be used with the students' own newspaper.

Newslab Kit I: Grades 4-8. Kit II: Grades 5-9 (Chicago: Science Research Associates).

The workbooks of many basal reading series contain numerous activities for reading in the content areas. The following are workbooks prepared specifically for content area reading strategies:

Be a Better Reader: Foundations A, B, C (Englewood Cliffs, NJ: Prentice-Hall).
Study Skills for Information Retrieval (Boston: Allyn & Bacon).
Beginning Stories to Study and *Stories to Study*. IA, IB, IIA, IIB (primary grades) (New York: William H. Sadlier).
Go: Reading in the Content Areas. Grades 4-8 (New York: Scholastic Books Services).
Understanding the News: In Newspapers, Magazines ... on Radio, TV. *Gathering the News:* For Newspapers, Magazines, Radio, TV (New York: Scholastic Book Services).

In addition, the following are sources of materials for developing reading skills for maps and other graphic aids:

Weekly Reader, Educational Center, 1250 Fairwood Avenue, Columbus, OH 43206
Using Charts and Graphs. Grades 3-6 (Cleveland: Modern Curriculum Press).

Many publishers produce books aimed at teaching functional reading and writing skills. Not all of them use actual representations of materials found in the real world. The following use fairly realistic materials:

Life Skills Reading Books. Grades 3-6 (Palo Alto, CA: Creative Publications). A series of books on making up favorite menus, using the telephone, using cereal boxes, reading menus, and using the yellow pages.
Building Life Skills. Grades 4-6 (Cleveland: Modern Curriculum Press). A series of books dealing with functional reading in the home, neighborhood, community, and country.

The following series are aimed at developing problem solving and thinking strategies while at the same time providing reenforcement of the basic arithmetic computational facts. Each lesson is organized as a story problem.

Story Problems. Grades 3-6. *Techniques of Problem Solving* (TOPS). Grades 3-12. *TOPS Developmental Workbooks* (to accompany TOPS) (Palo Alto, CA: Creative Publications).

One reading series devoted exclusively to applying reading skills in content area materials contains, at each grade level, units on general reading skills and reading social studies, mathematics, science, and literature.

Content Readers. Grades 1-8 (New York: Harper & Row).

The booklets that follow are titles in the International Reading Association's Reading Aids Series (P.O. Box 8139, Newark, DE 19711):

Earle, Richard A., *Teaching Reading and Mathematics* (1976).
Cheyney, Arnold G., *Teaching Reading Skills Through the Newspaper* (1971).
Gentile, Lance M., *Using Sports and Physical Education to Strengthen Reading Skills* (1980).
Thelan, Judith, *Improving Reading in Science* (1976).

Some publishers produce nonfiction books in series and reference materials geared toward the reading ability and cognitive maturity of elementary school students. Representative of such series are

Let's-Read-and-Find-Out Science Books (New York: Crowell Junior Books).
The Illustrated Science Encyclopedia. Grades 3 and up.
Read About Science. Grades 2-3.
Reading About Animals. Grades 2-3.
A Look Inside. Grades 4-12.
Machine World. Grades 2-4.
Look at Science. Grades K-3.
Life Cycles. Grades 1-2.
Animals of the World. Grades 4-9.
The Money Books. Grades 2-6.
  Milwaukee: Reaintree Publishing Group.

Discussion Questions and Activities

1. Explain what the following statement by Ned D. Marksheffel (1969) means to you in regard to reading in the content areas:

   Because reading has no subject matter of its own, whatever the reader reads is reading.

2. Explain what you think David L. Shepherd (1969) means by this statement:

   The scientific method is as applicable to student development in the skill of reading science material as in learning scientific understandings.

3. Obtain oral reading protocols of one upper elementary-grade student while reading a passage from a basal reader and a passage from a content area text. Score the miscue analyses of each and compare the results. Does the students' pattern of miscues differ on the two passages? If so, to what do you attribute the difference?

4. Select a passage from a content area textbook for middle grade-elementary students. Construct an author-idea map that
   a. Identifies the major concept of the passage.
   b. Shows the location of the important generalizations.

c. Indicates the location of the important information supporting the major concept and/or the generalizations.
5. Examine one chapter on the same topic in three different texts for the same grade level. Compare and/or contrast:
   a. The organization and format of the chapter.
   b. The use of graphic displays and their relationship to the text.
   c. The style of language and vocabulary diversity.
   d. The amount of information in subheadings that does not relate directly to them.

   Rate the three texts for their effectiveness in communicating with elementary- and/or intermediate level students.
6. Select a content area textbook and make a dialectical journal that students can use as a model for their own. Try out the procedures with the students. What kind of questions do they construct? How do their questions reveal what they do or do not understand about the text?

Further Readings

Those engaged in teaching the reading of content areas in the elementary school should have a background in and understanding of the concepts and generalizations in each area. The following texts provide teachers such information. The first is especially useful since it contains a series of "discovery lesson plans" that provide the basis for language experience units on a variety of topics at all grade levels. Within each lesson, the thinking processes for each lesson and the thinking processes for each activity and question are identified.

Carin, Arthur A., and Robert B. Sund, *Teaching Science Through Discovery,* 4th ed. (Columbus, OH: Chas. E. Merrill, 1983).
Copland, Richard W., *Mathematics and the Elementary Teacher,* 2nd ed. (Philadelphia: Saunders, 1972).
Welton, David A., and John T. Mallan, *Children and Their World: Strategies for Teaching Social Studies,* 2nd ed. (Boston: Houghton Mifflin, 1981).

The following texts were written primarily for secondary school students, though many of their ideas can be adapted for elementary and intermediate school students.

Herber, Harold L., *Teaching Reading in Content Areas,* 2nd ed. (Englewood Cliffs, NJ: Prentice-Hall, 1978).
Laffey, James, ed., *Reading in the Content Areas* (Newark, DE: International Reading Association, 1972).
Thomas, Ellen Lamar, and H. Alan Robinson, *Improving Reading in Every Class: A Sourcebook for Teachers,* 3rd ed. (Boston: Allyn & Bacon, 1982).

Chapter 11

DEVELOPING STRATEGIES FOR LITERATURE READING

Focus Questions

1. What is the purpose of a literature program in elementary school?

2. What are the different types of literature available for students to read?

3. How can literature of exceptional quality be identified?

4. How can the students and literature be brought together?

5. What means are available to assist teachers in selecting literature for their students?

A most important objective of literature reading program in elementary school is creating an environment so filled with books that students develop the desire to spend part of their lifetime in the act of reading. Reading literature (as part of a reading program) should lead students

1. To enjoy books and stories of all sorts.
2. To become acquainted with the literary heritage of their society.
3. To understand what constitutes "literature."
4. To apply knowledge gained from literature to their lives.
5. To evaluate and appreciate literature and develop a personal taste from among the wide varieties and forms of literature (Huus, 1975).

What actually constitutes "literature" is difficult to state. To one, it is classical or contemporary writing of such quality that children can understand what is read or heard (Huus, 1975). To another, it calls for power in using words and actions that lead to a well-knit plot, a strong theme that presents a basic truth, and realistic characters. It is seen as writing that reveals an author's knowledge of literary form and from which some wisdom may be apprehended (Painter, 1975). To still another, literature "portrays life and mind in language" and has three qualities: substance, sincerity, and memorable language (Lundsteen, 1976).

Precisely what constitutes literature probably could not be defined to the satisfaction of all; yet the three definitions have similarities. It is probably best to consider literature not as something good or bad but as a continuum on which all the writings of all authors reside. At one end can be found the writings that are almost universally accepted as representing what is meant by literature. The aim of this chapter is to consider the elements that most agree represent literary quality.

The United States has long been considered a melting pot in which various cultures meld. There is in American society, however, a growing appreciation of our pluralistic culture. Literature programs in elementary and intermediate schools should aim at studying and developing a respect for the contributions of all cultural groups to their literature and for the unique contributions of males and females in all aspects of society. The teaching of literature should seek to broaden and deepen the students' experience. When a reading program does not explore literature that reflects the varying segments of society and when a reading program consistently promotes sexism and sex stereotyping through the literature it offers, all students will be deprived of a fully rounded education.

Reading literature that treats society as pluralistic is not incongruent with the general purpose of any literature program. A literature program is one of the best ways in which students can learn to relive the experiences of others and broaden and deepen their own personal experiences (N. Smith, 1960). The study of literature that reflects the diverse cultural groups in American society can lead to an open-minded generation of students who accept the uniqueness and necessity of other life styles (Jenkins, 1973). It is by reading the literature of other cultural groups that one can understand the many similarities among those groups (Reed, 1976). By linking the understanding of linguistic sexism with the reading of literature of diverse cultural groups, students can understand the nature of cultural values in general and the nature of their own values in particular.

For minority group students the study of multiethnic literature is important to developing a healthy self-concept, which depends on a knowledge of and a sense of pride in one's family and cultural background and an understanding that one's own group is not the "center of the universe."

STRATEGIES FOR DEVELOPING A LITERATURE PROGRAM

The teaching of literature does not seem to be widely accepted as a critical part of the school reading program. A review of research on the teaching of literature reveals that literature is most often used to supplement other subject areas or as material for teaching reading skills (Cullinan, 1974). Children will not develop a sense of literature as enjoyment or as a means of understanding the world without specific guidance. They therefore need a planned, balanced program of literature instruction that offers

1. The free choice of reading materials. Free choice is the opportunity to select, read, and even stop reading something selected without any intervention from an adult.
2. The daily reading aloud of a story or poem by the teacher. The teacher conveys to students a feeling that something is "good" not by extolling its merits, but by putting enthusiasm and feeling into reading it. The selection can be one that will delight the children because of the magic of the author's words, or it may be one that gives the students a newer understanding of some aspect of life.
3. The guidance in finding a desired book. Teachers should help students find books. Through a teacher's or librarian's recommendation, students should be made aware of various books on a given topic or related to topics being studied in the content areas.
4. A focus on a common element in the literature through topical units. The units can focus on a specific topic or subject area, on a type or form of writing, or on a style of writing.
5. The creative sharing of the books. Children can become interested in the books they are reading or in the books others have read, as they share their ideas through discussion, reports, artwork, or dramatic presentations (Huus, 1975).

The planned literature program provision should be made for developing in the students

1. Strategies for distinguishing between real and make-believe.
2. Strategies for recognizing the author's craft.
3. Strategies for recognizing the mood, feeling, or tone of a story or poem.
4. Strategies for recognizing and interpreting figurative language.
5. Strategies for recognizing the major forms of fiction.
6. Strategies for extending one's personal reading interests.

While attempting to develop a planned literature program, teachers may face certain problems or difficulties (Huus, 1975). The lack of materials or the structure of the schoolwide program may not always permit students to have a "free" choice of reading matter. Solving the problem of limited materials may be easier than dealing with a situation in which students are restricted by a policy of required reading. While reading aloud, teachers should be careful not to inject their personalities into the story. Too often the focus of the daily reading may be on the performance and not on the literature. The guidance a student receives from teachers and librarians depends on their experience and expertise. The development of topical units may be limited by the availability of material on that topic and by the availablity of material appropriate and appealing to the intended students. Finally, the sharing of books all too often replaces the literature itself. Although reports, art projects, and dramatizations may be desirable, within the structure of the planned literature program they should not take precedence over the literature.

Recognizing the Categories of Literature

The literature in a balanced literature program should be drawn from both classic and new literature. Classic literature comprises those stories, poems, and plays that provide some continuity with the society's literary heritage. These consist of folk and fariy tales, myths and legends of other countries, and stories and books that have endured for long periods of time. The new literature is the modern fanciful stories and poems and the realistic works discussed previously. These, unlike the classics which tie the reader to a cultural heritage, more closely mirror the child's own world.

Children's literature can be studied in various ways. One way that the study of literature can be structured as through literary forms, structural elements of style, and use.

Recognizing Literary Forms

The major forms of writing in children's literature may be placed into quite arbitrary categories, and many books could be placed in more than one. However, the following categories are useful in a guided literature program:

Fiction   The forms of fiction include those that can be considered to be

   1. Realistic. In this classification are books and stories set in historical and contemporary periods. Many of these are the everyday adventure stories to which so many children are attracted. Also included are fictionalized biographies that portray real persons in realistic but fictional conversations and thoughts.

   2. Fantasy. In this classification are both the modern and the traditional stories of magic and romance. The traditional fairy tales, myths, legends, and folktales have withstood the test of time in their appeal to children. Modern fantasy, science fiction, and American folklore have the same magic found in the traditional fairy tales (Higgins, 1970). (Some authorities classify animals stories as a separate category of literature, and they are discussed below.)

   3. Pop literature. This category contains forms of literature that many would not consider literature—comics, jokes, chants in children's games, graffitti, and posters. However, there are many forms of pop literature, and many of them meet the criteria of literature.

   4. Picture books. These are the books intended primarily for young children. Their stories, although told in words, are carried through the sequence of illustrations. Once the story has been heard, the children can look at the pictures and retell the story.

5. Animal stories. Animal stories remain popular with children and adults. There are three types of animal stories: those in which the animals are talking beasts; those in which the animals act like animals but talk, and those in which the animals are seen objectively. The purpose of each is different. When the animals are talking beasts they really are humans in disguise portraying human foibles. Stories in which animals talk but are still animals are stories of fancy. When animals do not talk or act like humans, the author is not free to interpret the animals' emotions, attitudes, or intentions. The animals, central to the plot, remain animals, and the readers are free to interpret the animals' behavior (Lundsteen, 1976).

Nonfiction Classified as nonfiction are works that present information on topics in a literary style: biographies; personal narratives; technical or scientific explanations; essays; and books about other people, places, and cultures.

Poetry Poetry seems to be given little attention in class, is seldom read to children, and is infrequently encouraged as a writing form (Terry, 1972). One reason may be that teachers themselves are unfamiliar or uncomfortable with poetry.

A poem has a formal structure and a carefully chosen sequence of words. The structure and sequence of those words can have a variety of forms; some of the ones popular with elementary students are

1. *Haiku.* Haiku, a form of poetry composed in Japan, consists of a seventeen syllable statement about nature in which the topic is usually not named. The form is arranged so the first line has five syllables, the second line seven syllables, and the third line five syllables.

> Rustling green branches,
> Sweet music of singing birds
> Outside my window. (Fay et al., 1981).

2. *Cinquain.* Cinquain, a short poetic form of five lines:
a. Stating in the first line a single thing—a noun
b. Giving two words in the second line that tell what the thing might do—verbs
c. Describing the thing in the third line—adjectives
d. Stating in the fourth line a phrase that describes the thing
e. Repeating the word in the first line.

> Snow
> Floats, dances
> Cold white sparkling
> Sitting on my lashes
> Snow. (Fay et al., 1981)

3. *Limericks*. Limericks are nonsense rhymes that have five lines: lines 1 and 2 rhyme; 3 and 4 rhyme; and the last, rhyming with the first two, usually makes some humorous statement.

> There was an old man with a beard,
> Who said, "It is just as I feared!—
>   Two owls and a hen,
>   Four larks and a wren,
> Have all built their nests in my beard." (Lear, 1966).

4. *Narrative*. The narrative poem tells a long tale and may use a variety of forms and patterns.

5. *Free verse*. Free verse does not follow any rhyme patterns, but its poetry is obtained from the sound, rhythm, and cadence of its words and phrases.

6. *Quatrains*. Quatrains are poems in four-line units in which the second and fourth lines rhyme. Poems can contain several quatrains.

7. *Couplets*. Couplets are two-line rhyming units. Many poems have a number of couplets, sometimes of alternating rhythms, cadences, and rhymes.

Plays   One form of literature that students particularly seem to enjoy is plays. Like poetry, plays are intended to be read aloud and heard. Yet, when plays are read, they are literature.

Reading, seeing, and hearing plays can help students appreciate the amount of information that the reader has to supply in order to recreate the message intended by the author. Although there are various hints—stage directions and scene settings—the reader must provide much of the running commentary and interpretation that is usually provided in prose. Therefore, the study of plays for elementary students should be the study of the relationship between a playwright's scripts and the narrative of a prose writer. This experience can help prepare students to understand the dramas they will encounter in secondary school.

Recognizing Elements of Style

The study of *how* literature is constructed leads students to the full appreciation of the author's craft. Enjoyment is often derived from watching an artisan when one understands the intricacies of the craft and the criteria for judging the artistic quality of the product. A book is more than just a story when one follows the author in the development of a complex thought or the timbre of a phrase.

Characterization   In the development of believable characterizations, authors contend with three elements: credibility, portrayal, and uniqueness (Cullinan, 1971).

Copyright © 1975, United Feature Syndicate, Inc.

Characters are credible when they can be believed within the framework of the particular story. They must be integral parts of the author's story and make the action move in believable ways. Credibility ceases when a character performs some action or makes some statement that defies what the reader has been led to accept as the character's pattern.

Characters are portrayed in accordance with the author's intent. Some characters may be fully described, and so the reader little to construct in order to "know" the characters. Others may be vaguely delineated because they are not central to the plot or because the author wishes the character to be indistinct. In order to appreciate an author's character portrayals, students should be familiar with various personality types.

Each character in a story should have some qualities that set that individual apart from all the others; yet each should have some qualities that are common to all humans..

Plot Development In simplest terms, a plot is the basic story outline; the plot development is how the story unfolds. If the author does not provide for a purposeful sequence of events and a logical conclusion, readers are apt to dismiss the story as unbelievable. In most narration the order of the plot follows the sequence of introduction, development of a problem, solution of the problem, and conclusion.

Four basic plots have been identified in children's literature: romance, tragedy, irony-satire, and comedy (Sloan, 1975). Romance is literature in which wishes are fulfilled. The central character, or hero, is involved in a dangerous or marvelous journey, a struggle or ordeal, and a return. In children's literature, tragedy is the exploration of the limitation in the central character's ability to have or make wishes come true. Central to tragedy is the death or catastrophic fall of the hero. Irony and satire express the contrast that exists between ideals and reality—irony illustrating the limitations of humans, satire attempting the change of humans through ridicule. Comedy presents a positive view of the human experience, a picture of hope and renewal.

Figurative Language The craft of an author is most often appreciated through the language used. The author's choice of words determines how the reader constructs the images of the story's characters and settings. An author might use language that is straightforward in its reporting:

As Jock nudged the cow into the barn and locked the door behind her, the clouds opened and the rain dropped in a sudden torrent. The lightning stabbed through the clouds, and in its momentary brightness Jock could see the trees tossing wildly in the wind that howled through the river walls and roared across the highlands. He cringed in spite of himself at the exploding thunder as he ran toward the house. It sounded as if the earth were splitting behind him. (Emery, 1965).

Or an author might use language full of images:

The sea became a wildcat now, and the galleon her pray. She stalked the ship and drove her off her course. She slapped at her, rolling her victim from side to side. She knocked the spars out of her and used them to ram holes in her sides. She clawed the rudder from its sternpost and threw it into the sea. She cracked the ship's ribs as if they were brittle bones. Then she hissed and spat through the seams. (Henry, 1947).

The meaning of the story, both as intended and as perceived, is affected by the author's choice and use of words. Some of the ways to manipulate words are by alliteration, personfication, metaphor, and simile. In addition, an author can manipulate whole units of language to create moods.

Alliteration is the repetition of initial sounds in order to create an effect:

"creepy-crawly caterpillar"

>And a noise that's a growl,
>and a roar,
>and a wheeze,
>and a whistle all stirred together (Alexander, 1960).

Personfication is the portrayal of human traits in objects or animals:

The galleon shuddered. From bow to stern came an endless rasping sound! (Henry, 1947).

Seashell, whisper in my ear
All the secrets you hold dear. (Fay et al., 1981).

The wildcat sea yawned. She swallowed the men. (Henry, 1947).

Metaphor and simile are comparisons. Similes always use the words *like* or *as*.

The air was heavy, musky with an odor not unlike rotting fruit or aging garbage. (Monteleone, 1974).

It looked like a pile of broken twigs and oilcloth as it trembled and fluttered on the ground. (Monteleone, 1974).

The air about them quivered like a violin string. Then suddenly the string snapped, and the everyday world was all about once more. (Henry, 1947).

Moods are suggested by images and words:

For a while longer Tonka sat quietly on the mossy log in the sun, but the sun had little warmth even though it was late May. The last great Ice Age was over, but its cold lingered on. He drew his fox skin more tightly around his shoulders and looked away through the forest. Perhaps, he thought, he might see one of the beasts that the hunters of the tribe often killed and brought back to the cave where they all lived. But the forest was dark and forbidding, and he dared not venture beyond the stream to see what was there (Hutchins, 1965).

Theme Development The theme of a piece of literature provides the reader with the significance of the action or experience (Cullinan, 1971). It is the message of the story, the purpose for which the author took pen in hand and placed words upon the page. The theme is a presence that transcends the characters, the plot, and the setting. The themes of greatest impact are generally implicit in the plot and characterizations. An explicit theme may tend to create an impression of moralizing or preaching.

The range of themes that is found in children's literature is immense. In order to fully appreciate an author's theme, however, students need to first understand that themes exist in literature. After realizing that, students need to have experiences with themes to which they can relate. Unless they "know" a theme before it is encountered, there is no way that it will be recognized within a story. Students therefore, need exposure to various relevant themes so as to build a storehouse of universal ideas which they can relate to those found in their independent reading.

Uses of Literature

Children's literature can be categorized by the use to which it will be put (Cullinan, 1971). For example, the literature may be classified by an educational use—say, by age groupings or reading levels. Or it may be classified by the concepts that are to be developed—say, by cultures, occupations, or animal survival. Also, a work may be classified according to the influence it has on the reader. This use, called bibliotherapy, is discussed in greater length below.

Classifying children's literature by the manner it will be used is helpful only to the teacher. There is no real advantage to elementary students to understand this functional classification scheme because it provides them with no clear signals to the appreciation and understanding of an author's story and message. Therefore, although teachers will use this scheme for locating books, it is not one they would necessarily use for instructional purposes.

STRATEGIES FOR BRINGING CHILDREN AND LITERATURE TOGETHER

A successful literature program in the elementary and intermediate school is contingent on the teacher's possessing two qualities: a knowledge of children's literature, and a positive attitude toward reading. Of the two, the second quality may be more important because a teacher can always receive assistance in selecting reading material for students. A positive attitude towards reading is something that teachers must develop before they can instill it in their students. It is quite difficult to develop an appreciation for the author's craft without being a habitual, appreciative, discriminating reader oneself. As was indicated in Chapter 1, teachers need to have an awareness of the world beyond their technical training—and one way in which this is accomplished is through the reading of literature.

Using Library Resources

Wherever one teaches, the school library should function as an integral part of the classroom reading program. The teacher should be aware of what transpires in the library, and the librarian should know the activites taking place in the classroom. When the library is integrated with the classroom reading and literature programs, it provides effective service at varying levels. The library becomes an adjunct to the classroom, and the teacher becomes apprised of the availability of library materials and the librarian of the individual abilities of the students. This joint venture can lead to meaningful, effective, and valuable experiences for the students, the teachers, and the librarian.

Classroom libraries can be built up by borrowing books from the school library or the local public library. The librarian can help select the books and stories, or the teacher can refer to one of the resources indicated below. Classroom libraries can also be organized with books and other reading matter donated by the students. After their parents have given their permission, the students can lend the classroom library some of their books for the duration of the school year. Or they can be encouraged to join book clubs and leave their books in the class library until the year ends.

Whatever means is used, the students must have a source from which they can select reading material that varies in topics, difficulty, and interests, for example, books, short stories, magazines, plays, poems, and newspapers.

Selecting Children's Literature

The books, poems, plays, and stories chosen for the planned literature program should have literary merit. A review of often-used texts on the use of children's literature in the elementary school revealed that

1. The factors that determine literary quality in children's literature are the same as those in adult literature: plot, content, theme, characterization, style, and form.
2. The choice of subject matter and its treatment differentiate children's literature from adult literature, not the quality of writing or the depth of emotion expressed (Ladevich, 1974).

Besides selecting literature according to established criteria, literature can be judged to be of some merit when children themselves select the material for their independent reading. Children have a need to satisfy a basic desire to stretch beyond their surroundings and themselves (Fenwick, 1968). When they consistently choose from among the same core of books and stories, there is evidence that those materials have some measure of literary quality. Therefore, teachers should be sure to consider children's tastes when books are being labeled as fine literature (Darkatsh, 1974).

Teachers need some way to differentiate among the many books published each year. The following questions (from Huck & Kuhn, 1968) can be used to judge children's fiction:

Plot Does the book tell a good story? Will children enjoy it? Is the plot original and fresh? Is it plausibile and credible? Do the events logically follow one another? Is there an identifiable climax? How do events build to a climax? Is the plot well constructed?

Setting Where does the story take place? How does the author indicate the time? How does the setting affect the action, characters, or theme? Does the story transcend the setting and have universal implications?

Theme Does the story have a theme? Is the theme worth imparting to children? Does the theme emerge naturally from the story or is it stated too obviously? Does the theme overpower the story? Does it avoid moralizing?

Characterization How does the author reveal characters? Through narration? In conversation? By the thoughts of others? By the thoughts of the character? Through action? Are the characters convincing and credible? Do we see their strengths and their weaknesses? Does the author avoid stereotyping? Is the behavior of the characters consistent with their age and background? Is there any character development or growth? Has the author shown the causes of character behavior or development?

Style Is the style of writing appropriate to the subject? Is the style straightforward or figurative? Is the dialogue natural and suited to the characters? Does the author balance narration and dialogue? What are the main characteristics of the sentence patterns? How did the author create a mood? Is the overall impression one of mystery, gloom, evil, joy, security? What symbols or signs has the author used to communicate meaning? Is the point of view from which the story is told appropriate to the purpose of the book?

Format Do the illustrations enhance the story? Are the illustrations consistent with the story? How is the format of the book related to the text? What is the quality of the paper? How sturdy is the binding?

Other Considerations How does the book compare with other books on the same subject? How does the book compare with other books written by the same author? How have other reviewers evaluated this book?

The following questions (also from Huck & Kuhn, 1968) can be used to judge informational books for children:

Accuracy and authenticity What are the qualifications of the author? Are facts accurate? Is the book realistic? Are facts and theories clearly distinguished? Do text and illustrations avoid stereotypes? Is the book up to date? Are significant details omitted? Do generalizations go beyond present knowledge? Are differing viewpoints presented? In geographic books, is diversity revealed? In science books, is anthropomorphism omitted? Are phenomena given teleological explanations?

Content Is this a general survey book or one of some specific interest? Is the coverage of the book adequate for its purpose? Is the book within the comprehension and interest range of the age for which it is intended? Do experiment books lead to understanding science? Are experiments and activities safe and feasible? Does the book present interrelationships of facts and principles? Do science books indicate related social problems? Is the book fresh and original? Does the book help the reader understand the methods of science and social science?

Style Is information given directly or in story form? Is the text interesting and appropriate for the age level intended? Do vivid language and appropriate metaphor engender interest and understanding? Is the language pattern clear and simple or heavy and pedantic? Is there an appropriate amount of detail? Does the book encourage curiosity and further study?

Format and Illustrations Do illustrations clarify and add to the text? Do different types of media maintain clarity of concepts? Are illustrations explained by captions or labels? Are size relationships made clear? Do size of type and use of space contribute to clarity? Are end papers used effectively?

Organization Are subheadings used effectively? Do the table of contents and index help the reader locate information quickly? Does the bibliography indicate sources used by the author and sources for further reading by the children? Do appendixes extend information?

LITERATURE AND THE MEDIA

Television is often attacked as the source of many of society's problems. A common complaint is the effect of television viewing on students' reading performance. Parents and educators criticize the amount of time spent viewing television, the quality of the programming on television, and the impact of both television programs and product commercials have on students' academic success. Much of this criticism may be merely rhetoric, since research on the effect of television viewing on children's reading achievement is limited. (We do not condone all that appears on television or deny that there may be other effects on children from television viewing.)

A recent review of studies conducted between 1961 and 1976 revealed that the relationship between the amount of television viewing and reading acheivement is not statistically significant. The hours spent in front of the set seem to have a minor influence on achievement in reading and success in school. The conclusion is that television and reading can be moved into a symbiotic relationship where interest in one can effect interest in the other. Before any hard and fast conclusions can be made about any possible negative effects of televisiion viewing on reading, there should be more controlled studies of the context in which television is watched, including the presence or lack of parental guidance, and the types of programs viewed (Neuman, 1980).

There is no denying that media in any form can influence children's perceptions and behavior. The media are vehicles for communication, and to deny their potential impact is to deny the communication process itself (see Chapter 1). The implication is not to use television as a whipping post for other "crimes" present in society but to exert the influence of the school in developing the use of television, along with film, radio, and records, as forms of literature. is There is good and poor content in each yet, students can develop a "visual" literacy so the cognitive and affective strategies acquired in a reading program can be utilized for the selection and appreciation of information from these media.

Sources of ideas for activities aimed at linking television viewing and reading and for helping parents encourage the effective use of television at home can be found in the following:

Becker, George J., *Television and the Classroom Reading Program* (Newark, DE: International Reading Association, 1973).

Foster, Harold M., *The New Literacy: The Language of Film and Television* (Urbana, IL: National Council of Teachers of English, 1979).
Murray, John P., and Barbara Lonnborg, *Children and Television: A Primer for Parents* (Boys Town, NE: The Boys Town Center, n. d.)

The first source below contains articles and books on the use of television and other media, the second, on films. Both are annotated bibliographies.

Dillingofski, Mary Sue, *Nonprint Media and Reading.* (Newark, DE: International Reading Association, 1979).
May, Jill P., *Films and Filmstrips for Language Arts* (Urbana, IL: National Council of Teachers of English, 1981).

The major television networks offer instructional materials for specific programs and for television viewing in general. Additional information can be obtained from the sources below or from local commercial and public broadcasting stations.

Community Relations, ABC Television, 1330 Avenue of the Americas, New York, NY 10019
CBS Educational Relations Department, 51 West 52nd Street, New York, NY 10019
Educational Programming, NBC Television, 30 Rockefeller Plaza, New York, NY 10020
WNET/Thirteen Educational Division, 356 West 58th Street, New York, NY 10019
Although WNET serves the New York City area, it also provides materials for a number of programs shown on various PBS stations and for television viewing in general, notably, *Television and Your Family: A Viewing Guide.*

The following is a workbook for students to use with any television programm and to develop their "critical eye." It is a joint venture of WNET/Thirteen and the publisher.

Critical Television Viewing. Grades 3-9 (New York: Globe Book).

WRITING AND LITERATURE

Creative writing is the unique rearrangement of known linguistic and information elements into a new form or pattern that has not existed before. In this vein, all the writing of students is creative when it uses their own language. Two sets of schemas are needed to write creatively, language patterns and information. When students use what they know to produce something new, the act of creative writing has occurred. The readiness for creative writing is the acquisition of English language patterns, the structures of the different genre of literature, and a mental storehouse of information about a wide range of topics, events, and feelings.

Too often, creative writing is conceived as unstructured, free writing; a time in which students write without direction about a topic of their own choosing. Although some of these aspects are present in creative writing, students cannot create unless they have the means to do so. When students parody a limmerick, a television commercial, or a popular song, they are being creative. When they add to a list of events in an "add on" story such as "This Is the House That Jack Built," they are being creative. When they write "The Return of Goldilocks" or another Encyclopedia Brown mystery and pattern them after the original tales, they are being creative. Creative writing is all of these and more. It is the conscious rearrangement of the known into a form that may not have occurred elsewhere.

Resources for the Teacher

When teachers do not have the time, experience, or interest to assess all the books that will be made available to their students, there are other means that may be used to assist them in selecting reading material of exemplary literary quality. They can refer to professional texts, book lists, professional journals, and instructional materials.

Professional Texts

Professional texts written to inform teachers of the entire field of children's literature usually contain references to books, stories, plays, and poems of exceptional quality. Comprehensive references are

Arbuthnot, May Hill, and Zena Sutherland, *Children and Books,* 4th ed. (Glenview, IL: Scott Foresman, 1977).

Cullinan, Bernice E., *Literature and the Child* (New York: Harcourt Brace Jovanovich, 1981).

Cullinan, Bernice E., and Carolyn W. Carmichael, eds., *Literature and Young Children* (Urbana, IL: National Council of Teachers of English, 1977).

Huck, Charlotte S., *Children's Literature in the Elementary School,* 3rd ed. (New York: Holt, Rinehart & Winston, 1979).

A good reference available in paperback is

Larrick, Nancy, *A Parent's Guide to Children's Reading,* 4th ed. (New York: Doubleday, 1975). Available in paperback from Bantam Books.

A source of ideas for incorporating literature into a writing program is

Stewig, John W., *Read to Write: Using Children's Literature as a Springboard for Teaching Writing,* 2nd ed. (New York: Holt, Rinehart & Winston, 1980).

Book Lists

There are many books lists available for helping teachers select children's literature. These are "starter lists" to which other books of matching quality can be added. Some of the lists are general and others are specific, depending on the agency that compiled them. Two sources of general lists are

The Children's Services Division
American Library Association
50 East Huron Street
Chicago, IL 60611

The Children's Book Council
67 Irving Place
New York, NY 10003

An annotated list of books arranged by age and compiled by teams of teachers representing the Children's Book Council and the International Reading Association resulted from the field testing of books. The list contains those books that children either selected to read or asked to be read to them. The two organizations compile and publish an annual list of children's choices entitled "Classroom Choices: Children's Trade Books." Since 1974 these have been published in *The Reading Teacher,* and you can obtain single copies the Children's Book Council by sending them a large, stamped, self-addressed envelope.

Specialized lists are available that cover a wide range of topics. In developing literature programs for fostering an appreciation of the pluralistic nature of American society, the following lists may be useful. Others can be obtained from the ERIC Clearinghouse on Reading and Communication Skills, 111 Kenyon Road, Urbana, IL 61801.

Arth, Alfred A., and Judith D. Whittemore, "Selecting Literature for Children That Relates to Life, the Way It Is," *Elementary English* 50 (1973): 726-728, 744.

Reed, Linda, "Multi-Ethnic Literature and the Elementary School Curriculum," *Language Arts* 53 (1976): 256-261.

The following is intended for junior and senior high school students, but the material could be a source of materials for elementary students as well:

Stensland, Anna Lee, *Literature By and About the American Indian: An Annotated Bibliography* (Urbana, IL: National Council of Teachers of English, 1973).

There are many periodicals for children that can be found in

Guide to Children's Magazines, Newspapers, Reference Books. Washington, DC: Association for Childhood Education International.
Martin, Laura K., *Magazines for School Libraries* (New York: R.R. Bowker).

Professional Journals

Various journals list and review current publications. The first two references are devoted entirely to children's literature. The others contain regular reviews of children's literature.

Bulletin of the Center for Children's Books, University of Chicago Press, 5801 Ellis Avenue, Chicago, IL 60637.
The Horn Book Magaine, Horn Book, Inc. 585 Boylston Street, Boston, MA 02116.
Language Arts, National Council of Teachers of English, 1111 Kenyon Road, Urbana, IL 61801.
The Reading Teacher, International Reading Association, 800 Barksdale Road, Newark, DE 19711.
The School Library Journal, R.R. Bowker Co., 1180 Avenue of the Americas, New York, NY 10036.

Instructional Materials

There are a number of sources of materials for literature programs. Almost every major publisher has a children's book division which often makes books available in both hardcover and paperback. Some publishers reprint books in paperback and make them available to schools through book club plans.

Scholastic Book Services
   50 West 44th Street
   New York, NY 10017

Weekly Reader Paperback Book Club
   Education Center
   Columbus, OH 43216

Xerox Education Publication Book Clubs
   245 Long Hill Road
   Middletown, CT 06457

When teachers feel unsure about making selections, there are ready-made sources on which they can rely. Some of the publishers of basal reading series have literature anthology series. A good anthology series has selections with many topics, interests, styles, and forms.

One exemplary series is

Sounds of Language Readers New York: Holt, Rinehart & Winston.

Teachers who wish their literature program to be an individualized reading experience will find that some publishers also package books in what are infelicitously called "supplementary libraries." Each contains a variety of books, activity cards, and lessons. Representative of such libraries are

One-To-One: A Practical Individualized Reading Program. Tarrytown, NY: Prentice-Hall Media. (Junior edition for grades 1–4 and senior edition for grades 4–8.)
Individualized Reading (New York: Scholastic Book Service). (Units for each grade 1–6.)
Bill Martin's Instant Readers and *Noodles Instant Readers* (New York: Holt, Rinehart & Winston). (Sets of books for grades K–6.)
Random House Individualized Skill Pacers (New York: Random House). (Kits for each grade 1–6.)

The following two guides offer extensive plans for selected children's books. Included are a wide range of activities and suggested further readings for each theme and book. Teachers can develop their own lessons for other books following the format set out in the guides.

Reasoner, Charles F. *Releasing Children to Literature* (New York: Dell, 1968).
Reasoner, Charles F. *Where the Readers Are* (New York: Dell, 1972).

Activities for Developing Literary Appreciation

In order to encourage the development of literature-reading strategies, students should engage in activities designed to challenge their thinking, such as

☐ Construct a chart or "map" of a story's plot. They should draw in the main plot and any subplots, indicating how the important events are produced as these meet or diverge. The activity of the main and minor characters also can be traced in relation to the movement of the story's main event.

☐ Read or listen to a story up to a point near the climax. Have the students discuss possible endings of the story that would be logical for the flow of the events and the credibility of the characters. Finish reading the story and compare the students' endings with that of the author.

☐ Select vocabulary from some classic piece of children's literature and discuss whether the words are still used in the same manner today. Have the students suggest what words might be used to "modernize" the story.

☐ Analyze the illustrations that accompany some work of literature. Have the students decide whether the illustrations enhance the story of distract from it. Try to have them determine whether the illustration is appropriate in topic, style, and color to the particular story or poem.

☐ Analyze television programmes and movies using the same criteria for judging the quality of children's fiction. Have the students classify the program or movie according to its plot, theme, characterizations, and language style.

☐ Select a paragraph from a story and rewrite it by changing the vocabulary without changing the paragraph's meaning.

☐ Listen to two or more different recordings of the same story or poem. Have the students discuss the quality of the oral presentation in relation to the author's intended meaning.

☐ Compose stories and poems based on models that the students have studied. Students can begin by making parodies of some classic fairy tales by "extending" stories and poems that use repetitive elements. As they become familiar with plot structures, themes, and characterizations, they should compose their own stories and poems.

To extend students' understanding of characterizations and plot development ask them to

☐ Prepare a situation in which two or more characters from different books meet. The meeting should be a logical outcome of incidents in both books, and the conversation that ensues should be credible and consistent with the portrayal of the characters.

☐ Construct plot, events, and theme for the characters in a story. The students may be familiar with "spin-offs" that result from a minor character on a television series being highlighted in a new series. Have them create a spin-off based on a secondary character in a story.

☐ Select a plot from a familiar story and create a different theme. The students should decide how the characters might be protrayed differently in order for that theme to be significant.

In order to encourage students' interest in a variety of literary forms and styles, have them share their books through reports, art projects, and dramatizations. Ask them to

☐ Create collages, dioramas, "movie" boxes, posters, and book jackets that illustrate an important aspect of the story.

□ Select an event and dramatize it in a puppet show. The students should make the puppets to represent the characters in the story. The dialogue may be taken from the story, or it can be fictionalized.

□ Entice other students to read the book by means of written advertisements or book auctions in which succeeding portions of the story are revealed for "a price."

□ Study in depth one particular author or illustrator. Have the students read as many words as possible by that individual as well as any available biographies. Then have them write and/or illustrate their own stories in that person's style.

STRATEGIES FOR USING BIBLIOTHERAPY

Bibliotherapy is based on the premise that books are dynamic and can change the attitudes, habits, and skills of the individuals who read them (Shepherd & Iles, 1976). When a reader is engaged in appropriate and meaningful reading, his or her personality is affected by that particular book, story, or poem. The result is that the reader may develop (1) an enlarged sphere of interest, (2) an increased social sensitivity, (3) the realization that others have a life struggle, and (4) the realization that there is more than one solution to a problem (Corman, 1975).

As a process, bibliotherapy takes the reader through the stages of

1. Identification. The reader, vicariously participating with a character in a book or story, realizes that there is some common trait or bond between them. The reader identifies with the story character and becomes ready to "live the other's life."
2. Catharsis. After identification with a character is established, the reader can experience a release of emotions as the character works through a problem.
3. Insight. When the experience results in a shaping and changing of an individual's manner of thinking, then bibiliotherapy has been effective. The reader realizes that a transfer of the actions and/or attitudes of a story characters can be made to a real life situation (Corman, 1975).

Copyright © 1975 United Feature Syndicate, Inc.

The processes should not be viewed as a cure-all. There is no guarantee that a particular book will influence any particular student or that the influence, if it does occur, will be in the desired direction (Corman, 1975). Bibliotherapy seems to work best with individuals who are not severely maladjusted. Therefore, the following guidelines should be used whenever teachers attempt to change their students' interests, attitudes, or behavior by reading books:

1. Aim towards helping the child with a minor problems or question. Any seriously disturbed child should be referred to the school psychologist, guidance counselor, or nurse.
2. Avoid directly mentioning the problem. The intent is not that teachers become the therapeutic agents but that they merely arrange a situation that may have beneficial effects.
3. Select books the content, characterizations and situations of which are believable. Unless the book is real to the individual, there can be no identification with a character.
4. Create situations in which the students will select books without coercion. The individual must "happen" upon the book or story. Since all people, children and adults, live with a romanticized vision of themselves, any direct threat on that vision is greatly resisted. The best results seem to occur serendipitously (Shepherd & Iles, 1976).

In order to undertake the use of bibliotherapy in the classroom, teachers need books that naturally portray the problems and conflicts students encounter in their lives. Sometimes a teacher will wish to affect the attitudes of an entire class; at other times, there will be an interest in attending to the needs of just one student. The following is a major resource for locating literature appropriate for use in working out problems of human relations.

Tway, Eileen, ed. *Reading Ladders for Human Relations,* 6th ed. (Washington, DC: The American Council on Education, 1981). Available from: National Council of Teachers of English, 1111 Kenyon Road, Urbana, IL 61801.

A list of suggested books about bibliotherapy can be found in the following annotated bibliography.

Riggs, Corinne W. *Bibliotherapy: An Annotated Bibliography* (Newark, DE: International Reading Association, 1971).

Discussion Questions and Activities

1. Find out what children are reading. Visit a school and public library and interview children about their book selections. Find out why they are choosing

the books they do. Then interview teachers and librarians to find out what they think children *are* and *should be* reading. Compare the results of the two sets of interviews.
2. Investigate the criteria by which books are given awards. Information can be obtained from the Children's Book Council and the American Library Association. Select one year's awards and compare the winner and the runners-up. Would your decision have been the same as the judges'?
3. Investigate the current movement in the media arts toward "visual literacy." In what ways do the criteria for quality and understanding differ between the judging of a visual story and a written story?
4. Explain what Charlotte Huck (1968) meant in the following:

   The ultimate experience of a story or a poem lies in the way it is told, not in just the facts or events it relates.

5. Is it true, as John Barrett (1968) states, that

   Only that book which helps the student to clarify and thus to define is going to be seen by him as relevant and will thus be for him an experience that has meaning; all other books will be irrelevant and meaningless.

6. Plan a topical unit for students in a particular grade level. Develop the theme of the unit by means of a variety of literary forms and styles. Be sure to include selections appropriate to a wide range of reading abilities.
7. Plan a bulletin board display to be used introduce students in the primary grades to the different types of literary forms.
8. Plan a book fair and contact local merchants or book suppliers about contributing books. Then plan a campaign to encourage elementary students and their parents to attend. If possible, work with a local parents' or teachers' organization to hold the book fair.
9. Explain what this statement by Helen Koss (1972) means to you: "Relevance is a matter of applicability."
10. What is your definition of literature? Investigate how various authors define the term and then write your own definition.

Further Readings

The first reference discusses the place of literature in elementary education. The author presents a theory with practical instructional suggestions for unifying the language arts so that literature becomes the center of language studies.

Sloan, Glenna Davis, *The Child as Critic: Teaching Literature in the Elementary School* (New York: Teachers College Press, Columbia University, 1975).

Those who wish to find out more about the effects of reading on the individual should read

Russell, David H., *The Dynamics of Reading,* ed. Robert B. Ruddell (Waltham, MA: Gin, 1970).

The following text organizes and discusses children's literature in terms of social issues:

Rudman, Masha Kabakow, *Children's Literature: An Issues Approach* Lexington, MA: D. C. Heath, 1976).

The following monograph, although it uses examples mostly from the secondary school level, contains ideas that can be used at all grade levels:

Weiss, M. Jerry, Joseph Brunner, and Warren Heis, eds., *New Perspectives on Paperbacks.* Monograph no. 1. The College Reading Association, 1973 (May be obtained from Strine Printing Co., 391 Greendale Road, York, PA 17403.)

The International Reading Association (Newark, DE) has published a number of collected articles on topics relating to the teaching of children's literature.

Carlson, Ruth Kearney, ed., *Folklore and Folktales Around the World.* (1972).
Catterson, Jane H., ed., *Children and Literature (1970).*
Huus, Helen, *ed., Evaluating Books for Children and Young People* (1968).
Painter, Helen W., *Poetry and Children* (1970).
Painter, Helen W., ed., *Reaching Children and Young People Through Literature* (1971).
Sebasta, Sam Leaton, ed., *Ivory, Apes, and Peacocks* (1968).
Strickland, Dorothy S., ed., *The Role of Literature in Reading Instruction: Cross Cultural Views* (1981).
Tanyzer, Harold, and Jean Karl, eds., *Reading Children's Books, and Our Pluralistic Society* (1972).

The following, all published by the International Reading Association, are meant to help teachers with children who have problems about themselves as readers and learners.

Alexander, J. Estill, and Ronald C. Filler, *Attitudes and Reading* (1976).
Quandt, Ivan, *Self Concept and Reading* (N.D.)
Shapiro, Jon E., ed., *Using Literature and Poetry Effectively* (1979).
Spiegel, Dixie Lee, *Reading for Pleasure: Guidlines* (1981).

Periodically, *Language Arts* focuses on various themes related to children's literature. For example, the April issues of volumes 55 (1978); 56 (1979); 57

(1980); and 58 (1981) all are on children's literature. Earlier volumes should be consulted for other related themes.

In addition to the articles on sex stereotyping in literature that occasionally appear in *The Reading Teacher* and *Language Arts,* the following are good sources of information about how to recognize it, how to teach students about it, and how to keep it out of your own and your students' writing:

Nilsen, Alleen P., et al., *Sexism and Language* (Urbana, IL: National Council of Teachers of English, 1977).

Sheridan, E. Marcia, ed., *Sex Stereotypes and Reading: Research and Strategies* (Newark, DE: International Reading Association, 1982).

Chapter 12

STRATEGIES FOR STUDENTS WITH SPECIAL NEEDS

Focus Questions

1. What problems in learning to read and write are faced by speakers of divergent dialects?

2. How can nonnative speakers of English become effective readers and writers of English?

3. What are the characteristics of reading and learning disabilities?

4. How can students with special needs be instructed in the regular classroom?

Our main point in our discussion of students with special needs is that their inability to function in school is due to an inability to receive and transmit information effectively.[1] Since the vehicle for communication is language, an understanding of the nature of verbal and nonverbal communication (such as that given in Chapter 2) is essential to understanding students' ineffectiveness in learning to read in school.

We will talk about four types of students with special needs—speakers of divergent dialets, students for whom English is a second language, students with difficulties in learning to read, and students who are considered gifted and talented.

THE NEEDS OF DIVERGENT DIALECT SPEAKERS

In every major language there can be found variations among its speakers in the pronunciation of sounds, formation of sentences, and the use of meanings assigned to words. When these variations are consistently used by an identifiable group of speakers, they are called a dialect. American English speech is a family of dialects and each dialect is a legitimate form of communication for its speakers (Goodman, 1969c). Within a language group, dialects have two dimensions

---

[1]The first edition of this chapter was written with Michele K. Heiman.

(Foerster, 1974b). One is geographic and is observable in regional dialect variations such as those heard in Maine, New York, and Texas. The other is closely allied with individuals' socioeconomic status. At one extreme of this dimension is the speech of the poor and disenfranchised and at the other is the speech of the affluent and the highly educated. Between them lie many other dialects. These two dimensions intersect so that each regional grouping has its own socioeconomic variations.

A dialect is not "slang," which is a deliberate word substitution in a dialect. All dialects can have expressions that are considered slang.

Standard American English is just one dialect that has been arbitrarily set by society as the language of business, government, and mass communication. Standard American English is that language most commonly used by announcers and newscasters and heard on most national radio and televison news and informational programs. It does not differ sharply from most other main dialects, and there is no one region that solely possesses this variety of the English language. The reason for this seems to be the extreme regional and social mobility within the general society. The word *standard* in regard to this language variety is probably unfortunate and misleading. Just as a standardized test score does not represent an ideal toward which all instruction should aim, the standard dialect should not be so conceived either. Even the written form does not represent any extensively used spoken form and should not be used as the basis for oral language instruction.

Black American Dialects

The largest group of divergent dialects in American society is black American English. An understanding of how black dialects evolved should help clarify the differences between black American English and standard American English. The history of black American English can be summarized as follows (Stewart, 1966):

Africans were among the first immigrants to colonial America, being brought in as slaves. As were all immigrants, they were faced with the problem of acquiring the language of the new nation. As a result of slave trade, a kind of pidgin was formed. (Pidgins are hybrid languages used by native speakers of other languages.) Many Africans who were brought to America already spoke an English pidgin, as did many of the Americans engaged in the slave trade. The policy of slave owners and slave buyers to mix Africans of different language and cultural groups forced the Afro-Americans to rely on this means rather than their native tongue to maintain communication with others. The pidgin flourished and affected the English spoken by both slaves and slave owners.

Today, communities in many urban and rural areas display a range of dialects. Much dialect blending occurs as members of the different linguistic communities become mobile.

Unquestionably, the term *black American English* is stereotypical, but many features of pronunciation, grammar, and lexicon are shared by a large number of speakers (Labov, 1966). These features are acquired socially and perpetuated socially. Research on the forms of these features has indicated how black American English and Standard American English differ (Baratz, 1968). Examples of these differences can be found in Table 12-1. It should be noted that not all researchers agree on the form and frequency in which these features are

Table 12-1 Features of Black American English

Phonological Features

Certain sounds may be omitted from medial and/or final positions:
  /r/ from words such as *guard* (becoming /god/).
  /l/ from words such as *tall* and *help* (becoming /taw/ and /hep/).
  /t/, /d/, /s/, and /z/ in final clusters in words such as *past, bites, nest* (becoming /pass/, /bite/, and /nes/).
  Some final consonants may be lost in words such as *bat* and *hand* (becoming /bah/ and /han/).
Certain sounds may be similarly pronounced or interchanged:
  /m/ and /n/ may be indistinguishable in words such as *ram* (becoming /ran/).
  /th/ in initial position may become /d/ in words such as *them* (becoming /dem/).
  /sk/ in medial or final position may become /ks/ in words such as *ask* (becoming /aks/).
  /th/ in final position may become /v/ or /f/ in words such as *breathe* and *both* (becoming /breev/ and /bohf/).
  /sk/ may be substituted for /st/ in initial position in such words as *street* (becoming /skreet/).
  /e/ and /i/ may become indistinguishable in words such as *pen* and *pin* (becoming /pin/ and /pin/).

Syntactic Features

Certain transformations may occur in verb forms:
  The present tense, third person: *He walks* becomes *He walk.*
  The present progressive: *She is singing* becomes *She sing.*
  The past tense irregular: *He took it* becomes *He taken it.*
  Past perfect irregular: *He has taken it* becomes *He have took it.*
  Future: *I am going to do it* may become *I'm a do it.*
  Present habitual: *She is* (always) *doing it* may become *She be doing it.*
  Past habitual: *He used to do it* may become *He been doing it.*
Certain transformations may occur in sentence structure:
  Negation: *They don't have any* may become *They don't got none.*
  Questions
  Indirect: *I asked if he fixed it* may become *I asked did he fix it?*
  Direct: *How did you do that* may become *How you do that?*
  The subject: *My mother is there* may become *My mother, she there.*
  Plural nouns: *Those pencils* may become *Them pencils.*
  Possessive: *Phillip's book* may become *Phillip book.*

Source: Based on information presented in Miles V. Zintz, *The Reading Process: The Teacher and the Learner,* 2nd ed. (Dubuque, IA: William C. Brown, 1975).

found in black American English. It might be best to look on these features as those that are often used by a majority of the speakers in black urban communities. No one would probably use them all, all of the time.

Barriers to Comprehension

Barriers to effective communication were discussed in Chapter 2. Two factors discussed then are relevant to the discussion here: communication may be hindered because of different linguistic codes or because of "emotional static." The first barrier occurs when two or more individuals attempt to communicate in the belief that their utterances are mutually intelligible. The other may occur when attitudes toward the backgrounds of students with divergent dialects interfere with the acceptance of their ideas and contributions in school.

For many years, speakers of divergent dialects—which usually meant speakers of black American English but also may have included other minorities—were considered "disadvantaged" learners. Many people felt that their "disadvantagedness" resulted from their "substandard" speech and thinking. Sometimes the term *culturally disadvantaged* was applied to indicate that the students were not prepared by the preschool environment to cope with school situations. These however, are definitely misnomers, since group members which society has so labeled have learned to function as well as any other group members among their peers. (Wheat, 1974). The label becomes the reality when individuals are taken from a familiar environment and placed in a system that seems alien.

Students from minority cultures who speak a divergent English dialect may come to school not having had some experiences that the school presumes they have had. Success in school is therefore hindered, not because the pupils cannot do the school tasks, but because they understand them differently. This then compounds the students' unfamiliarity with certain linguistic conventions used in school. The result is an apparent lack of understanding and an inability to perform school tasks.

As to the effect on reading achievement, especially on comprehension, of being a speaker of black American English, reviews of the literature indicate that the picture is not clear. Although there is evidence of a high incidence of poor achievement in reading among black English speakers, there is no definitive evidence that it is due primarily to their language patterns (Rupley & Robeck, 1978; Dillingofski, 1979: Barnitz, 1980; Eberwein, 1982; and Schwartz, 1982). There is some evidence of an attitudinal interference, as many teachers hold negative attitudes toward "nonstandard language" (Monteith, 1980).

The question of whether or not black American English interferes with understanding in school is futher complicated by the introduction of a legal interpretation, in addition to the educational interpretation. In 1979, a federal district court judge in Michigan ruled that black English is more than a dialect, that it is a language different from standard American English. The judge ruled that because of this different linguistic background, black English speakers in Ann Arbor, Michigan, were receiving an inferior education. Although he did not rule that materials, written in black English were to be used for instruction, he did rule that the teachers in the Ann Arbor school district should receive training in raising their sensitivity to the needs of black English speakers. The judge indicated that a problem existed when teachers refuse to recognize and accept in school the existence of a language that is acceptable in the child's home environment and community (Monteith, 1980; Padak, 1981).

There are a number of important learnings which are prerequisites to successful school achievement (see Chapter 6). The students who receive sensory and intellectual stimulation of the kind upon which school learning is based generally possess these prerequisites. However, some students may be deprived of this background or may have received markedly different instruction which may interfere with their school achievement (Edwards, 1969). It is *not* that they cannot speak and think; it is just that what they do think and speak about is different from what they may be asked to do in school. Their cognitive and linguistic backgrounds are different, not inferior.

Students come to school able to communicate with others in their immediate social environment. It is when some students are confronted with the unfamiliarity of the school code and experiences that they find a barrier to communicating and comprehending. Researchers have discovered that if two communicators who do not share many experiences or points of view try to communicate, they need to use an elaborated code—one that employs extensive language signals. The factor controlling the extent to which a message needs an elaborated code is the extent to which the communicators share attitudes and experiences, or "context" (Erickson, 1968). High shared context situations allow the use of a restricted code, since there is considerable overlap of experience and points of view between the communicators. Low shared context situations necessitate the use of the elaborated codes. "As context increases the volume of necessary communication signals decreases" (Erikson, 1968).

Developing Comprehension Across Dialects

Three alternative views have been offered by various authorities for developing literacy among speakers of different dialects: (1) teach standard American English before teaching the students to read and write, (2) create instructional materials using the dialect patterns, and (3) allow the students to retain their dialect patterns while reading and writing standard patterns.

Those who advocate teaching standard American English prior to formal reading and writing instruction generally recommend that the standard dialect be taught as a second language. Many instructional plans use foreign language-teaching procedures. Others imply that standard forms should be learned because the dialects represent stunted language growth (Bereiter &

Englemann, 1966; Englemann, 1969). This is pure nonsense. Every language and dialect is a highly complex system capable of ordering and categorizing the world, though each might do it a little differently. The fact that some ideas are difficult to express in a dialect also holds true for the standard dialect. Thus, although no one disagrees on the advantage of being familiar with standard English patterns, there is little evidence that they must be spoken before learning to read and write. The creation of basal series in dialect patterns is probably one of the most volatile issues in the black literacy controversy. Some people have almost immediately rejected their use because they picture them as texts in the style of Harris's *Tales of Uncle Remus*. But the dialect basals are intended as transition texts: a step toward reading standard English.

However, the process of this transitional step may be unnecessary and prolong the time until students are able to function in "regular" school texts. Using a dialect text may also be impractical. Black American English dialects may have certain common features, but they do vary. A text appropriate for blacks in northern urban centers may have little value for blacks in southern rural areas.

The third alternative, allowing the students to retain their dialectal patterns but to receive instruction in standard language patterns, is what generally occurs in most schools with most students. The written dialect transcends all spoken dialects and permits effective communication between speakers of all dialects of American English. The use of standard written forms together with the students' dialectal spoken forms becomes ineffective only when the teachers and students do not share a common context: when teachers do not recognize, accept, and understand the language patterns, and the students are made to feel that their language patterns are inappropriate for academic success.

Instruction for speakers of divergent dialects should teach them about the structure of the material they will be asked to read and write. They should learn how to use their own knowledge of language to predict what will be found in the books they read. They must be taught that they can approach the printed page with confidence and that they have the tools to discover the author's meaning (Lloyd, 1969). Learning to read for speakers of divergent dialects, then, should be not different than for speakers of standard dialect. When readers can predict a great deal of the meaning in the printed matter the result is "comprehension." Predictability is as crucial for divergent dialect speakers as it is to other speakers. If predicatability is desirable, then it seems logical to suggest that any student who can speak a language but who has no reading ability can be best guided *in the initial acquisition of literacy* by the use of predictable written language—that is, by written language which at least comes close to matching the oral language patterns used. (See Chapter 7.)

The implications of the above discussion for teaching students with divergent dialects are

1. Regardless of which alternative teachers select for instructing speakers of black American English, or any other divergent dialect, they should be

prepared to meet some opposition. They should choose their instructional procedures after analyzing the local school situation and evaluating each school's particular needs.
2. Whatever instructional approach they choose, teachers should improve their understanding of the English language and its many varieties. The language that each student brings to school should be accepted as a legitimate means for communication.
3. If there is a difference between the students' normal speech patterns and that used in the school, then it seems incumbent on the school personnel to determine which items of language require attention because communication is inhibited. Analyze, do not criticize!
4. The development of literacy in all the students should be accomplished through the mutual involvement of teachers and students. Together they should attempt to understand the alternatives available to them and to select those that seem comfortable and appropriate to the situation.

THE NEEDS OF SPEAKERS OF ENGLISH AS A SECOND LANGUAGE

School programs for students for whom English is not a native language exist in a variety of forms and for a variety of purposes. Some programs are intended to teach students to speak English. These are generally known as "English as a Second Language" programs (ESL). They are conducted in much the same way as are the foreign language programs found in many high schools and in a few elementary schools. Other programs for nonnative speakers of English try to provide instruction in two languages. These bilingual programs conduct certain instructional periods in the native language and others in English. For instance, public school bilingual programs sometimes conduct instruction in mathematics, social studies, and science in the native language and language arts instruction in English. Some parochial school programs give religious studies in one language and secular studies in English. A third kind of program for nonnative English speakers is given in English but takes into account the linguistic and cultural features of the native language. These programs are sometimes labeled "education of the bilingual."

It should be apparent that bilingual education and education of the bilingual as here used are two different things. Our discussion will focus on the later: the education of pupils for whom English is not a native language but who have achieved a degree of proficiency in spoken English so that they can receive reading instruction in English.

When an individual becomes bilingual, a language continuum is created (Ching, 1976). When proficiency in both languages is attained, it is possible for the speaker to "glide" at will from one end of the continuum to the other. What becomes evident to many teachers is the apparent mixing of the two languages by students who have not become totally bilingual. In some areas the pejorative terms *TexMex* and *Spanglish* are used to denote the language of individuals who mix Spanish and English. What teachers need to realize is that it may not be the language differences or the mixing of language forms that interferes with reading. What may interfere with the students' learning is the influence that the language of such speakers has on teachers and through them on the learning environments (Gumperz & Hernandez-Chavez, 1972).

There is evidence that code switching—alternating between two languages—persists wherever a minority language group comes in contact with a majority language group under conditions of rapid social change (Gumperz & Hernandez-Chavez, 1972). Alternating between languages seems to serve definite and clearly understandable communicative ends. It does not represent "errors" on the part of the speaker; rather, the creative use of alternative language forms conveys specific meanings. At this time, there seems to be no way to predict when a switch in linguistic form will occur or to predict its particular meaning. The use of alternative language forms of different languages is akin to the process in which a speaker will choose certain words rather than their synonyms because of their connotations or because of the effect they will have on the listener. It is a verbal strategy used in the same way that one can adjust his or her speech to the various degrees of formality or informality of a situation. Teachers therefore should accept speech varieties as potentially meaningful and should attempt to interpret them in relation to the context of the situation in which they occur.

To be able to interpret a message contained in a mixed code, speakers must share a cultural and linguistic context. They need to have had common experiences, which may be functions of home background, peer group experiences and education. For teachers who do not speak their students' native language, communicating may be extremely difficult.

How then can teachers instruct bilingual pupils? One thing they can do is learn as much as possible about the students' language and culture.

When dealing with nonnative speakers of English, teachers should be acutely sensitive to the students' cultural values: their aspiration levels, their value orientations, and their process of socialization. Whenever there are differences between the cultural values of the schools and those of the local culture, a breakdown in the communication between teachers and students is likely. Effective communication is hindered when the teacher fails to consider these differences, since "the basis for using language for information, action, or emotion in educational content is the assumption that the child has already mastered the essentials" of language (Mackey, 1973).

Teachers should develop a learning situation in which nonnative speakers of English have many opportunities to develop a sense of security, acceptance and recognition. Actually, this should not be difficult, since all students need these for successful school experiences.

In dealing with the language of nonnative speakers, teachers should become aware of the differences in how experiences and concepts are encoded, the similarity or difference in phonemes, the vocabulary, and the syntax. An analysis of the languages can reveal potential sources of confusion and barriers to effective communication. For example, some students may be reluctant to speak or write English because they are unsure of or confused by language forms that do not exist in their native language. Or some may be unfamiliar with the connotations of certain words or the appropriateness of certain words or phrases in a given situation. The result is embarrassment or frustration whenever they are required to use English in situations for which they do not possess adequate English language skills. Teachers can avoid potentially emotional situations only through an understanding of the language system of the students.

Strategies for Teaching

There are various approaches to working with students for whom English is a second language. Since the purpose here is to discuss the bilingual student who has not developed proficiency in English similar to that of a native, no attempt will be made to discuss ESL or bilingual programs. The focus of the discussion is how to provide instruction in reading for the bilingual student in typical classroom situations.

Before adequate instruction can be provided, teachers need some means for identifying the English proficiency of the students. After a discussion of assessment instruments and procedures, attention will be given to instructional strategies and then to resource materials.

Assessment Teachers can use formal and informal means of assessing the students' English language proficiency. Formal means consist of standardized instruments that measure the students' skills in English and/or in the native language. Informal means consist of teacher-made tests and inventories for measuring the students' understanding and use of English forms.

The following are standardized tests that rate the students' bilingual skills. They use comparable forms in English and Spanish and measure similar skills in both languages. They can be used for assessing the students' strengths in using similar strategies in different linguistic contexts.

Bilingual Syntax Measure (New York: Test Department, Harcourt Brace Jovanovich).
Hoffman Bilingual Schedule (New York: Teachers College Press, Columbia University).
Cooperative Inter-American Tests (Princeton, NJ: Educational Testing Service).

When standardized instruments are unavailable, teachers can construct their own means for determining students' readiness for reading instruction. The performance rating scale shown in Figure 12-1 is one means for localizing the aspects of language which may hinder progress in learning to read English.

	LISTENING	SPEAKING	READING	WRITING
Pronunciation/ Spelling		_____		_____
Vocabulary: Word Meanings	_____	_____	_____	_____
Morpholical Units	_____	_____	_____	_____
Sentence Patterns	_____	_____	_____	_____
Intonational Patterns:				
Oral Usage Related to Written Form		_____		_____

Ratings: The student compared with age-level peers, understands and/or uses standard American English patterns:

1. Like a local native speaker.
2. With accent and some situationally inappropriate forms.
3. In most situations but must make conscious effort to avoid code switching with native language forms.
4. To small degree or haltingly.
5. Not at all.

Figure 12-1 Performance Scale for Assessing Language Skills of Nonnative English Speakers

The scale is used by observing the students in a variety of social and educational situations. Or, the teacher can set up a series of games in which the students are asked to perform tasks revealing their language proficiency. For example, games can be played that reveal whether the students can auditorily distinguish between similar English phonemes—/*shin*/ and /*chin*/—or between contrastive elements in English and the native language—/*hump*/ and /*jump*/. Similarly, activities can be designed to reveal the students' proficiency in speaking, reading, and writing. In all cases, the standard against which the nonnative English speaker is judged is the performance of native English speakers of that person's age.

In addition, the exercises and activities in the following section on instructional strategies can be modified for use as informal testing procedures.

The mistakes that students make during these activities undoubtedly should mean more to someone who knows the learner's native language than to someone unfamiliar with it. Just as native speakers pass through stages of development that can be identified by analyzing their performance, so can the development of nonnative speakers be assessed. Consider your students' "errors" as miscues that may have resulted from their inability (1) to deal with contrastive forms of the two languages, (2) to understand a particular English language form, (3) to realize the ambiguity of a speech form, or (4) to use certain irregular English forms. Only by being aware of the linguistic and cultural features of the students' native language can teachers effectively assess the importance and meaning of their language divergences.

Instructional Strategies The activities and exercises in the ensuing discussion are not exhaustive but are presented as representative of the type that can be assist those students who have at least a rudimentary knowledge of English. Such students would receive scores of three and four on a performance scale like the one in Figure 12-1. As students are taught the various structures and forms of English, they should be told how these differ from or parallel those in their native languages.

The first step in improving the bilingual student's reading proficiency is to link their oral language with reading and writing acts. This is accomplished by using the language experience approach. The ideas in Chapter 6 for developing readiness for reading instruction and those in Chapter 7 for using the language experience approach to introduce students to literacy can be used with students for whom English is a second language.

Oral and written language proficiency can be developed through activities that direct the students' attention to significant features of English. Bilingual students can become fluent in English through tasks that have them

1. Practice a series of pattern drills (Saville-Troike, 1973) that include
   a. Mimicry. The students imitate a sentence attempting to use the teacher's intonational pattern. These sentences can be used until the students memorize them.
   b. Chain drill. This activity is similar to the game of "Follow the Leader." One student makes a statement that is then repeated by the other students.
   c. Substitution. Students are asked to substitute a word or phrase for another with the same grammatical function.
   d. Replacement. Students are to replace a word or phrase with a substitute word, in most cases, a pronoun.
   e. Conversion. Students change the tense of the sentences in a predetermined manner.
   f. Expansion. A word or group of words is added to a sentence.
   g. Transformation. The word order of a sentence is changed so that a sentence becomes a question, an affirmative becomes a negative, or an active becomes a passive.
2. Develop a sense adjectival modifaction by expanding noun phrases. The students should learn the order of modifiers: nationality, color, shape, size, quality, cardinal, ordinal, defining, and indefinite or inclusive.

3. Develop a sense of adverbial modification through tasks requiring the placement of adverbs in sentences. A distinction should be made between adverbs that move without changing a sentence's meaning and those that qualify only a particular unit within the sentence.
4. Develop an understanding of common, multiple-use function words such as *have* and *do*. Students should become acquainted with constructions using *have:*

    have + infinitive (to show necessity)
    have + to have (to show necessity)
    have + noun (to show causative action)
    have + noun + verb (to show directives)

Resources Cities and states with populations containing a large number of pupils for whom English is a second language often develop instructional guides to meet the needs of these students. The following are series designed to introduce and develop English for nonnative speakers. The criteria presented in Chapter 5 should be used to assess their appropriateness for your situation.

I Like English. Intended grades: K–6 (Glenview, IL: Scott Foresman).
English for a Changing World Program. Intended grades: 5–8 (Glenview, IL: Scott Foresman)
Reading Out. Intended grades: lower elementary (Riverside, NJ: Macmillan).
Steps to English. Intended grades: K–6. (New York: Webster Division/McGraw-Hill).

THE NEEDS OF STUDENTS WHO HAVE DIFFICULTY LEARNING TO READ

The reading act is quite complex, and many characteristics of child growth and development have a bearing on reading success. A single causal interpretation of reading difficulty does not, therefore, seem to be possible. Each student who has difficulty learning to read may do so for several reasons. The assessment of each case requires studying the student in a particular social and educational setting.

There is a growing trend among school personnel to label students having difficulties as *learning disabled*. When the difficulty is learning of reading strategies, the term dyslexia is used. Other terms have been and are being used, but the one that seems to persist is dyslexia. Among its users, the term is often used in ways that may seem confusing. Depending on the individual's conceptual background, the term can have several different meanings.

Historically, interest in dyslexia began in the various branches of preventive and rehabilitative medicine, remedial reading, and the study of learning disabilities in the area of special education. Now, those who study dyslexia include researchers in fields that are tangential to reading behavior, including those studying the sociological, psychological, political, and economic effects of reading failure. Basically, there are two separate approaches, the medical and the educational, to the study and instruction of dyslexia (Lerner, 1981). Medically,

dyslexia is viewed as an inability to read because of brain damage or central nervous system dysfunction. Educationally, dyslexia is viewed as an inability to read when no specific causes are evident.

Reviews of the literature on researchers' use of the term dyslexia show that it is used in many ways. One review reveals that dyslexia defines a pupil's performance when there exists (1) evidence of brain damage, (2) behavioral manifestations of central nervous system dysfunctions, (3) evidence of a genetic or inherited problem, (4) maturational lag, (5) reading retardation, and (6) an inability to learn through regular classroom methods (Lerner, 1981). Other reviews also show a wide lack of agreement among professionals about the criteria for identifying individuals with learning and reading problems (Harber, 1981; Kavale & Nye, 1981; Olsen & Mealor, 1981).

Most educators define dyslexia to conform with the Education for All Handicapped Children Act, Public Law 94-142, which states that children with learning disabilities are

... children who have a disorder in one or more of the basic psychological processes involved in understanding or in using language, spoken or written, which disorder may manifest itself in imperfect ability to listen, think, speak, read, write, spell, or do mathematical calculations. such disorders include such conditions as perceptual handicaps, brain injury, minimal brain dysfunction, dyslexia, and developmental aphasia. Such terms do not include children who have learning problems which are primarily the result of visual, hearing, or motor handicaps, of mental retardation, of emotional disturbance, or environmental, cultural, or economic disadvantage.

According to this definition, dyslexia is a learning disability for which no cause is known. What results is that the students become the victims of a blind label. A review of the literature reveals many inconsistencies in the definition of dyslexia (McCarthy & McCarthy, 1971). Defining it as a single "disease" is unacceptable because so many different manifestations of it are possible. Educators also feel that there are many possible causes for students' learning difficulties—social problems, emotional maladjustments, general health status, and defective teaching. However, the definition in Public Law 94-142 says that no such causes can be considered in defining a dyslexic child.

To dispel the confusion about learning disabilities, a revised definition was created by a committee with representatives from six national organizations serving learning-disabled students. The committee drew up a definition that, they stated, does not imply a standard approach to assessment and educational management, that recognizes learning disabilities as a problem not just in young children, that states the cause of learning disabilities, and that does not exclude other handicapping conditions or cultural factors (Hammill et al., 1981; NJCLD, 1981). The proposed definition states that

... learning disabilities is a generic term that refers to a group of disorders manifested by significant difficulties in the acquisition and use of listening, speaking, reading, writing, reasoning or mathematical abilities. These disorders are intrinsic to the individual and presumed to be due to central nervous system dysfunction. Even though a learning disability may occur concomitantly with other handicapping conditions (e.g., sensory impairment, mental retardation, social and emotional disturbance) or environmental influences (e.g., cultural differences, insufficient/inappropriate instruction, psychogenic factors), it is not the direct result of those conditions or influences.

There are many myths about dyslexia because there are no established criteria for determining who really has a learning disability. In fact, the phenomenon identified as dyslexia may in actuality be that which educators for many years labeled reading disability. "There is little if any difference between learning by disabled children and many of the other children being seen by the reading specialist. A false dichotomy has been created because the two specialists imply different terms, different diagnostic approaches, and different remedial methods" (Hartman & Hartman, 1973; see also the research of Taylor et al., [1979]; and Harris, [1980].)

Identification of the Reading Disabled

The most common means of determining whether students are reading disabled is by establishing some relationship between their ability levels and their performance levels. Ability is determined by using a mental maturity or intelligence measure, and reading ability by using standardized reading instruments. Through an index or formula, a ratio between performance and ability is computed. When students' performance levels are more than two years below their potential or anticipated performance level, then they are considered reading disabled. When there is no direct evidence of a cause for their apparent inability to read, they are labeled by many as dyslexic.

This labeling procedure is not as simple as it appears. From the discussion in Chapter 4 it should be evident that standardized intelligence and reading tests have serious limitations. It may not always be factors associated with the students that cause low scores. The use of various indexes also can produce varying results (Reed, 1970; Samuels, 1970). First, there is a large discrepancy among the results of different formulas and indexes. The index used to establish reading retardation not only influences the pattern of the relationship between verbal and nonverbal intelligence scores found among retarded readers, but it also affects the incidence of retarded readers for any given population. There is disagreement as to how great a discrepancy between actual and potential achievement should be used as an index of disability. The cut-off figure of two years is an arbitrary point, but there is no empirical evidence that this identifies the instance of disability.

The prevalence of learning disability in school settings is not at all clear (Bruininks et al., 1971). It seems that the learning problems found among different general school populations vary widely in proportion and characteristics in the students so labeled. The reviewers of the literature ascribe the cause of these variations to the influence of differences in (1) the defining criteria, (2) the instrumentation used for measurement, (3) the methods used to analyze the data, (4) the characteristics of the sample drawn from school populations, and (5) the quality and extent of the subjects' instructional history. Their conclusion is that few current estimates of the prevalence of students with school-learning problems are supported by findings from empirical studies.

Those adhering to a medically influenced model of reading disability advocate as a possible cause the inability to achieve intersensory transfer or intersensory perceptual shifting. Intersensory transfer is the translation of information from the terms of one sensory channel to those of another. Perceptual shifting is the changing of attention from one sensory channel to another. A review of the research literature in these areas points out some limitations in applying the conclusions of research findings to reading achievement (Jones, 1972). In regard to intersensory transfer and reading achievement, the evidence suggests that it is highly probable that ability to associate intersensory stimuli is significantly related to the ability to read. However, the research investigating the relationship of cross-model transfer skills and intelligence is conflicting. There is a general softness in the studies, as they do not control visual clues during presentation of auditory stimuli, and, there are possible variations in stimulus patterns owing to human error. Many of the sample populations also do not represent normal school populations. In regard to intersensory perceptual shifting and reading achievement, the research is insufficient to draw any conclusions. In regard to model preference and reading achievement, the conclusions of the research indicate that the presentation of information through printed or oral channels under various conditions is pertinent to learning in general but not to learning to read. One major problem is the identification of a preferred modality through a valid test of modal preference.

In conclusion, it seems that modality deficiencies, congitive deficits, aptitude weaknesses, and the relation of verbal to nonverbal performance abilities will vary according to the method of identifying the retarded reader. The fact that different criteria will yield different results makes it clear that the final truths about retarded readers may be difficult to discover. The particular pattern of deficits may be only an artifact of the investigator's decision to use one measure of potential instead of another (Reed, 1970). Most of the studies do not take into account the adequacy of the instruction given to such students (Samuels, 1970). Finally, there is considerable evidence to suggest that despite all the testing and data collecting, they have little influence on actual decisions to label a student learning disabled. It seems the decisions may be made independent of the data and despite whether or not the decisions are supported by the data (Ysseldke et al., 1982).

A Developmental Concept of Disability

There seem to be two common frameworks in which reading and/or learning disabilities are placed. One may be termed the *deficiency concept* and the other the *developmental concept*. The deficiency concept assumes that students who lack certain vital skills cannot function. The adherents to this concept postulate one or more traumas occurring in the students lives that have interfered with their ability to perform some educational tasks. Taking their cue mainly from the medical profession, the proponents of the deficiency model suggest that once the causative factors have been identified, correction procedures can be instituted. This thinking is, of course, very much like that prevalent at the on set of the compensatory programs for the educationally disadvantaged. It is notable that these programs seemed to have failed whenever they were built on an erroneous concept of "disadvantagedness."

The developmental concept of learning disability posits that students may not achieve in school because they are not ready to perform certain tasks. This concept demands that any single performance be evaluated in relation to preceding or subsequent performances. Since human behavior is a function of structure, individuals seem to behave largely because of the way they have developed (Ames, 1968). Behavior, therefore, is patterned, predictable, and ordered, as is the physical organism.

The students who exhibit learning disabilities are usually considered different; yet they may not be as different from other students as is usually thought. It may just be more a matter of timing than of actual difference in potential (Ames, 1968). To understand the students (and to be able to work toward preventing disruptions in learning), each student's developmental history should be known. It is important to measure and identify the stage of development that the students have reached. Those lacking the appropriate readiness will appear to be learning disabled; yet all that might be missing is the prerequisite conceptual background in thinking and motor abilities. For those who seem to be having a great deal of difficulty with learning, their problem may be "rooted in some aspect of the child's basic individuality or learning ability" (Ames, 1968).

The maturational process is linked to age. For some students maturational lag, the slow or delayed development of those brain areas that mediate the acquisition of age-linked development skills, may be the cause of the apparent disability. Rather than representing a unique syndrome or disturbance, the pattern of deficits observed in dyslexic students often resembles the behavior patterns of chronologically younger students who have not yet developed certain skills. In such cases, the patterns of deficits vary as a function of the age at which certain skills first develop (Satz & Sparrow, 1970).

In addition to differing developmental growth patterns, students may also differ in their approaches to problem solving (Wagner & Wilde, 1973). Students' cognitive styles and/or conceptual tempos may influence their problem-solving strategies, and this may result from a blending of perceptual, cognitive, and personality factors. Individual problem-solving strategies may range along a psychologically differentiated continuum. Where on the continuum the students' strategies are located many explain their attempts to organize their environment in meaningful ways. They might differ in their cognitive styles depending on where they lie on the following continuums:

Locus of Control (approach to the environment)
    External _____ Internal
Field Articulation (organization of experiences)
    Dependence _____ Independence
Mode of Conceptual Tempo (problem-solving reaction time)
    Impulsivity _____ Reflective
Preferential Mode of Perceptual Organization and Conceptual Categorization (processing of stimuli)
    Relational _____ Analytic

Locus of control has received increased attention in the past few years. Some students seem to attribute their failure or inability to learn to factors beyond their control. They have, in fact, learned to be helpless (Grimes, 1981; Stipek & Weisz, 1981. Thomas, 1979). These students seem to react to failure by lowering their expectancies of success and to respond to problems according to sensory-perceptual information rather than to an internal analysis of the information.

If further research reveals that there are differences in how students undertake problem solving, teachers might be able to understand that all students can be "disabled" when expected to perform tasks in a manner not consistent with their particular approach to processing information. For an extended discussion of the development of human thinking, refer to Chapter 2.

Assessment of Disability and Instruction

When problems exist, individuals are apt to seek out a cause. Chapter 4 contains a full examination of the nature and uses of analytical teaching. Our discussion here will focus on two types of assessment, or diagnosis, for students exhibiting reading disabilities (Brown & Botel, 1972).

Status assessment is like making an inventory: it may be used to find the range and content of students' repertoires of responses. It is usually undertaken with one or more standardized "diagnostic" instruments designed to distinguish the tasks or items that students do know from those they do not.

In regard to identifying or diagnosing students with learning disabilities associated with reading, the instruments most commonly used are predictive. Norm-referenced instruments attempt to predict those students who will not succeed, on the assumption that a severe disability already exists and that intervention is necessary. Two examples of instruments commonly used are the

Developmental Test of Visual Perception (Frostig, 1964) and the *Illinois Test of Psycholinguistic Abilities* (ITPA) (Kirk et al., 1968). The *Developmental Test of Visual Perception* contains five subscores and a total that are used to identify those students who may have a high chance of failure. It is then implied that those five so-called perceptual skills are the prerequisites for learning to read. So far, there is no empirical evidence that those five subtests have anything to do with the learning to read process. The test is a predictive instrument that explains nothing about why or how students are not performing. (Refer to Chapter 4 for a discussion of the use of predictive tests for determining causality.)

The ITPA is a popular diagnostic instrument used extensively in schools with students who have various learning difficulties. The test writers say that it measures abilities necessary for language development. Yet the reliability and validity of the various subtests have not been clearly established. There is no specific information about the relationship between poor performance on the subtest and reading disability; therefore, its use might be rather limited (Ekwall, 1976). Two researchers who reviewed studies in which the ITPA was used concluded that its use for individual diagnosis is not supported and recommended that the test should not be used for

1. Determining the cause of academic failure.
2. Devising strategies for remedying academic problems.
3. Selecting instructional programs that are psycholinguistically appropriate.
4. Screening individual students to find those who have a high probability of failing basic school subjects (Newcomer & Hammill, 1975).

The second type of assessment, *process analysis,* is related more closely to children's natural behavior. In process analysis, one attempts to analyze the sequence of steps or structures the individual learner uses to produce any given response (Brown & Botel, 1972). Unlike status assessment, in which students might provide the "right" answer for the wrong reason, the process framework seeks to evaluate any single performance in relation to preceding or subsequent functioning. The key to understanding process analysis is the ability to understand functional relationships.

Process analysis is used when teachers attempt to determine *how* students perform the reading act and why they might not be proficient at it. The psycholinguistic perspective set forth in this text should provide the framework in which to undertake this assessment. Process-oriented assessment techniques, such as those explained in Chapter 5, should give teachers a starting place.

Those concerned with learning disabilities have become more aware of the importance of whole language approaches to learning and to instruction based on the principles of psycholinguistics (Leigh, 1980; Reid & Hresko, 1981). One important effort to meet the needs of disabled pupils is called Instrument Enrichment (Feuerstein, 1979, 1980). Although the program is intended primarily to develop the congitive abilities of individuals classified as mentally retarded, it can be used with any individual who could benefit from planned, guided instruction aimed at developing cognitive strategies. The program is based on Piagetian principles, with the exception of one important principle, the universality of cognitive development without any direct environmental influence. Instrumental Enrichment occurs when there are direct, purposeful interactions between an adult and a child to modify the child's cognitive behavior. This activity is called a Mediated Learning Experience (MLE). MLE is an interaction between the child and the environment that includes cultural transmission, since behaviors are partly culturally determined and partly triggered by situational events and circumstances.

The child is guided in a learning event to master a given situation through (1) coping with a sequence of events situated in time and space, (2) disassociating the means of problem solving from the actual goal, and (3) indulging in anticipatory representational thought. The mental act of learning has four phases. The first, *input,* has the individual gather both quantitative and qualitative data with which to solve a problem or even to appreciate the nature of a problem. This is the readiness-for-response phase. The second, *elaboration,* uses the collected data in "thinking," that is, the "internalized, organized coordinated set of actions in terms of which we elaborate upon information" (Feuerstein, 1979, 1980). It is reorganizing, classifying, and serializing existing information and applying it to new data. The third phase, *output,* is the communication of any and all solutions. The last phase, *affective,* deals with motivational factors involved in learning.

Instrumental Enrichment cannot be used by all teachers unless they undergo extensive training in the philosophy of MLE and the use of the special materials. This can be a very limiting factor to its wider dissemination and use. However, much of Instrumental Enrichment and MLE can and should be used to identify and teach students with learning problems. In many ways it is consistent with the perspective presented in this text, and its influence, when more widely felt, should be an important one for the education of all students, not only those with learning problems.

In conclusion, learning disabilities should not be viewed as strange phenomena that must be approached with reverence and awe. The teacher's task is not to require students to meet any shortsighted, rigid requirements for which they may not be ready. Their task is to adjust instructional expectations to fit the students' developmental pattern and to provide alternative learning procedures appropriate for their stage of development and cognitive style.

THE NEEDS OF THE GIFTED AND TALENTED

The idea that gifted and talented students are individuals with special needs has been exemplified in a variety of ways. One is the passage of the Gifted and

Talented Children's Education Act of 1978. In this federal law, gifted and talented means that

... children and, whenever applicable, youth who are identified at the preschool, elementary, or secondary level as possessing demonstrated or potential abilities that give evidence of high performance responsibility in areas such as intellectual, creative, specific academic, or leadership ability, or in the performing and visual arts, and who by reason thereof, require services or activities not ordinarily provided by the school.

The concern here is: Should gifted and talented students be given different educational programs for learning to read and write? Journal articles on this topic, organizations or special interest groups in major educational organizations, and conferences devoted to this topic all attest to an affirmative response to the question. Many educators view the needs of the gifted and talented, especially in regard to reading and writing programs, as different. These needs include more rapid pacing and timing; "going deeper" into a topic; a less rigidly structured learning environment; the provision for critical thinking, reading and writing; and responses to ideas completely different from those of more ordinary students (Frezise, 1978).

However, if one examines the factors that are supposed to differentiate gifted and talented students' reading and writing instruction from others', one is likely to answer our question negatively. First, there is some question as to whether gifted students read earlier than do nongifted students. Evidence exists to show that they may not and that they even may have some difficulty acquiring literacy, despite the readiness they exhibit when entering school (Cassidy & Vukelich, 1980). Other recommended strategies are similar to those discussed throughout this text and recommended for all students, regardless of their performance and ability. The instructional progrms for the gifted and talented are to (1) provide less dependence on word recognition programs and more on comprehension, (2) encourage the habit of reading widely through independent and recreational reading, (3) break away from the lock-set use of basal readers and their accompanying workbooks, (4) select well-written instructional materials that focus on ideas and events relevant to the students, (5) develop creative and critical reading skills, and (6) use peer groupings to discuss authors' ideas and styles (Labuda, 1974; Trezise, 1978, Witty, 1971).

To repeat an idea presented in Chapter 2 at the conclusion of our discussion of Piaget's stages of development: in general, the results of Paiget's work seem to indicate that children at each stage of development would benefit more from enriching activities than from attempts to speed up their education. If this premise is accepted, then reading and writing programs for the gifted and talented do not differ in kind from what is proposed for all students; they differ only in degree. Gifted and talented pupils will benefit from an expansion of their abilities rather than an acceleration of them. They should not be pushed to higher levels of materials; they should be guided to gain greater maturity at their level of performance through a wider (not different) range of experiences and activities. Some gifted and talented students also may need to develop a sense of the naturalness of failure or what may seem to them as failure—the incomplete assignment, the need for multiple revisions during the composition of a message, and the possibility that a prediction about an author's message or intent may result in an understanding different from that discovered by others.

What can be expected from many gifted and talented students is a well roundedness and a success orientation that may not be present in other students. This difference—level of performance—can separate them from their peers and even threaten some teachers. Therefore, teachers and students should be as sensitive to the gifted and talented as they are to other students with special needs. They can be done by using the bibliotherapy techniques discussed in Chapter 11. The following books discuss awareness of and sensitivity to the needs of gifted and talented students:

Fein, Ruth L., and Adrienne H. Ginsburg, "Realistic Literature About the Handicapped," *The Reading Teacher* 31 (1978): 802–805.
Lass, Bonnie, and Marcia Bromfield, "Books About Children with Special Needs: An Annotated Bibliography," *The Reading Teacher* 34 (1981): 530–538.
Tway, Eileen, "The Gifted child in Literature," *Language Arts* 57 (1980): 14–20.

Discussion Questions and Activities

1. Someone proposes to you that your students who speak black American English be placed in a "special" class because they do not have the usual conceptual background, an adequate vocabulary, and the experiences handling written verbal symbols needed to remain in a heterogeneously grouped class. How would you answer?
2. Examine reading materials written in a black American English dialect. In what ways do these materials meet or fail to answer the questions about reading materials given in Chapter 5?
3. The following statement about reading readiness is from Chapter 6. How can it be rewritten to replace "reading readiness" with "learning disability" so that the basic intent and meaning of the statement is retained?

    In a Piagetian sense, readiness means possessing those skills and abilities of a preceding stage of development.

4. What factors need to be taken into consideration when administering, scoring, and interpreting the informal language assessment procedures (including the

miscue analysis) for bilingual and bidialectal speakers? How could features of their language patterns be misconstrued as errors?
5. Examine at least three definitions of dyslexia from current texts or journal articles. Do they contain common aspects? Prepare a statement for a parents' meeting that interprets these definitions in light of the information presented in this chapter and Chapters 2 and 3.

Further Readings

Much of the recent literature on teaching speakers of divergent dialects also concerns teaching speakers of English as a second language. The references below should be helpful to teachers who want additional information about either of these topics.

Benderly, Beryl L., "The Multilingual Mind," *Psychology Today* (March 1981): 9–12.

Cazden, Courtney B., *Child Language and Education,* Chapter 7, "Dialect Differences and Bilingualism" (New York: Holt, Rinehart & Winston, 1972).

Ching, Doris C., *Reading and the Bilingual Child* (Newark, DE: International Reading Association, 1976).

Crowley, Sharon, ed., *The English Language: Issues in Study and Teaching* (Urbana, IL: National Council of Teachers of English, 1977).

Feitelson, Dina, ed., *Mother Tongue or Second Language? On the Teaching of Reading in Multiligual Societies* (Newark, DE: International Reading Association, 1979).

Fox, Robert P., ed., *Essays on Teaching English as a Second Language and as a Second Dialect* (Urbana, IL: National Council of Teachers of English, 1973).

Harber, Jean R., and Jane N. Beatty, *Reading and the Black English Speaking Child: An Annotated Bibliography* (Newark, DE: International Reading Association, 1978).

Johns, Jerry L., ed., *Literacy for Diverse Learners: Promoting Reading Growth at All Levels* (Newark, DE: International Reading Association, 1974).

Laffey, James L., and Roger W. Shuy, eds., *Language Differences: Do They Interfere?* (Newark, DE: International Reading Association, 1973).

Office for Minority Education, *An Approach for Identifying and Minimizing Bias in Standardized Tests: A Set of Guidelines* (Princeton, NJ: Educational Testing Service, 1980).

Reed, Carroll E., *Dialects of American English,* revised ed. (Urbana, IL: National Council of Teachers of English, 1977).

Seitz, Victoria, *Social Class and Ethnic Group Differences in Learning to Read* (Newark, DE: International Reading Association, 1977).

Thonis, Elanor W., *Literacy for America's Spanish Speaking Children* (Newark, DE: International Reading Association, 1976).

There is much material available about learning and reading disabilities. However, much of it contains the unfounded assumptions discussed in this chapter. The text below is a good general reference that surveys the field and gives the reader a background in the various diagnostic procedures and teaching strategies.

Lerner, Janet W., *Children with Learning Disabilites: Theories, Diagnosis, and Teaching Strategies,* 3rd ed. (Boston: Houghton Mifflin, 1981).

The following is a critical examination of some programs used for children with learning disabilities and contains a good template for evaluating other programs:

Kaufman, Maurice, *Perceptual and Language Readiness Programs: Critical Reviews* (Newark, DE: International Reading Association, 1973).

Additional information about the Instrumental Enrichment progrm can be obtained from the texts below. Both contain information about the program's philosophical and theoretical assumptions. The first treats the principles of assessment, and the second explains the instructional program and materials.

Feuerstein, Reuven, *The Dynamic Assessment of Retarded Performers* (Baltimore: University Park Press, 1979).

Feuerstein, Reuven, *Instrumental Enrichment: An Intervention Program for Cognitive Modifiability* (Baltimore: University Park Press, 1980).

For information about the relationship between learning problems and the functioning of the mind, many of the chapters in the following are excellent sources:

Chall, Jeanne S., and Allan F. Mirsky, eds., *Education and the Brain: The Seventy-Seventh Yearbook of the National Society for the Study of Education* (Chicago: University of Chicago Press, 1978).

A source of other books about learning disabilities is the following annotated bibliography:

Lee, Grace E., and Allen Berger, comp., *Learning Disabilities with Emphasis on Reading* (Newark, DE: International Reading Association, 1978).

The following contain articles with direct instructional applications for finding books for readers with problems learning:

Ciani, Alfred J., ed., *Motivating Reluctant Readers* (Newark, DE: International Reading Association, 1981).

Suggestions for instructional programs for the gifted and talented are discussed in the following:

Labuda, Michael, ed., *Creative Reading for Gifted Learners* (Newark, DE: International Reading Association, 1974).

Witty, Paul A., ed., *Reading for the Gifted and The Creative Student* (Newark, DE: International Reading Association, 1971).

References

Aiken, Lewis R., Jr. 1972. "Language Factors in Learning Mathematics." *Review of Educational Research,* 42, 359-385.

Albert, Burton, Jr. 1971. "Purple Marbles and Little Red Hula Hoops." *The Reading Teacher 24:* 647-651.

Alexander, Anne. 1960. *Noise in the Night.* Chicago: Rand McNally.

Allen, Roach Van, and Claryce Allen, 1970. *Language Experiences in Reading.*

Ames, Louise B. 1968. "Learning Disability: The Developmental Point of View." *Progress in Learning Disabilities* Ed. Helmer R. Myklebust. New York: Grune & Stratton.

Anastasiow, Nicholas. 1979. *Oral Language: Expression of Thought.* Newark, DE: International Reading Association and ERIC Clearinghouse on Reading and Communication Skills.

Andre, Thomas. 1979. "Does Answering Higher-Level Questions While Reading Facilitate Productive Learning." *Review of Educational Research* 49: 280-318.

Armentrout, William A., ed. 1970. *What Should the Purpose(s) of American Education Be? A Collection of Notable Responses on the Subject.* Dubuque, IA: Kendall/Hunt.

Arth, Alfred A., and Judith D. Whittemore, 1973. "Selecting Literature for Children That Relates to Life the Way It Is." *Elementary English* 50: 726-728, 744.

Aulls, Mark W. 1970. "Context in Reading: How It May Be Depicted." *Journal of Reading Behavior* 3: 61-73.

Balow, Irving H., Roger Farr, Thomas Hogan, and George Prescott. 1979. *Manual for Administering and Interpreting the Metropolitan Achievement Test: Reading, Intermediate Level.* New York: Psychological Corporation.

Baratz, Joan C. 1968. "Linguistic and Cultural Factors in Teaching Reading to Ghetto Children." *Elementary English* 45: 199-203.

Barnitz, John G. 1980. "Black English and Other Dialects: Sociolinguistic Implications." *The Reading Teacher* 33: 779-786.

Barret, John. 1968. "Relevancy of Content to Today's Students." In *Evaluating Books for Children and Young People.* Ed. Helen Huus. Newark, DE: International Reading Association.

Beattie, Sara S., and Dolores Greco, 1980. *Ourselves and Others, Windows on Our World,* Houghton Mifflin Social Studies. Boston: Houghton Mifflin.

Beck, Isabel L., and Margaret G. McKeown, "Developing Questions That Promote Comprehension: The Story Map." *Language Arts* 58: 913-918.

Bell, Wendell. 1974 "Social Science: The Future as a Missing Variable" In *Learning for Tomorrow: The Role of Future in Education.* Ed. Alvin Toffler. New York: Random House

Bercari, Joan. 1975. Personal correspondence.

Bereiter, Carl. 1980. "Development in Writing." In *Cognitive Processes in Writing.* Ed. Lee W. Gregg and Erwin R. Steinberg. Hillsdale, NJ: Erlbaum.

Bereiter, C., and S. Englemann, 1966. *Teaching Disadvantaged Children in the Preschool.* Englewood Cliffs, NJ: Prentice-Hall.

Berger, Carl F., et al. 1979. *Houghton Mifflin Science, Level 3.* Boston: Houghton Mifflin.

Berger, Carl F. et al. 1979. *Houghton Mifflin Science, Level 6.* Boston: Houghton Mifflin.

Berry, Mildred F. 1980, *Teaching Linguistically Handicapped Children.* Englewood Cliffs, NJ: Prentice-Hall.

Black, Janet K. 1980. "Those 'Mistakes' Tell Us a Lot." *Language Arts* 57: 508-513.

Blanton, William E. 1972. *Preschool Reading Instruction: A Literature Search, Evaluation and Interpretation. Final Report.* Washington, DC: National Center for Educational Communication/DHEW.

Blitz, Barbara. 1973. *The Open Classroom: Making It Work.* Boston: Allyn & Bacon.

Bloom, Benjamin S. 1969. "Some Theoretical Issues Relating to Educational Evaluation." In *Educational Evaluation: New Roles, New Means.* Ed. Ralph W. Tyler. Chicago: University of Chicago Press.

Bormuth, John R. 1968. "The Cloze Readability Procedure." In *Readability in 1968.* Ed. John R. Bormuth. Urbana, IL: National Conference on Research in English.

Bormuth, John R. 1969a. "An Operational Definition of Comprehension Instruction." In *Psycholinguistics and the Teaching of Reading.* Ed. Kenneth S. Goodman and John T. Fleming. Newark, DE: International Reading Association.

Bormuth, John R. 1969b. "Research on Literal Comprehension." Paper read at the Symposium on Application of Psycholinguistics to Key Problems in Reading. International Reading Association, Kansas City.

Bormuth, John R. 1975. "The Cloze Procedure." In *Help for the Reading Teacher: New Directions in Research.* Ed. William D. Page. Urbana, IL: National Conference on Research in English and ERIC Clearinghouse on Reading and Communication Skills.

Branson, Margaret Stimmann. 1980. *Around Our World, Windows on Our World.* Houghton Mifflin Social Studies. Boston: Houghton Mifflin.

Brewer, A.C., Nell Garland and **Jerome J. Notkin** 1972. *Elementary Science: Learning by Investigating.* Chicago: Rand McNally.

Britton, James et al. 1975. *The Development of Writing Abilities.* Urbana, IL: National Councils of Teachers of English.

Brown, Ann L., 1981. "Learning to Learn: On Training Students to Learn from Texts." *Educational Researcher* 10: 14-21.

Brown, Roger, and **Ursula Bellugi.** 1966. "Three Processes in the Child's Acquisition of Syntax." In *Language and Learning.* Ed. Janet A. Emig, James T. Gleming, and Helen M. Popp. New York: Harcourt Brace Jovanovich.

Brown, Virginia and **Morton Botel.** 1972. *Dyslexia: Definition or Treatment?* ERIC/CRIER Reading Review Series.

Bruininks, Robert H., Gertrude M. Glaman, and **Charlotte R. Clark.** 1971. *Prevalence of Learning Disabilities: Findings, Issues, and Recommendations.* Project No. 332185, Grant No. OE-09-332189-4533(032). Washington, DC: DHEW/OE Bureau of Education for the Handicapped.

Bruland, Richard A. 1974. "'Learnin' Words: Evaluating Vocabulary Development Efforts." *Journal of Reading* 18: 212-214.

Bruner, Jerome S. 1966. *Toward a Theory of Instruction.* New York: W. W. Norton.

Bruner, Jerome S., Jacqueline J. Goodnow, and **George A. Austin.** 1956. *A Study of Thinking.* New York: John Wiley.

Burke, Carolyn L. 1973. "Preparing Elementary Teachers to Teach Reading." In *Miscue Analysis: Applications to Reading Instruction.* Ed. Kenneth S. Goodman. Urbana, IL: National Council of Teachers of English and ERIC Clearinghouse on Reading and Communication Skills.

Burke, Carolyn L. 1975. "Oral Reading Analysis: A View of the Reading Process." In *Help for the Reading Teacher: New Directions in Research.* Ed. William D. Page. Urbana, IL: National Conference on Research in English and ERIC Clearinghouse on Reading and Communication Skills.

Burns, Paul C., and **Betty L. Broman** 1983. *The Language Arts in Childhood Education.* 5th ed. Boston: Houghton Mifflin.

Burns, Paul C., and **Leo M. Schell.** 1975. "Instructional Strategies for Teaching Usage of Context Clues." *Reading World* 15: 89-96.

Burrows, Alvina T., Dianne L. Monson, and **Russell G. Stauffer.** 1972. *New Horizons in the Language Arts.* New York: Harper & Row, Pub.

Byers, Paul, and **Happie Byers** 1972. "Nonverbal Communication and the Education of Children." In *Functions of Language in the Classroom.* Ed. Courtney B. Cazden, Vera P. John, and Dell Hymes. New York: Teachers College Press, Columbia University.

Cambourne, Brian. 1981. "Oral and Written Relationships: A Reading Prespective." In *Exploring Speaking-Writing Relationships: Connections and Contrasts.* Ed. Barry M. Kroll and Roberta J. Vann. Urbana, IL: National Council of Teachers of English.

Carroll, John B. 1966. "Words, Meanings, and Concepts." In *Language and Learning.* Ed. Janet A. Emig, James T. Fleming, and Helen M. Popp. New York: Harcourt Brace Javonovich.

Cassidy, Jack, and **Carol Vukelich** 1980. "Do the Gifted Read Early? *The Reading Teacher* 33: 578-581.

Ching, Doris C. 1976. *Reading and the Bilingual Child.* Newark, DE: International Reading Association.

Chomsky, Carol. 1971. "Write First, Read Later." *Childhood Education* 47: 296-299.

Chomsky, Carol. 1973. "Reading, Writing, and Phonology." In *Psycholinguistics and Reading.* Ed. Frank Smith. New York: Holt, Rinehart & Winston.

Chomsky, Carol. 1979. "Language and Reading." In *Applied Linguistics and Reading.* Ed. Robert E. Shafer. Newark, DE: International Reading Association.

Chomsky, Noam. 1965. *Aspects of the Theory of Syntax.* Cambridge, MA: MIT Press.

Christapherson, Steven, L. 1974. "The Effect of Knowledge of Discourse Structures on Reading Recall." Paper read at the Annual Meeting of the American Educational Research Association, Chicago. ERIC No. ED 090 531.

Church, Marilyn. 1974. "Does Visual Perception Training Help Beginning Readers?" *The Reading Teacher* 27: 371-374.

Clay, Marie M. 1975. *What Did I Write?* Exeter, NH: Heinemann Educational Books.

Clay, Marie M. 1982. "Learning and Teaching Writing: A Developmental Perspective." *Language Arts* 59: 65-70.

Cleland, Craig J. 1981. "Highlighting Issues in Children's Literature Through Semantic Webbing." *The Reading Teacher* 34: 642-646.

Cohen, Alice Sheff, and **Elaine Schwartz,** 1975. "Interpreting Errors in Word Recognition." *The Reading Teacher* 28: 534-537.

Cohen, Elizabeth G. 1972. "Sociology and the Classroom: Setting the Conditions for Teacher-Student Interaction." *Review of Educational Research* 42: 441-452.

Cohn, Margot. 1981. "Observations of Learning to Read and Write Naturally." *Language Arts* 58: 549-555.

Combs, Arthur W. 1958. "Seeing Is Behaving." *Educational Leadership* 16: 21-26.

Combs, Arthur. 1973. "Educational Accountability from a Humanistic Perspective." *Educational Researcher* 2: 19-21.

Combs, Arthur W. and **Donald Snygg.** 1959. *Individual Behavior:* A Perceptual Approach to Behavior. New York: Harper & Row.

Congreve, Willard J., and **George J. Rinehart.** eds. 1972. *Flexibility in School Programs.* Worthington, OH: Charles A. Jones.

Corman, Cheryl. 1975. "Bibliotherapy—Insight for the Learning Handicapped." *Language Arts* 52: 935-937.

Cramer, Ronald L. 1970. "Setting Purposes and Making Predictions: Essential to Critical Reading." *Journal of Reading* 13: 259-262, 300.

Cramer, Ronald L. 1971. "Dialectology—A Case for Language Experience." *The Reading Teacher* 25: 33-29.

Crist, Barbara I. 1975. "One Capsule a Week—A Painless Remedy for Vocabulary Ills." *Journal of Reading* 19: 147-149.

Cullinan, Bernice E. 1971. *Literature for Children: Its Discipline and Content.* Dubuque, IA: William C. Brown.

Cullinan, Bernice E. 1974. "Teaching Literature to Children, 1966-1972." In *Teacher Effectiveness in Elementary Language Arts: A Progress Report.* Ed. H. Alan Robinson and Alvina Truet Burrows. Urbana, IL: National Council on Research in English/ERIC-RCS.

Darkatsh, Manuel. 1974. "Who Should Decide on a Book's Merit?" *Elementary English* 51: 352-354.

Davis, O.L., et al. 1971a. *Exploring the Social Sciences: Asking About the U.S.A. and Its Neighbors.* New York: American Book.

Davis, O.L. et al. 1971b. *Exploring the Social Sciences: Investigating Communities and Cultures.* New York: American Book.

Deighton, Lee C. 1959. *Vocabulary Development in the Classroom.* New York: Bureau of Publications, Teachers College, Columbia University.

Diehl. William. 1978. "A Critical Summary of Rumelhart's Interactive Model of Reading." In *Secondary Reading: Theory and Application.* Ed. William Diehl. *Language and Reading Studies* Monograph No. 1, The 1978 Lily Conference on Secondary Reading.

Dillingofski, Mary Sue. 1979. "Sociolinguistics and Reading: A Review of the Literature." *The Reading Teacher* 33: 307-312.

Donlan, Dan. 1975. "Teaching Words Through Sense Impression." *Language Arts* 52: 1090-1093.

Downing, John. 1975. "What Is Decoding?" *The Reading Teacher* 29: 142-144.

Downing, John, and **Peter Oliver.** 1973. "The Child's Conception of 'A Word'" *Reading Research Quarterly* 9: 568-582.

Downing, John, and **John Sceats.** 1974. "Should School Dictionaries Be Banned?" *Elementary English* 51: 601-603.

Duchastel, Philippe C., and **Paul F. Merrill** 1973. "The Effects of Behavioral Objectives on Learning: A Review of Empirical Studies." *Review of Educational Research* 43: 53-69.

Durkin, Dolores. 1968. "When Should Children Begin to Read?" In *Innovation and Change in Reading Instruction*. Ed. Helen M. Robinson. Chicago: University of Chicago Press

Durkin, Dolores. 1974. "Phonics: Instruction That Needs to Be Improved." *The Reading Teacher* 28: 152-156.

Durkin, Dolores. 1981. "Reading Comprehension Instruction in Five Basal Reader Series." *Reading Research Quarterly* 14: 515-544.

Durr, William K., et al. 1983. *Moonbeams*. Houghton Mifflin Reading Program. Boston: Houghton Mifflin.

Eberwein, Lowell. 1982. "Do Dialect Speakers' Miscues Influence Comprehension?" *Reading World* 21: 255-263.

Edwards, Thomas J. 1969. "Learning Problems in Cultural Deprivation." In *Elementary Reading Instruction—Selected Materials*. Ed. Althea Beery, Thomas C. Barrett, and William R. Powell. Boston: Allyn & Bacon.

Ehri, Linnea C., Roderick W. Barron, and **Jeffrey M. Feldman.** 1978. *The Recognition of Words*. Newark, DE: International Reading Association.

Eisenhardt, Catheryn T. "The Structure of Meaning." Paper read at the Annual Meeting of the International Reading Association, New Orleans. ERIC No. ED 095 484.

Ekwall, Eldon E. 1976. *Diagnosis and Remediation of the Disabled Reader*. Boston: Allyn & Bacon.

Elkind, David. 1972. "Ethnicity and Reading: Three Avoidable Dangers." In *Reading Children's Books, and Our Pluralistic Society*. Ed. Harold Tanyzer and Jean Karl. Newark, DE: International Reading Association.

Elkind, David. 1974. *Children and Adolescents: Interpretive Essays on Jean Piaget*. 2nd ed. New York: Oxford University Press.

Elkind, David. 1976. "Cognitive Development in Reading." In *Theoretical Models and Processes of Reading*. Ed. Harry Singer and Robert B. Ruddell. 2nd ed. Newark, DE: International Reading Association.

Emery, Anne. 1965. *A Spy in Old West Point*. Chicago: Rand McNally.

Englemann, Siegreid. 1969. *Preventing Failure in the Primary Grades*. New York: Simon & Schuster.

Erikson, Frederick D. 1968. " 'F' get You Honkey!" A New Look At Black Dialect and the School." *Elementary English* 45: 495-499, 517.

Esposito, Dominick. 1973. "Homogeneous and Heterogeneous Ability Grouping: Principal Findings and Implications for Evaluating and Diagnosing More Effective Educational Environments." *Review of Educational Research* 43: 163-179.

Fay, Leo, and **Paul S. Anderson.** 1981. *The Rand McNally Reading Program. Level 11, Twirling Parallels,* Teacher's Edition. Chicago: Riverside.

Fay, Leo, Ramon Royal Ross and **Margaret LaPray.** 1981. The Rand McNally *Reading Program, Level 6, Red Rock Ranch,* Teacher's Edition. Chicago: Riverside.

Feininger, Andreas. 1966. *Successful Color Photography*. Englewood Cliffs, NJ: Prentice-Hall.

Fenwick, Sara Innis. 1968. "Selecting and Evaluating Materials for Recreational Reading." In *Ivory, Apes, and Peacocks: The Literature Point of View*. Ed. Sam Leaton Sebasta. Newark, DE: International Reading Association.

Feuerstein, Reuven. 1979. *The Dynamic Assessment of Retarded Performers*. Baltimore: University Park Press.

Fillmore, Charles. 1968. "The Case for Case." In *Universals in Linguistic Theory*. Ed. E. Buch and R. Harms. New York: Holt, Rinehart & Winston.

Fiske, Edward B. 1981. "Reading Analysis Is Called Lacking." *New York Times* (November 12).

Foerster, Leona. 1974a. "Idiomagic!" *Elementary English* 51: 125-127.

Foerster, Leona M. 1974b. "Language Experiences for Dialectally Different Black Learners." *Elementary English* 51: 193-197.

Foerster, Leona M. 1975a. "Kindergarten—What Can It Be?" *Elementary English* 52: 81-83.

Foerster, Leona M. 1975b. "Teach Children to Read Body Language." *Elementary English* 52: 440-442.

Frase, Lawrence T. 1977. "Purpose in Reading." In *Cognition, Curriculum, and Comprehension*. Ed. John T. Guthrie. Newark, DE: International Reading Association.

Frezise, Robert L. 1978. "What About a Reading Program for the Gifted?" *The Reading Teacher* 31: 742-747.

Frostig, Marrianne. 1974. *Developmental Test of Visual Perception*. Chicago: Follett.

Furth, Hans G. 1970. *Paiget for Teachers*. Englewood Cliffs, NJ: Prentice-Hall.

Furth, Hans. G. 1975. *Paiget and Knowledge: Theoretical Foundations*. 2nd ed. Englewood Cliffs, NJ: Prentice-Hall.

Gagne, Robert M. and Richard T. White. 1978. "Structure and Learning Outcomes." *Review of Educational Research* 48: 187-222.

Gelb, Larry. 1975. "Developing an Experiential Reading Program." Unpublished manuscript, Queens College of the City University of New York.

Gephart, William J., 1970. Application of the Convergence Technique to Basic Studies of the Reading Process. Final Report, Project No. 8-0737, Grant No. OEG-0-8-080737-4335. Washington, DC: U.S. Office of Education/DHEW.

Gere, Anne R., and Eugene Smith. 1979. *Attitudes, Language and Change*. Urbana, IL: National Council of Teachers of English.

Geyer, John J. 1972. "Comprehensive and Partial Models Related to the Reading Process." *Reading Research Quarterly* 7: 541-587.

Glass, Gerald. 1965. "The Teaching of Word Analysis Through Perceptual Conditioning." In *Reading and Inquiry*. Ed. John Figurel. Newark, DE: International Reading Association.

Glass, Gerald G., and Elizabeth H. Burton. 1973. "How Do They Decode? Verbalizations and Observed Behaviors of Successful Decoders." *Education* 94: 58-64.

Gombrich, E. H. 1974. "The Visual Image." In *Media and Symbols: The Forms of Expression, Communication, and Education*. Ed. David R. Olson. Chicago: University of Chicago Press.

Goodlad, John L. 1969. "The Schools vs. Education." *Saturday Review (April 19)*, pp. 59ff.

Goodman, Kenneth S. 1967. "Reading: A Psycholinguistic Guessing Game." *Journal of the Reading Specialist* 6: 126-135.

Goodman, Kenneth S. 1968. "The Psycholinguistic Nature of the Reading Process." In *The Psycholinguistic Nature of the Reading Process*. Ed. Kennth S. Goodman. Detroit: Wayne State University Press.

Goodman, Kenneth S. 1969a. "Analysis of Oral Reading Miscues: Applied Psycholinguistics." *Reading Research Quarterly* 5: 9-30.

Goodman, Kenneth S. 1969b. "A Communicative Theory of the Reading Curriculum." *Elementary English* 46: 290-298.

Goodman, Kenneth S. 1969c. "Let's Dump the Uptight Model in English." *Elementary School Journal* 70: 1-13.

Goodman, Kenneth S. 1972. "Orthography in a Theory of Reading Instruction." *Elementary English* 49: 1254-1261.

Goodman, Yetta M. 1981. "Test Review: Concepts About Print Test." *The Reading Teacher* 34: 445-448.

Goodman, Yetta M. and Carolyn L. Burke. 1972. *Reading Miscue Inventory: Manual*. New York: Macmillan.

Gorman, Alfred H. 1974. *Teachers and Learners: The Interactive Process of Education*. 2nd ed. Boston: Allyn & Bacon.

Graesser, Arthur C. 1981. *Prose Comprehension: Beyond the Word*. New York: Springer-Verlag.

Gray, William M. 1978. "A Comparison of Paigetian Theory and Criterion Referenced Measurement." *Review of Educational Research* 48: 223-249.

Grimes, Lynn. 1981. "Learned Helplessness and Attribution Theory: Redefining Children's Learning Problems." *Learning Disability Quarterly* 4: 91-100.

Guilford, John P. 1967. *The Nature of Human Intelligence*. New York: McGraw-Hill.

Guilford, John P., and Ralph Hoepfner. 1971. *The Analysis of Intelligence*. New York: McGraw-Hill.

Gumperz, John J., and Eduardo Hernandez-Chavez. 1972. "Bilingualism, Bidialectalism, and Classroom Interaction." In *Functions of Language in the Classroom*. Ed. Courtney B. Cazden, Vera P. John, and Dell Hymes. New York: Teachers College Press, Columbia University.

Guthrie, John T. 1978. "Inventing to Read." *The Reading Teacher* 31: 964–966.

Guthrie, John T. 1980. "The 1970's Comprehension Research." *The Reading Teacher* 33: 880–882.

Hacker, Charles J. 1980. "From Schema Theory to Classroom Practice." *Language Arts* 57: 866–871.

Hall, Mary Anne. 1972. "Linguistically Speaking, Why Language Experience?" *The Reading Teacher* 25: 328–331.

Hall, Mary Anne. 1981. *Teaching Reading as a Language Experience*. 3rd. ed. Columbus, OH: Chas. E. Merrill.

Halliday, Michael. 1975. *Learning How to Mean: Explorations in the Development of Language*. New York: Elsevier.

Halliday, Michael, and R. Hasan. 1976. Cohesion in English. London: Longman.

Hammill, Donald D., and others 1981. "A New Definition of Learning Disabilities." *Learning Disability Quarterly* 4: 336–342.

Harber, Jean R. 1981. "Learning Disability Research: How Far Have We Progressed?" *Learning Disability Quarterly* 4: 372–381.

Harker, W. John. 1973a. "Classroom Implications from Models of Comprehension." Paper read at the Annual Meeting of the International Reading Association, Denver. ERIC No. ED 089 226.

Harker, W. John. 1973b. "Teaching comprehension: A Task Analysis Approach." *Journal of Reading* 16: 379–382.

Harris, Albert J. 1980. "An Overview of Reading Disabilities and Learning Disabilities in the U.S." *The Reading Teacher* 33: 420–425.

Harste, Jerome. 1978. "Instructional Implications of Rumelhart's Model." In *Secondary Reading: Theory and Application*. Ed. William Diehl, Monograph No. 1. *Language and Reading Studies*. The 1978 Lily Conference on Secondary Reading.

Hartman, Nancy C., and Robert K. Hartman 1973. "Perceptual Handicap or Reading Disability?" *The Reading Teacher* 26: 684–695.

Havighurst, Robert J. 1964. "Characteristics and Needs of Students That Affect Learning." In *Meeting Individual Differences in Reading* Ed. H. Alan Robinson. Chicago: University of Chicago Press.

Heckinger, Fred M. 1980. "Improvement in Reading Linked to Broad Support for the Basics." *New York Times* (September 16).

Henderson, Edmund H. 1974. "Correct Spelling—An Inquiry." *The Reading Teacher* 28: 176–179.

Henderson, Edmund H., and James W. Beers. eds. 1980. *Developmental and Cognitive Aspects of Learning to Spell: A Reflection of Word Knowledge*. Newark, DE: International Reading Association.

Henry, George H. 1974. *Teaching Reading as Concept Development: Emphasis on Affective Thinking*. Newark, DE: International Reading Association.

Henry, Marguerite. 1947. *Misty of Chincoteague*. Chicago: Rand McNally.

Herber, Harold L., and Joan B. Nelson. 1975. "Questioning Is Not the Answer." *Journal of Reading* 18: 512–517.

Higgins, James E. 1970. *Beyond Words: Mystical Fancy in Children's Literature*. New York: Teachers College Press, Columbia University.

Hittleman, Daniel R. 1973. "Seeking a Psycholinguistic Definition of Readability." *The Reading Teacher* 26: 783–789.

Hittleman, Daniel R. 1978. "Readability, Readability Formulas, and Cloze: Selecting Instructional Materials." *Journal of Reading* 22: 117–122.

Hittleman, Daniel R. 1980. "Adaptive Assessment for Nonacademic Secondary Reading." In *Disabled Readers: Insights, Assessment, Instruction*. Ed. Diane J. Sawyer. Newark, DE: International Reading Association.

Hittleman, Daniel R., and H. Alan Robinson. 1975. "Readability of High School Text Passages Before and After Revision." *Journal of Reading Behavior* 7: 265–282.

Holt, Suzanne L., and **JoAnne L. Vacca.** 1981. "Reading with a Sense of Writer, Writing with a Sense of Reader." *Language Arts* 58: 937-941.

Horowitz, Robert A. 1979. "Psychological Effects of the 'Open Classroom'." *Review of Educational Research* 49: 71-86.

Horton, Raymond Joseph. 1972. "The Construct Validity of Cloze Procedure: An Exploratory Factor Analysis of Cloze, Paragraph Reading, and Structure-of-Intellect Tests. Ph.D. Dissertation, Hofstra University.

Huck, Charlotte. 1968. "Reading Literature Critically." In *Ivory, Apes, and Peacocks: Literature The Point of View.* Ed. Sam Leaton Sebasta. Newark, DE: International Reading Association.

Huck, Charlotte S., and **Doris Y. Kuhn.** 1968. *Children's Literature in the Elementary School.* 2nd ed. New York: Holt, Rinehart & Winston.

Hutchins, Ross. 1973. *Tonka, the Cave Boy.* Chicago: Rand McNally.

Huus, Helen. 1975. "Approaches to the Use of Literature in the Reading Program." In *Teachers, Tangibles, Techniques: Comprehension of Content in Reading.* Ed. Bonnie Smith Schulwitz. Newark, DE: International Reading Association.

Jacobs, Leland B. 1971. "Humanism in Teaching Reading." *Phi Delta Kappan* (April), pp. 464-467.

Jenkins, Esther C. 1973. "Multi-Ethnic Literature: Promise and Problems." *Elementary English* 50: 693-699.

Johns, Jerry. 1980. "First Graders' Concepts About Print." *Reading Research Quarterly* 15: 529-549.

Johnson, Joyce Elaine. 1979. "Back to Basics? We've Been There 150 Years." *The Reading Teacher* 32: 644-666.

Johnson, Ronald E. 1975. "Meaning in Complex Learning." *Review of Educational Research* 45: 425-459.

Jones, John Paul. 1972. *Intersensory Transfer, Perceptual Snifting, Modal Preference and Reading.* Newark, DE: International Reading Association.

Jones, Margaret B., and **Edna C. Pikulski.** 1974. "Cloze for the Classroom." *Journal of Reading* 17: 423-438.

Jongsma, Eugene A. 1980. *Cloze Instruction Research: A Second Look* Newark, DE: International Reading Association.

Karlsen, Bjorn, Richard Madden, and **Eric F. Gardner.** 1976. *Manual for Administering and Interpreting the Stanford Diagnostic Reading Test, Green Level.* New York: Psychological Corporation.

Kavale, Kenneth, and **Chad Nye.** 1981. "Identification Criteria for Learning Disabilities: A Survey of the Research Literature." *Learning Disability Quarterly* 4: 383-388.

Kean, John M., and **Carl Personke.** 1976. *The Language Arts: Teaching and Learning in the Elementary School.* New York: St. Martin's Press.

King, Frederick, et al. 1971. *The Social Studies and Our Country: Concepts in Social Science.* River Forest, IL: Laidlaw Brothers.

Kingston, Albert J. 1969. "So the Advantages of the Ungraded Schools Outweigh the Disadvantages?" In *Current Issues in Reading.* Ed. Nila B. Smith. Newark, DE: International Reading Association.

Kintsch, Walter. 1979. "On Modeling Comprehension." *Educational Psychologist* 14: 3-14.

Kintsch, Walter. 1980. 1980. "Learning from Text, Levels of Comprehension, or: Why Anyone Would Read a Story Anyway." *Poetics* 9: 87-98.

Kintsch, Walter, and **Teun A. van Dijk.** 1978. "Toward a Model of Text Comprehension and Production." *Psychological Review* 85: 363-394.

Kirk, Samuel A., J. J. McCarthy, and **Winifred D. Kirk.** 1968. *The Illinois Test of Psycholinguistic Abilities.* Revised ed. Urbana: University of Illinois Press.

Koss, Helen G. 1972. "Relevancy and Children's Literature." *Elementary English* 49: 991-992.

Kumar, V. D. 1971. "The Structure of Human Memory and Some Educational Implications." *Review of Educational Research* 41: 379-418.

Labov, William. 1966. "Some Sources of Reading Problems for Negro Speakers of Non-standard English." Unpublished paper, Columbia University. ERIC ED 010688.

Labuda, Michael, ed 1974. *Creative Reading for Gifted Learners.* Newark, DE: International Reading Association.

Lacey, Patricia A., and Philip E. Weil. 1975. "Number—Reading—Language." *Language Arts* 52: 776-782.

Ladevich, Laurel. 1974. "Determining Literary Quality in Children's Literature." *Elementary English* 51: 983-986.

Lapp, Diane. 1972. *The Use of Behavioral Objectives in Education.* Newark, DE: International Reading Association.

Lear, Edward. 1966. *The Complete Nonsense Book.* New York: Dodd, Mead.

Lee, Doris, and Roach Van Allen. 1963. *Learning to Read Through Experience.* 2nd ed. New York: Appleton-Century-Crofts.

Lehr, Fran. 1981. "Integrating Reading and Writing Instruction." *The Reading Teacher* 43: 958-961.

Leigh, James E. 1980. "Whole Language Approaches: Premises and Possibilities." *Learning Disability Quarterly* 3: 62-69.

Lerner, Janet W. 1981. *Children and Learning Disabilities: Theories, Diagnosis, and Teaching Strategies.* 3rd. ed. Boston: Houghton Mifflin.

Linden, Michelle, and M. C. Wittrock. 1981. "The Teaching of Reading Comprehension According to the Model of Generative Learning." *Reading Research Quarterly* 14: 44-57.

Lindfors, Judith W. 1980. *Children's Language and Learning.* Englewood Cliffs, NJ: Prentice Hall.

Lindsay, Peter H., and Donald A. Norman. 1977. *Human Information Processing: An Introduction to Psychology.* 2nd ed. New York: Academic Press.

Lloyd, Helen M. 1969. "Progress in Developmental Reading for Today's Disadvantaged." In *Elementary Reading Instruction—Selected Materials.* Ed. Althea Beery, Thomas C. Barrett, and William R. Powell. Boston: Allyn & Bacon.

Lohmann, Idella. 1968. "Reactions to Using Language Experience in Beginning Reading." In *A Decade of Innovations: Approaches to Beginning Reading.* Ed. Elaine C. Vilscek. Newark, DE: International Reading Association.

Lundsteen, Sara W. 1974a. "Levels of Meaning in Reading." *The Reading Teacher* 28: 268-272.

Lundsteen, Sara W. 1974b. "Questioning to Develop Creative Problem Solving." *Elementary English* 51: 645-650.

Lundsteen, Sara W. 1976. *Children Learn to Communicate: Language Arts Through Creative Problem Solving.* Englewood Cliffs, NJ: Prentice-Hall.

McCarthy, James J., and Joan F. McCarthy. 1971. *Learning Disabilities.* Boston: Allyn & Bacon.

McDonell, Gloria. 1975. "Relating Language to Early Reading Experiences." *The Reading Teacher* 28: 438-444.

McLuhan, Marshall. 1964. *Understanding Media.* New York: Signet Books.

MacGinitie, Walter H. 1969. "Evaluating Readiness for Learning to Read: A Critical Review and Evaluation of Research." *Reading Research Quarterly* 4: 396-410.

MacGinitie, Walter H. 1973. "What Are We Testing?" In *Assessment Problems in Reading.* Ed. Walter H. MacGinitie. Newark, DE: International Reading Association.

Mackey, William F. 1973. "Language and Acculturation." In *Essays on Teaching English as a Second Language and as a Second Dialect.* Ed. Robert P. Fox. Urbana, IL: National Council of Teachers of English.

Madden, Richard, Eric F. Gardner, Herbert C. Rudman, Bjorn Karlsen, and Jack C. Merwin. 1973. *Manual for Administering the Stanford Achievement Test: Reading, Intermediate Level I.* New York: Psychological Corporation.

Maeroff, Gene I. 1981. "Reading Results Give the Schools a Lift." *New York Times* (September 6).

Maffei, Anthony C. 1973. "Reading Analysis in Mathematics." *Journal of Reading* 16: 546-549.

Malmstrom, Jean. 1977. *Understanding Language: A Primer for the Language Arts Teacher.* New York: St. Martin's Press.

Manzo, Anthony V., and J. K. Sherl. 1971. "Some Generalizations and Strategies for Guilding Vocabulary Learning." *Journal of Reading Behavior* 4: 78-89.

Marksheffel, Ned D. 1969. "Reading in the Content Areas: A Framework for Improvement." In *Fusing Reading Skills and Content.* Ed. H. Alan Robinson and Ellen Lamar Thomas. Newark, DE: International Reading Association.

Marquardt, William F. 1965. "Linguistics and Reading Instruction: Contributions and Implications." In *Developments in Reading.* Ed. H. Alan Robinson. Chicago: University of Chicago Press.

Marshall, Hermine H. 1981. "Open Classrooms: Has the Term Outlived Its Usefulness?" *Review of Educational Research* 51: 181-192.

Maya, Antonia Y. 1979. "Write to Read: Improving Reading Through Creative Writing." *The Reading Teacher* 32: 813—817.

Mayer, Jeri E. 1975. "Evaluating Reading Readiness: A Reply" *Elementary English* 52: 343-345.

Melear, John D. 1974. "An Informal Language Inventory." *Elementary English* 51: 508-511.

Menzel, Peter. 1970. "On the Linguistic Bases of the Theory of Writing Items." Appendix to John R. Bormuth, *On the Theory of Achievement Test Items.* Chicago: University of Chicago Press.

Merla, Patrick. 1972. " 'What is *Real*?' Asked the Rabbit One Day." *Saturday Review* (November 4), pp. 43-50.

Michaelis, John O. 1972. *Social Studies for Children in a Democracy: Recent Trends and Developments.* 5th ed. Englewood Cliffs, NJ: Prentice Hall.

Mickish, Virginia. 1974. "Children's Perceptions of Written Word Boundaries." *Journal of Reading Behavior* 6: 19-21.

Miller, George, ed. 1973. *Communication, Language, and Meaning: Psychological Perspectives.* New York: Basic Books.

Miller, John W. 1974. "Linguistics and Comprehension." *Elementary English* 51: 853-854, 857.

Mishler, Elliot G. 1972. "Implications of Teacher Strategies for Language and Cognition: Observations in First Grade Classrooms." In *Functions of Language in the Classroom.* Ed. Courtney B. Cazden, Vera P. Johns, and Dell Hymes. New York: Teachers College Press, Columbia University.

Moffett, James. 1968. *Teaching the Universe of Discourse.* Boston: Houghton Mifflin.

Moffett, James, and Betty Jane Wagner. 1976. *Student Centered Language Arts and Reading K-13: A Handbook for Teachers.* 2nd ed. Boston: Houghton Mifflin.

Monteith, Mary K. 1980. "Black English, Teacher Attitudes, and Reading." *Language Arts* 57: 908-912.

Monteleone, Thomas F. 1974. "The Thing from Ennis Rock." In *More Science Fiction Tales.* Ed. Roger Elwood. Chicago: Rand McNally.

Morine, Greta, and Harold Morine. 1973. "Teaching." In *The Elementary School in the U.S.* 72nd Yearbook of the National Society for the Study of Education. Ed. John L. Goodlad and Harold G. Shane. Chicago: University of Chicago Press.

Neuman, Susan B. 1980. "Television: Its Effect on Reading and School Achievement." *The Reading Teacher* 33: 801-805.

Newcomer, Phyllis L., and Donald D. Hammill. 1975. "ITPA and Academic Achievement: A Survey." *The Reading Teacher* 28: 731-742.

NJCLD. 1981. "U.S. National Joint Committee on Learning Disabilities Urges Revised Definition of LD." *The Reading Teacher* 35: 134-135.

Northcut, Norvell et al. 1975. Adult Functional Competence. Austin: Adult Performance Level Project, Industrial and Business Training Bureau, University of Texas.

Nuthall, Graham and Ivan Snook, 1973. "Contemporary Models of Teaching." In *Second Handbook of Research on Teaching* Ed. Robert M. W. Travers. Chicago: Rand McNally.

Oliver, Marvin E. 1970. "Organizing for Reading Instruction." *Elementary School Journal* 71: 97-104.

Olmo, Barbara G. 1975. "Teaching Students to Ask Questions." *Language Arts* 52: 116-119.

Olsen, Judy L., and David J. Mealor. 1981. "Learning Disabilities Identification: Do Researchers Have the Answer?" *Learning Disability Quarterly* 4: 389-392.

Olson, David R. 1981. "Writing: The Divorce of the Author from the Text." In *Exploring Speaking-Writing Relationships: Connections and Contrasts.* Ed. Barry M. Kroll and Roberta J. Vann. Urbana, IL: National Council of Teachers of English.

Otto, Wayne, Robert Chester, John McNeil, and Shirley Myers. 1974. *Focused Reading Instruction.* Reading, MA: Addison-Wesley.

Padak, Mancy D. 1981. "The Language and Educational Needs of Children Who Speak Black English." *The Reading Teacher* 35: 144-151.

Page, William D. 1976. "Pseudocues, Supercues, and Comprehension." *Reading World* 4: 232-238.

Painter, Helen. 1975. "Literature Develops Reading Skills." In *Teachers, Tangibles, Techniques: Comprehension of Content in Reading.* Ed. Bonnie Smith Schulwitz. Newark, DE: International Reading Association.

Pauk, Walter. 1973. "Two Essential Study Skills for the Community College Student." *Reading World* 12: 239-245.

Pavlak, Stephen A. 1974. "Significant Research on Comprehension (1948-72)." Paper read at the Annual Meeting of the International Reading Association, New Orleans. ERIC No. ED 095 506.

Pearson, P. David, and Johnson, Dale D. 1978. *Teaching Reading Comprehension.* New York: Holt, Rinehart & Winston.

Pehrsson, Robert. 1975. "The OP-IN Procedure." Paper read at the Preconvention Institute, "Psycholinguistics and Reading Instruction," New York State Reading Association Annual Conference, Kiamisha Lake.

Peltz, Fillmore K. 1975. "Handling Questions About Reading Materials." Paper read at the Preconvention Institute, "Psycholinguistics and Reading Instruction," New York State Reading Association Annual Conference, Kiamisha Lake.

Pezdek, Kathy. 1980. "Arguments for a Constructive Approach to Comprehension and Memory." In *Reading and Understanding.* Ed. Joseph Danks and Kathy Pezdek. Newark, DE: International Reading Association.

Piaget, Jean, and Barbel Inhelder. 1973. *Memory and Intelligence.* New York: Basic Books. Trans. Arnold J. Pomerans.

Pikulski, John J. 1974a. "Assessment of the Pre-reading Skills: A Review of Frequently Employed Measures." *Reading World* 13. 171-197.

Pikulski, John J. 1974b. "Criterion Referenced Measures for Clinical Evaluation." *Reading World* 14: 116-128.

Postman, Neil. 1973. "The Politics of Reading." In *The Politics of Reading: Point-Counterpoint.* Ed. Rosemary Winkeljohan. Newark, DE: International Reading Association/ERIC-RCS.

Powers, Anne. 1981. "Sharing a Language Experience Library with the Whole School." *The Reading Teacher* 34: 892-895.

Pyrczak, Fred. 1972. "Objective Evaluation of the Quality of Multiple Choice Test Items Designed to Measure Comprehension of Reading Passages." *Reading Research Quarterly* 8: 62-71.

Randhawa, Bikkar S., and Lewis L. W. Fu. 1973. "Assessment and Effect of Some Classroom Environmental Variables." *Review of Education Research* 43: 303-321.

Raven, Ronald, and Richard Slazer. 1971. "Piaget and Reading Instruction." *The Reading Teacher* 24: 630-639.

Reed, James C. 1970. "The Deficits of Retarded Readers—Fact or Artifact?" *The Reading Teacher* 23: 247-252.

Reed, Linda. 1976. "Multi-Ethnic Literature and the Elementary School Curriculum." *Language Arts* 53: 256-261.

Reid, D. Kim, and **Wayne P. Hresko.** 1981. *A Cognitive Approach to Learning Disabilities.* New York: McGraw-Hill.

Robinson, H. Alan. 1969. "Reading in the Total School Curriculum." In *Reading and Realism.* Ed. J. Allen Figurel. Newark, DE: International Reading Association.

Robinson, H. Alan. 1978. "Facilitating Successful Reading Strategies." Paper presented at the Annual Conference of the International Reading Association, Houston.

Robinson, H. Alan 1983. *Teaching Reading, Writing and Study Strategies: The Content Areas.* 3rd ed. Boston: Allyn & Bacon.

Robinson, Helen M. 1975. "Children's Behavior While Reading." In *Help for the Reading Teacher: New Directions in Research.* Ed. William D. Page. Urbana, IL: National Conference on Research in English and ERIC Clearinghouse on Reading and Communication Skills.

Rude, Robert T. 1973. "Readiness Tests: Implications for Early Childhood." *The Reading Teacher* 26: 572–580.

Rumelhart, David E. 1976. "Toward an Interactive Model of Reading." Technical Report No. 56. San Diego: Center for Human Information Processing, University of California.

Rumelhart, David E. 1981. "Schemata: The Building Blocks of Cognition." In *Comprehension and Reading.* Ed. John T. Guthrie. Newark, DE: International Reading Association.

Rupley, William H., and **Carol Robeck.** 1978. "Black Dialect and Reading Achievement." *The Reading Teacher* 31: 598–601.

Ryan, Allen B., and **Melvyn L. Semmel.** 1969. "Reading as a Constructive Language Process." *Reading Research Quarterly* 5: 59–83.

Samuels, S. Jay. 1970. "Reading Disability?" *The Reading Teacher* 24: 267, 271, 283.

Sapir, Edward. 1967. "Communication." In *The Psychology of Language, Thought, and Instruction.* Ed. John P. deCecco. New York: Holt, Rinehart & Winston.

Sargent, Eileen E., Helen Huus, and **Oliver Andresen,** 1970. *How to Read a Book.* Newark, DE: International Reading Association.

Satz, Paul, and **Sara S. Sparrow.** 1970. "Specific Developmental Dyslexia: A Theoretical Formulation." In *Specific Reading Disability—Advances in Theory and Method.* Ed. Dirk J. Bakkar and Paul Satz. Rotterdam: University of Rotterdam Press.

Saville-Troike, Muriel R. 1973. "TESOL: Methods of Materials in Early Childhood Education." In *Essays on Teaching English as a Second Language and as a Second Dialect.* Ed. Robert P. Fox. Urbana, IL: National Council of Teachers of English.

Sawyer, Diane J. 1975. "Readiness Factors for Reading: A Different View." *The Reading Teacher* 28: 620–624.

Schafer, John C. 1981. "The Linguistic Analysis of Spoken and Written Texts." In *Exploring Speaking-Writing Relationships: Connections and Contrasts.* Ed. Barry M. Kroll and Roberta J. Vann. Urbana, IL: National Council of Teachers of English.

Schaff, Adam. 1973. *Language and Cognition.* New York: McGraw-Hill.

Schwartz, Judy I. 1975. "A Language Experience Approach to Beginning Reading." *Elementary English* 52: 320–324.

Schwartz, Judith I. 1982. "Dialect Interference in the Attainment of Literacy." *Journal of Reading* 25: 440–446.

Simons, Herbert D. 1971. "Reading Comprehension: The Need for a New Perspective." *Reading Research Quarterly* 6: 338–363.

Sims, Rudine. 1976. "What Else Are Kids Reading?" Paper presented at the Preconvention Institute, "What Could/Should Kids Be Reading?" at the 21st Annual Convention of the International Reading Association, Anaheim, CA, May 10.

Shepherd, David L. 1969. "Reading and Science: Problems Peculiar to the Area." In *Fusing Reading Skills and Content.* Ed. H. Alan Robinson and Ellen Lamar Thomas. Newark, DE: International Reading Association.

Shepherd, Terry, and **Lynn B. Iles.** 1976. "What Is Bibliotherapy?" *Language Arts* 53: 569–571.

Sloan, Glenna Davis. 1975. *The Child as Critic: Teaching Literature in the Elementary School.* New York: Teachers College Press, Columbia University.

Slobin, Dan. 1979. *Psycholinguistics.* 2nd ed. Glenview, IL: Scott Foresman.

Smith, Frank. 1971. "Overloading the Competent Reader." Paper read at the National Council of Teachers of English Annual Conference, Las Vegas. ERIC No. 085674.

Smith, Frank 1972. "Phonology and Orthography: Reading and Writing." *Elementary English* 49: 1075-1088.

Smith, Frank. 1975a. *Comprehension and Learning.* New York: Holt, Rinehart & Winston.

Smith, Frank. 1975b. "The Role of Prediction in Reading." *Elementary English* 52: 305-311.

Smith, Frank. 1978, *Understanding Reading: A Psycholinguistic Analysis of Reading and Learning to Read.* 2nd ed. New York: Holt, Rinehart & Winston.

Smith, Frank. 1982. *Writing and the Writer.* New York: Holt, Rinehart & Winston.

Smith, James A. 1972. *Adventures in Communication: Language Arts Methods.* Boston: Allyn & Bacon.

Smith, Nila Banton. 1960. "Literature for Space-Age Children." *Education Magazine,* pp. 1-4.

Smith, Nila Banton. 1964a. "Patterns of Writing in Different Subject Areas: Part I." *Journal of Reading* 8: 31-37.

Smith, Nial Banton. 1964b. "Patterns of Writing in Different Subject Areas: Part II." *Journal of Reading* 8: 97-102.

Stauffer, Russel. 1971. "The Quest for Maturity in Reading." In *Language, Reading, and the Communication Process.* Ed. Carol Brown. Newark, DE: International Reading Association.

Stauffer, Russel G. 1975. *Directing the Reading Thinking Process.* New York: Harper & Row, Pub.

Stauffer, Russell G., and John J. Pikulski. 1974. "A Comparison and Measure of Oral Language Growth." *Elementary English* 51: 1151-1155.

Stewart, William A. 1966. "Nonstandard Speech Patterns." *Baltimore Bulletin of Education,* pp. 52-66.

Stipek, Deborah J., and John R. Weisz. 1981. "Perceived Personal Control and Academic Achievement." *Review of Educational Research* 51: 101-138.

Strang, Ruth. 1969. *Diagnostic Teaching of Reading.* 2nd ed. New York: McGraw-Hill.

Strange, Michael. 1980. "Instructional Implications of a Conceptual Theory of Reading Comprehension." *The Reading Teacher* 33: 391-397.

Strickland, Dorothy S. 1972. "Black Is Beautiful, White Is Right." *Elementary English* 49: 200-223.

Taylor, H. Gerry, Paul Satz, and Janette Friel. 1979. "Developmental Dyslexia in Relation to Other Childhood Reading Disorders: Significance and Clinical Utility." *Reading Research Quarterly* 15: 84-101.

Terry, Ann. 1972. *Children's Poetry Preferences: A National Survey of Upper Elementary Grades.* Urbana, IL: National Council of Teachers of English.

Thomas, Adele. 1979. "Learned Helplessness and Expectancy Factors: Implications for Research in Learning Disabilities." *Review of Educational Research* 49: 208-221.

Thompson, William Irwin. 1972. *At the Edge of History: Speculations on the Transformation of Culture.* New York: Harper & Row.

Toffler, Alvin. 1974. "The Psychology of the Future." In *Learning for Tomorrow: The Role of Future in Education.* Ed. Alvin Toffler. New York: Random House.

Toothaker, Roy. 1974. "Developing an Action-Packed Vocabulary." *Elementary English* 51: 861-897.

Torrence, E. Paul, and R. E. Myers. 1972. *Creative Learning and Teaching.* New York: Dodd, Mead.

Tuinman, J. Jaap. 1973. "Determining the Passage Dependency of Comprehension Questions in Five Major Tests." *Reading Research Quarterly* 9: 206-223.

Vargas, Julie S. 1972. *Writing Worthwhile Behavioral Objectives.* New York: Harper & Row, Pub.

Vendig, Anne. 1974. "Reading' in the Kindergarten." Unpublished manuscript. Great Neck, NY: Great Neck Public Schools.

Vilscek, Elaine C. 1968. "What Research Has Shown About the Language Experience Program." In *Decade of Innovative Approaches to Beginning Reading.* Ed. Elaine C. Vilscek. Newark, DE: International Reading Association.

Vogel, Susan A., and **Harold J. McGrady.** 1975. "Recognition of Melody Patterns in Good and Poor Readers." *Elementary English* 52: 414-418.

Wagner, Steven R., and **John Wilde.** 1973. "Learning Styles: Can We Grease the Cogs in Cognition?" *Proceedings of the Claremont Reading Conference,* pp. 135-141.

Wardhaugh, Ronald. 1977. *Introduction to Linguistics.* 2nd. ed. New York: McGraw-Hill.

Waugh, R. P., and **K. W. Howell.** 1975. "Teaching Modern Syllabication." *The Reading Teacher* 29: 20-25.

Weaver, Wendell W., and **A. C. Bickley.** 1967. "Sources of Information for Responses to Reading Test Items." *Proceedings,* 75th Annual convention, American Psychological Association.

Wehmeyer, Lillian M. 1975. "It Must Be Right ... I Read It in the Encyclopedia!" *Language Arts* 52: 841-842.

Weiner, Roberta. 1974. "A Look at Reading Practices in the Open Classroom." *The Reading Teacher* 27: 438-442.

Weinstein, Carol S. 1979. "The Physical Environment of the School: A Review of the Research." *Review of Educational Research* 49: 577-610.

Wheat, Thomas. 1974. "Reading and the Culturally Diverse." *Elementary English* 51: 251-256.

Wiemann, John M., and **Philip Backlund.** 1980. "Current Theory and Research in Communicative Competence." *Review of Educational Research* 50: 185-199.

Williamson, Leon E. 1974. "Teach Concepts, Not Words." Paper read at the Annual Meeting of the Western College Reading Association, Oakland, CA: ERIC No. ED 092 925.

Wilson, Marilyn J. 1981. "A Review of Recent Research on the Integration of Reading and Writing." *The Reading Teacher* 34: 896-901.

Winkley, Carol K. 1971. "What Do Diagnostic Tests Really Diagnose?" In *Diagnostic Viewpoints in Reading.* Ed. Robert Leibert. Newark, DE: International Reading Association.

Witty, Paul A. 1971. *Reading for the Gifted and the Creative Student.* Newark, DE: International Reading Association.

Wood, Barbara S. 1981. *Children and Communication: Verbal and Nonverbal Language Development.* 2nd ed. Englewood Cliffs, NJ: Prentice-Hall.

Ysseldke, James E., and others 1982. "Declaring Students Eligible for Learning Disability Services: Why Bother with the Data?" *Learning Disability Quarterly* 5: 37-44.

Zintz, Miles V. 1975. *The Reading Process: The Teacher and the Learner.* 2nd ed. Dubuque, IA: William C. Brown.

Zuck, L. V. 1974. "Some Questions About The Teaching of Syllabication Rules." *The Reading Teacher* 27: 583-588.

Index

Academic potential, 103, 109
Accommodation, 43
Adult Performance Level Project, 301
Advance organizers, 61
Aiken, Lewis R., 293
Albert, Burton, Jr., 281, 283
Allen, Claryce, 174
Allen, Roach Van, 174, 179
American English, *see* English language
Ames, Louise B., 357
Analytical teaching, 87*f*, 107
Anaphora, *see* Referents
Anastasiow, Nicholas, 55
Anderson, Paul, 191
Andre, Thomas, 49, 50, 52
Ann Arbor decision, 345
Armentrout, William, 12
Assessment
    formative, 87
    process analysis, 359
    silent reading, 127*f*
    status, 358
    summative, 87
Assimilation, 43
Aulls, Mark, 248
Author idea map, 224
Author's craft, 320
Author's message, activities for reconstructing, 231*f*

Backlund, Philip, 55, 59
Balow, Irving H., 92
Baratz, Joan C., 343
Barnitz, John G., 344
Barrett, John, 337
Basal reading series, 183
Beattie, Sara S., 287, 289
Beck, Isabel L., 184
Beers, James W., 259
Bell, Wendell, 3
Bellugi, Ursula, 54
Bercari, Joan, 177
Bereiter, Carl, 345
Berger, Carl F., 279, 306, 308
Berry, Mildred F., 53, 282
Bibliotherapy, 335*f*, 362
Bickley, A.C., 99
Bilingual programs, 347
Bilingual Syntax Measure, 349
Black American English, 342
Blanton, William E., 140, 143
Bloom, Benjamin, 101

Boehm Test of Basic Concepts, The, 160
Bormuth, John, 130, 131, 135, 198, 207
Botel, Morton, 358, 359
Branson, Margaret S., 285, 308
Britton, James, 144
Broman, Betty L., 243, 244
Brown, Roger, 78
Brown, Virginia, 358, 359
Bruininks, Robert H., 356
Bruner, Jerome, 5, 40
Burke, Carolyn, 111, 115, 119
Burns, Paul C., 243, 244, 248
Burrows, Alvina T., 184, 185
Burton, Elizabeth H., 257
Byers, Happie, 19, 20
Byers, Paul, 19, 20

Cambourne, Brian, 84
Carroll, John B., 40
Cassidy, Jack, 361
Characterization, 225, 320
Children's Book Council, 15, 321
Ching, Doris C., 347
Chomsky, Carol, 82, 257, 259, 261
Chomsky, Noam, 23, 144
Christapherson, Steven L., 207
Church, Marilyn, 143
Classroom organizational patterns, 6, 8*f*
Clay, Marie M., 144, 161
Cleland, Craig J., 229, 230
Cloze procedure, 129, 204
Code switching, 348
Cognition, 42
Cognitive Abilities Test, 103
Cognitive styles, 357
Cohen, Elizabeth G., 10
Coherence, 37
Coherence graph, 76
Cohn, Margot, 142
Combs, Arthur, 78
Communication, 2, 17*f*
    barriers to, 19*f*, 344
    cultural situation, 17
    paralinguistic, 19
    social context of, 26
Composing, *see* Writing
Comprehension, 35, 76, 83, 183, 197, 207
    listening, 109
    prediction strategies, 200
    see also Communication
Comprehensive Tests of Basic Skills, 94
Concepts, 40, 145, 242. *See also* Schemas

Concepts About Print Test, 161
Concrete operations, 45
Congrave, Willard J., 8
Consonants, 30
Content area reading
    activities, 290*f*
    guided reading, 283
    materials, 274
    resources, 310
    writing patterns, 277*f*
Content words, 36
Context signals, 248
    activities, 257*f*
Cooperative Inter-American Tests, 349
Corman, Cheryl, 335, 336
Cramer, Ronald L., 172, 200
Crist, Barbara I., 247
Cullinan, Bernice, 155, 316, 320, 323
Culturally disadvantaged, 344

Darkatsh, Manuel, 326
Davis, Flora, 62
Davis, O. L., 277, 279, 308
Decoding, 68. *See also* Graphophonological information; Word recognition
Deep structure, 24
Degrees of Reading Power Test, 96
Deighton, Lee C., 247, 248, 249, 259
Deletion procedure, 204
Developmental stages, 46
Developmental Test of Visual Perception, 359
Dialect, 172, 341
    comprehension barriers, 344
    divergent speakers, 120
Dictionary, 37
    activities, 266
    resources, 267
Diehl, John A., 74
Dillingofski, Mary Sue, 344
Discovery learning, 6
Directed reading lesson, 185. *See also* Guided reading-thinking lesson
Donlan, Dan, 244
Downing, John, 155, 256, 261, 262
Duncan, E. R., 276
Durkin, Dolores, 140, 144, 183, 253
Durr, William K., 279
Dyslexia, 352

Eberwein, Lowell, 344
Education for All Handicapped Children Act, 354

Edwards, Thomas J., 345
Ehri, Linnea, 261
Ekwall, Eldon E., 359
Elkind, David, 46, 83, 140
Emery, Anne, 322
Encoding, 68. *See also* Spelling
Encyclopedia, 296
Englemann, S., 346
English language
    coherence, 37
    graphic features, 38
    history, 26
    phonological features, 29
    pragmatics, 37*f*
    semantic features, 35*f*
    syntactic features, 32
English as a second language
    assessment, 349
    instruction, 357
    resources, 352
Equilibration, 44
Erickson, Frederick, 345
Esposito, Dominick, 10

Fagan, William T., 161
Fay, Leo, 110, 190, 191, 202, 211, 226, 252, 319, 322
Feiniger, Andreas, 62
Fenwick, Sara Innis, 326
Feuerstein, Reuven, 359, 360
Fiction, 318
Figurative language, 321
Fillmore, Charles, 26
Fiske, Edward B., 3
Foerster, Leona, 144, 153, 246, 342
Formal operations, 46
Frase, Lawrence T., 192
Frezise, Robert L., 361
Fu, Lewis L., 11
Function words, *see* Structure words
Functional literacy, 301
Furth, Hans G., 43, 44

Gagné, Robert M., 50, 52, 53
Gardner, Eric F., 91
Gates-MacGinitie Reading Tests, 94
Gelb, Larry, 173
Generative semantics, knowledge domains, 25*f*
Gephart, William J., 4
Geyer, John J., 66
Gifted and Talented Education Act, 361
Glass, Gerald, 257, 258

Gombrich, E. H., 2
Goodlad, John, 13
Goodman, Kenneth S., 5, 68, 78, 110, 111, 269, 341
Goodman, Yetta, 115, 161
Gorman, Alfred H., 163
Grade equivalent, 90
Graesser, Arthur C., 25, 40*f*, 53, 78
Graphics
    reading problems of, 282
    recall from, 282
    types of, 280
Graphophonological information, 253*f*
Gray, William M., 44
Greco, Dolores, 287, 289
Grimes, Lynne, 358
Groups, 162*f*
    classroom organization, 9*f*
Guided reading, 172*f*
    content area, 283*f*
Guided reading-thinking lesson, 284
Guilford, John P., 46, 78
    structure-of-intellect model, 46*f*
Gumperz, John J., 348
Guthrie, John, 67, 83

Hacker, Charles J., 40
Hall, Mary Ann, 173
Halliday, Michael, 55
Hammill, Donald, 354, 359
Harber, Jean R., 354
Harker, W. John, 197, 198, 238
Harris, Albert J., 355
Harste, Jerome, 74
Hartman, Nancy C., 355
Hartman, Robert K., 355
Havighurst, Robert J., 7, 8
Heckinger, Fred M., 1
Heiman, Michele Kaye, 341
Henderson, Edmund, 259
Hennings, Dorothy G., 194
Henry, George H., 210
Henry, Marguerite, 322, 323
Herber, Harold, 292
Hernandez-Chavez, Eduard, 348
Higgins, James, 318
Hittleman, Daniel R., 78, 110, 119, 129, 131
Hoffman Bilingual Schedule, 349
Holt, Suzanne L., 199
Horowitz, Robert A., 10
Horton, Raymond J., 130

Howell, K. W., 255
Hresko, Wayne, 359
Huck, Charolette, 326, 327, 337
Human thinking, 39
Hutchins, Ross, 323
Huus, Helen, 315, 317

Iles, Lynn B., 335, 336
Illinois Test of Psycholinguistic Abilities (ITPA), 359
Illustrations, *see* Graphics
Inhelder, Barbel, 53
Inquiry lesson, 206
Instrumental enrichment, 359
Intelligence, 44, 102
International Reading Association, 14
Invented spelling, 144, 261
Iowa Tests of Basic Skills, 94

Jacobs, Leland, 4, 12
Jenkins, William A., 264, 265, 316
Johns, Jerry L., 161
Johnson, Dale, 192, 228, 230
Johnson, Ronald E., 1, 238
Jones, John Paul, 356
Jones, Margaret B., 131
Jongsma, Eugene A., 204

Karlsen, Bjorn, 91
Kavale, Kenneth, 354
Kean, John M., 30
Kernel sentences, 33*f*
Kingston, Albert J., 10
Kintsch, Walter, 75, 80
Kirk, Samuel A., 359
Knowledge domains, 25, 40
Koss, Helen, 337
Kuhn, Doris Y., 326, 327
Kumar, V. D., 49, 52, 61

Labov, William, 343
Lacey, Patrica A., 293
Ladervich, Laurel, 325
Language
    case grammar, 26
    competence, 59
    development of, 54
    domains, 26*f*
    educational implications, 59
    functions, 22
    generalizations, 21*f*
    generative semantics, 25
    paralinguistic features, 58

pragmatics, 25
semantic development, 57
signaling meaning, 21f
structure, 23f
syntactic development, 56
transformational grammar, 23
Language experience approach, 172f
 resources, 181f
LaPray, Margaret, 110, 190, 202, 226, 252
Lear, Edward, 320
Learning, 5,
 school organization for, 8
 see also Problem solving
Learning disability, 352
 assessment, 358f
 definitions, 354, 355
 developmental concept of, 357f
Learning theories, 6
Lee, Doris, 179
Lehr, Fran, 83
Leigh, James E., 359
Lerner, Janet, 353, 354
Library, 295
 card catalog, 295
 classroom, 325
Life Skills: Tests of Functional Competencies in Reading and Math, 96
Linden, Michelle, 67, 199
Lindfors, Judith W., 55, 58
Lindsay, Peter H., 49, 52
Listening-thinking lesson, 151
Literacy, readiness for, 143f
Literary forms, 318f
Literature
 activities, 333
 categories, 318
 definition, 315
 judging fiction, 326
 judging nonfiction, 327
 and media, 328
 program objectives, 317
 resources, 330
 uses of, 323
Lloyd, Helen M., 346
Locating information, 294f
Lohmann, Idella, 194
Long term memory, 52f
Lundsteen, Sara W., 141, 201, 315, 319

McCarthy, James J., 354
McCarthy, Joan F., 354
McDonell, Gloria M., 141, 142, 155

MacGinitie, Walter, 99, 100, 140, 160
McGrady, Harold J., 160
McKeown, Margaret G., 184
Mackey, William F., 348
McLuhan, Marshall, 1
Macrostructure, 75
Madden, Richard, 91, 98
Maeroff, Gene I., 1
Maffei, Anthony C., 290
Main idea, 207, 212
Malmstrom, Jean, 23, 29
Manzo, Anthony V., 242
Maps, 297f
Marksheffel, Ned D., 312
Marquardt, William F., 22
Marshall, Hermine H., 10
Maya, Antonia Y., 83
Mayer, Jeri E., 144
Mealor, David J., 354
Meaning, 68. *See also* Comprehension
Mediated learning experience, 360
Memory, 40, 49
 long term, 52, 71, 76
 retrieval, 53
 sensory register, 49
 short term, 51, 68
Metropolitan Achievement Tests, 94
Michaelis, John O., 273
Microstructure, 75
Miller, George, 61
Miller, John W., 238
Miscue analysis, 109f
 information material, 119
 narrative material, 111f
Miscues, 72
Mishler, Elliot G., 142, 151
Moffett, James, 144, 259, 261, 262
Monteith, Mary K., 344, 345
Monteleone, Thomas F., 323
Morine, Greta, 7
Morine, Harold, 7
Morphemes, 36. *See also* Word recognition
Myers, R. E., 188, 193

National Assessment of Educational Progress, 3
Nelson, Joan, 292
Neuman, Susan B., 328
Newcomer, Phyllis L., 359
Newspaper reading, 298f
Nonfiction, 319
Normal curve equivalent (NCE), 92
Norman, Donald, 49, 52

Northcut, Norrell, 301
Nuthall, Graham, 6
Nye, Chad, 354

Oliver, Marvin E., 9
Oliver, Peter, 155
Olmo, Barbara G., 206
Olsen, David R., 354
Olsen, Judy, 38
Oral reading
    assessing, 110
    retelling, 127*f*
Organizing information, 304*f*
Otis-Lennon School Ability Test, 103
Outlining, 305*f*

Padak, Nancy D., 345
Painter, Helen, 315
Paragraph
    functions, 216*f*
    patterns, 212*f*
    structures, 277*f*
Parish, Peggy, 21
Paulk, Walter, 290
Pearson, P. David, 192, 238, 230
Pedzek, Kathy, 67
Pehrsson, Robert, 204
Peltz, Fillmore, 233
Performance Assessment in Reading, 96
Personke, Carl, 30
Phonemes, 29*f*
    confusion about, 30
Phonics instruction, 254
Phonological component, 23
Piaget, Jean, 42, 53
Pikulski, John J., 101, 131, 160, 173
Plays, 320
Plot, 150, 225, 321
Poetry, 319
Postman, Neil, 1
Powers, Anne, 194
Pragmatics, 25, 37*f*
Predictable language, 346
Prediction of meaning, 284, 287
    cloze, 204
    deletions, 204
    strategies for, 200*f*
Preoperational stage, 44
PRI/Reading Systems, 94
Problem solving, 5, 39, 141, 274
Professional organizations, 14
Propaganda, 279

Psycholinguistics, 22
Pyrczak, Fred, 99

Questioning, 187*f*. *See also* Miscue analysis
Questions
    different thought processes, 187
    schema implicit, 192
    text explicit, 192
    text implicit, 192

Randhawa, Bikkar, 11
Raven, Ronald, 60, 67
Readability, 75, 129
Readiness, 77, 139*f*
    activities, 146*f*
    affective factors, 151
    assessment, 159*f*
    cognitive factors, 146*f*
    defined, 140
    group activities, 162
    linguistic factors, 155*f*
    psychomotor factors, 153
    resources, 165*f*
    tests, 160*f*
Reading
    act, 65, 78*f*
    activities, 231
    author idea map, 224
    basal series, 183
    bottom-up models, 66
    comprehension, 35
    defined, 4
    disability, 355
    environment, 81
    Goodman model, 68
    guided, 171
    implementing strategies, 224*f*
    instruction, 5
    interactive model, 72*f*
    interactive process, 4, 83
    longer discourse, 216*f*
    oral assessment, 110*f*
    paragraph structures, 211*f*
    parents and, 141
    process 4, 65
    programs, 3*f*
    purposes for, 77, 200
    relationship of writing, 82
    resources, 235*f*
    role in society, 2
    semantic webs and maps, 228*f*
    sentence strategies, 208

setting purposes, 200
text comprehension model, 75f
top-down models, 66
Reading-thinking lesson, 184f
self-guided, 201f
Recall, 76, 290
from graphics, 282
see also Assessment; Comprehension; Retelling
Recoding, 68
Reed, James C., 355, 356
Reed, Linda, 316
Referents, 207, 243, 286
Reid, D. Kim, 359
Reliability, 93
Resource units, 180
Retelling, 115f, 127. See also Recall
Retrieval, 53. See also Recall
Rinehart, George J., 8
Robeck, Carol, 344
Robinson, H. Alan, 13, 80, 82, 110, 212, 278
Robinson, Helen, 135
Ross, Ramon Royal, 110, 190, 202, 226, 252
Rude, Robert T., 160
Rumelhart, David E., 40, 72, 80
Rupley, William H., 344
Ryan, Ellen, 67, 68

Salzer, Richard, 60
Samuels, S. Jay, 355, 356
Sapir, Edward, 18, 19, 20
Sargent, Eileen E., 286
Satz, Paul, 357
Saville-Troike, Muriel R., 351
Sawyer, Diane J., 155, 160
Sceats, John, 261, 262
Schafer, John C., 37
Schaff, Adam, 23
Scheiner, Robert, 105
Schell, Leo M., 248
Schemas, 40f, 73, 76, 140, 146
Schiller, Andrew, 264, 265
Schwartz, Judy I., 173, 344
Seifert, Mary, 136
Semantic component, 23
Semantic maps and webs, 228
Semantics, 35
Semmel, Melvyn L., 67, 68
Sensorimotor stage, 44
Sensory register, 49
Sentence reading, 208f
Sequential Tests of Education Progress, 94

Shared context, 345
Shepherd, David L., 312, 325
Shepherd, Terry, 335, 336
Sherk, J. K., 242
Short term memory, 51f
Silent reading, 127
Simons, Herbert, 198
Slazer, Richard, 60, 67
Sloan, Glenna D., 321
Slobin, Dan, 54
Smith, Frank, 25, 109, 200, 201, 238, 254, 256, 259
Smith, James A., 145
Smith, Nila B., 274, 277, 278, 316
Snook, Ivan, 6
Sparrow, Sara S., 357
Speech development, 54f
Spelling, 29, 254, 259f. See also Word recognition
Spoken prose, 38
SQ3R, 286f
Standard American English, 342
Standard error of measurement, 93
Standardized tests, 89
criterion referenced, 92
effective use of, 102
limitations, 96
norm referenced, 90
reading, 94
Stanine, 91
Stauffer, Russell, 67, 123, 184, 185
Stewart, William A., 342
Stipek, Deborah J., 358
Story organization, 225
Strang, Ruth, 98, 103
Strange, Michael, 193
Strategy learning lesson, 219f
Structure-of-intellect model, 46f
Structure words, 32, 36
Style, see Author's craft
Surface structure, 24
Syllabication, 254
Syntactic component, 23

Taylor, H. Gerry, 355
Teachers
being informed, 11
roles, 6
Test of Cognitive Skills, 103
Textbooks, using, 273
Thematic units, 180
Theme, 150, 225, 323

Thesaurus, 263
Thinking, 42
    conclusions about, 53
    developmental stages, 43
    See also Problem Solving
Thompson, William Irving, 3, 11
Topic development, 278
Torrence, E. Paul, 188, 193
Transformational grammar, 23
Transformations, 24, 33*f*, 57
Tuinman, J. Jaap, 98
Tway, Eileen, 336

Understanding, 42. *See also* Comprehension

Vacca, Joanne, 199
Validity, 93
Vocabulary
    activities, 245*f*
    content areas, 275
    development, 243*f*
    referents, 207, 243, 286
    resources, 268*f*
Vogel, Susan A., 160
Vowels, 30, 242, 257
Vuckelich, Carol, 361

Wagner, Betty Jane, 259, 261, 262
Wagner, Steven R., 357
Wardaugh, Ronald, 22
Waugh, R. P., 255
Weaver, Wendell W., 99
Wehmeyer, Lillian M., 296
Weil, Philip E., 293

Weinstein, Carol S., 10
Weisz, John R., 358
Wheat, Thomas, 344
White, Richard T., 50, 52, 53
Wienmann, John M., 55, 59
Wilde, John, 357
Williamson, Leon E., 243
Wilson, Marilyn J., 83
Winkley, Carol K., 100
Wittrock, M. C., 67, 199
Witty, Paul, 361
Wood, Barbara S., 38, 39, 55, 58, 59
Word meaning, contextual signals of, 248*f*
Word recognition, 241
    immediate, 256
    letter clusters, 257
    morphological units, 258
Writing, 2, 198
    assessment, 132*f*
    in beginning reading, 144
    as comprehension strategy, 193*f*
    in content areas, 309
    functional literacy, 302
    and literature, 329
    relation to reading, 82
    role in society, 2
    stages, 144

Ysseldyke, James E., 356

Zintz, Miles V., 343
Zuck, L. V., 254, 255

Student Response Form

The author and editors of *Developmental Reading, K-8: Teaching from a Psycholinguistic Perspective* would like your opinion of the book after you have read it. Your comments will help us not only in improving the next edition of the text but also in developing other books. We would appreciate it if you would take a few minutes to respond to the following questions and return the form to: College Marketing, Houghton Mifflin Company, One Beacon Street, Boston, MA 02108.

1. We would like to know your reaction to the following features of the text:

	Excellent	Good	Adequate	Poor
a. General interest level of the book compared to other educational texts.	____	____	____	____
b. Writing style and readability.	____	____	____	____
c. Clarity of presentation of ideas.	____	____	____	____
d. Value of the suggested teaching strategies and activities.	____	____	____	____
e. Value of the models of reading and thinking.	____	____	____	____
f. Value of the suggested readings at the ends of chapters.	____	____	____	____
g. Helpfulness of actual examples of students' texts.	____	____	____	____
h. Your overall evaluation of the book.	____	____	____	____

2. Check one or more of the responses. I am currently

    ____ a teacher of preschoolers.   ____ a teacher of primary children.

    ____ a teacher of intermediate-school children.   ____ a supervisor.

    ____ a graduate student.   ____ an administrator.

    ____ an undergraduate in a four-year college.   ____ an undergraduate in a two-year college.

    ____ a librarian.

    ____ other. Explain _____

    _____

    _____

STUDENT RESPONSE FORM

3. Check one or more of the responses and complete the information requested. I read *Developmental Reading* as part of

   ____ an undergraduate course called _____

   ____ a graduate course called _____

   ____ a workshop called _____

   ____ my personal reading.

   ____ other. Explain: _____

4. Do you intend to keep the book as part of your professional library? Yes   No   Maybe

   Please tell us why _____
   _____
   _____

5. Please indicate the numbers of the chapters you found most helpful to you as an educator or educator-to-be. _____

   Why did you find these chapters most helpful? _____
   _____
   _____

6. Please indicate the numbers of the chapters you found least helpful to you.
   _____

   Why did you find these chapters least helpful? _____
   _____
   _____

7. What did you like best about this book? _____
   _____
   _____

8. What did you like least about this book? _____
   _____
   _____